BRITISH
SECRET PROJECTS

JET FIGHTERS SINCE 1950

To my dear parents
Len and Betty

British Secret Projects – Jet Fighters since 1950
© Anthony Leonard Buttler, 2000
ISBN 1 85780 095 8

First published in 2000 by
Midland Publishing
24 The Hollow, Earl Shilton,
Leicester, LE9 7NA, England.
Tel: 01455 847 815 Fax: 01455 841 805

Midland Publishing is an imprint of
Ian Allan Publishing Limited.

Worldwide distribution (except North America):
Midland Counties Publications
Unit 3 Maizefield, Hinckley Fields
Hinckley, Leics. LE10 1YF, England
Tel: 01455 233747 Fax: 01455 233737
E-mail: midlandbooks@compuserve.com

North America trade distribution by:
Specialty Press Publishers & Wholesalers Inc.
11605 Kost Dam Road
North Branch, MN 55056, USA
Tel: 651 583 3239 Fax: 651 583 2023
Toll free telephone: 800 895 4585

Design concept and editorial layout
© Midland Publishing.

Printed by Ian Allan Printing Limited
Riverdene Business Park, Molesey Road
Hersham, Surrey, KT12 4RG, England.

Photograph on previous page:
**Lovely view of a lovely aeroplane –
the pale green Hawker Hunter prototype WB188
on an early test flight.** BAe Farnborough

Photograph on title page, opposite:
**An artist's impression of the Saunders-Roe P.163
proposed supersonic research aircraft to ER.134T,
from May 1953. The design was developed into the
P.177, a mixed-power interceptor, which in turn
became the SR.177 and was ordered for the RAF
and Royal Navy before being cancelled in stages
between April and December 1957.** GKN Westland

BRITISH
SECRET PROJECTS
JET FIGHTERS SINCE 1950

TONY BUTTLER

Midland Publishing

Contents

Introduction

Many books have been written about the fighters designed and built in Britain since the war, either collectively or featuring individual types, so one imagines that this offering may well provoke the comment 'not again!' Well I hope the reader looks a little more deeply because this work makes extensive use of previously unpublished primary source material held by museums and record offices and in company and private collections, much of it recently declassified. Examination of these papers has given the opportunity to describe in more detail the Ministry's side of events and give an insight into a secret world where the public had little idea of what was going on, while at the same time presenting something of a coherent nationwide picture of fighter development and evolution. Particular emphasis is placed on the tender design competitions between companies and their projects, an important driving force and an aspect often ignored, and some of the events that led to certain aircraft either being cancelled or chosen for production and service.

Until the Second World War, fighters were cheap and could be built relatively quickly and a new specification often brought forth a selection of prototypes for a fly-off, with the best chosen for production. Jet engines and rockets, swept and delta wings, guided weapons, advanced materials and sophisticated avionics changed that situation so that by the 1950s, fighters had became an expensive commodity (though still cheap by today's standards). The driving force behind this progress was the types of threat posed by the Soviet Union and the methods and effort needed to deal with them; the state of the art moving swiftly. Now fighter competitions took place with 'paper-planes' where companies submitted detailed brochures of their proposals which included full information on construction methods, performance estimates from tunnel testing and equipment.

A huge number of fighter projects have been drawn by British companies over the last 50 years, in particular prior to the 1957 White Paper, but with few turned into hardware, little has been published about most of them. One reason was that all military brochures remained classified once a winner was chosen and many copies were destroyed as secret waste. Any survivors could not be released for public scrutiny until at least 30 years had passed. Further to this, the amalgamation of firms into British Aerospace with the consequent closure of a number of factories brought the destruction of great quantities of records. This book brings together many little known projects within a full narrative of fighter development, but some designs are still missing and are probably lost forever. There are other gaps too, of course, as the complete story would take a dozen volumes, but many aspects previously ignored are revealed for the first time.

Fighter design is constantly evolving – look at the difference in capability between the Meteor and Eurofighter. But individual projects can be developed markedly and there are many examples where production fighters were quite different from their prototypes, and where the F Mk.G was far superior to the F Mk.A. At the earliest stages, there were often many dissimilar layouts under the same project number so parameters have to be set for what can be included here, otherwise drawings would be queuing by the thousand to get in. The main criterion for acceptance is that any project must have an 'official' number and be in its ultimate form(s). In other words, projects actually submitted to the Ministry for consideration become automatic entries; private venture designs appear in final form when work stopped, usually after consuming a reasonable amount of time and effort.

This is a general rule; there are exceptions and occasionally the chance is taken to illustrate a line of development in full (Hawker's P.1103 / P.1116 / P.1121 series for example). One difficulty comes from strike fighters and multi-role types whose dual role might not necessarily represent real fighter capability. Here a demarcation line for qualification is difficult and judgement is made as we go along. Only products from recognised firms and design teams are included; ideas such as the Griffith supersonic fighter of 1946 are omitted. Many projects had short lives and drawings were often part of an experiment, even a training exercise for a new draughtsman ('boy racer' 3-views).

Picking the important ones has at times been difficult, many of the Kingston P and HS series have little significance except to show an idea under consideration at a specific time. A good proportion of the arrangements drawn would be tunnel tested, but it is impossible to say from the evidence available if they would work. Few that did not at least reach wind tunnel testing are worthy of historical attention. Some projects are 'what ifs?'; a firm is following a main line of advance but needs to cast to either side just in case. 'Paper' aircraft, of course, commit no sin and conceal their weaknesses. It is worth remembering also that fighter development work was usually so secret that relatively few members of a firm's staff would know anything about new designs until the hardware stage.

One senses that working with Ministry and Treasury officials must at times have been hell for those in the industry and many politicians were clearly uncomfortable with, and incapable of making, the big decisions necessary in military aviation. But these were the folk who dished out the orders and the cash, so their opinions are important. Few publications even reveal the names of 'the Men from the Ministry' whereas the careers of such as Sydney Camm are well documented. Contrary to popular belief, there were some outstanding people in Whitehall and St Giles' Court, especially those with the ability to see weaknesses in a design, and a design team, quicker than the firms themselves.

Project data throughout is manufacturer's estimates. If submitted to the Ministry, the figures would normally be re-assessed by specialists and often changed; weights in particular would regularly increase. But using company data as much as possible provides a common factor in presenting figures. I have long been fascinated how and why designers working to the same specification could produce such different projects, yet often cover the same ground or invent or use the same feature. This data will allow others to make comparative judgements on designs that are now maybe 40 or 50 years old.

An accurate sub-title was a problem but 1950 was chosen because none of the types featured in depth in the main text flew in the 1940s, despite so much design work being completed before the new decade.

Twenty-five years ago, Derek Wood's book *Project Cancelled* was published and provided a big stimulant in discovering the history of British aviation. I am lucky to have had access to many declassified documents denied to Mr Wood in 1975.

Many records have been lost or destroyed, but it is amazing how much material has survived or been saved by determined individuals. Researchers like myself are so much in their debt. It is also pleasing to see the establishment of Heritage Centres at several British Aerospace sites for cataloguing and protecting their archives and I hope very much that they flourish.

The RAF Museum has long been a major source of information but other museums like Brooklands have also assembled large and important archives.

The fighter is one of man's most spectacular and glamorous creations. Perhaps it is wrong to describe in such terms what is in essence a killing machine, but one considers them more defensive than offensive in nature. Each design possesses its own character and I hope I never lose the thrill of seeing and hearing such machines as they cavort around the sky. It has been immensely enjoyable to write about some of my favourite aircraft, even more to uncover previously unknown designs and information. When an original document contradicts information that has been published previously, one knows what journalists feel like when they have a scoop

and I urge any readers who may have any contribution, great or small, to add to the information in this book, to write to me via the publisher, so that any further knowledge can be published in due course. Photographs and other information will be gratefully received, acknowledged and returned on request.

Finally, I hope that those of you reading this work, either experts, enthusiasts or general readers, will find the result enjoyable. British Fighter development has been, and still is, a long, complex and often tortuous story, but here goes . . .

Tony Buttler MA, AMRAeS, AMIM   July 1999

Acknowledgements

To produce such a work such as this, to find so much new material and to access the opinions and memories of experts requires the assistance of many kind and helpful people. To begin I must thank the authors of the Putnam series of books on British Aircraft Manufacturers, and selected other titles listed in the bibliography, who included in their works a list of unbuilt projects. In doing this they gave me a framework from which to begin my own research, a task that otherwise would have been quite impossible.

I wish to express my sincere thanks to the following for their help in dealing with countless requests for information, drawings and photographs, and for permission to publish material. I hope I have not left anyone out:

Wing Commander Ron Allen; Peter Amos (Folland archive); Fred Ballam and David Gibbings (GKN Westland Yeovil); Wing Commander Roland 'Bee' Beamont; Ken Best and Joan Grenville (Short Bros.); Terry Blacow and Colin Charnley (BAe Warton), and Andrew Bunce (BAe Warton) for clearance to publish the Eurofighter text; Pete Bishop; Roy Boot; Phil Bowden (BAe Dunsfold); Michael J F Bowyer; Alec Brew (Boulton Paul Association); Derek G Brown; Phil Butler; Ian Butcher (MoD); David Charlton, Mike Fish & Duncan Greenman (BAe Airbus, Filton); Bob Coles;

Peter Elliot, Ray Funnel, Ken Hunter & Anna McIlwaine (RAF Museum); Bob Fairclough, Ian Lawrenson and colleagues of the North West Heritage Group (BAe Warton); Peter Green; Mike Goodall, Julian Temple and the late Mike Harries of the Brooklands Museum (who also gave permission to photograph some 1/24th scale models on loan from BAe Military Aircraft, Dunsfold).

Stan Field, Steve Gillard and the staff of the BAe Brough Heritage Centre; Jim Fletcher; the late Dr John Fozard; Pam and Barry Guess, Barry Pegram and John Strange (BAe Farnborough); Bill Gunston; John Harrington (Cranfield University); Bill Harrison (Fairey archive); Roy C Hofschneider; Barry Hygate; Derek James; Peter G Jeffery; George Jenks (BAe Woodford); Roff Jones, Tim Kershaw and Don Tombs of the Gloucestershire Aviation Collection's Jet Age Museum; Midland Air Museum, Baginton; Arnold Nayler & Brian Riddle (Royal Aeronautical Society); Ann O'Brien (Loughborough University); Sir Freddie Page; Peter Pavey (Rolls-Royce Bristol); Ashok and Gitta Prema; Public Record Office; Tony Roden (Westland Cowes); Charles Ross (Lightning Association); Mike Salisbury; Ray Sturtivant (Air-Britain); Peter A Ward; Ray Wheeler; Les Whitehouse; Ray Williams (Armstrong Whitworth archive) and Derek Wood.

I am particularly grateful to: Chris Farara (Brooklands Museum) and Ralph Hooper for filling gaps and checking the accuracy of the Kingston story for 1975 onwards, and David Walley for his similar treatment of the Warton text for the same period; Brian Kervell for letting me tap into his huge knowledge of British aeronautical history; my old mate Clive Richards whose knowledge of the archives held in the RAF Museum and MoD Air Historical Branch alerted me to anecdotes, articles and one or two 'scoops' which filled in the story so much better than it might have been; dear Eric Morgan who made available his archives and realised I'm as daft about the subject as he is; and Ken Ellis who, besides seeing a book in all of this and encouraging me to write it, gave me the opportunity to develop a new career. Thanks to Keith Woodcock for a marvellous cover painting and Pete West for his splendid colour artwork; also I wish to thank Chris Salter and the production team at Midland Publishing for their help in bringing this book to fruition.

Finally, I must add that in 1995 *Air Enthusiast* published two of my articles on fighter projects and received a very large mail bag in response. This proved to be a big factor in the book going ahead and I thank all of those readers who took the trouble to write in.

British Secret Projects: Jet Fighters

Chapter One

A Long Haul

Naval All-Weather Fighter Development: 1945 to 1957

By the time the Second World War ended in 1945, Britain had made great progress in the development of jet engines and jet fighters. Three aircraft types had flown. The first was the ground breaking Gloster E.28/39 research aircraft that took the Allies' opening steps into jet flight on 15th May 1941. George Carter's team at Gloster followed with its Meteor twin jet fighter, a conventional machine but the right choice with which to begin wartime service experience. De Havilland flew the single engined Vampire on 20th September 1943 but this type did not enter squadron service until after the armistice. These were all-new aeroplanes but others in the pipeline such as Supermarine's Attacker could trace their origins back to earlier piston engined fighters. Official specifications were written around each of these craft, but they were all 'one-off' designs without competition.

The jet was to revolutionise aircraft design and it was only to be expected that the fighter would benefit first. This new source of power was relatively simple compared to the highly complicated mechanics within the piston engine and the instant removal of the propeller suddenly brought the prospect of previously unheard of speeds. Britain's wartime jets were of the centrifugal type with aluminium impellers in the compressor that utilised known technology from supercharged piston engines, but they were inefficient. The first axials had many rows or stages of blades and were heavy and bulky and poor performers. Not until the Avon and Sapphire were perfected after long developments did top quality axials become available, so the centrifugal jet engine had a vital role to play for some years beyond the war. The desperately difficult development problems of the Avon were, to an extent, unexpected and many early projects specified the engine. Early jets lacked acceleration and, for a period, rockets were added anywhere and everywhere, particularly

XN684 was the interim prototype Sea Vixen FAW Mk.2, rebuilt from FAW Mk.1 standard with extended tail booms and four Red Top air-to-air missiles. This aircraft first flew on 1st June 1962, and the picture, taken on 6th September 1963, allows comparison with the DH.110 (on page 18) in terms of structure change and weapon load.
BAe Farnborough

to help rate of climb, a vital property for most fighters.

The Navy's quest for a radar equipped all-weather fighter was to become a very drawn out affair. Ten years were to pass from the earliest requirement to the first flight of a production Sea Vixen (yet today we would be delighted with such a timescale). The first jet to land and take-off from a carrier had been the second Vampire prototype on 3rd December 1945. The Navy's first jet fighter was the Attacker which served for just a short period in the 1950s but gave vital experience in jet operation. It was followed by Hawker's

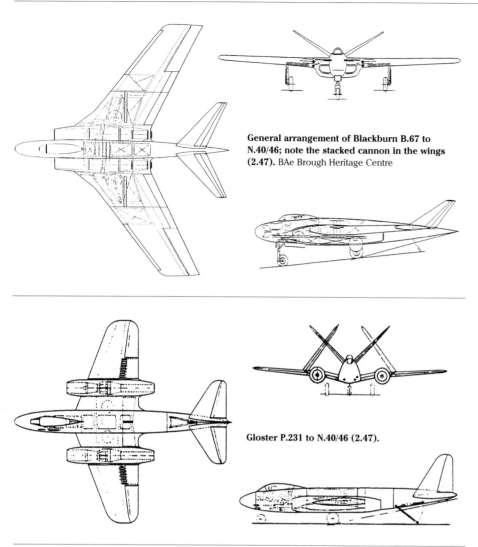

General arrangement of Blackburn B.67 to N.40/46; note the stacked cannon in the wings (2.47). BAe Brough Heritage Centre

Gloster P.231 to N.40/46 (2.47).

Sea Hawk, an altogether better and more successful machine that was to lead directly to the Hunter. In September 1946 the first draft of Naval Staff Requirement NR/A.14 was written and, under specification N.40/46, issued for design studies to Blackburn, Gloster, Hawker and Westland on the last day of January 1947.

N.40/46
(and Operational Requirement OR.246)
This requested a twin-jet naval night fighter to replace the Sea Hornet with a top speed at least 500 knots (575mph/927km/h) from sea level to 20,000ft (6,096m), and a maximum all-up-weight of 30,000lb (13,608kg). Span limit was 55ft (16.8m) (18ft [5.5m] folded) and length 43ft (13.1m). The best possible manoeuvrability was needed and the aircraft had to be able to land and take-off from carriers by day or night. It was accepted some form of take-off assistance might be needed and the armament was to be 30mm cannon. All bar Hawker submitted.

Blackburn B.67
This swept-wing swept V-tail project had de-rated Avons of only 5,000lb (22.2kN) thrust mounted in the lower wing roots. Outside them were a pair of cannon, the wing being so thick that they could be stacked one above the other. Sea level rate of climb 5,200ft/min (1,585m/min); 7.0 minutes to 25,000ft (7,620m); practical ceiling 41,000ft (12,497m).

Gloster P.231
One of many projects derived by Gloster from the successful Meteor, here with a swept-wing and V-tail. It was really based on the two-seat P.228 to F.44/46 (Chapter 4) which had a conventional tail. Three cannon in lower fuselage; sea level rate of climb 10,700ft/min (3,261m/min); 3.4 minutes to 25,000ft; practical ceiling 45,800ft (13,960m).

Westland N.40/46
(Drawing PJD.129). Possibly the first jet fighter design to have two stacked engines, a format duly made famous by the Lightning, this project was a flying wing reminiscent of de Havilland's DH.108 research aircraft but having wingtip fins and rudders like Armstrong Whitworth's AW.52. The second crewman faced rearwards and the three cannon were mounted underneath the cockpit. Sea level rate of climb 5,300ft/min (1,615m/min); 6.0 minutes to 25,000ft; practical ceiling 51,000ft (15,545m).

—

During the Tender Design Conference held at Thames House (MoS) on 4th March 1947 it became clear that the need for manoeuvrability in a pursuit curve interception could not be fully met for four to five years and would probably involve the use of suction applied to the wings, itself a major item of research and development. It was recommended that the requirement should be reviewed by the Admiralty and CNR, and a revised issue was sent in June to the three firms plus de Havilland and Fairey. Fairey was included thanks to the cancellation of its N.16/45 turboprop strike aircraft competitor to the Westland Wyvern.

Maximum all-up-weight was reduced to 28,000lb (12,701kg) but new arrestor gear was being designed for 30,000lb (13,608kg) so this was not a rigid limit. The guns were replaced by 20mm Hispano cannon. As a consequence, new studies from Fairey, de Havilland and Westland were forthcoming. Blackburn did not submit new proposals but instead offered an idea for an approximate scale model to study the problems before embarking on a full scale project. As its original brochure was, however, not unsuited to the new requirements, it remained under consideration. All proposals carried eight rocket projectiles (RPs); none were classed as official tenders.

Blackburn B.67
Although proposed with derated AJ.65s, RAE scaled up the aircraft and its figures to the full Avon rating of 6,500lb (28.9kN). Sea level rate of climb became 8,600ft/min (2,621m/min); critical Mach number 0.88.

De Havilland DH.110
An adaptation of the night fighter to F.44/46 submitted the previous March. The first clues that the DH.110 existed came when a modified DH.108 wing tunnel model fitted with twin fins and rudders and inverted V-shaped tail was tested at Farnborough. Initial engine choice was two Metropolitan Vickers F.9's but by Conference time the Rolls-Royce 'Avon' AJ.65 had become the preferred engine. DH's Vampire and DH.108 experience had led to the conclusion that wing sweepback was essential to achieve the required Mach 0.87 of

the F.44/46 Night Fighter and so a 40° sweep angle would easily cover the Mach 0.82 of N.40/46 with ample margin. A small span, which was 5ft (1.5m) less than the Mosquito, combined with power boost ailerons and a low wing loading (41.5lb/ft² [202.6kg/m²] at normal all-up take-off weight) were expected to give an extremely manoeuvrable aeroplane.

The twin tail boom layout was chosen for the following reasons:

1. On a relatively small aircraft like this with two powerful engines it was necessary to fit them as close to the aircraft's lift coefficient as possible for good single engine control;
2. The tail-less format was abandoned because of difficulties in achieving slow landing speeds and possible vices at high Mach numbers;
3. A layout with partially buried engines in a conventional fuselage had been investigated but resulted in an extremely difficult structure and very bad accessibility to the engines;
4. A tail boom layout removed these difficulties and resulted in a straightforward structure. Engine change was simple as they were not hemmed in by stressed structures.

The firm considered the tail boom arrangement to have been entirely successful on the Vampire with no penalty in weight and drag and with this experience, plus the knowledge gained from the sweptback wing of the DH.108, felt it should be possible to produce this aeroplane without a long period of research and development. Adapting the night fighter would save development effort and expenditure.

The two crew sat side-by-side and slightly staggered with the four Hispanos under the cabin floor. The night fighter had four 30mm Adens and de Havilland suggested using two Adens in the N.40/46. Provision was made for two 1,000lb (454kg) bombs or eight 60lb (27kg) RPs mounted near the wing root, plus drop tanks. An AI.9D radar with 28in (71cm) scanner was in the nose; a 40in (102cm) scanner would require a much bigger aeroplane. Stowage of the Red Hawk AAM had not been investigated because little was known about the weapon.

The wing had a single fold and used a single spar to take the main bending loads at the root, the spar dying out along the span until the whole bending load was taken by thick skin and stringers. It was proposed to fit full span slots with a possible development to boundary layer suction later on. Fowler type high lift flaps and short span, large chord

ailerons with power boost were used. A trimming tailplane was mounted in tail booms very similar to the Vampire and the possibility of an all moving tailplane was to be investigated in high speed tunnel tests. The fins were built integral with the booms and the aircraft was all-metal. Sea level rate of climb was 8,500ft/min (2,590m); critical Mach number 0.94; total internal fuel 1,050gal (4,773lit) plus drop tanks 300gal (1,364lit).

Fairey N.40/46

No drawing is available at the time of writing for this project, but the wing was swept 25° Rate of climb at sea level 8,600ft/min (2,621m/min); critical Mach number 0.835; total fuel 1,140gal (5,183lit).

Westland N.40/46

Westland produced three drawings to the modified specification: PJD.142, 143 and 144. The main offering, PJD.144 was similar to the earlier PJD.129 with stacked engines and tip fins but the wings had greater chord towards the tip thanks to a reduced leading edge sweep from 45 to 38° Fin tip area was also increased. The other drawings were similar and used the same wing but side-by-side engines; PJD.142 with a centre fin but no horizontal tail surfaces, 143 a T-tail. As before, Westland quoted two 4,860lb (21.6kN) engines but to keep things on the same level, RAE recalculated using AJ.65 Avons. Rate of climb became 8,800ft/min (2,682m/min) at sea level; critical Mach number 0.85. 950gal (4,319lit) of fuel were carried internally. Westland had looked closely at blown flaps having done a good deal of early work on boundary layer control for Supermarines.

As none of the projects were official tenders, a Design Study Conference was held on 15th December 1947 chaired by Stuart Scott Hall, PDTD(A). It was noted that Hawker, although reminded frequently, had not expressed interest in the project, and it was also agreed that six years would be a realistic date for introduction into service due to the time needed to develop AI equipment. The Westland design was discarded on the grounds that it showed badly on performance, was likely to have a high approach speed and be subject to all the uncertainties associated with developing a tail-less layout, the lack of a tail being criticised.

Low approach speed was more important than all-up-weight because of the night fighter role. RAE had commented that although one drawing did show a tail, it had not been given serious thought and if the correct tail volume were provided, the weight and drag advantages of the tail-less design would disappear. J E Serby, DMARD, explained how Westland was warned after the earlier conference of the hazards of the tail-less layout but it appeared they still preferred this feature. Tip stalling could well be a problem.

The performance of the survivors was compared on the basis of the Avon engine. The DH.110 failed to reach the required approach speed in present form but the RAE were sure it could be achieved by increasing wing area by 10%. Blackburn's B.67 offered less performance than the DH.110 for about the same development risk; Fairey's project was more conventional so had less risk and, although of lower performance, met all the stated requirements. The B.67 was inferior in all respects except top speed at sea level and the

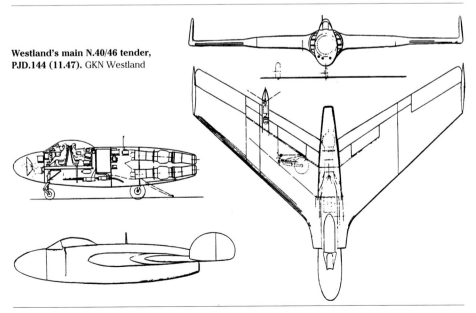

Westland's main N.40/46 tender, PJD.144 (11.47). GKN Westland

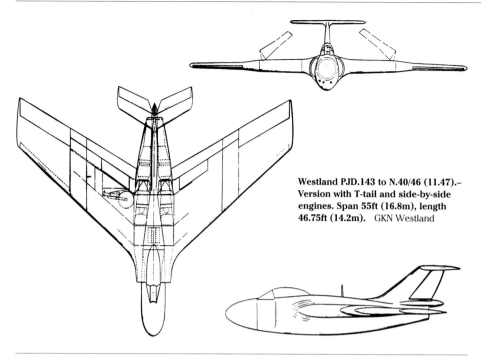

**Westland PJD.143 to N.40/46 (11.47).–
Version with T-tail and side-by-side
engines. Span 55ft (16.8m), length
46.75ft (14.2m).** GKN Westland

proposal to build a 10,000lb (4,536kg) model
of a 28,000lb (12,701kg) aircraft was not justified. Test results would be needed before design work on the full scale machine could
commence and consequently this would not
start for another two or three years. The B.67
was thus eliminated.

Choosing between de Havilland and Fairey
rested on an acceptable development risk
bearing in mind the differing sweep angles of
40 and 25° The greater sweep of the DH.110
gave a speed advantage which reached
46mph (74.1km/h) at altitude, a top speed of
Mach 0.93 placing it on a par with shore based
aeroplanes when the Avon still had some
thrust in hand. Fairey's Mach 0.86 might be a
bit low in six years and this aircraft would be
unable to take advantage of engine thrust developments, but the lower sweep angle required less attention to tip stalling, stability
and control. On past experience, de Havilland
was the more likely to meet the estimated
performance, but while Fairey's project could
take both the 40in (102cm) scanner and the
small search scanner, the DH.110 could not
handle the bigger dish (DH had made allowance for a larger fuselage if required).
From the catapulting aspect, Fairey's design
was the most attractive.

De Havilland had the most design work on
hand of the two but could still take on the additional commitment and do the work as
quickly as Fairey. Its production arrangements were, however, tending to become
overloaded but the scheme to make the type
an F.44/46 variant showed overall economy
of productive effort. It was agreed that the de

Havilland design with 10% extra wing area
was preferred on technical grounds and that
DMARD would approach the firm and advise
them to adopt this modification.

After some give and take with de Havilland,
a contract was placed in October 1948 for a
DH.110 prototype programme that would
equally serve N.40/46 and F.4/48 (previously
F.44/46). Alternative versions from Fairey
were still being examined. In March 1949
NR/A.14 was brought up to date under a new
Specification N.7/49 and then almost immediately N.14/49, agreement having been
reached to rewrite N.40/46 and call for the
same factors and speeds as F.4/48. Four
months later three naval DH.110 prototypes
were ordered (two night fighter, one strike) to
bring the total DH.110 order to 13 aircraft. A
dove-tail trials programme for the Royal Navy
and RAF was agreed but in November the
naval aircraft were dropped through economic pressure on the research and development (R&D) programme. The CNR had
intended to let the RAF carry the weight with
de Havilland while the Navy supported
Fairey's aircraft. De Havilland had also experienced difficulty in converting the aircraft to
fold within the box dimensions of the specification so Fairey was left in possession of the
N.14/49 field.

Fairey N.14/49 twin engine
A strike derivative of the N.40/46 was submitted in September 1948 and then, resulting
from discussions with Messrs Cohen and Ross
of MoS, the N.40/46 fighter was updated on
16th November to include new equipment

and information on increased engine weights.
All-up-weight rose by 4,300lb (1,950kg) and
the aircraft's dimensions were increased to
compensate. The likelihood of a change in
maximum level speed was assessed as negli-
gible since this was limited by the rise in compressibility drag.

In January 1949, DMARD advised Fairey that
certain items of equipment and armament
may be deleted in order to effect a reduction
in weight to get the machine below
a new top limit of 28,000lb (12,701kg). For
example the Avon's weight could now be
assumed as 2,130lb (966kg) instead of the
2,400lb (1,089kg) previously calculated. Fairey
observed this could reduce span to 52ft
(15.9m) and area to 526ft² (48.9m²), but considered that a better all-round aircraft would
result by leaving the original dimensions to
take advantage of the gain in climb, ceiling
and cruise performance. The changes did
allow a reduction in fuselage depth and width
for a useful saving in cross sectional area.
Final all-up-weight was given as 28,000lb, sea
level rate of climb 8,280ft/min (2,524m/min),
time to 25,000ft (7,620m) 4.1 minutes, ceiling
46,300ft (14,112m), 1,195gal (5,434lit) of fuel
was carried but top speed remained unchanged. Soon afterwards the project was
renumbered N.14/49.

During the two year period 1947/48, Air
Staff thinking on the subject remained somewhat fluid and a short term emphasis on
strike as the primary function reverted back
to the fighter role (N.8/49 and NR/A.18 called
for an N.14/49 strike variant). Following the
changes to Fairey's original design, agreement was slowly reached with the Admiralty
on the aircraft's final form and an Advisory
Design Conference was held on 5th April. By
now Fairey had many staff occupied on the
project yet it was 10th August before an official letter arrived stating prototypes were to
be ordered. Design work was stepped up in
anticipation of a three aircraft order, but the
economy drive duly had its effect on this
programme as well. Fairey was informed on
2nd November that work should be held up
on the N.14/49 as a result of economies being
imposed by the Treasury. It was hoped the
embargo would only be temporary.

J E Serby, who wrote the embargo letter,
was extremely worried about the whole position and most anxious that a gap should not
be left in the Navy's development programme. He argued with Fairey that, as economy was likely to be the watchword for
several years, it might be possible to get the
whole programme moving again if the firm
put forward an acceptable design based on a
single Avon instead of two (a feature in fact of

all Fairey's previous work). Such an aircraft might be cheaper and lighter and thus solve a number of carrier installation problems. Two alternative single engine designs were, therefore, prepared by the end of the year.

Fairey N.14/49 single engine

D L Hollis Williams sent his firm's brief preliminary investigation for a single-seat F.14/49 on 23rd December stressing this was not yet a serious design effort due to a lack of time. To make the version more attractive, Fairey based it on some preliminary and unofficial figures for an improved Avon known as the RA.5; the Sapphire was an alternative. There were two layouts, Schemes A and B, one with normal fuselage construction and long tail pipe, the other with tail booms and short tail pipe. The firm thought it would most likely persevere with the long pipe version as this gave the possibility of using afterburning later on. The disposition of radar, crew and armament, wing plan and the low wing remained as proposed for the twin since Fairey concluded no advantage could be gained by changing any of them.

Scheme A used a tricycle undercarriage and all fuel was carried internally. Reheat was not envisaged yet since the increase in all-up-weight was unjustified compared to the performance improvement achieved. For engine removal, the rear portion of the fuselage was swung laterally and the engine wheeled aft through the open end.

Scheme B introduced twin tail booms each with fin and rudder. The tail plane was of the all-moving constant chord type without sweep-back and pivotally attached to the twin fins. The wing and wing fold mechanism, tricycle chassis, fuel and armament were all similar to Scheme A's, and engine withdrawal was effected by removal of cowling panels over the aft portion of the fuselage.

An initial comparison of the two by their designers indicated that the increase in structure weight of Scheme B from the booms would be more than compensated for by deletion of the long jet tail pipe necessary in Scheme A. Further weight saving was achieved by the reduction in total aircraft drag and consequently the investigation suggested Scheme B was about 200lb (91kg) lighter. This was prior to a detailed structural investigation but the Twin Boom Scheme was clearly feasible. Performance was substantially similar but B had slightly the better climb and a sea level speed about 9mph (14.5km/h) more. A's rate of climb at sea level was 6,100ft/min (1,859m/min) and 680gal (3,092lit) fuel were carried. Ceiling was about 42,000ft (12,802m).

January 1950 brought a suggestion whether the Navy's fighter projects were really needed and the Naval Staff had to prepare a justification paper. Fairey's single engine design had received support but the Naval Staff seized on the hold up as an opportunity to make further drastic revisions to the requirement and, deciding to drop the strike alternative altogether, concentrate on a day and night all-weather fighter of greatly improved performance. Work began on a new specification but the need for one or two engines and installation of the radar scanner was a source of argument. N.14/49 had called for a minimum top speed of 500kts (575mph/927km/h) but this was now raised to 540kts (622mph/1,001 km/h) at 30,000ft (9,144m).

The naval projects to N.14/49 and N.9/47 (Supermarine day fighter, Chapter 2) were examined at Thames House on 3rd April, the discussion conducted in light of the vital need for economy except when the compelling interests of defence demanded expenditure. The twin engine Fairey N.14/49 was now seen to be incapable of producing the 540kts demanded and the introduction of reheat or a scaled down single engined version would still fail to reach the limit. The single or twin showed little difference in probable performance except the latter would have a better rate of climb. The main flaw was the 25° sweep 12% thick wing which aerodynamically limited top speed and no increase could be expected without increased sweep as

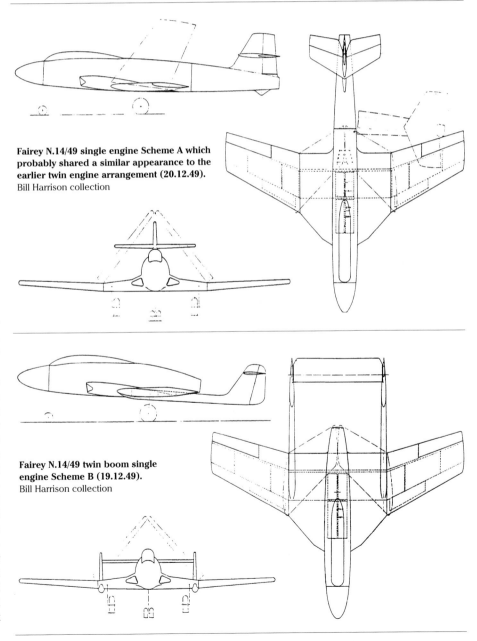

Fairey N.14/49 single engine Scheme A which probably shared a similar appearance to the earlier twin engine arrangement (20.12.49).
Bill Harrison collection

Fairey N.14/49 twin boom single engine Scheme B (19.12.49).
Bill Harrison collection

provided on de Havilland's fighter. A high rate of climb was not so important here.

All Fairey's N.14/49 studies had an AI.9C radar but now it was desired to use the AI.16 and it was realised that neither twin nor single engine could accommodate its 35in (89cm) scanner. This observation brought surprise and significantly influenced the subsequent decision. As no Fairey project was under construction, revised design studies could be made economically on both engine arrangements and it was agreed the firm should be told that none of its designs were acceptable and a new study be requested based on a single engine. There was concern that the same large expenditure was being devoted to the N.14/49 as to the N.9/47, but for much smaller requirements.

The MoS asked the Admiralty if developing the carrier-borne N.9/47 and N.14/49 day and

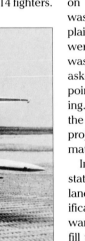

The Mikoyan MiG-15 that influenced British fighter design so much during this period.
Ken Ellis collection

night fighters was necessary since both were expensive high performance types designed to specifications comparable to the most advanced land-based fighters intended for UK air defence. It was explained they were based on the need to maintain sea communications through the Mediterranean in the face of attacks from captured airfields by the types of enemy aircraft expected in service by 1957. The Naval Staff felt the Venom would be an adequate day/night fighter for trade protection on ocean routes for some time yet; it was also suitable for the service's smaller carriers and relatively cheap. It was convinced, however, that nothing but a ship-borne fighter of the highest quality would effectively protect shipping in the restricted waters of the Mediterranean once the enemy could threat-

en with modern advanced shore-based air-forces. Unfortunately, the F.3/48 and F.4/48 fighters (Hunter and Javelin, Chapters 3 & 4) were, for technical reasons, unsuited for carrier operation, but the Admiralty wished to see them fully developed for the RAF.

The Ministry doubted whether any future carrier force would at all times be able to sustain protracted air operations within range of powerful and numerous enemy shore-based air forces, either in the Mediterranean or anywhere else. But if the Royal Navy was called on to undertake this formidable task (history indicating that it may well be necessary), it was essential that they had the best possible equipment. Assuming the strategic requirement for the defence of Britain's sea communications through the Mediterranean would remain firm, the Ministry felt bound to support the requirement for the N.9 and N.14 fighters.

It also considered the naval strike aircraft situation because the turboprop Wyvern was about to come into service. This would be outclassed by 1957 and development of suitable variants of the N.9 and N.14 appeared essential if maritime strike was to continue as a naval aviation role. It was debatable whether the ability to operate either shore-based or ship-borne maritime strike forces was an essential requirement for the defensive strategy that would almost certainly be adopted during the opening phase of a future war against Soviet Russia, despite a definite need in some areas. To abandon naval strike aircraft development would permanently relieve naval aviation of the strike role since fighters could not carry a torpedo and anti-submarine aircraft lacked the necessary performance. This was a vital decision for the future.

Breaking into the sequence of events for a moment, is it fascinating to see how situations develop. Here we have one of the armed forces trying to get the best equipment

in spite of a Treasury policy for economy, a common situation throughout British military history but compounded on this occasion by the cost of the big advances in weapons technology. Just a few months later came the outbreak of the Korean War which was to last for three years, reveal the latest Soviet weaponry such as the MiG-15 and heavily involve the Navy, often with just piston aircraft. In truth, these latest navy fighters would not have been ready in time, but the drive for economy went out of the window and the MiG-15 was to influence British fighter design for a long time. Panic stations became the order of the day at the Ministry of Supply (MoS), but the Admiralty appeared unmoved, progressing with their advanced fighter plans at, so it would appear, the same steady pace.

Fairey's C H Chichester-Smith wrote to Serby on 10th February demanding to know what was going on and why all the delay. It was explained that the main faults of Fairey's project were the 25° sweep wing and a fuselage that was not big enough for the radar. The Ministry asked for the revised project to rectify these points two days after the naval aircraft meeting. Fairey expressed much disquiet about the technical uncertainties surrounding the project but was told to keep quiet while the matter was with the Chiefs of Staff.

In September a Staff Requirement was stated for a navalised version of the de Havilland Venom fighter under NR/A.30 and specification N.107. The Navy had decided it wanted the Sea Venom as soon as possible to fill the unacceptably wide gap between the Sea Hornet and the N.14/49 that threatened to leave the fleet without an efficient night fighter for many years. The usefulness of the Venom as a general purpose trade route fighter would outlive its role as a night fighter while production of the naval variant would give the Australian Navy something to replace its Sea Furies. A production order for Sea Venoms was given in January 1951 and, in the event, Australia ordered 39 as well.

N.14/49 as originally conceived was withdrawn entirely on 19th July 1950 as a new specification and requirement were prepared. There was indecision as to whether to put this document direct to Fairey or fully out to tender again, but it was agreed in October that a three to six month delay could be accepted and the latter option taken. Prompted by the fresh start and likely re-tendering, a strongly worded letter from Fairey on 14th September revealed the pent-up frustration generated by the 'non' go-ahead of its fighter. It described in depth the firm's heavy naval fighter and strike design effort since 1944, starting with the Spearfish prototype torpedo bomber to O.5/43, which had not been rewarded with any production orders. The Spearfish was turned into the losing competitor to the Westland Wyvern strike aircraft under N.16/45 before the long series of N.40/46 and N.14/49 studies began.

Fairey had spent £53,000 on design work to the two jet fighter specifications and, 'due to the absence of other programmes', did not terminate work in their drawing office on the twin Avon N.14/49 until 19th May. The firm observed 'As this company has devoted so much effort and thought to the Navy's fighter and strike aircraft, it has become very familiar with the multiplicity of problems involved. It would seem the best way of securing an economy of time and public money would be to capitalise all this previous thinking into a new design to meet the latest Naval Air Staff requirements. If the whole matter is put to open tender, there is no reason to suppose that a repetition of the previous long periods of indecision will not recur before a start is finally made'. This assumption was to prove correct.

N.114T (and NR/A.14)

In January 1951 the new specification was issued officially to de Havilland, Vickers, Gloster, Fairey, Blackburn and Westland; the last three plus Saunders Roe and Shorts submitting designs in July. The specification covered day and night fighting and requested a two-seat machine with AI.18 radar. Top speed in clean condition was 540kts (622mph/1,001 km/h) minimum at 30,000ft (9,144m), minimum ceiling 40,000ft (12,192m), sea level rate of climb 10,000ft/min (3,049m/min) and maximum all-up-weight 28,000lb (12,701kg). Required patrol time was 1.5 hours and power was to come from Sapphire or RA.7 Avon engines with reheat to 1,500K although other proposals would be welcome. Armament mix was four 30mm Aden cannon, two Aden plus an air-to-air rocket battery or two Aden plus four Blue Sky AAMs. Red Deans were added later. Before tendering, the firms were informed carriage of Blue Sky or Red Hawk missiles was to be disregarded for the time being, but some brochures did include guided weapons.

Concern was expressed in March by Mr Evans, the Director of Naval Air Warfare, about the ever growing gaps in the naval fighter programme with no swept fighter likely until 1957. Both the N.9/47 (Chapter 2) and N.14/49 were unlikely to be available before then when the current performance of their predecessors, Sea Hawk and Sea Venom, was inadequate to allow them to remain in service for so long. As a consequence, suit-

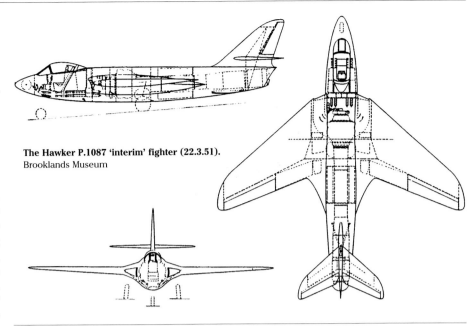

The Hawker P.1087 'interim' fighter (22.3.51).
Brooklands Museum

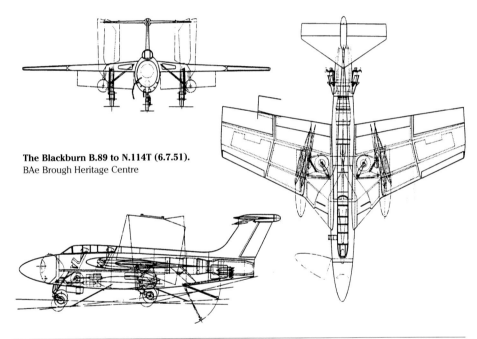

The Blackburn B.89 to N.114T (6.7.51).
BAe Brough Heritage Centre

able interim day and night fighters were suggested for service entry in 1955 but, to save time, without the prototyping and evaluation procedure. Prospective day fighters included a modified Sea Hawk, a hooked Swift and Hunter, and the P.1087 (navalised P.1081 with four cannon under the cockpit).

Supermarine's Swift was seen as the best day fighter candidate and NR/A.34 and N.105 were written around a hooked Swift. P.1087 was ruled out on grounds of risk, but RAE felt the Swift was an equally risky development. An all-weather night fighter was more of a problem as the Sea Venom had reached its limits and was beyond development. No interim fighter was ordered. These discussions

were concurrent with N.114T to which the following were submitted, all conventional construction with aluminium alloy spars and skins.

Blackburn and General B.89

An aircraft with T-tail, root intakes and double wing fold and developed from the earlier brief B.82 company study to N.14/49. The wing had compound sweep (sweep at different angles), then a feature of much interest at Brough for giving the desired aerodynamics, and thus had a variable t/c ratio of 10 to 6.5%. The Aden cannon were placed below the cockpit floor and the rocket batteries carried internally. Alternative engines were the Avon

Model of the Blackburn B.89. All the models pictured in this book, in wood to 1/24th scale, were made by the manufacturers specifically for tender to the Ministry alongside their brochures. Only the most important projects enjoyed the luxury of being modelled.
BAe Brough Heritage Centre

The one beneficiary of N.114 was the Blackburn B.103 Buccaneer strike aircraft which ended the line of development opened by the B.89. This view shows the fourth development aircraft XK489 with its distinct wing shape.

RA.12R or Bristol Olympus Ol.3. Sea level rate of climb with reheat 10,320ft/min (3,146m/min); ceiling over 45,000ft (13,716m); 870gal (3,955lit) fuel internally, maximum capacity 1,170gal (5,319lit). Prototype first flight was expected 3.5 years after ITP.

Fairey N.114

A mid-wing cantilever monoplane powered by a single unreheated Olympus Ol.3. Wing root intakes, double wing folding and a tricycle undercarriage were employed and two Adens were housed in each inner wing leading edge. Sea level rate of climb 7,250ft/min (2,210m/min); ceiling 44,550ft (13,579m); internal fuel 700gal (3,182lit), maximum with overload tanks 1,076gal (4,892lit). Prototype first flight to be three years after ITP. RAE felt that Fairey had overestimated by some margin the aircraft's weights so for the Tender Conference it also prepared new figures with a reheated Sapphire 4 (12,200lb/54.2kN) to ease comparison. Sea level top speed became 712mph (1,145m/h) and rate of climb 9,630ft/min (2,935m/min); ceiling 42,850ft (13,061m).

Saunders-Roe P.148

This had a shoulder-high wing with the Avon mounted in a straight duct above and behind the wing, with a T-tail above that. Single folding and tricycle undercarriage. The crew were accommodated side-by-side with the raised pilot's canopy on the port side but the navigator's nearly flush with the fuselage in an arrangement very similar to the eventual Sea Vixen. The four Adens were underneath the cockpit; the two batteries of 36 rocket projectiles on doors in the lower fuselage. Internal fuel was 760gal (3,455lit) with 390 (1,773) more in two outboard tanks. First flight 2.5 years from ITP.

No performance data survives for the Avons, but thanks to the RAE, comparative figures are available with a reheated Sapphire 4 – at sea level maximum speed was 709mph (1,142km/h) and rate of climb 10,420ft/min (3,176m/min); ceiling 42,350ft (12,908m).

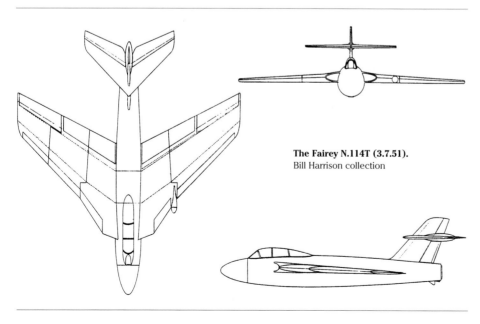

The Fairey N.114T (3.7.51).
Bill Harrison collection

Short P.D.5

An aircraft capable of conventional deck or flexible deck landing, the P.D.5 had a low aspect ratio thin wing set mid-position on the fuselage with a single fold. The tailplane was all-moving without an orthodox rudder and radar scanners were mounted both in the nose and on top of the fin. Tricycle undercarriage; four Adens in lower fore-body of fuselage; 52 rocket projectiles in fuselage and four Blue Sky or two Red Dean AAMs on underwing pylons. Sea level rate of climb 9,910ft/min (3,021m/min); ceiling 42,850ft (13,061m); internal tankage 850gal (3,864lit) but two rigid overload tanks could be carried. First flight 2.5 years from ITP.

Westland W.37

This had a compound sweep single fold wing of near delta formation with bifurcated leading edge intakes, T-tail and tricycle undercarriage. A completely detachable nose containing the entire radar installation, not just the scanner, was felt practical as the set was still in a state of development. The cannon were mounted below the pilot outside the main structural members while the rocket batteries and air-to-air missiles were carried externally under each wing joint outboard of the undercarriage legs. Rate of climb (Avon / Sapphire) 10,800 / 10,500ft/min (3,292 / 3,200m/ min); Ceiling (Sapphire) 43,400ft (13,228m). The high internal fuel load of 950gal (4,319lit) avoiding the need for external tanks, but a 90gal (409lit) ventral drop tank could be fitted if required. First flight two years four months from ITP. Westland built a mock-up of the W.37 and offered the afterburning Avon RA.12 as the main engine, but the Sapphire 4 could be fitted without major structural change. The firm considered the machine conventional but still up-to-date having the heavy sweepback necessary to achieve maximum speed. A two-seat operational trainer was projected.

The Tender Design Conference was held at Thames House on 9th October 1951, but, prior to this, the weights were re-calculated by the Ministry and came out slightly higher. This was significant for, in the overload all-up-weight condition, each project was overweight by 4,000 to 6,000lb (1,814 to 2,722kg). Shorts and Saro were unsatisfactory due to high approach speeds; Fairey's was poor because of very high structure weight which raised the question why such an established firm with a good reputation should be so seriously astray with this estimate. Blackburn and Westland both met the performance despite excess weight and, hence, a preference lay

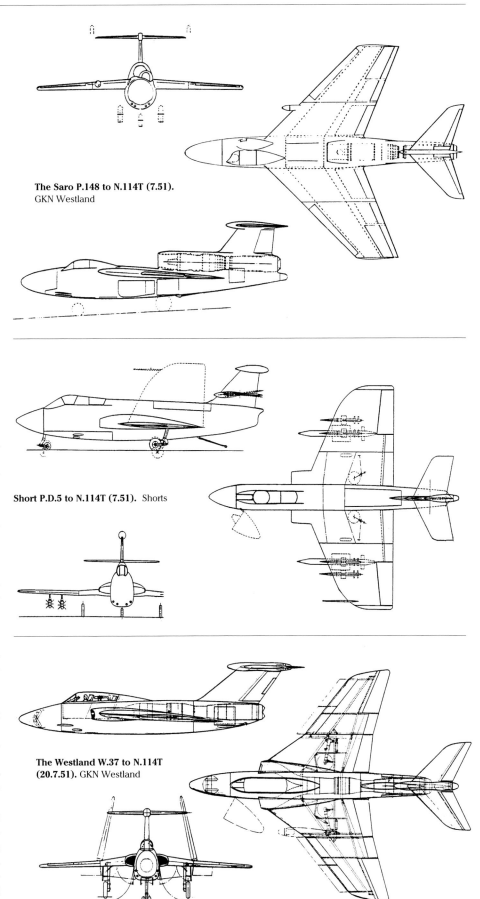

The Saro P.148 to N.114T (7.51).
GKN Westland

Short P.D.5 to N.114T (7.51). Shorts

The Westland W.37 to N.114T
(20.7.51). GKN Westland

Impression of Westland's 'Javelin'; the W.37 could be mistaken for Gloster's fighter from some angles. GKN Westland

between either internal or external carriage of the rocket batteries. Clean, the W.37 was quickest, but the slower with external rockets.

Fairey's project was considered worse than Westland's in all respects, worse than Blackburn's in all respects bar top speed, for its fairly high trailing edge sweepback was an expensive structural method of getting the required high Mach number characteristics. Both Blackburn and Westland had made a more careful choice of wing design parameters, the former by spanwise variation of maximum thickness position, the latter by using high sweepback on the root leading edge and small sweepback on the trailing edge. Short's P.D.5 might be improved by fitting more effective flaps but it would still be inferior to the B.89. Little could be done for Saro's P.148 because of its high wing loading while the engine position high to the rear might adversely affect directional control in the approach. This, coupled with the narrow wheel track, would make deck-landing more difficult.

No preference was expressed for choice of engine. The Avon was more likely to be available than the Olympus which was being considered as an alternative on two current bomber projects but so far without a firm decision to use it. The RAE representative thought the Olympus would be a good powerplant for a high-altitude fighter but any of the engines selected could be put in any of the submitted designs. The importance at interception altitude of a small turning circle as a performance requirement was emphasised. This was primarily a function of wing loading and, from this point of view, the B.89 was best and the P.148 worst.

It was doubted if Blackburn could recruit the extra staff needed to achieve a first flight in three and a half years because designing a new version of the Beverley freighter would

clash with the N.114 if both were required; a freighter production order would seriously affect delivery rates at Brough. An order for Short's would disturb the Canberra programme while Fairey's capacity would be fully occupied with the Gannet for some time to come. The Blackburn B.89 and Westland W.37 appeared to be the best in all technical respects with the B.89 narrowly rated first, but a final outcome could not be decided due to other considerations. Saunders-Roe's effort was considered particularly fine for a firm new to this type of design.

On 5th November the PDTD(A), S Scott Hall, reported that the Admiralty had serious doubts whether it wanted an aircraft to N.114T. In any event they would like one produced by one of the leading fighter firms as they had little confidence in either of those who came top at the Conference. Woodward Nutt, DMARD, confirmed this stating how the Admiralty doubted whether it could deal with an aeroplane of such size and weight. He referred to the 'interim' fighter above and the 'putting off of N.114T' until something much better can be presented, but stressed how the Admiralty had no clear idea of what this 'something' could be. By now, de Havilland had aroused interest in its Super Venom described shortly, but Woodward Nutt felt that machine could not be in service before 1957. Choosing this was an unwise move for its availability was little different to N.114T itself. However, the willingness to consider the Super Venom implied that the Admiralty was ready to reduce its requirements.

A final notice on 21st January 1952, stated all submissions fell short of N.114T so the Admiralty would not proceed with the project and no further work was to be undertaken. It was impractical to produce an aircraft to meet these stringent limits to an acceptable weight and, in December, N.114T was declared 'dead'. N.114T.2 was, however, raised the following May to study naval fighters fitted with jet deflection to increase lift.

Fairey's prediction had come true but sadly their comments go unrecorded (fortunately perhaps as they were probably unprintable). Not all the N.114 work went to waste however, despite the designs being too heavy for deck operations. The Blackburn Design Project Office continued investigations on this type of aircraft and in October 1951 produced an undercarriageless version, the B.94, for use on flexible decks (wing area 575ft² [53.4m²]). Since it had been favourably considered to N.114T, the B.89 was re-examined in March 1952 with a view to producing a lighter version. Much thought went into a revision called the B.95 with all-up-weight of 20,000lb (9,072kg) and wing area 425ft² (39.5m²) that showed sufficient promise to be put before the Company's board with a view to development as a 'private venture', but rejected on account of cost.

In late 1952 the B.102 naval all-weather interceptor fighter with 'mixed' powerplant followed still based on B.89/B.95 thoughts. Power was supplied by Bristol Orpheus jets but using a de Havilland Spectre rocket for climb and combat. One day in November, a routine visit to the Ministry and Navy Staff revealed that the Navy had a requirement for a strike aircraft designated NA.39 and Blackburn were advised to carry out a design study. The Project Office produced the B.103 with the same salient features of the B.89 and B.95 (the crescent wing and high tail), but (initially) using Sapphires shrouded in the wing roots and employing jet deflection to improve take-off and landing. The B.103 was started in January 1953 and subsequently won the requirement. As the Gyron Junior and the Spey powered Buccaneer it brought the Brough factory work right through to the 1990s.

In late summer 1951, R E Bishop of de Havilland visited America and, as a result of the lessons he learnt, changed his ideas about improving the Sea Venom. He could now completely re-design it with thinner swept-back wings and a reheated RA.12 Avon. Having informed the Ministry what was possible, it was agreed in September that he should prepare a design study on his own initiative which became known, to the Ministry at least, as the Super Venom. With the death of N.114

a new Staff Requirement NR/A.38, replacing NR/A.14, was written around the Super Venom in March 1952 and formally accepted by the Ministry in July, a new Specification N.131T following.

N.131T was actually sent to de Havilland, Fairey, Saro, Short and Westland for possible tendering of new designs by 1st November, a step taken on Woodward Nutt's advice so that the MoS and Admiralty would not lose what might be considerable 'face' with the industry. Theoretically, all the N.114Ts failed to meet the requirements but he knew that the main reason for this was that they were too severe. Rejecting the tenders and subsequently accepting another firm's design to less severe limits would be most unfair to those firms who had spent a great deal of time and money in carefully preparing their N.114 projects, which they had every reason to believe were honestly wanted. However, no tendering took place. Maximum speed was to be at least 620kts (714mph/1,149km/h) at sea level; ceiling 48,000ft (14,630m). Blue Jay missiles later became part of the weapon requirement for a fighter that was to be in service by 1958.

De Havilland DH.116 Super Venom

A design resembling the Venom only in the nose and cockpit area thanks to removal of the twin booms for a reheated Avon and all-through jetpipe; when the brochure was completed in January 1952 the latest Avon RA.14 was specified. This proposal presented a much smaller aircraft than the DH.110 with better performance but some sacrifices in equipment, armament and endurance. Thin highly swept wings and an all-moving T-tail contrasted sharply with earlier Venom practice and resulted in a level flight Mach number just over 1.0; nose slots were placed all along the leading edge and Fowler flaps were used with all controls power operated. The wing fold was placed just outboard of the intakes and main undercarriage for a narrow 12ft (3.66m) folded span. Super Venom would have an advanced AI.17 or APS.21 radar and two Aden cannon beneath the cockpit which, to save design time, was itself near identical to the Sea Venom.

All 562gal (2,555lit) of internal fuel were carried in the deep centre section but an additional 120gal (546lit) could go in internal wing tanks and a pair of 100gal (455lit) drop tanks were also available. This centre section lent itself to simple construction and good stiffness and the front fuselage and intake were divorced from the main wing to offer a relatively simple change to a single-seater if required. Sea level rate of climb was predicted to be 9,900ft/min (3,018m/min) on dry power; at 2,000K reheat this became 29,600 ft/min (9,022m/min) with time to 45,000ft (13,716m) 4.1 minutes and operational ceiling 51,500ft (15,697m). Dry thrust gave a top 698mph (1,123km/h, Mach 0.92) at sea level rising to 740mph (1,191km/h, Mach 0.975) with full reheat. Bishop pointed out that aircraft usually became obsolete because of performance and seldom on account of their equipment, but this improved Venom would not be obsolete on performance grounds and could operate from all Fleet and Light Fleet Carriers.

Two prototypes were ordered but shortly afterwards Bishop privately informed the Navy's Chief of Staff (Air), and formally the Fifth Sea Lord, that due to an error of judgement, de Havilland could not cope with the new project. A lack of design staff was the reason and in November 1952 DH suggested a navalised DH.110 in its place, the firm subsequently being asked to offer it in answer to the specification. So the DH.110 was back in the picture except that it had changed a bit since first submitted to N.40/46. Two prototypes to the RAF night fighter specification F.4/48 had been flown but, after the horrible crash at the 1952 Farnborough Show, it had lost favour and so by now was seeking a role. The general feeling within the MoS was that the DH.110 was all that could be offered without the very considerable delay of going out to tender yet again.

The DH.110 was assessed at St Giles Court on 5th March 1953 to see how far a navalised version could meet the Navy's requirement. There were doubts whether the AI.18 radar could be installed even with a small scanner and the strength factors provided by DH were on bottom limit and would need modifying for ground attack operations. The Admiralty wanted four Blue Jay missiles, two was insufficient. There was a poor opinion of the ability of the de Havilland team at Christchurch to do the work in quick time and the CS(A) release date for service use needed to be put back by one year, a decision made on the basis of the third prototype being fully representative of the requirement which prevented delivery until August 1956. Go-ahead was frozen until NR/A.38 was reconciled with the DH.110 and the firm had submitted a new and more detailed brochure. N.139D and P were duly drafted around the aircraft with AI.18 a firm requirement. The standard for the third (naval) prototype (serial XF828), to be constructed from F.4/48 components, was agreed with DH in August and First Level Priority was requested for producing it.

Confirmation came from the Admiralty in September that it definitely wanted the aircraft having made financial provision for 400 and an Advisory Design Conference was held on 21st December. A year later came Treasury approval for an order for 75 (reduced from 100) and it was confirmed that carriage of Red Dean would be required in later production orders (the missile was later cancelled). Redesign by W A 'Bill' Tamblin's team resulted in changes to 80% of the original DH.110 and the third navalised prototype first flew from Christchurch on 20th June 1955. The 'new' aircraft had an Avon RA.14, an all-moving tail and the AI.18 radar complete with a small scanner. Four Blue Jay (Firestreak) missiles were carried and when the Sea Vixen FAW Mk.1 entered service in

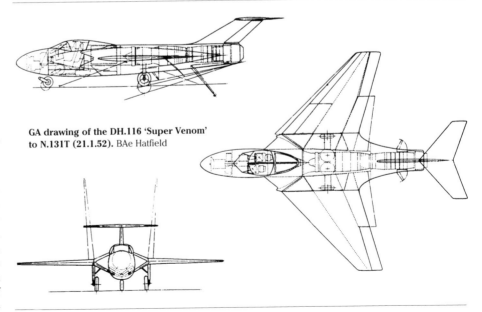

GA drawing of the DH.116 'Super Venom' to N.131T (21.1.52). BAe Hatfield

1959 it became the first British aircraft to use guided weapons as primary armament. The Adens were replaced by Microcell 2-inch (5.1cm) rocket packs putting the Sea Vixen alongside several American interceptors in the 'no guns' category; a popular concept in the US.

In 1954 the DH.110 was to be officially called Pirate (to complement Blackburn's Buccaneer), but this was stalled. As early as 1949, DH was calling the 110 the Vixen; the idea of a night hunter (as the DH.110 then was) being a Vixen was plausible and the Hornet people liked the idea of finding things at night in 'bolt holes'. Eventually approval came for Sea Vixen (and Scimitar for Super-

marine's Type 544, Chapter 2) in March 1957. The Sea Vixen served in two versions until 1973, but proposals to fit new engines (1965), a long range AI pulse radar (1966) and new long range AAMs (1968) came to nothing. In about 1960 the Long Range Air-to-Air Missile had been intended solely for the '1970' fighter, a new aircraft that was to replace the Sea Vixen that year.

Besides the three DH.110 prototypes, a total of 119 FAW Mk.1s were built plus 29 of the FAW Mk.2 version, originally proposed in February 1960 to a tentative Naval Air Staff requirement for an interceptor/strike aircraft for 1965/1970. This initially had two RB.168 engines (later named Spey) of 11,060lb (49.1kN)

dry thrust and 19,250lb (85.6kN) reheated plus bigger intakes. Extended booms offered more fuel while the Firestreak AAM and its support systems were replaced by Red Top. Maximum take-off weight with four Red Tops and full fuel was 46,341lb (21,020kg), maximum level Mach number 0.985 and in a dive 1.5. In the event, the FAW Mk.2 kept its Avons and 67 FAW Mk.1s were rebuilt to the later standard.

The result of all of the delay was that US contemporaries to the Sea Vixen, the near Mach 2 Chance-Vought F8U Crusader, was flown before the third DH.110, and the Mach 2.2 McDonnell F4H Phantom II was flown in May 1958. Consequently the Sea Vixen has been looked on as something of an inferior aircraft when really it was a high class machine that, had it been in service five years earlier, would today enjoy a fine reputation. It had a great rate of turn and, despite some speed restrictions due to control problems, was popular in FAA circles and elsewhere; many considered it superior to the RAF's Javelin.

Writing this long story one is struck by the continual lack of push from the Admiralty; surely if it really knew what it wanted, then a new all-weather fighter could have entered service long before 1959. So many designs were prepared that failed the requirements but, driven hard enough, surely one firm must have been able to put together a satisfactory answer. This made such a contrast to the NA.39 / M.148T strike aircraft requirement so quickly satisfied by the Buccaneer. Perhaps if Hawker or Supermarine had shown real interest, this saga might have been very different, but Hawker was full with Sea Hawk and Hunter work while Supermarine had the Attacker and Swift, plus a day fighter requirement that was ultimately satisfied by the Scimitar (in the next Chapter).

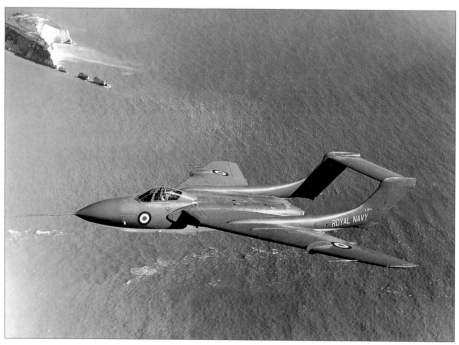

DH.110 second prototype WG240 in ocean colours.
Eric Morgan collection

XJ474 was the first production Sea Vixen FAW Mk.1 to N.139 and was flown for the first time on 20th March 1957. BAe Hatfield

Naval All-Weather Fighter Projects – Estimated Data

1: To Specifications N.40/46 and N.14/49

Project	Span ft (m)	Length ft (m)	Wing Area ft² (m²)	t/c %	All-Up-Weight lb (kg)	Powerplant Thrust lb (kN)	Max Speed / Height mph (km/h) / ft (m)	Armament
Blackburn B.67	51.5 (15.7)	43.0 (13.1)	590 (54.8)	12	29,160 (13,227)	2 x scaled AJ.65 5,000 (22.2)	614 (988) at sea level	4 x 30mm Aden cannon
Gloster P.231	48 (14.6)	42.0 (12.8)	605 (56.2)	9	28,000 (12,701)	2 x F.9 7,000 (31.1)	636 (1,024) at sea level	3 x 30mm Aden cannon
Westland N.40/46 (PJD.129)	51.0 (15.5)	42.0 (12.8)	610 (56.7)	15	25,500 (11,567)	2 x Arm Siddeley 4,860 (21.6)	620 (998) at sea level	3 x 30mm Aden cannon
Blackburn B.67 (RAE estimates)	51.5 (15.7)	43.0 (13.1)	590 (54.8)	12	29,450 (13,358)	2 x AJ.65 6,500 (28.9)	668 (1,075) at sea level	4 x 30mm Aden cannon
de Havilland DH.110	49.5 (15.1)	52.0 (15.8)	640 (59.5)	10	28,950 (13,131)	2 x AJ.65 6,500 (28.9)	656 (1,056) at sea level	4 x 20mm Hispano cannon
Fairey N.40/46	53.0 (16.2)	50.0 (15.2)	520 (48.3)	12	25,000 (11,340)	2 x AJ.65 6,500 (28.9)	633 (1,019) at sea level 613 (986) at 20,000 (6,096)	2 x 30mm Aden cannon
Westland N.40/46 (PJD.144)	55.0 (16.8)	43.5 (13.3)	745 (69.2)	15	27,260 (12,365)	2 x AJ.65 6,500 (28.9)	632 (1,017) at sea level	3 x 30mm Aden cannon
Fairey N.14/49 (ex- N.40/46 - 16.11.48)	55.0 (16.8)	50.0 (15.2)	583 (54.2)	?	29,300 (13,290)	2 x AJ.65 6,500 (28.9)	619 (995) at sea level 586 (943) at 20,000 (6,096)	3 x 30mm Aden cannon
Fairey N.14/49 (Scheme A)	46.0 (14.0)	49.5 (15.1)	470 (43.7)	?	21,500 (9,752)	1 x Avon RA.5 8,300 (36.9)	570 (917) at sea level 598 (962) at 20,000 (6,096)	3 x 30mm Aden cannon
Fairey N.14/49 (Scheme B)	48.5 (14.8)	46.5 (14.2)	?	?	21,300 (9,662)	1 x Avon RA.5 8,300 (36.9)	579 (932) at sea level	3 x 30mm Aden cannon

2: To Specifications N.114T, N.131T and N.139

Project	Span ft (m)	Length ft (m)	Wing Area ft² (m²)	t/c %	All-Up-Weight lb (kg)	Powerplant Thrust lb (kN)	Max Speed / Height mph (km/h) / ft (m)	Armament
Blackburn B.89	50.5 (15.4)	53.7 (16.4)	700 (65.0)	6.5 to 10	26.940 (12,220)	1 x Sapphire 4 9,760 (43.4) dry 12,200 (54.2) reheat	698 (1,123) at sea level	3 x 30mm Aden cannon, 80 RP
Fairey N.114T	46.0 (14.0)	50.0 (15.2)	645 (59.9)	8	29,800 (13,517)	1 x Olympus 3 12,1500 (54.0) no reheat	692 (1,114) at sea level 656 (1,056) at 20,000 (6,096)	3 x 30mm Aden, 70 RP, 4 Blue Sky or 2 Red Dean
Saro P.148	38.5 (11.7)	50.0 (15.2)	500 (46.5)	8	28,000 (12,701)	1 x Avon RA.10R or RA.12	c.690 (1,110) at sea level	4 x 30mm Aden, 72 RP
Short P.D.5	44.0 (13.4)	54.25 (16.5)	641 (59.6)	6.5	28,000 (12,701)	1 x Sapphire 4 12,200 (54.2) reheat	698 (1,123) at sea level	4 x 30mm Aden, 52 RP, 4 Blue Sky or 2 Red Dean
Westland W.37	42.25 (12.9)	56.0 (17.1)	600 (55.7)	8	28,000 (12,701)	1 x RA.12R or Sapphire Sa.4 ? / 12,200 (54.2) reheat	715 (1,151) at sea level 691 (1,112) at sea level, respectively	4 x 30mm Aden, 2 x RP packs, 4 Blue Sky or 2 Red Dean
de Havilland DH.116	34.0 (10.36)	44.0 (13.4)	370 (34.4)	5 to 7	21,405 (9,709)	1 x Avon RA.14 9,500 (42.2) dry c.14,000 (62.2) reheat	685 (1,102) Mach 1.01 at 30,000 (9,144)	2 x 30mm Aden cannon
de Havilland DH.110 Sea Vixen FAW Mk.1 (flown)	50.0 (15.2)	55.6 (16.9)	648 (60.3)	10	42,000 (19,051)	2 x Avon 208 11,250 (50)	645 (1,038) at 10,000 (3,048)	4 x Firestreak, bombs or RPs

Chapter Two

Ship-Borne Supermarines

Naval Day Interceptors: 1945 to 1957

The story of the Navy's day fighter development during the 1950s is an altogether more straightforward affair, but gives away nothing in timescale to the Sea Vixen. In February 1945 N E Rowe, DTD, requested from Joe Smith, Supermarine's Chief Designer, a scheme for an advanced jet propulsion interceptor, the Ministry having studied new project ideas for Royal Air Force and Fleet Air Arm use. The fighter was to have the best possible performance and be suitable for landing on the spring deck or 'carpet' then being designed (see Chapter 13). Smith replied that with the end of the war in Europe imminent, it was assumed that Drawing Office work would decrease and the extra draughtsmen required for the experimental shop would, therefore, be available.

Supermarine Type 505

This initial proposal was a radical V-tail pro-

ject, essentially for the Royal Navy but also available to the RAF. It used the accelerated take-off equipment (i.e. catapult) in conjunction with the landing 'carpet' under development at RAE, the feeling being that great advantages could be gained with the 'carpet' in respect to the saving of the undercarriage weight making possible a very real improvement in performance. Particular emphasis was placed on a high rate of climb and Supermarine had endeavoured to pack the greatest possible power into the smallest and lightest possible airframe, the power plant selected consisting of two AJ.65s.

Substantial investigation had centred on a single engine arrangement plus rockets, but the addition of a rocket booster would be associated with a sweptback wing and both features were excluded until they had been perfected. Uncertainties associated with wing sweep included lateral control at high lift coefficients and, a serious unknown, distortion effects at high speeds, so this was regarded as a refinement to be introduced later. The decision to use two jets was also neces-

Supermarine Type 508 VX133 to N.9/47 flown on 8th August 1951.

sary to accommodate the armament while simplifying construction of the fuselage.

The best possible advice had been sought regarding armament and the 30mm Aden cannon was chosen as it appeared to have reached a more advanced stage of development than two other guns currently proposed, the internally housed 5.9in (15.0cm) rocket gun or the 4.5in (11.4cm) recoilless gun. Provision for these alternatives was made using what little information was available. An initial flying shell prototype could be provided within 15 months of receipt of contract with armament and equipment installation proceeding as test flying progressed. Provision was made for a fixed jury tricycle undercarriage to facilitate early flying and explore the aircraft's behaviour up to about 400mph (644km/h). The reduction in weight allowed use of the thinnest possible wing for an estimated increase in speed and rate of climb of 13% and 19%.

The all-moving V-tail provided a convenient way of getting the tail out of the jet-stream and simplified the structural problems connected with surfaces of very low thickness/chord ratio (6% on the tail). It also provided protection to the rear structure when landing on a flexible deck. Fore and aft control at high speeds was provided by altering the incidence of the whole surface whilst elevators were also brought into action for landing. Directional control came from the elevators' moving differentially. Spoilers were also available for landing approach, power operated wide chord ailerons for lateral control and plain flaps to help lift. Dive recovery flaps were mounted under the wings. A nose flap was extended across the complete span for extra lift, but the possibility of replacing this with boundary layer control was being explored.

The exceptionally small t/c ratio had made it necessary to employ steel spar flanges and an unusually thick light alloy skin for the torsion box making for an extremely robust construction. The fuselage was light alloy throughout. Additional wing tip fuel tanks could be carried. Fitting the engines side-by-side saved 20% on frontal area and was safer in the event of engine failure on take-off, the resulting fuselage shape was laterally stable on the landing 'carpet'. The top speed of 685mph (1,102km/h) at sea level was a pure estimate from the data available as it was impossible with the then current knowledge to predict with certainty an accurate maximum speed as Mach number approached 1.0. At 13,500lb (6,123kg) load, sea level rate of climb was estimated to be 27,300ft/min (8,321m/min), time to 45,000ft (13,716m) 3.0 minutes. Internal fuel totalled 405gal (1,841lit).

At a meeting to consider ordering the Type 505 on 9th August 1946, the decision was taken not to go-ahead, mainly because flexible deck trials were yet to take place and converted carriers would not be ready for production aircraft. In fact it was becoming apparent that sprung deck trials would take longer than originally thought. M S Slattery, Vice Controller Air, said to order now was not justified and perhaps the project could be shelved for 12 to 18 months to get Supermarine busy on a pure jet naval strike aircraft, the one remaining project he had to fill in the 1947/48 development programme. The alternative was a naval fighter to be transferred from the 1947/48 programme to 1946/47 because he liked the idea of converting the Type 505 into a conventional fighter with undercarriage. The undercarriageless option was to be kept in mind for some time as this always appealed to the Navy.

A hedge against possible failure of the Hawker N.7/46 (later the Sea Hawk) was needed, as considerable difficulty was being experienced with the Kingston aircraft. Hence, a new brochure was prepared for a fighter called Type 508, a project initially very close in appearance to the 505 except for more wing area (310ft² [28.8m²]) and an undercarriage.

Supermarine Type 508

This was a big aeroplane, particularly for a ship-borne fighter, with a near straight (8° sweep) wing and the distinct butterfly V-tail which performed the dual role of tailplane and fin. Supermarine was still confident of the success of the 'carpet' experiments that were to go ahead as fast as possible and thus arranged the 508's undercarriage for rapid removal if required. The only limitation placed upon the design was that approach speed (1.15 x stall speed) should not exceed 121 mph (195km/h). The addition of a tricycle undercarriage plus the increase in wing area to meet the approach speed requirement had increased weight appreciably. The wing was thickened to 9% to reduce structure weight

and size and provide more room for the accommodation of flap, spoiler, aileron and wing-fold mechanism. At the brochure stage, length remained as the 505, but span had increased to 40.0ft (12.2m) while the retraction of the wheels into the lower fuselage resulted in a deeper body. The estimated maximum speed at sea level was 660mph (1,062km/h), 25mph (40km/h) less than the 505, and normal loaded weight 17,500lb (7,938kg). Sea level rate of climb 18,700ft/min (5,700m/min).

The project was discussed in January 1947 and three prototypes were ordered in August to the new Naval Staff Requirement NR/A.17 and Specification N.9/47 issued in April. Four 30mm Aden cannon were to be fitted below the air intakes, but in the event only the second aircraft actually received the guns. Joe Smith had seriously considered fitting a tail wheel instead of the nose wheel as the latter had such an enormous load thrown onto it after engaging the arrestor wire, but ultimately chose the tricycle arrangement as this assisted pilot view.

The mock-up was examined officially on 24th September 1948 and construction of the first prototype, VX133, began in mid-1949.

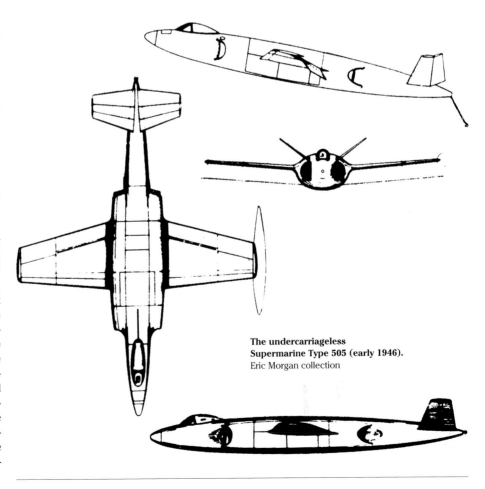

**The undercarriageless
Supermarine Type 505 (early 1946).**
Eric Morgan collection

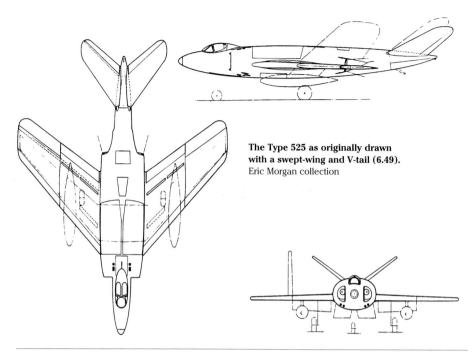

The Type 525 as originally drawn with a swept-wing and V-tail (6.49).
Eric Morgan collection

The completed aircraft was larger than that proposed in the brochure with a wing area of 340ft² (31.6m²) and a successful first flight was made on 31st August 1951. Take-off and climb performance proved to be excellent but top speed was only 603mph (970km/h) at 30,000ft (9,144m). The main criticism came with certain lateral and directional characteristics, some of which appeared to be inherent with the butterfly tail. VX136 received some minor modifications and was renumbered Type 529. First flown on 29th August 1952, it reached 607mph (977km/h), Mach 0.92, at 30,000ft.

Well before flight test, the Thames House meeting on 3rd April 1950 that examined the N.14/49 situation also looked into N.9/47 progress. RAE pointed out how new Sapphire and Avon (RA.6) developments offered such an improvement in performance that an aircraft powered by either would probably be speed limited aerodynamically and not by lack of power, and they questioned the desirability of continuing with twin engines when by using one of these later engines a smaller and cheaper aircraft would meet the requirement. It was unanimously agreed that whichever project was decided upon, swept-back wings would have to be employed in order to raise the aerodynamic limitations as high as possible.

However, it was likely to be three to four years before the new engines gave a higher top speed than two RA.3s and designing a single engine version would put it 2.5 years behind the present project if started *now*. This was unacceptable and it was agreed that the third Type 508 prototype, VX138, should be al-

tered to embody sweep back and reheat in order to obtain the best possible performance from the project at the earliest possible date. Concurrently the MoS would, as a research project, initiate a design study of a single engined alternative.

Supermarine Type 525

Such a redesign had already been proposed by Supermarine in June 1949 with wing and butterfly tail both swept. Supermarine explained that projected developments in carrier arresting and catapulting equipment, coupled with the tractability at approach speeds of its own swept wing aircraft (the Type 510), suggested that the position was distinctly encouraging. The firm had accordingly investigated converting the Type 508 to a swept configuration for naval use. Estimates suggested approach speed would not increase with the required endurance unimpaired, but sea level speed using reheat was now expected to be over 700mph (1,127 km/h) with supersonic potential at altitude. A drooped nose flap to the leading edge was planned with trailing edge flaps of the NACA double slotted type between aileron and fuselage. Sea level rate of climb was 13,000ft/min increasing to 22,200ft/min (3,962 and 6,767m/min) with reheat. NR/A.17 was duly revised in November 1950.

Go-ahead was given for the 525 but the swept V-tail became a problem structurally as the stresses in the pivot holding on the whole tail were excessive and a cruciform tail with all-flying horizontal surfaces was substituted. Many projects of this period had V-tails, V or T types each having their supporters. The V-tail

reduced drag over the T-tail, but because the latter was horizontal, it also acted like a wing and prevented loss of airflow from the fin. Aircraft design has always entailed a difficult balancing act between aerodynamics, drag and structural weight.

VX138's maiden flight took place on 27th April 1954. Two Avon RA.7s each of 7,500lb (33.4kN) thrust were fitted but the planned addition of reheat never happened. Despite the great amount of installed thrust, the Type 525 was still subsonic at its top speed of 647mph (1,041km/h), Mach 0.954, at 30,000 (9,144m), but it was supersonic in a shallow dive reaching Mach 1.08 by 1st November. Time to height did not improve and there were some handling problems. Flight testing revealed serious trouble with engine surging and pitch-up characteristics and the fin had to be redesigned to assist directional stability.

The question arose for ordering further N.9/47 prototypes when in fact the Type 525 had failed to fully meet the specification. Ordering a fourth prototype would probably mean cutting the number of Gloster Javelin prototypes for the RAF. A new specification N.113D was the result and Supermarine's response, the Type 544, was a full redesign which really resembled the 525 only in shape. The wing tips were subtly re-shaped to postpone the onset of compressibility drag rise which, working in tandem with a waisted fuselage (not area ruled), moved up the maximum Mach number a fraction.

DMARD was disappointed the swept N.9 differed so much from the final N.113 and refused a request for Boscombe Down to get involved clearing up those problems peculiar only to the 525. As events transpired, the Boscombe pilots refused to fly it from Chilbolton anyway. The Type 525 spun into the ground and was destroyed on 5th July 1955 after just 61 hours flying and really proved useful to N.113D only in the investigation and development of flap blowing or 'supercirculation'. Modifying the 525 to provide the supersonic blowing of air over the flap was approved in May 1954, the air being bled from the engine compressor and projected as a slim high pressure jet through a tiny slot along the trailing edge slightly ahead of the flap.

The idea of blowing very high velocity air over extended flaps is to re-energise the airflow remaining in contact with the wing and flap upper surfaces, preventing it breaking away. Lift is improved quite dramatically and thus, stalling speed is reduced. Without blowing, the upper surface airflow can break up becoming turbulent at low speeds leading to a loss of lift and increase in drag.

The 'Attinello flap', pioneered in America by NACA under the leadership of John D Attinello, was taken aboard several contemporary American aircraft. In Britain, early boundary layer control research had been performed by Westland for Supermarine before the fighter firm made a full investigation in October 1953. Schemes looked at blowing out of the flap shroud or suction applied at the flap leading edge and the former was selected as the more promising. The Buccaneer strike aircraft was to take 'flap-blowing' a stage further in spanning the whole wing plus the tail which reduced the size of both horizontal surfaces quite markedly, an important benefit for a carrier aeroplane.

The 525 first flew with the blown flaps operating in June 1955 and preliminary results showed its use reduced approach speed by about 12mph (19km/h) and much improved stability and control at low speeds, but any detailed assessment was prevented by the loss of the aircraft. In April 1955 it was decided to fit blown flaps to the Type 544 in place of double slotted flaps, but the first machine did retain the latter.

N.113D

Issued on 16th July 1951, this called for a swept-wing fighter capable of 720mph (1,158 km/h) at sea level and 610mph (982km/h) at 45,000ft (13,716m) without reheat and carrying four Aden cannon, an air-to-air rocket battery and Blue Sky or Red Dean missiles. The whole question of armament was so fluid that the only known fitting was the cannon, the guided weapons and air-to-air rockets were to be installed during production but the aircraft was to have four under-wing hardpoints to accept them and other weapons. N.113P followed in May 1953 for the production aircraft and included RA.23 engines and the additional capability of long range low level bombing and strike. WT854, the first of three Type 544 prototypes, made its maiden flight on 19th January 1956. Initial plans for 100 of what became the Scimitar received financial approval in December 1952 but, in the event, only 76 were built. The first series aircraft flew on 11th January 1957.

The Sea Vixen was eventually to take on most of the Navy's interception duties leaving the Scimitar for strike work which included carriage of the Red Beard tactical nuclear bomb (Target Marker Bomb), conventional iron bombs or Bullpup air-to-surface guided missiles. It was, however, adapted to take the Sidewinder AAM and retained the cannon. On entering service in June 1958 it was the UK's fastest in-service fighter but was only supersonic in a dive. Its service life was to last just eight years. The Scimitar possessed phenomenal power and take-off acceleration, was an immensely noisy beast and was the first single-seat swept-wing fighter, the first equipped with nuclear weapons and the biggest and heaviest single-seat fighter the Fleet Air Arm ever had. It was also capable of releasing most of its weapons at pretty well its full performance limits.

Supermarine Type 556

Second generation Scimitars included the Type 556 two-seat all-weather fighter of March 1954. Adapted to carry two Red Dean or four Blue Jay air-to-air missiles, four cannon or a Blue Jay/gun mix, it had a fatter nose for AI.18 radar and side-by-side seating and was a response to a Ministry request of 17th February. The wider cockpit allowed splayed engines which made room for equipment between the compressors and intake ducts. Supermarine felt this substantially met NR/A.38 in terms of speed, climb and ceiling. A single prototype, XH451, was ordered to NR/A.38 in September, but after construction of a mock-up, work was suspended the following April and cancelled in July after the Sea Vixen was ordered into production. Span was 37.17ft (11.3m), length 58.5ft (17.8m), wing area 478ft² (44.5m²), maximum take-off weight (long range fighter – two guns, two Blue Jay and two drop tanks) 41,852lb (18,984kg). With reheated RA.24s, sea level climb rate was 43,600ft/min (13,289m/min), top sea level speed was 766mph (1,232km/h) and 690mph (1,110km/h) at 40,000ft; service ceiling was 52,150ft (15,895m).

The Type 558 Mark 2 Scimitar project of April 1955 used developments of the RA.24 and had the span increased to 43.3ft (13.2m), length 54.15ft (16.5m). Firestreak was the main weapon.

A possible interim Scimitar development with reheated RB.146 and Airpass radar was suggested in 1959. However, with a primary FAA role of strike, any development of the Scimitar became pointless once the Buccaneer had arrived.

Artist's impression of the V-tail Type 525.
Eric Morgan collection

Top left: **The Type 525 VX138 photographed on 8th June 1955. This aircraft was the third N.9/47 prototype and flew for the first time on 27th April 1954. It was lost on 5th July shortly after the picture was taken.** Eric Morgan collection

Top right: **WT854 was the first Scimitar prototype and made its maiden flight on 19th January 1956. It is shown in mid-1956 with a modified nose but still with the dihedral tail of the first prototypes.** Eric Morgan collection

Above: **XD212 was the first Scimitar F Mk.1 production aircraft and this lovely shot shows the anhedral tailplane is now fitted.** Eric Morgan collection

Naval Day Interceptor Projects to Specifications N.9/47 and N.113 – Estimated Data

Project	Span ft (m)	Length ft (m)	Wing Area ft² (m²)	t/c %	All-Up-Weight lb (kg)	Powerplant Thrust lb (kN)	Max Speed / Height mph (km/h) / ft (m)	Armament
Supermarine Type 505	35.0 (10.7)	46.75 (14.2)	270 (25.1)	7	15,500 (7,031)	2 x AJ.65 6,500 (28.9)	685 (1,102) at sea level	2 x 30mm Aden cannon
Supermarine 508 (flown)	41.0 (12.4)	50.0 (15.2)	340 (31.6)	9	18,850 (8,550) (normal load)	2 x Avon RA.3 6,500 (28.9)	603 (970) at 30,000 (9,144)	4 x 30mm Aden (not fitted)
Supermarine 529 (flown)	41.0 (12.4)	50.5 (15.4)	340 (31.6)	9	22,584 (10,244)	2 x Avon RA.3 6,500 (28.9)	607 (977) at 30,000 (9,144)	4 x 30mm Aden cannon
Supermarine 525 (V-tail – as proposed)	42.0 (12.8)	52.0 (15.8)	490 (45.5)	8	21,650 (9,820)	2 x Avon RA.3 6,500 (28.9)	679 (1,093) at sea level 702 (1,130) reheat	4 x 20mm Hispano cannon
Supermarine 525 (flown)	37.2 (11.3)	53.0 (17.4)	450 (41.9)	8	19,910 (9,031) [28,169 (12,777) max overload]	2 x Avon RA.7 7,500 (33.3)	647 (1,041) at 30,000 (9,144)	None fitted
Supermarine 544 Scimitar F Mk.1 (flown)	37.2 (11.3)	55.25 (16.8)	485 (45.1)	8	23,962 (10,869) [34,200 (15,513) max overload]	2 x Avon 202 11,250 (50.0)	737 (1,186) at sea level	4 x 30mm Aden, Bombs, Red Beard, AAMs, ASMs

Chapter Three

Day-Fighters for the RAF

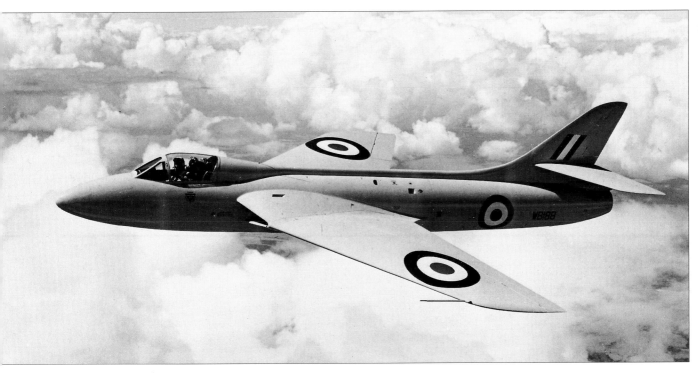

Land-Based Fighter Progress 1946 to the mid-1950s: Part 1

What were some of the factors needing to be taken into account when developing a fighter in the early 1950s? For a naval fighter, a large speed range was an important consideration with the emphasis on control and stability at slow speeds for deck work, especially when this had to be carried out by day and by night. This was not so vital for an aircraft with access to long concrete runways. From a fuel consumption point of view, jet aircraft operated most economically at their service ceiling making performance at maximum altitude of primary importance to ensure altitude supremacy. Lightness was another factor despite the power and quality of the engine. The fighter with the lowest wing loading would have the advantage in manoeuvrability at all heights regardless of thrust to weight ratio; the effect at high Mach numbers could be very pronounced. The criterion for the 1950s interceptor fighter was high Mach number limit combined with low wing loading to give maximum advantage.

New engines gave more power which increased speeds and rate of climb, but performance limits also depended on the quality of airframe design including wing shape. Researchers digging through the records of Nazi Germany directly after the war found proof from flight or tunnel testing of the help swept and delta wings could give to high speed aeroplanes. Sweeping the wings to reduce drag had been proposed at a High Speed Flight Congress in Rome during 1935 by a German called Busemann. Four years later Albert Betz, a Swiss, revealed sweepback could delay the advance of compressibility during transonic flight and by the war's end many German fighter projects had swept wings. The delta was another feature developed by German engineers, this time by Professor Alexander Lippisch, and benefited high speed flight by reducing the rate of transonic drag rise and improving manoeuvrability.

With so much valuable data available, designers around the world began to introduce these features into their new projects and, after a year or two, British designers too moved on from their early 'conservative' jet fighters to fully absorb the German lessons.

The first P1067 prototype on an early test flight. BAe

The information saved both research time and expense. As time progressed into the 1950s, the designer's job was not helped by the need to carry new weapons such as air-to-air missiles and stuffing the machine with radars and other electronics (avionics), but the seeds were now laid for some fine aircraft.

The development of the RAF's fighters over this period splits quite neatly into two groups, day and night fighters. The RAF's earliest jet fighter, the Meteor was followed by the de Havilland DH.100 Vampire and then by a faster 'thin wing' development which became the DH.112 Venom fighter-bomber first flown on 2nd September 1949 to Specification F.15/49.

The Meteor was turned into a night fighter by Armstrong Whitworth in 1949 in the form of the 'long-nose' NF Mk.11 to F.24/48. But these were interim gap-fillers and the quest for more advanced fighters was already well underway. The stories become inter-linked

once specifications F.43/46 and F.44/46 for day and night fighters respectively were issued together in January 1947 and we will look at the day job first.

F.43/46 (and OR.228)

The primary role of this day interceptor was the destruction of high-speed, high-altitude bombers as soon as possible after initial detection by radar. From a button start, the fighter was to reach 45,000ft (13,717m) in no more than six minutes. The margin of speed over enemy bombers was not likely to be great so the fighter was to be equipped primarily with a long range cannon, namely the 4.5in (11.5 cm) non-recoil gun. The Air Staff set great store by this weapon, but it had stipulated alternative armament comprising two 30mm cannon in case the 4.5in was not successful or its proximity fuse proved susceptible to jamming. Swept wings were preferred but it was appreciated they might lead to

Late 1940s fighter design was influenced by the information on advanced combat aircraft acquired from Germany after the end of the war, knowledge already utilised to an extent in the Messerschmitt Me262.

delay so wing design could be changed on later models. Top speed at 45,000ft had to be approximately 547kts (630mph/1,014km/h), Mach 0.953, or 500kts (575mph/925km/h) for a more conventional design should there be swept wing design difficulties; service ceiling 50,000ft (15,240m). The aircraft was to replace the Meteor.

Early jet engines had several limitations but the most serious were:

i) high fuel consumption, especially at low altitudes (long distances meant a stack of fuel);

ii) restricted operating conditions for giving maximum efficiency. The jet engine could be comparatively efficient, provided it was working under its favoured conditions of high

speed and great height. Although the thrust itself decreased with height, aircraft drag decreased in a greater proportion while both the thermal and overall efficiency of the engine increased appreciably.

As a consequence, the first jet bombers were also limited by these restrictions and therefore, those designed by the Soviet Union were expected to attack at height. The great threat posed by the jet bomber was also brought home by the capabilities of English Electric's superb Canberra tactical bomber. The need to make fast interceptions at height became paramount.

The maximum figures quoted for combat aircraft (top speed, maximum ceiling etc.) were usually of no real importance to a fighter pilot. More relevant were rate of climb and the aircraft's performance at different heights compared to a likely opponent. In the first generation Meteor and Vampire the benefits from jet propulsion on climb rate were not as great as one might have expected. Piston fighters with very powerful engines like the de Havilland Hornet could climb near vertically and 'hang on their props' whereas the early jets had to climb at a shallower angle which nullified some of the extra speed. Not until the arrival of higher power-to-weight ratios in the later generation jet fighters did vertical climb start to become a reality again.

The late 1940s and early 1950s saw remarkable work in the development of fighter guns. The standard RAF armament since the middle war years had been the 20mm Hispano cannon which had proved immensely successful. Aircraft structures, however, were gradually and continuously increasing in weight and strength and the 20mm would eventually provide inadequate lethality. A new gun was needed and the Armament Development Establishment and Royal Small Arms Factory, Enfield, (AD and EN) worked together to produce an answer. The result was the Aden cannon of 30mm calibre which duly became the RAF's new standard. Initially it was planned to allow the Aden to use 20mm or 30mm ammunition simply by changing the barrel and feed, the 20mm having less destructive power but greater accuracy from a much higher muzzle velocity.

Hispano responded with its own 30mm called the 825 which was selected for trials aboard the sixth production Swift F Mk.1 in 1952. The aircraft, WK199, was technically considered a full prototype but never actually flew with the gun as initial trials in a Meteor during late autumn revealed the 825's blast was rather greater than the Aden's. The 825 was briefly considered as an insurance for the Aden and for the period when the effects of

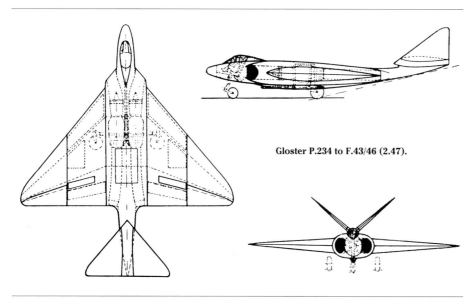

Gloster P.234 to F.43/46 (2.47).

blast were under examination, the whole future of UK gun and interceptor design depended on the result, but Hispano's cannon was abandoned. WK199 had been altered from a two to four gun format and the time taken to do this brought Supermarine some criticism. The firm's record in carrying out manufacture work for research purposes was described as 'very bad'.

The 4.5in (11.5cm) recoilless gun was the brainchild of the Chief Engineer and Superintendent of Armament Design (CEAD), Fort Halstead, and was prepared in mock-up form by May 1947. The gun was fundamentally a tube in which the recoil was absorbed by the backwards ejection of a counterweight when the shell was fired. Seven proximity fused shells were carried capable of lethal effects within a 100ft (30.5m) diameter circle. The barrel was 10ft (25.4cm) long but proved difficult to produce and this weapon was never brought to an operational state. De Havilland's R E Bishop, however, stated emphatically that the 4.5in needed some redesign before it was at all suitable for installation in an aeroplane. He felt the diameter of the feed mechanism (a swinging revolving chamber) needed to be reduced.

Four firms were invited to tender to F.43/46 and three, Gloster, Hawker and Supermarine submitted projects.

Gloster P.234

A progression from the Meteor introducing a delta wing and delta V-tail. Two Rolls-Royce AJ.65 engines were placed inside the fuselage and fed by very large side intakes and the 4.5in gun was mounted on the bottom fuselage centre-line. The firm estimated the P.234 should be capable of supersonic speed.

Hawker P.1054

Hawker's preliminary proposals for a swept wing interceptor fighter with 4.5in gun were submitted in brochure form during September 1946 under P.1054. For Hawker, with its usual emphasis on style, this was a particularly garish layout with twin AJ.65 engines placed in the lower forward fuselage and fed by split intakes with the gun 'threaded' between, the barrel passing directly beneath the cockpit. This was done to get frontal area down, the accent being placed on aerodynamic refinement with structure a secondary consideration. The result was a very complex fuselage structure. Because of the mid-wing arrangement, wing structure was adversely effected by the jet pipes passing through the spars and any addition of reheat, necessitating as it would a larger jet pipe diameter, would make this worse. Span was 36.0ft

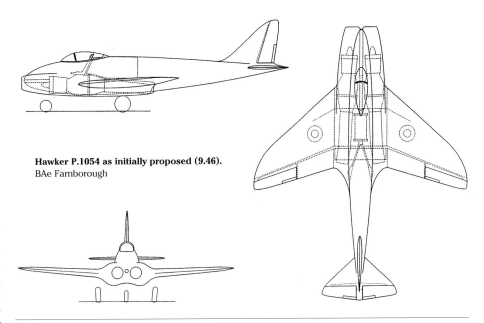

Hawker P.1054 as initially proposed (9.46).
BAe Farnborough

(11m), length 44.6ft (13.6m), gross wing area 354ft^2 (32.9m^2) and total internal fuel 400gal (1,818lit).

Three weeks later the decision was taken to proceed with the P.1052 project (swept-back version of the P.1040 – see later) rather than start detailed work on the P.1054. Scott-Hall wrote to Camm at the end of October stressing a desire to get the earliest possible experience on swept-back wings. Pressing on rapidly with the P.1052 would save many months of work and Hawker would get the P.1054 fighter into the air much earlier. It was also stated that any future high-speed aircraft must be equipped with pilot-ejection. Camm replied that the swept-back version of the P.1040 was originally submitted in October 1945 (the P.1047) and if the project had been put in hand then, much time could have been saved. The P.1054 project proved to have quite an influence on Ministry thinking and F.43/46 reflected the capabilities set by the Hawker design. Hawker's proposal to the specification was a modified P.1054.

Hawker's Vivian Stanbury visited Fort Halstead in early May 1947 to see the working 4.5in (11.5cm) gun mock-up, the first time anyone from the aircraft firm had seen it. He felt the large size made the P.1054 appear rather small and estimated that the weapon's weight of 2,000 to 2,300lb (907 to 1,043kg) would push all-up-weight from 15,000lb (6,804kg) up to about 18,000lb (8,165kg). The blast pressure from both the muzzle and recoil jets was alleged to be 'most formidable'.

Hawker P.1061

J E Serby, DMARD, visited Kingston on 26th April and asked Hawker to look at a conversion of the P.1054 with straight wings instead of swept with, if possible, a 20in (51cm) radar dish fitted. The result was a brochure submission on 10th June for the P.1061 project. Engine and cannon arrangement were unchanged but intake shape was altered to allow for a small nose extension to house the radar dish. The project if anything looking uglier than the P.1054. There was an estimated loss of speed over the swept P.1054 but structurally and aerodynamically the project was more straightforward. Hawker closed its investigations into the P.1054 and P.1061 projects in July 1947.

Supermarine Type 508 variant

This was a modification of the firm's naval fighter which, considering F.43/46's requirement to get the heaviest possible armament up to 45,000ft (13,716m) in the shortest possible time, was considered to be the smallest and lightest design that would satisfactorily house the 4.5in (11.5cm) gun. The two AJ.65s ensured that the maximum possible power was available for a top speed at 45,000ft of 580 mph (933km/h). Internal fuel totalled 415gal (1,887lit). Rocket boosting was omitted but the firm could foresee no difficulty in introducing a rocket in the fuselage tail when such units were perfected. As the 30mm cannon appeared at the time to have reached a more advanced stage of development than the 4.5in, it was anticipated that 30mm armament would be fitted initially. Metrovick's F.9 engine was a possible alternative.

To achieve the higher speed required by the Air Staff, Supermarine considered it necessary to employ back-swept wings and a design investigation on this was already in hand. An additional drawing of a 'swept' Type 508 was included with a span of 41.0ft (12.5m), length

48.0ft (14.6m) and wing area 450ft² (41.8m²); the airframe being convertible. It was felt, that there were still a number of unknowns connected with this type of wing and it was preferred therefore to regard sweep-back as a refinement to be introduced at a further stage in development. At the time such wings were being fitted to the Type 392 Attacker (as the Type 510) and it was expected that trials would do much to clarify the position.

Because of these unknowns, the conventional straight wing used was designed to delay compressibility effects to the highest possible Mach number and, as t/c ratio was the overriding parameter in this respect, the thinnest aerofoil possible was used at 9%. Aerofoil section was constant throughout the span so that initial stall should occur at the wing/body junction and it was felt that tip stalling should be completely avoided. Supermarine wished to see model tests at high Reynolds numbers to confirm this. Estimated speeds over Mach 0.85 were difficult to predict with current knowledge.

–

The F.43/46 Tender Design Conference was held on 9th April 1947. Despite Hawker's design employing a swept-back wing, Gloster's project consisting of a delta wing plus tail, was the most advanced. Supermarine's aircraft had not yet been ordered by the Navy and it was not clear any such order would be forthcoming. In a sense the F.43/46 was an interim fighter pending the longer term development of the Red Hawk air-to-air missile at which stage a two-seat day and night fighter would probably become standard. It was thought a large production order would follow the prototype to entirely re-equip Fighter Command for two or three years.

Supermarine's project had a wing loading of about 50lb/ft² (244kg/m²) and was likely to be the less manoeuvrable of the three types and would not reach the stipulated full speed. The swept version had a loading of 36lb/ft² (176kg/m²) and would achieve the speed with better manoeuvrability as well. The Hawker P.1054 had a wing loading of 38lb/ft² (186 kg/m²) while Gloster's P.234 was just 25lb/ft² (122kg/m²) thanks to the delta planform and without a high price in structure weight. The P.234 was likely to have the best manoeuvrability thanks to a low lift coefficient and it exceeded or almost reached the other specified limits. All projects came within specification for climb to 45,000ft (13,716 m) with estimated times of 4.5, 5.75 and 5 minutes for P.1054, P.234 and Type 508 respectively.

At the time it was impossible to say which would be the faster project, Gloster's or Hawker's, nor which would prove to be the more practical, there being no reliable data at the very high Mach numbers involved. Both had problems of control and stability, as did the swept Type 508, and it was possible a top speed limit might come from aileron ineffectiveness at perhaps around Mach 0.93. The P.234 could have the advantage, thanks to its lower wing tip t/c ratio and greater sweep.

Both swept and delta projects introduced aero-elastic problems which were being tackled theoretically and on several experimental aircraft currently under construction (Boulton Paul P.111, Hawker P.1052 and Supermarine Type 510), but it was unlikely these would provide high speed flight data in less than two years. Some useful but inconclusive full scale data was available from the DH.108 research aircraft and low and high speed results had been recorded for swept-back wings, but no flight or high speed tunnel data was available for delta wings. A tunnel programme for the latter was in hand, but it was acknowledged that much more was currently known about swept wings than deltas.

To the author, this review suggests a lack of hard knowledge and aerodynamic experience in these new wing shapes was available to UK aircraft designers at the time, despite

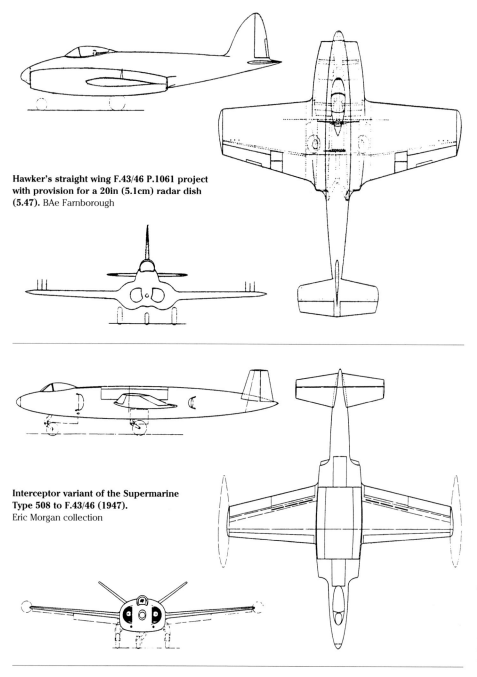

Hawker's straight wing F.43/46 P.1061 project with provision for a 20in (5.1cm) radar dish (5.47). BAe Farnborough

Interceptor variant of the Supermarine Type 508 to F.43/46 (1947). Eric Morgan collection

the material found in Germany and discussed in Chapter 6. The desire to use them seems to be there, but maybe with a lack of confidence. This presented great difficulties in producing new fighters capable of dealing with the expected future threat from the Soviet Union and a single sentence in the Conference minutes highlights the problem beautifully, 'From the low speed tunnel work so far the delta wing might present a worse lateral stability problem, and in any case nobody yet knows the effect at high subsonic speeds of placing a tail behind such a wing'. After some discussion it was agreed that the question of a tail would be settled later if it were decided to order the Gloster design.

The objective was to have an aeroplane much better than the Meteor in service in four or five years and these estimates were made for first flights: Gloster, December 1949 (assuming basic delta wing aerodynamic data was immediately available); Hawker, November 1949; Supermarine, January 1949 (allowing for the fact that the design had been underway for some time. It would, however, be set back by redesign of the tail plane). On technical grounds the Gloster design appeared the most attractive in view of its large wing root dimensions, low wing loading and the scope for development that the layout offered. On the other hand, after redesign of the intakes and tails, both the Hawker and swept Supermarine would be backed by a greater volume of research information.

Much discussion centred on the ordering of two aircraft, one to offer the highest possible performance and the other to act as an insurance. It was agreed that an order should be placed with Gloster for its delta design, the number of prototypes to be settled later. The straight wing Supermarine appeared a useful insurance, but there would be serious objection to ordering a prototype which it was hoped would never go into service. However, it was felt if the Navy ordered the aircraft, an RAF version would share costs and swept wings could be fitted in due course. This was left as a possible solution.

Martin-Baker F.43/46

Another F.43/46 project but apparently not submitted; it received no consideration at the Conference. This delta's wing would today be considered fairly conservative, but putting the pilot in a pressurised cockpit faired into the base of the fin was quite unusual though having much in common with early Lippisch ideas. As a consequence, the fin root was very thick. Estimated performance was Mach 0.84 at sea level, Mach 0.91 (600mph [966km/h]) at 45,000ft (13,716m) with 6 minutes to reach

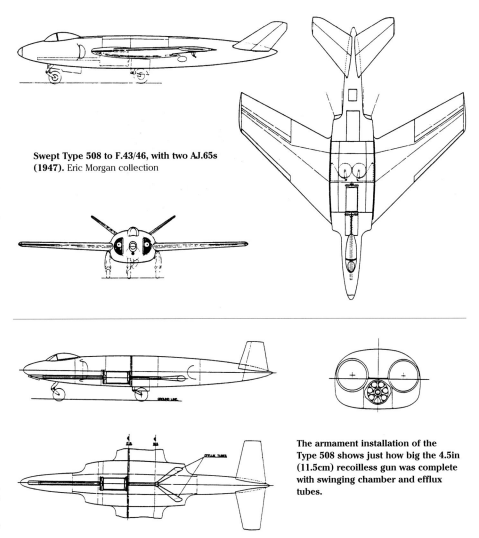

Swept Type 508 to F.43/46, with two AJ.65s (1947). Eric Morgan collection

The armament installation of the Type 508 shows just how big the 4.5in (11.5cm) recoilless gun was complete with swinging chamber and efflux tubes.

45,000ft. Internal fuel was 300gal (1,364lit) and armament comprised one Hispano cannon in each wing root. The aircraft had a cigar shaped fuselage and nose intake.

By incorporating an ejector seat, Martin-Baker made use of another of its pioneering achievements which eventually made the name world famous. Despite the project appearing in model form at the 1947 SBAC Show at Radlett, there was no way the firm could realistically build such an advanced aircraft, despite previous success with piston types, and it chose instead to work on ejector seats for high performance aircraft. This was the easiest and safest way of getting a crew out of a stricken aircraft at high speeds and/or low level and, with such big advances in performance, a new market opened up. So successful was Martin-Baker in perfecting its seats that they have been used in a large percentage of the western world's fighters ever since.

–

Gloster was informed during June 1947 that prototypes were to be ordered and a meeting

at Bentham in late July confirmed a proposal to construct the first two prototypes as flying shells, without vital equipment, for early aerodynamic and handling tests. The layout had been revised with the 4.5in (11.5cm) gun emerging at the extreme nose of the fuselage. But in September the Air Staff asked for a change of requirement which forced contract action to be suspended on the 23rd. A much revised F.43/46 layout was discussed with Gloster during November as were new schemes with Hawker and one with de Havilland, inter-linking again with the F.44/46 night fighter specification.

Gloster P.248 and P.250

These August 1947 drawings represented a major redesign with all trace of Meteor ancestry having departed. They were the same aircraft except the P.248 had the 4.5in gun with barrel protruding from the nose centre and the latter carried two nose mounted Adens. Still single-seat aircraft, the addition of a T-tail represented the first step towards the

VW120

De Havilland's DH.108 was a research aircraft designed to probe the unknowns of transonic flight and it became the first British aircraft to produce a supersonic bang, albeit while completely out of control. Eric Morgan collection

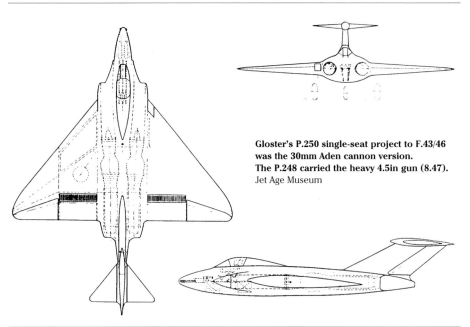

Gloster's P.250 single-seat project to F.43/46 was the 30mm Aden cannon version. The P.248 carried the heavy 4.5in gun (8.47). Jet Age Museum

final Javelin arrangement. They were very short lived, however, as a Ministry of Supply report called for drastic changes to F.43/46 by leaving out the 30mm cannon and replacing the 4.5in recoilless gun with one or more Red Hawk air-to-air missiles. An AI search radar and 42in (107cm) nose scanner was now required and another brochure had been put together by 1st October.

Gloster P.258 and P.259

Gloster's fighter now became a two-seater and was altogether much bigger. Little information was available to the firm regarding shape, size and weight of Red Hawk and housing it satisfactorily was likely to be difficult. The P.258 drawing showed what Gloster thought Red Hawk might look like when carried semi-conformally beneath the fuselage, the missile being lowered into the free air stream before launching. Another version

carried six RPs in the wing roots while the full general arrangement P.259 retained the 4.5in gun in the port wing. Alternative engines, grouped closely together for adequate single engine control, were Metrovick Sapphires or Rolls Avons.

Gloster understood that the Sapphire could be developed to 7,500lb (33.3kN) thrust which would reduce time to 45,000ft (13,716m) by 45 seconds and raise ceiling to 56,000ft (17,069m). Even at 7,000lb (31.1kN), this was 500lb (2.2kN) more than the AJ.65 Avon giving an estimated time of 8.25 minutes to 45,000ft compared to 8.6 and a speed of 628mph (1,011km/h – Mach 0.95) at that height. Besides the large nose scanner, a fixed 10in (25cm) scanner was placed in the rear of the tail junction torpedo. Provision of a small trimming tailplane was felt desirable due to the large trim changes associated with a speed range of 100 to 700mph (161km/h to

1,126 km/h). Structure was mainly light alloy based on a conventional single wing spar arrangement with subsidiary rear spar.

–

The alterations to F.43/46 made renumbering a sensible move and by February 1948 it was retitled F.3/48. Hawker reviewed various alternatives for interceptor fighter aircraft during early 1948 and these were gathered together for discussion with the Ministry at Kingston on 10th March. A brochure submitted in February had given the firm's opinions on the merits of jet engines, reheat and rocket motors and Hawker doubted whether a twin engine design to F.3/48 requirements would be successful owing to the comparatively large frontal area. They suggested a more efficient design would be obtained with a single engine plus rocket motor. Further, the recoilless gun with single barrel and several rounds did not provide an easy installation for a high performance fighter and a multiple barrel layout with single rounds was preferable.

In the past, the main objection to the use of rocket motors had been the difficulty in handling the special fuels (some of which were particularly volatile and nasty chemicals), but Hawker contended that the design of high performance fighter aircraft had reached the stage where any difficulties had to be overcome. A scheme for the experimental installation of the Armstrong Siddeley rocket motor in the N.7/46 naval fighter was being investigated by the firm. This related to a 2,000lb (8.9kN) Snarler rocket fitted in the tail fuselage of the P.1040 prototype VP401 as an addition to its Rolls-Royce Nene engine, the project being renumbered P.1072. In this guise, the aircraft flew on 20th November 1950 after flying on the 16th under turbojet power only. Despite an impressive climb performance, the machine made just six flights with the rocket before the Ministry gave preference to afterburning jet engines.

Hawker considered that a twin Avon design would have a comparatively large frontal area and drag without the additional problems of the 4.5in (11.5cm) gun; the aircraft would be just too big. The single engine plus rocket alternative undoubtedly resulted in a smaller aircraft, particularly when 20mm or 30mm cannon were used instead of the big 4.5in weapon, with a performance as good as the twin Avon design. Hawker studied a series of proposals including the P.1054, a night fighter project to the F.44/46 requirement (the P.1057 fitted with a T-tail which had poor engine access plus frontal area up to 41ft² [3.8m²]) and the group below. Great emphasis was placed on achieving the smallest frontal area possible, the figure for the P.1054 at 38ft² (3.5m²) being the target to beat.

Hawker P.1064

Compared to the P.1054, aerodynamic refinement was not allowed to dictate in this layout, primary consideration was a simple structure. The wing was of the straight through type capable of having any number of spars in any position, the only restriction coming from the retracted undercarriage. The fuselage sat on top of the wing in the fashion of the piston engine Fury with the engines resting in the junction between them. The recoilless, or alternative, gun armament was forward of the pilot and unencumbered by any other items. Thus engine and gun accessibility or interchangeability were excellent, but the aerodynamics were poor. The flaps were uninterrupted from aileron to aileron but the design was unconventional in that the heavy weights were strung out and the tail arm was short. Frontal area was 45ft² (4.2m²).

Hawker P.1065

This project shared similar wing and tail surfaces to the P.1064 but with cut back intakes, tail jet pipe for a single AJ.65 and provision for a rocket motor of either 2,000 or 4,000lb (8.9 or 17.8kN) thrust. It was a smaller machine than those with two engines, a fact reflected in the frontal area figure of 24.5ft² (2.3m²).

Hawker P.1063 (?)

Besides P.1054 and P.1064, two more un-numbered twin Avon layouts had their engines slung under either straight or swept wings with a T-tail. All twin Avon designs had a disproportionately large frontal area, a situation caused by the need for balance by placing the engines near the centre of gravity, at which position was also placed the fuel. But this project, believed to come under P.1063 and also associated with the Navy's N.9/47 requirement, though not confirmed, achieved the small frontal area of 32ft² (3.0m²) by moving one engine forward and the other back thereby preserving balance.

The lead engine was placed right inside the port intake level with but below the cockpit; the rearward engine in the upper fuselage fitted just ahead of the tail and was fed entirely by the starboard intake. The exhausts stayed

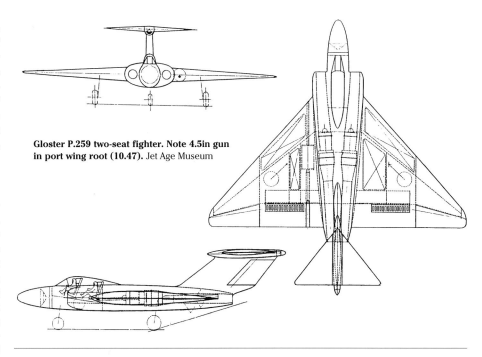

Gloster P.259 two-seat fighter. Note 4.5in gun in port wing root (10.47). Jet Age Museum

separate resulting in a 'stacked' jet pipe. Consequently the aircraft had an elongated fuselage with air ducts and jet pipes occupying a large amount of space such that fuel tanks were very dispersed and of uneconomical shape, the armament installation was very cramped and the undercarriage had to be in the wings. The aerodynamics were very good with minimum interference to the wing, but engine efficiency and access were poor.

–

The F.43/46 and F.44/46 Design Conferences had selected Gloster to build the single-seat day fighter and de Havilland the two-seat night fighter. Hawker was also to build a two-

seater if possible. A memorandum dated 26th January 1948, from J E Serby, DMARD, reported that after much discussion with the Air Staff and the firms concerned, it had been agreed that Gloster's delta layout lent itself better to the two-seat aeroplane, chiefly because the large chord wings could conveniently house the greater fuel and equipment required. Moreover, Hawker had considerable difficulty in producing an attractive two-seat layout but had tabled a good single-seater. The following orders were therefore proposed: F.43/46 three prototypes from Hawker; F.44/46 three prototypes from both Gloster (later four) and de Havilland.

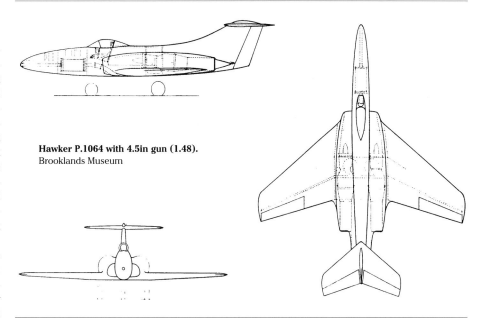

Hawker P.1064 with 4.5in gun (1.48). Brooklands Museum

F.3/48 (still OR.228)

F.43/46 was shortly to become F.3/48 and essentially written around Hawker's new P.1067 project. Formally issued on 15th October 1948, the required 547kts (630mph/1,014 km/h) at 45,000ft (13,716m) and six minutes to that height were unchanged. A single Avon or Sapphire was specified with provision for reheat, and two or four 30mm Aden cannon.

Way back in early November 1944, DOR (Mr Wardle) and DTD (N E Rowe) visited Sydney Camm at Claremont House to discuss single engine jet fighter aircraft. Camm had available the bifurcated pipe scheme (a split jet pipe at the trailing edge wing roots) which was sent to Rolls-Royce for investigation on the 14th. The idea proved satisfactory and a proposal called P.1040 fitted with a Nene engine was declared by the Ministry a considerable advance on present types. The aircraft was eventually ordered as the Sea Hawk naval fighter to Specification N.7/46 and over 500 were built. During early October 1945 a new tender was submitted for a swept-back version with an additional rocket motor called P.1047 and throughout the first half of 1946 discussion centred on construction of a swept-back N.7/46. Go-ahead was given in late August and the aircraft (VX272) was built as the P.1052 to experimental specification E.38/46, flying on 19th November 1948. It proved a very pleasant aircraft to fly.

On 30th July 1948, data was submitted to J E Serby on two interim fighter versions of

the P.1052 and P.1040 called P.1062 and P.1068 respectively with a Rolls-Royce Nene 4 engine and straight exhaust pipe. Three months later a full proposal followed to develop the P.1062 as an interim fighter. In the first stage the P.1052 was taken as it stood with the Nene II plus the addition of armament; the P.1062 was to be the second stage with a Rolls-Royce RB.44 (Tay) engine complete with reheat. The project was not adopted and closed on 5th November.

Exactly a year later Hawker proposed to the MoS a P.1052 with straight through pipe as a private venture. Air Marshal Sir Alec Coryton, CS(A), welcomed the idea and Serby agreed it was well worth doing as the bifurcated jet pipe did not lend itself to reheat making the all-through pipe essential. The second prototype P.1052, VX279, was rebuilt from aft of the rear engine bay from April 1950 onwards and included the swept variable incidence tailplane first tested on the P.1052; the forward fuselage and wing panels were unchanged. This aircraft, now called P.1081, made its second maiden flight on 19th June. A Rolls-Royce Tay R.Ta.1 centrifugal turbojet of 6,250lb (27.8kN) dry thrust was to be fitted with reheat, but the aircraft crashed on 3rd April 1951, before the standard Nene could be replaced. The aircraft displayed good handling up to Mach 0.93.

There had been some production plans for the P.1081 to satisfy a possible Australian order. These came to nothing but by now Hawker had collected a good deal of swept

wing knowledge and experience with the P.1052 and P.1081 and were well placed to prepare a top of the range single-seat day fighter. Redrafting the specification into F.3/48 confirmed the requirement had settled down and the firm could start some metal bashing.

Hawker P.1067 Hunter

Hawker's day fighter studies finally came together in this project with a single Avon engine. Preliminary investigations were completed in January 1948 for an aircraft weighing 12,000lb (5,443kg) and armed with two 30mm cannon, and on the 26th Serby gave instructions to go ahead in accordance with the new requirements set out by the Air Staff. After very long term discussions an armament of four 30mm cannon was accepted with the possible use of the Armstrong Siddeley Sapphire as an alternative engine. The Avon was to have 20% reheat.

One of the earliest P.1067 drawings had a nose intake with four cannon placed low down in a bulbous forward fuselage. This quickly turned into the attractive circular fuselage P.1067/1 of August 1948 to accommodate a bigger Martin-Baker ejection seat, fuselage diameter rising by 2in (5.1cm), and a brochure was prepared. There were doubts as to the final position of the tailplane because of the high speeds envisaged, large changes in trim and the possibility of the elevator becoming ineffective. Hawker's intention was to build one prototype with the tail on top of the fin and another with it placed a little above the fuselage; the latter showed certain structural advantages but the high position was felt to be much better aerodynamically. A low tail would have to be bigger but would shield the rudder and reduce its effectiveness. It was felt imperative that the tail should in some way be adjustable in flight which would probably need power operation and information was expected from an investigation already underway on a Sea Fury. Both ailerons and rudder had spring tabs.

The circular nose intake divided forward of the cockpit and reconverged just forward of the compressor entry on the engine. Only two of the cannon (at this point still 20mm Hispano but with provision for 30mm) stayed underneath, the others moving to the wing roots. Care was taken to ensure adequate stiffness at the high speeds expected with the number of large holes cut to a minimum, despite this creating the need to remove the entire rear fuselage for an engine change. For the same reason the wings (and rear fuselage) were covered in thick gauge skin which also provided sufficient bending resistance to

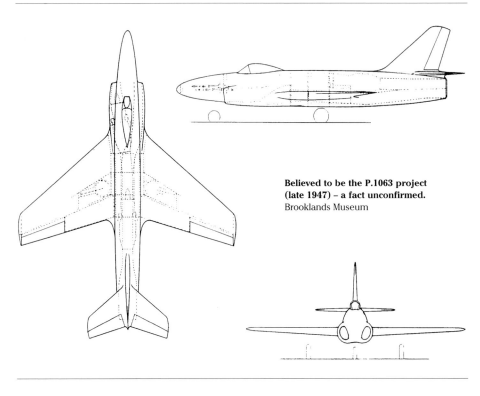

Believed to be the P.1063 project (late 1947) – a fact unconfirmed.
Brooklands Museum

P.1052 prototype VX272 in original configuration with unswept tail. Eric Morgan collection

This view of the Hawker P.1081 shows the important features – swept wing, swept tail and all-through jet pipe. Eric Morgan collection

cut down wing structure in a manner already used successfully on the P.1040 and P.1052. Wing taper ratio was moderate and the wing was not expected to suffer unduly from tip stalling. The large landing flaps were of the ordinary split type, the outer portions together with the upper surface flaps also acting as air-brakes.

Internal fuel, carried in wing tanks and a small fuselage tank, totalled 300gal (1,364lit) but there was no provision for external tanks since Hawker felt these were inadmissible on such a high performance aeroplane. Rate of climb at sea level was 16,400ft/min (4,999m /min) and at 45,000ft (13,716m) 3,300ft/min (1,006m/min); climb to 45,000ft was expected to take 5 minutes from leaving the ground with the operational ceiling 53,000ft (16,154m). On 8th September the firm received a contract for a full Design Study on this transonic aircraft.

It was agreed in January 1949 that Avons should be fitted in the first two prototypes and a Sapphire in the third. Only a radar gun ranging sight was carried inside the small conical intake centre-body but now TRE showed interest in a radar installation ahead of the intake. By March the gradual growth of equipment, notably radar, four cannon and ejector seat, made it apparent the air intake could no longer remain in the nose position. Accordingly a sketch was drawn with leading edge entry and a meeting with Mr Serby discussed the subject on the 11th. This situation was so serious that abandonment was a possibility until the solid nose and well known bifurcated wing root intake were laid out by Harold Tuffen. Approval to proceed with these changes came on the 22nd.

The 8th August saw the inspection of the full mock-up with the final aerodynamic arrangement near complete, but in October a final change confirmed the low tail position. The front fuselage assembly jig was constructed on 5th December and prototype manufacture began. The first intimation of a production order came in late September 1950 by which time manufacture of the outer wings was well advanced, a draft production specification arriving on 1st December. The first aircraft, WB188, made its maiden flight on 20th July 1951.

A national daily newspaper held a contest to name the fighter and its readers chose 'Demon', just at the time the US Navy picked the same name for its new McDonnell F3H interceptor flown on 7th August, so the alternative 'Hunter' was chosen. The Hawker Hunter was to suffer numerous development problems with aerodynamics, gun firing and engine, but it eventually became one of the most popular of all British fighter aircraft. It was supersonic in a modest dive and highly respected by all who flew it and was put into service by the RAF, Royal Navy and numerous overseas customers. Nearly 2,000 were produced in many versions. Despite F.3/48 being prepared around Hawker's day fighter, both Gloster and Supermarine also submitted designs to the specification, but these were never considered for construction.

Gloster P.275

Another rather odd delta design, this project from April 1948 was not dissimilar to Martin-Baker's F.43/46. Gloster's W G Carter wrote to Serby explaining it 'was included for general interest as an advanced design study.

Further consideration had been made to the same general plan but with jet-cum-rocket and we will send this if you wish to see it'. The project had been re-planned on more advanced lines compared to Gloster's earlier F.43/46 studies because new information indicated it was likely to be a good deal more difficult to achieve the required design Mach number at 45,000ft (13,716m) in level flight than previously expected. This single engine design was based on a 12,000lb (53.3kN) reheated axial engine with two-stage compressor turbine, but it was thought drag rise might limit Mach number to 0.95 at 45,000ft. The power installation was chosen to meet the climb requirement when reheated.

Gloster explained much simplification was achieved by housing the pilot in the leading edge of the highly swept fin making it possible to suppress the glass hood to minimum dimensions without impairing the pilot's view, except to the rear. The all-moving tail was deleted for simplicity, this being possible by using rotating wing tip control surfaces for longitudinal control. The same surfaces also satisfied the lateral handling aspect by differ-ential control. Four Adens were housed in pairs in the wing around mid-distance from the root and a gun laying radar scanner was in the centre of the nose entry duct. Internal fuel was 600gal (2,728lit), this being sufficient to give a reasonable margin of capacity over F.3/48 requirements to permit the use of re-heat in manoeuvres for short periods, in addition to making full use of it in intercept climb. Time to 45,000ft (13,716m) was 7.4 min, top speed at 45,000ft 672mph (1,081km/h, Mach 0.94), and as stated the specified 6 minutes could be met with the thrust increased another 20% by afterburning. Absolute ceiling was estimated to be 62,000ft (18,898m).

Supermarine Type 526

This interceptor version of the back-swept V tail Type 525 N.9/47 aircraft was modified to F.3/48 requirements (it had been denavalised) and submitted 9th August 1949. Essentially the two aircraft looked identical and were basically the same bar deletion of wing folding, arrestor gear, catapult hooks and other specialised equipment; factors when coupled with a reduced fuel requirement that made possible a smaller wing area. This was done by clipping the main plane tips, cutting area from 490 to 450ft² (45.5 to 41.8m²). The main spar was arranged to occupy the same position as the 525, wing torque being taken by a nose rib attached to the fuselage side. 'Droop nose' leading edge flaps, NACA double slotted trailing edge flaps and power assisted slotted ailerons were fitted.

Fuselage alteration was minimal; the front engine frame was strengthened for the wing torque attachment and the fuel tank housing had to be re-disposed as the CofG was approximately 12in (30.5cm) behind that on the 525. Avon engine installation was identical but provision was made for reheat. 630gal (2,864lit) of internal fuel was available; weights and performance were quoted for four 20mm Hispano cannon, but 30mm Adens could be carried. Sea level rate of climb was 16,670 ft/min (5,081m) – 25,650 [7,818] with reheat; 45,000ft could be reached in 6.45 minutes (4.65 with reheat), top speed at this height 617mph (993km/h) or 643 (1,035) with reheat. The Ministry considered the Type 526 seemed attractive as a high performance subsonic fighter for daylight duties and felt it was an appreciable improvement over the Kingston design.

Supermarine Type 541 Swift

In the event, the rival to Hawker's Hunter was not the Supermarine 526 / Scimitar family, but the same firm's Swift, an aircraft that had passed through similar 'stages' of evolution

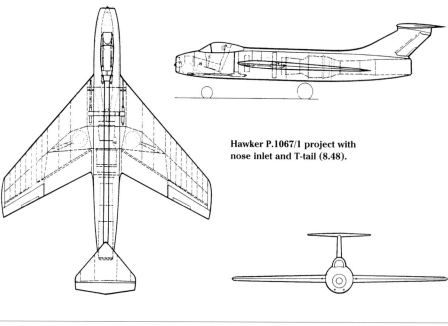

Hawker P.1067/1 project with nose inlet and T-tail (8.48).

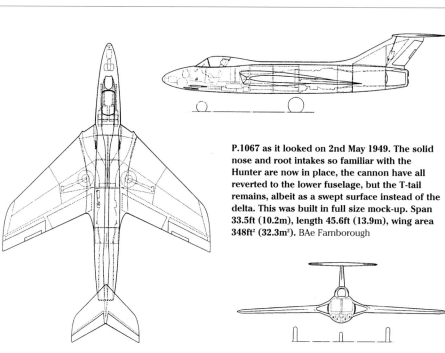

P.1067 as it looked on 2nd May 1949. The solid nose and root intakes so familiar with the Hunter are now in place, the cannon have all reverted to the lower fuselage, but the T-tail remains, albeit as a swept surface instead of the delta. This was built in full size mock-up. Span 33.5ft (10.2m), length 45.6ft (13.9m), wing area 348ft² (32.3m²). BAe Farnborough

British Secret Projects: Jet Fighters

ut without the competition. The firm's first et fighter was the Attacker flown in 1946. Although inferior to Hawker's Sea Hawk, it can be considered as Supermarine's straight wing quivalent and was a year in advance of the Kingston machine. An obvious step was to fit wept wings and the resultant Type 510 to .41/46 flew right at the end of 1948 and just over a month later than the P.1052. Some official documents, incidentally, referred to the ype 510 as the Swift. Step three was to fit the econd 510 with a reheated Nene engine as he Type 528 before the aircraft, VV119, was rebuilt with a tricycle undercarriage as the ype 535, flying in this form on 23rd August 950. The P.1081 can be considered as Hawker's equivalent aeroplane. Reheating the 510 vas felt a most suitable step forward and sea evel speed was estimated to be 680mph 1,094 km/h), a bit more than was actually achieved. The reheat work was undertaken as a private venture by Supermarine.

On the basis of flight tests with the experimental Type 535, a production order was placed in September 1950 for an adaptation to broadly meet the same requirements as he Hunter. Two prototypes were ordered a month later to Specification F.105P2 (F.105P was written around the Type 535), the first virtually a 535 with Avon RA.7 instead of the Nene, the second to production standards, and Supermarine called the aircraft the Type 541. The first aircraft flew on 1st August 1951 but there was a need to continue using the research 535 as well as the 541s. The Type 535 became the forerunner of the Swift proper and was needed for fighter assessment; it achieved a maximum Mach number of 0.99.

Until the outbreak of the Korean War in June 1950, the only swept wing day fighter on order for the RAF was the Hunter. The appearance of the Mikoyan MiG-15 brought panic to the Ministry and RAF, and the western world in general, and its performance superiority over the Meteor made it highly desirable to introduce into service a fighter of better performance as soon as possible. As already stated, the MiG-15 was to govern the direction of fighter design for some time to come. The development work already done on the 510 and 535 gave reason to believe that the Swift would be available earlier than the Hunter and a concession to fit only two Adens in the Swift was given since it did not seem four could be accommodated, but later versions did get the four guns.

Although its performance was expected to be a little inferior to the Hunter, the Air Council was concerned to increase the effective strength of the RAF front line by every possible means as quickly as possible. Its anxiety,

and that of the Government, to increase effective strength was graphically illustrated by a decision to embark on a substantial programme of refurbishing Spitfires. The Hunter was thought to have great promise but possible technical delays made an alternative important and the Swift was therefore in the nature of an insurance. Thanks to Type 510 and 535 test flying, the Swift was expected to be brought into service without serious development delays, its performance could be superior to the MiG-15 and would represent a big material advance on the Meteor.

Both Supermarine and the Ministry of Supply felt the Swift was a safe bet but this proved very optimistic. 150 Swifts were ordered before the aeroplane had been fully tested, there being insufficient flying time available to finish testing the design's aerodynamic qualities; neither were there enough prototypes. Early problems included poor low speed characteristics, poor manoeuvrability at high altitudes and wing flexing at speed prior to aileron flutter at Mach 0.93. Later it was realised engine surge under certain flight conditions was also present and the Swift F Mk.2 had a pronounced tendency to tighten in turns at height.

The placing of a large production order tended to 'freeze' a design early which resulted in big problems if major modifications needed to be introduced. On the Swift it was thought these problems were 'the usual run of development troubles' and so production was allowed to continue. In May 1954 all marks of Swift were grounded following a fatal

accident apparently caused by the aileron power controls reverting to manual control under certain circumstances. In the eyes of the Government, the aircraft was a failure and in April 1955 all Mk.3, 4 and 6 aircraft were cancelled. Continued construction with so many problems still outstanding was considered particularly bad practice but there was heavy criticism towards many aspects of the programme.

Eventually, the larger span F Mk.7 (Type 552) proved a far better aircraft and the two prototypes and 12 production machines successfully tested the Fairey Blue Sky (Fireflash) AAM. But it was too late and those fighters already in service were swiftly withdrawn, a total approaching 200 having been built. With the end of the Korean conflict, cancellation was probably the best course of action, but this became something of a habit over the next ten years. For a fighter, the Swift lacked what today is called agility, but it could be taken through the 'sound barrier' in a shallow dive.

One achievement of the Swift was to help add a new word to the vocabulary, 'Superpriority'. A policy had been declared in 1945 that no war was likely for ten years and no substantial re-equipping was to take place, rather new equipment for all three Services would be limited but designed to still perform its role in ten years time. Money was needed elsewhere and the pace of new development and manufacture was allowed to drop off thanks to the lack of urgency; these opening chapters show how slow some of the progress became. But building production aircraft also

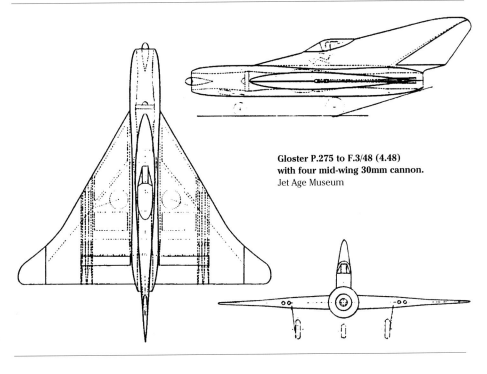

**Gloster P.275 to F.3/48 (4.48)
with four mid-wing 30mm cannon.**
Jet Age Museum

began to take excessive time, not least because of the long periods needed to get parts made. The industry became run down and when Korea began, was in a poor condition to respond.

The Government took until 1952 to find a way of getting things moving; the solution was Superpriority. The plan was to select the most important aeroplanes and give them priority over all others with maximum urgency to prevent delay. The Hunter and Swift were included in what was really a cosmetic exercise as the system was incapable of finding extra skilled staff, materials or tooling when there was a shortage in all areas. The close of the Korean War in 1953 relieved the pressure in the short term and Superpriority died away.

With Korea over, the long term problem was still how to deal with the Soviet threat. It was the mid-1950s before Hunters began to appear in numbers and the short term gap was eventually filled by an overseas purchase.

Top: **View of the Type 535 VV119.** Rolls-Royce

Centre left: **The Supermarine E.10/44 prototype TS409 photographed in September 1946. When navalised to E.1/45 it was called the Attacker.**

Centre right: **The first Supermarine Type 510, VV106, a swept wing modification of the Attacker.**

Bottom left: **An early Hawker Hunter F Mk.1 taken in 1956.**

America's main swept wing fighter was the North American F-86 Sabre which first flew on 1st October 1947. It was built in vast numbers, was very successful in Korea against the MiG-15 and, to provide the RAF with a swept wing interceptor to combat Russian short range fighters, 430 were acquired by Britain. The first examples arrived in late 1952 from the Canadian production line and in due course a dozen squadrons, mostly based in Germany, received Sabres before they were

British Secret Projects: Jet Fighter

placed by Hunters by 1956. The majority
were then transferred abroad. The decision
to buy them was much criticised and must
have got right under the skin of some Ministry,
Air Force and industry people, but it proved a
wise move in a period of tense East-West relations. The RAF gained vital transonic experience from a fighter that was much liked by
its pilots and a delight to fly, and which also
revealed important weaknesses in British
fighter design and manufacture.

Before moving to the night fighter scene, it
is worth taking a look at the advances in engines and weaponry associated with these
new fighters. By the time the Hunter and Swift
flew in production form, the Armstrong Siddeley Sapphire and Rolls-Royce AJ.65 Avon
axial jets had reached a degree of 'maturity',
but there were to be problems during development flying. It had taken several years for
the Avon to reach 6,500lb (28.9kN) of thrust
with the RA.3, which entered RAF service as
the 100 series Mk.101. Thrust ratings increased and the Mk.115 (RA.21) reached just
over 8,000lb (35.6kN).

Metropolitan-Vickers (Metrovick) was the
original designer of the F.9 Sapphire but the
engine was taken over by Armstrong Siddeley
Motors at Coventry in 1947. This too had its
troubles but the compressor was superior to
the Avon 100 series. In 1950 Rolls took the opportunity to absorb some of the best elements
from its rival's compressor in a full redesign of
the Avon, the opportunity to examine the Sapphire coming when the Coventry firm asked
for help with blade failure problems. This became the Avon 200 series and exceeded
10,000lb (44.4kN) thrust for the first time. Sydney Camm adopted the Mk.203 (RA.28) for
the F.6 (P.1099) Hunter without reheat and
versions found their way into the Scimitar
(Mk.202) and Sea Vixen (Mk.208), both rated
at over 11,200lb (49.8kN). When the Sapphire
was released from the Secret List it was the
world's most powerful jet engine at 7,200lb
(32kN) thrust, but it never eclipsed the Avon
from the number one spot.

An important addition to total engine
power came from the introduction of afterburning or reheat. This provided an opportunity to increase thrust without increasing the
engine's frontal area and made use of the unburnt oxygen still present in the jet exhaust.
Additional fuel was burnt in the jet pipe to increase exhaust velocity and, therefore, increase the engine's thrust which was vital for
rate of climb and to enable an aircraft to go
supersonic. To compliment this, development of the convergent/divergent nozzle also
proved beneficial in allowing the expanding
gases to exert a reaction against the rear-

The second Type 541 Swift prototype, WJ965,
the first Vickers-Supermarine aircraft to exceed
Mach 1 in a dive. Eric Morgan collection

ward-facing divergent walls and, hence, give
even more thrust. This feature, however, was
more important to the highly supersonic aircraft discussed in Chapter 6.

The first British air-to-air missile was code-named Red Hawk and work began in 1947 to
OR.1056. It was initially to be an all-singing all-dancing all-weather AAM intended to be fired
from any angle relative to the target but, as the
difficulty of achieving this became apparent,
it was changed to a cone behind the target
weapon as an interim scheme pending development of a homing system that might
take over five years to produce. All methods
of guidance were under consideration and no
official general arrangement was completed.

The RAE was heavily involved and in October did produce a draft drawing of what Red
Hawk might look like to help designers assess
the problems of carriage and launch from
their aircraft. Total weight of a complete round
was 420lb (191kg) with length 8.5ft (2.59m).
The outline showed four boost rockets
placed around the rear body, for the missile
as drawn was purely a dart. Following acceleration to Mach 2 in a few seconds, when the
rocket's solid fuel became exhausted, the
boost and fin assembly was jettisoned leaving
the manoeuvrable unpowered dart to coast
to its target. Beam-riding was the simplest
radar guidance method, the missile following a beam visually aimed and continuously
held on the target throughout the attack by
the parent aircraft's radar ranging.

R E Bishop was asked to fit Red Hawk on
the DH.110 night fighter, but he proposed that
the store should be completely cleaned up
with wings and fins made retractable, the
four rockets reduced to one central rocket,
and the whole thing 'made generally so clean
that one could be carried on each wing tip'.
Otherwise he feared grave trouble from a
launch made beneath a fighter's fuselage.
During a meeting at de Havilland on 15th November 1947 it was agreed with the MoS that
the drag of the missile should be measured
both in model and full scale form, Bishop offering to do a full scale test on a DH.108.
DOR(A), Air Commodore T G Pike, felt such a
weapon would be a very useful supplementary
armament. He was to prove correct, for the
AAM was to supplant the cannon as the primary fighter armament and for a period guns
were omitted altogether, until it was realised
such an extreme move was a grave error.

Industrial involvement became necessary
to accelerate the national guided weapon
programme and the interim Red Hawk was
split off in 1949 as new beam-riding missile
called Blue Sky (later Fireflash) to OR.1088
under the control of Fairey Aviation. Fireflash
was designed for stern attack by day within a
+/-15° cone and on launching accelerated to
about Mach 2.4 in less than two seconds
being unguided during the boost period; once
burnt the motors were again jettisoned. Primary targets were large piston engine bombers and optimum range was 6,000ft (1,829m),
but a launch could be made up to 10,000ft
(3,048m) away at heights between 15,000
and 35,000ft (4,572 and 10,668m). A complete
Fireflash weighed 330lb (150kg) and was 9.3ft

(2.83m) long. Meteor NF Mk.11s were used as test-beds before the Swift F Mk.7 became the high speed test vehicle. Trials were spread over four years before the weapon was approved for limited service use on 11th April 1957.

Fireflash was rather a clumsy concept and had a very draggy configuration. Red Hawk continued in its more advanced form before finally being split into two further AAMs in 1951, the infra-red homing Blue Jay and radar guided Red Dean (Chapter 6). Work on Blue Jay began at de Havilland Propellers under OR.1117. Named Firestreak in 1957, it became the standard RAF and Navy AAM aboard the Javelin, early marks of Lightning and Sea Vixen.

Blue Jay homed onto a heat source using an infra-red (IR) sensor; with fighters now powered by jets or rockets there was plenty of heat to aim for, the homer looking through a glass nose. This passive (non-emitting) method of detection could not be detected by an enemy and once fired and locked-on, the weapon was left to fly to the target by itself at over Mach 2, enabling the attacker to attack something else. Firestreak was 10.4ft (3.17m) long, weighed 300lb (136kg) and entered service in 1959. Maximum range was 5 miles (8.0km). The title Blue Jay is more often used here as it was the preferred name in Ministry documents.

A striking difference existed between tl design of high speed fighters and AAMs; tl missile basically opted out of all the problen of take-off and landing. As fighter speeds i creased, more attention was needed to e sure they could fly at speeds slow enough f a safe landing; an AAM had no take-off landing speed problems to worry about. also avoided most of the difficulties of brea ing the 'sound barrier' since the rapid boo given after launch accelerated the weapc through the speed of sound so quickly that r serious transonic problems arose.

RAF Day Fighter Projects – Estimated Data

1: To Specification F.43/46

Project	Span ft (m)	Length ft (m)	Wing Area ft² (m²)	t/c %	All-Up-Weight lb (kg)	Powerplant Thrust lb (kN)	Max Speed / Height mph (km/h) / ft (m)	Armament
Gloster P.234	41.0 (12.5)	48.0 (14.6)	615 (57.1)	?	15,600 (7,076)	2 x AJ.65 6,500 (28.9)	c. Mach 1	1 x 4.5in (11.5cm) gun
Hawker P.1054 (F.43/46 submission)	37.5 (11.4)	?	382 (35.5)	?	14,200 (6,441)	2 x AJ.65 6,500 (28.9)	615 (990) Mach 0.93	1 x 4.5in (11.5cm) gun
Hawker P.1061	39.0 (11.9)	42.0 (12.8)	378 (35.1)	?	?	2 x AJ.65 6,500 (28.9)	c. 600 (966)	1 x 4.5in (11.5cm) gun
Supermarine 508 (Straight wing)	40.0 (12.2)	46.5 (14.2)	310 (28.8)	9	16,000 (7,257) 17,250 (7,824) with 4.5in gun	2 x AJ.65 6,500 (28.9)	661 (1,064) at sea level	2 x 30mm guns or 1 x 4.5in (11.5cm) gun
Martin-Baker F.43/46	26.0 (7.9)	39.5 (12.0)	360 (33.4)	8	8,710 (3,951)	1 x AJ.65 6,500 (28.9)	640 (1,030) at sea level Mach 0.84	2 x 20mm Hispano cannon
Gloster P.259	52.0 (15.8)	53.5 (16.3)	900 (83.6)	10.5	21,000 (9,525) Sapphire 20,400 (9,253) Avon	2 x Sapphire 7,000 (31.1) or 2 x Avon 6,500 (28.9)	702 (1,130) at sea level	1 x 4.5in (11.5cm) gun, RPs or projected AAM
Hawker P.1064	41.5 (12.6)	50.5 (15.4)	450 (41.8)	?	?	2 x Avon 6,500 (28.9)	?	1 x 4.5in gun or 4 x 30mm Aden
Hawker P.1065	38.0 (11.6)	47.6 (14.5)	370 (34.4)	?	?	1 AJ.65, 6,500 (28.9) + 2,000 or 4,000 (8.9/17.8) rocket	?	4 x 30mm Aden cannon
Hawker 'P.1063'	42.0 (12.8)	55.5 (16.9)	480 (44.6)	?	?	2 x Avon 6,500 (28.9)	?	4 x 30mm Aden cannon

2: To Specifications F.3/48 and F.105

Project	Span ft (m)	Length ft (m)	Wing Area ft² (m²)	t/c %	All-Up-Weight lb (kg)	Powerplant Thrust lb (kN)	Max Speed / Height mph (km/h) / ft (m)	Armament
Hawker P.1067/1	33.5 (10.2)	42.0 (12.8)	340 (31.6)	10 tip 8.5 root	12,970 (5,883)	1 x Avon 6,500 (28.9)	710 (1,142) at sea level 610 (981) at 40,000 (12,192)	4 x 20mm Hispano or 4 x 30mm Aden
Hunter F Mk.1 (flown)	33.67 (10.3)	45.9 (14.0)	340 (31.6)	8.5	16,200 (7,348)	1 x Avon RA.7 (Mk.113) 7,500 (33.3)	702 (1,130) at sea level	4 x 30mm Aden cannon
Gloster P.275	45.5 (13.9)	48.0 (14.6)	750 (69.7)	8	18,500 (8,391)	1 x 12,000 (53.3) jet with re-heat	668 (1,075) at sea level Mach 0.88	4 x 30mm Aden cannon
Supermarine 526	35.5 (10.8)	52.0 (15.8)	450 (41.8)	8	18,000 (8,165) 20,000 (9,072) re-heat	2 x Avon 6,500 (28.9)	685 (1,102) at sea level 710 (1,143) re-heat	4 x 20mm Hispano cannon
Swift F Mk.1 (flown)	32.33 (9.9)	41.5 (12.6)	306 (28.5)	10	19,764 (8,965)	1 x Avon RA.7 7,500 (33.3)	709 (1,141) at sea level	2 x 30mm Aden, cannon

Chapter Four

Night Fighters for the RAF

Land-Based Fighter Progress 1946 to the mid-1950s: Part 2

The RAF's requirement for a night fighter has squeezed into the story several times already, so it is time for a full account. Specification F.44/46 was issued on 24th January 1947, the same day as its day fighter counterpart.

F.44/46 (and OR.227)

This prototype night fighter landplane was to have sufficient performance to intercept enemy aircraft flying at 40,000ft (12,192m), an enemy assumed to have a maximum speed of 550mph (885km/h) and cruising at 500mph (805km/h) and 25,000ft (7,620m). Top speed at 25,000ft had to be 525kts (605mph/973 km/h) (Mach 0.87) and from a push button start, 45,000ft (13,716m) was to be reached within ten minutes with ceiling to be at least

that height. An endurance of two hours (twice F.43/46) was requested to include a climb to 25,000ft and 15 minutes combat. Crew was to comprise pilot and radar operator and armament four 30mm fixed forward-firing cannon. The aircraft was urgently needed to replace the Mosquito which was now very out of date.

De Havilland DH.110

This aircraft was described in Chapter 1 under de Havilland's submission to the naval N.40/46 requirement. In essence the projects were the same apart from specific naval equipment but the RAF project had a straight tail when originally proposed to F.44/46 in March 1947 and Metrovick F.9 engines. The later swept forward tail surface was expected to be better structurally and aerodynamically but was dependent on high speed tunnel tests. Four Aden cannon were mounted beneath the cabin floor. Sea level rate of climb

WD804, the first Gloster G.A.5 prototype, banks towards the camera during a test flight in early Summer 1952.

(RAE figure) 11,300ft/min (3,444m/min) and time to 45,000ft just over 10 minutes. Internal fuel totalled 900gal (4,091lit).

Gloster P.228

This was also a very similar design to Gloster's N.40/46 (the P.231 which was actually developed from this project) but with an orthodox tail and fin and a fourth 30mm in the lower fuselage. Forward of the tail they were in fact identical bar wing folding and gun arrangement. Sea level rate of climb 10,700 ft/min (3,261m/min) with 11.25 minutes needed to reach 45,000ft. Somewhat like the Meteor, this was Gloster's 'conventional' F.44/46 layout and was designed to be convertible to the delta planform.

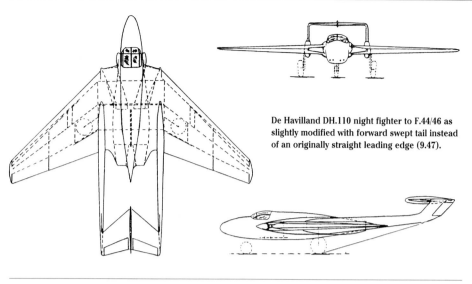

De Havilland DH.110 night fighter to F.44/46 as slightly modified with forward swept tail instead of an originally straight leading edge (9.47).

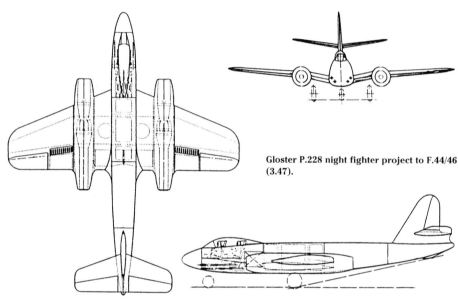

Gloster P.228 night fighter project to F.44/46 (3.47).

Gloster Delta Wing F.44/46

A project (number unknown) similar to the firm's P.234 F.43/46 day fighter proposal but larger and with an orthodox tail. Rate of climb was 10,300ft/min (3,140m/min) at sea level with 10.5 minutes to 45,000ft.

Hawker P.1056

A project that one might call the Hawker Meteor as this aeroplane appearance-wise had much in common with Gloster's highly successful product. The two Avons, however, were placed more forward of the wing leading edge and the tail was lower down the fin. The cannon were housed below the cockpit, the spot chosen in fact for all the F.44/46 projects. Total fuel capacity was 700gal (3,182lit), sea level rate of climb 10,800ft/min (3,292 m/min), time to 45,000ft (13,716m) 9.3 minutes. The P.1056 design was discontinued in May following the Design Conference.

Hawker P.1057

Early ideas for this project showed a swept wing version of the P.1056 with a 41ft (12.5m) span and 49.5ft (15.1m) length. However, when submitted the design was a cross between the P.1054 (to F.43/46) and a swept wing Sea Hawk, the engines still well ahead of the c.g but with a rounded fuselage and wing root jet pipes. Total fuel capacity 730gal (3,319lit), sea level rate of climb 10,000ft/min (3,048m/min), time to 45,000ft 9.8 minutes.

Supermarine Type 511

This comprised two designs, one swept, the other straight winged. The former had the considerable advantage of a 57mph (92km/h) speed increase at the quoted operational height of 25,000ft (7,620m) but, in order to meet the climb requirement it needed a rocket booster which was to be started once the 511 was flying. The straight wing met the

climb factor without a rocket by virtue of it lighter weight and it just met the speed limit The swept variant's main undercarriage wa housed within the wings, in the straight type i retracted into the fuselage as the wings hac insufficient depth. In other respects the de signs were similar having twin Avons in a stressed skin fuselage, the usual under-fuse lage four gun housing and a V-tail. Superma rine considered the arrangement with two engines side by side in the fuselage to be the most economical scheme in respect of both drag and structure weight, but due to the se vere requirements specified, the designs were large by current fighter standards. It was not possible to make them smaller. The Avon's thrust of 8,000lb (35.6kN) was an improved rating expected in the near future.

For the back-swept version, time to 45,000ft (13,716m) was 8.6 minutes, service ceiling 48,000ft (14,630m), sea level rate of climb a all-up-weight [32,000lb/14,515kg] 9,800ft/min (2,987m/min) and with rocket boost (37,000lb [16,783kg] auw) 10,000ft/min (3,048 m/min) The rocket was housed in the extreme rear fuselage. Total internal fuel was 1,055gal (4,796lit) but on this machine the 5,175lb (2,347kg) of underwing rocket fuel could be replaced by two 300gal (1,364lit) drop tanks On the straight wing these figures became almost 10 minutes to 45,000ft, ceiling 49,300ft (15,027m), sea level climb rate 10,900ft/min (3,322m/min). Internal fuel totalled 1,014gal (4,610lit) with two wing drop tanks of 270gal (1,227lit) also available. For space and weight purposes, on both designs carriage of the AI Mk.9 radar was assumed but it was hoped that smaller equipment would become available once detail design commenced.

After the Type 508 variant to F.43/46, Supermarine now appeared to have a touch more confidence in swept wings as these projects shared equal billing, the firm sensing the most serious difficulty associated with a large wing sweep was probably to provide satisfactory stability and control at the stall. In the swept 511 the firm provided automatic leading edge slats over the outer wing but by keeping the aspect ratio down it was hoped to ultimately dispense with them. As a further step to making the stall gentle, a large leading edge radius was chosen. The back-swept wing had the same aspect ratio, aerofoil section and taper ratio as that being fitted to the Type 510 and split flaps were used over the inner wing trailing edge. Light alloy was employed almost exclusively in the wing with as much as possible employed as a torsion box for stiffness. The fuselage was of normal light alloy monocoque construction and the tail was fixed with wide-chord flaps which worked together as elevators and differentially as rudders.

For the straight wing, the parameters affecting F.43/46's Type 508 were applicable here and the same solution, lowest possible thickness and a constant section, was employed. It was felt lateral stability at the stall should be exceptionally good. A full span nose flap deflected downwards through 25°, inner span trailing edge plain flaps having 60° deflection and wide chord slotted ailerons arranged to droop by 10° were used as high lift devices, the latter also supplying lateral control. Longitudinal control was achieved by altering the incidence and camber of the all-moving V-tail surface while directional control came when the trailing edge flaps were moved differentially, each half of the tail being mounted on a single rotatable spar cantilevered from the fuselage. The small t/c ratio made it necessary to employ steel spar flanges in the wing which, with an unusually thick light alloy skin for the torsion box, provided an extremely robust but simple construction.

–

The Tender Design Conference was held on 29th April 1947. Originally the Air Staff had asked for a Mosquito replacement to be available in something like three years, but as it was advised that a new aircraft could not be ready in quantity that quickly, it was felt the best design on offer should be chosen subject to it involving only a small risk in either development or production. Of the principal performance features, ceiling and speed were listed as most important since the fighter must be able to deal with aircraft corresponding to the British bombers now coming forward, while rate of climb was less so since it was likely that interception would be from standing patrols and not from the ground. Extra endurance over the two hour minimum would be very welcome.

In terms of performance, of the three conventional designs only Supermarine's had a real chance of achieving the required speed and that by virtue of a wing loading near 55lb/ft² (269 kg/m²); but all could meet take-off, landing and ceiling demands. Of the three swept-back types, all had a margin in hand on top speed and could therefore keep their loading down to around 42lb/ft² (205kg/m²). After reassessment by RAE when the manufacturer's estimates were 'corrected', no design met the 10 minute to 45,000ft (13,716m) limit but it was thought the DH.110 with Metropolitan-Vickers F.9 engines would have the best chance of approaching the figure. There might also be an advantage in using the F.9 since so many other designs were scheduled to have the AJ.65.

The Gloster delta proposal, though similar to their F.43/46 day fighter tender but larger, possessed the same uncertainties regarding aerodynamic features and it also failed the climb limit. RAE thought the need for a quick design ruled out the Gloster delta, but it might have long term possibilities for a combined day and night fighter with new weapons.

The Type 511s used a scaled up AJ.65 engine and it was queried whether this would be available and the project feasible. The AJ.65 had now run on the test bed and there was no reason why the engine should not be available at its designed rating of 6,500lb (28.9kN) in time for this aircraft. But at present there was no proposal to develop it to 8,000lb (35.6kN) thrust and if it were decided to use such an engine, it would not be ready at full rating for over three years. There was

also some uncertainty about the future of the Metrovick F.9. Metropolitan Vickers was not anxious to remain in the aero engine field but the Air Staff wished F.9 development to continue and, therefore, the project might be transferred to another firm (Armstrong Siddeley Motors eventually took it on). If this happened, the F.9 was unlikely to achieve its design performance within two to three years since a new design firm would have to familiarise themselves with it.

The 2,500lb (11.1kN) rocket booster was in the design stage and a similar time period away and DOR(A), Air Commodore T G Pike) stated there were operational objections to using such a rocket in the service. H F Vessey, AD/ARD(Research), thought the proposal a mistaken use of the rocket since it appeared to be correcting a bad rate of climb and not

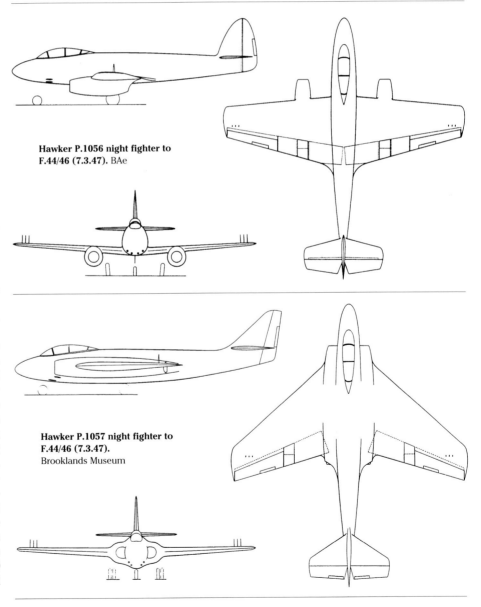

Hawker P.1056 night fighter to F.44/46 (7.3.47). BAe

Hawker P.1057 night fighter to F.44/46 (7.3.47). Brooklands Museum

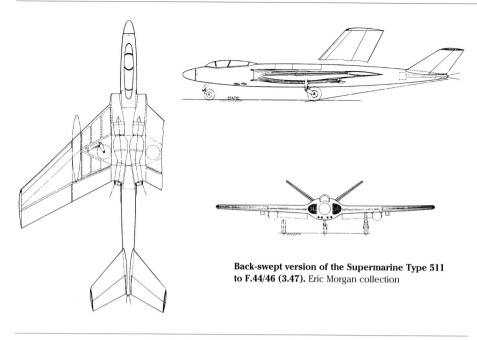

Back-swept version of the Supermarine Type 511 to F.44/46 (3.47). Eric Morgan collection

providing some large additional thrust. Consequently, thanks to the use of a non-programmed engine and rocket boost (contrary to Air Staff Policy), Supermarine's designs were ruled out and no further consideration given to them.

Next it was queried whether the Gloster Delta fitted within the need that the chosen type should carry little development risk and DOR(A) stated that since the present standard RAF night fighter would be obsolete much sooner than the present day fighter, a correspondingly smaller degree of risk was permissible in the length of time required to bring a replacement into service. On these grounds the meeting therefore decided to rule out the Gloster Delta. No further interest was shown towards the P.228 either, since it was not up to the performance requirements. The DH.110 and Hawker designs remained. Hawker's appeared slightly better from a radio and radar point of view, but the gun installation on the DH.110 was the best on paper (all the tenders offered reasonable gun arrangements). On general considerations of interception and attack, it was observed that a small turning circle, and hence a low wing loading, were essential since all attacks would be on a curve of pursuit or from astern and here the DH.110 was also slightly better.

It was agreed the de Havilland DH.110 appeared the best proposal on technical grounds through its lower wing loading and better crew arrangement. Moreover it constituted a logical follow-on to previous de Havilland work, namely a combination of the swept wing demonstrated on the DH.108 and the tail boom layout proved on the Vampire. In addition the firm had considerable past ex-

perience in designing night fighter aircraft. Disadvantages were a cramped equipment layout, a need for extra vertical fins to house the radio aerials, and the fact that F.9 development was behind the AJ.65.

The last point favoured the swept Hawker P.1057 which could be in the air some six months before de Havilland's prototype. There would be conflict at de Havilland between the Brabazon IV civil airliner (the Comet) and the F.44/46 that would prevent the drawing office reaching full strength on the fighter until the end of 1947 (during subsequent discussions with the firm it was suggested setting back other work and flying the first prototype with Avon engines). It was emphasised that if an aircraft was needed quickly, the Hawker P.1056 should be chosen as a prototype as this would fly at least six months earlier than any other and be in production a year earlier. The Kingston firm was better placed in manufacturing capacity than de Havilland.

The DH.110 was made first choice but further discussion examined the need for an insurance type, and the need to keep Hawkers in work. DOR(A) welcomed a second night fighter design and ordering from Hawker would bring a quicker and cheaper result and give the firm some night fighter experience. Pike thought it would be a good move if the extra cost could be accepted and it was thus agreed to order the P.1057 to compete with the DH.110, subject to confirmation that the cost of designing and building two sets of prototypes could be entertained. On May 22nd J E Serby sought approval to order three prototypes of each and in June Hawker was informed its tender had been accepted, orders

for a mock-up, jigs and tools, and three prototypes of the P.1057 following on 7th July.

However, the Advisory Design Conference, set for 26th August 1947, was cancelled and the preliminary mock-up dismantled. An effort was made to reduce frontal area (achieved by re-disposition of fuel) before Serby wrote on 13th September to tell the firm to suspend work. In November Serby requested alternative layouts with the 4.5in (11.4cm) recoilless gun or one or possibly two Red Hawk weapons and new schemes were sent to the Ministry on the 24th. Early in December all P.1057 work stopped and, on the 20th, Serby met the Kingston team to inform them that emphasis was now placed on a single-seat fighter. They were asked to carry out investigations into the optimum size for this type of aeroplane which led to the studies described in Chapter 3, and eventually the Hunter.

Following the order for three DH.110s, a DH.110 Advisory Design Conference was held at Thames House on 15th August 1947, where de Havilland's R E Bishop stated he would like a better shape to the nose than the spherical fairing usually fitted with the Mk.9D radar. It was thought perhaps a rocket weapon such as Red Hawk could be carried but the 4.5in gun was for the F.43/46 only. An addendum with the 4.5in did follow in November with all-up-weight 27,914lb (12,662kg). More accurate estimated figures now gave the standard DH.110's all-up-weight as 28,013lb (12,707kg) and sea level rate of climb 9,640ft/min (2,938m/min), but maximum speed was unchanged. The possibility of fitting reheat to the engines was forwarded in January 1948, but by now the armament and radar requirements were under drastic review alongside the F.43/46 day fighter changes.

F.4/48

Heavy discussion centred on armament and radar fitting and the specification duly reappeared as F.4/48 (still under OR.227). Now the minimum top speed of 525kts (605mph/973km/h) was set at 40,000ft (12,192m), a rate of climb of 1,000ft/min (305m/min) at 45,000ft (13,716m) had been added, but the four 30mm armament stayed.

In Chapter 3, development of the Gloster F.43/46 had advanced to a state more suited to the night fighter role. Consecutive Advisory Design Conferences held on 20th and 21st May 1948, examined the de Havilland and Gloster F.4/48s respectively and resulted in a full prototype programme. Three de Havilland F.4/48s were 're-ordered', the first as a flying shell and the others fully equipped, together with three (later four) Gloster aircraft.

By January 1949 it was intended to adapt the basic DH.110 to meet four separate operational requirements – F.4/48, F.5/49 (a short lived long range fighter for the RAF), N.40/46 (naval night fighter) and N.8/49 (naval strike aircraft). At least two more prototypes were needed for naval carrier trials and as the naval strike fighter differed considerably from the N.40/46 thanks to the extra roles it had to perform, so another prototype was needed here. The 1949 specification numbers were as yet unallocated, but the intention was to develop the four types concurrently so they could be brought into service with minimum delay.

On 3rd January it was proposed to order, in addition to the three F.4/48 DH.110s, four more F.4/48s for common RAF/RN use on armament, radar and instrument clearance, plus two each to N.40/46, the naval strike and the RAF long range fighter requirements. There was concern at the financial implications of ordering so many prototypes which might well preclude ordering future prototypes for projects such as Fairey's N.40/46 (later N.14/49). In such an event it would be necessary to abandon the present practice of ordering insurance aircraft, a dangerous policy, but despite these implications there was no alternative and the programme was to go ahead. The DH.110 had become just about the most important project in the UK.

By July all 13 prototypes were on order but the naval aircraft were cancelled in November through economic pressures and F.5/49 was also discontinued. In August 1950 efforts were made to accelerate the plane but, for the time being, only two prototypes were to fly, the first becoming airborne on 26th September 1951. During that month, the aircraft was also publicly unveiled and the first photographs released. On 20th October 1952, after examining the DH.110 crash at Farnborough and the current situation and costs with de Havilland, the MoS decided not to complete the third aircraft. The Gloster project had become the more favoured and the DH.110 programme languished until re-taken up by the Royal Navy (Chapter 1).

Gloster's delta wing fighter had been left in Chapter 3 at the end of its day fighter 'career' having advanced into the P.258 and P.259, both large enough for the night fighter role. J E Serby wrote to Gloster's RTO on 24th February 1948 to explain that at the end of July 1947 it had still been planned to accelerate progress by proceeding with the first two F.43/46 flying shell prototypes without military equipment. Since then the conception of the aeroplane had undergone considerable change, it was now a two-seat aircraft and would be designed to a freshly numbered specification

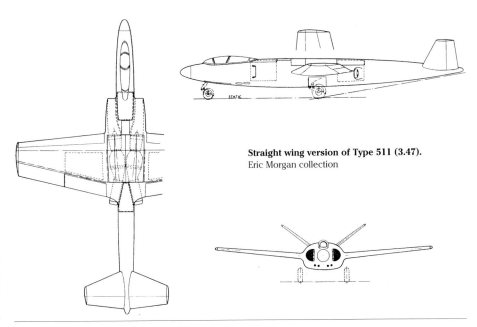

Straight wing version of Type 511 (3.47).
Eric Morgan collection

The second DH.110 prototype to F.4/48, WG240, viewed in flight on 2nd September 1953.
BAe Farnborough

(F.4/48). The plan was to order prototypes in May, but in June Gloster pointed out the alarming growth in weight that was forcing a need for larger or additional engines.

Gloster P.272

Gloster's first official project to F.4/48 dated 15th April 1948, and based on earlier twin jet studies. It had become necessary to take account of a big 39in (99cm) diameter radar scanner in the nose, the bulky housing and side intakes making the body rather larger than was desirable in view of the expected Mach number performance. The firm estimated all-up-weight to be substantially on the high side at 25,500lb (11,567kg) compared to 20,500lb (9,299kg) previously, most of the rise

coming from revised engine weights, increased military load and fuel. It was found necessary to retain separate controls for longitudinal, lateral and directional stability, a small all-moving slab tailplane being used to give ample powerful manoeuvrability while at the same time counteracting trim changes resultant from flight throughout a large speed range and Mach number. Lateral control came from rotating wing tip 'ailerons' instead of normal ailerons as there was little available information on delta wing lateral control.

Total internal fuel was 900gal (4,091lit), climb rate at sea level 9,600ft/min (2,926 m/min), and at 45,000ft 1,800ft/min (549 m/min). 11.4 minutes were needed to reach 45,000ft but the ten minute limit could be achieved with a 10% increase in thrust from afterburning. The four Adens were mounted in the wings (a variant actually had four 4.5in [11.4cm] guns in the wings).

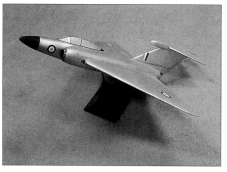

Two views of a Gloster project to F.4/48 probably based on the P.272 but with fixed ailerons.

Gloster P.279

The weight increase that worried Gloster so much resulted in the P.279 of July 1948. Further changes to F.4/48 since the April brochure (P.272) brought this further increase in size as an alternative to that design. Gloster's Project Department had been occupied with various basic designs for two, three and four engines over a three week period before the new brochure went to Serby. Level speed at 40,000ft (12,192m) was limited to Mach 0.89 down

from 0.92 as the thrust needed increasing, the expedient to obtain this extra thrust was to incorporate reheat.

Rolls-Royce claimed afterburners would increase static thrust by 20% and rate of climb by 30% for a modest 200lb (91kg) weight increase. Still theoretical at the time, it was expected that engines of 9,000lb (40kN) thrust would be available in the future; according to Armstrong Siddeley a scaled-up Sapphire enlarged to 40in (102cm) diameter was predicted to give 9,000lb. This would give a sea level climb rate of 11,800ft/min (3,597m/min) and a ceiling of 56,000ft (17,069m). In the event of the airframe being ready before the engines, the P.279 would initially use two 7,500lb (33.3kN) Sapphire Sa.2 engines limiting top speed to 633mph (1,018km/h) at sea level (Mach 0.83) and 593mph (954km/h) at 40,000ft.

Gloster P.280

It is believed the Gloster P.276 was the first drawing to fully represent what was to become the G.A.5 Javelin night fighter. A final F.4/48 brochure in late July called P.280 saw the Sapphire Sa.2 substitute the AJ.65 Avon and introduce normal control surfaces on the wings instead of the wing tip type. Sea level climb rate was 12,100ft/min (3,688m/min), time to 45,000ft (13,716m) the required 10 minutes and ceiling 55,000ft (16,764m). The P.280 brochure was updated in March 1951 as more reliable performance and weight estimates were now available with the 7,500lb (33.3kN) thrust Sa.3. Top speed had sharpened to 687mph (1,105km/h) or Mach 0.90 at sea level, 608mph (978km/h) or Mach 0.92 at 40,000ft (12,192m). This information really made reference to the Service aircraft.

The Javelin is a classic case of an aircraft evolving over a period of time from several design studies. It is hard to put a date on what would be the inception of design work on the Javelin rather than Meteor project developments, but it seems likely the delta attracted George Carter in 1945 as soon as German information in this direction became available. In November 1949 the number of Gloster F.4/48s had been halved to two both for economy reasons and for the fact that it was regarded as an insurance against trouble on the DH.110 which was preferred for production as a more conventional aeroplane and easier to build. But in March 1951 three additional prototypes were ordered (making five all told) on the grounds that Gloster's aircraft now had greater development potential than the DH.110 and the Air Staff wished to accelerate the programme.

The first G.A.5 Javelin prototype made its maiden flight on 26th November 1951 and it became one of a number of fighter aircraft including the DH.110 to make supersonic bangs in dives over Britain. The FAW Mk.1 entered RAF service in 1956 and the Javelin was to remain on strength for 12 years in nine versions, production exceeding 430 aircraft. Later versions introduced the 11,000lb (49kN) Sapphire Sa.7R reheated to give 12,300lb (54.7 kN) thrust and carried four Firestreak AAMs. Many within the RAF were happy with the Javelin because it was just what they wanted to knock down Soviet bombers but there were others who felt the DH.110 would have been a better choice; another of aviation's long argued but never to be answered disputes.

As fighter development advanced, another argument centred on the number of crew required and the equipment needed, and a little anecdote finished this story rather nicely. In February 1955 the then Minister of Supply (Mr Selwyn Lloyd) declared during a House of Commons debate that the RAF 'do not use single-seat night fighters' and 'there are great advantages in having twin-seat night fighters'. This caused quite a fuss since there was a growing school of thought that felt a single-seat aircraft equipped with radar had its place in the UK's all-weather defence. Lloyd stated during his next Commons speech that he did not believe a one seat fighter could operate in UK climatic conditions, but he was eventually forced to withdraw. There were arguments for and against, but the RAF always liked its two-seater and persisted with it right through to the Tornado ADV.

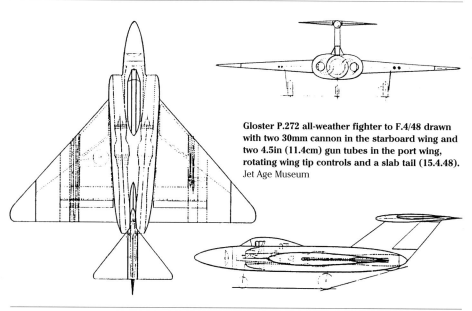

Gloster P.272 all-weather fighter to F.4/48 drawn with two 30mm cannon in the starboard wing and two 4.5in (11.4cm) gun tubes in the port wing, rotating wing tip controls and a slab tail (15.4.48). Jet Age Museum

British Secret Projects: Jet Fighters

Left: **Javelin FAW Mk.7 XH710 with unreheated Sapphire 7s and four de Havilland Firestreak (Blue Jay) air-to-air missiles.**

Above: **Javelin FAW Mk.8 XH966 shot by Gloster photographer Russell Adams in 1958. Also carrying four de Havilland Firestreak guided missiles, this mark had reheated Sapphire engines, as indicated by the modified jet pipe.**

RAF Night Fighter Projects to Specifications F.44/46 and F.4/48 – Estimated Data

Project	Span ft (m)	Length ft (m)	Wing Area ft² (m²)	t/c %	All-Up-Weight lb (kg)	Powerplant Thrust lb (kN)	Max Speed / Height mph (km/h) / ft (m) x 1,000	Armament
de Havilland DH.110	49.5 (15.1)	47.9 (14.6)	640 (59.5)	10	26,350 (11,952)	2 x F.9 7,000 (31.1)	656 (1,056) Mach 0.86 at sea level 625 (1,006) Mach 0.90 at 25.0 (7.6)	4 x 30mm Aden cannon
Gloster P.228	48.0 (14.6)	57.0 (17.4)	605 (56.3)	9	26,000 (11,794)	2 x F.9 7,000 (31.1)	650 (1,046) at sea level 605 (973) at 25.0 (7.6)	4 x 30mm Aden cannon
Gloster F.44/46 (Delta)	54.0 (16.5)	62.0 (18.9) ?	1,000 (93.0)	9	25,000 (11,340)	2 x F.9 7,000 (31.1))	720 (1,158) at sea level 656 (1,056) Mach 0.95 at 25.0 (7.6)	4 x 30mm Aden cannon
Hawker P.1056	50.0 (15.2)	50.25 (15.3)	500 (46.5)	10	22,100 (10,025)	2 x AJ.65 6,500 (28.9)	680 (1,094) at sea level 617 (993) at 25.0 (7.6)	4 x 30mm Aden cannon
Hawker P.1057	48.0 (14.6)	53.5 (16.3)	600 (55.8)	10	24,000 (10,886)	2 x AJ.65 6,500 (28.9)	720 (1,158) at sea level 671 (1,080) at 25.0 (7.6)	4 x 30mm Aden cannon
Supermarine 511 (Swept)	51.5 (15.7)	67.0 (20.4)	750 (69.8)	10	32,000 (14,515)	2 x AJ.65 (dev) 8,000 (35.6) plus 1x2,500 (11.1) rocket	671 (1,080) at 10.0 (3.0) 663 (1067) at 25.0 (7.6)	4 x 30mm Aden cannon
Supermarine 511 (Straight)	47.0 (14.3)	63.0 (19.2)	515 (47.9)	9	29,000 (13,154)	2 x AJ.65 (dev) 8,000 (35.6)	647 (1,041) at sea level 606 (975) at 25.0 (7.6)	4 x 30mm Aden cannon
de Havilland DH.110 (flown)	51.0 (15.4)	52.1 (15.9)	648 (60.3)	10	32,000 (14,515)	2 x Avon RA.7 7,500 (33.3)	710 (1,142) at sea level	4 x 30mm Aden Not fitted when flown
Gloster P.272	52.0 (15.8)	53.5 (16.3)	900 (83.7)	10	25,500 (11,567)	2 x AJ.65 6,500 (28.9)	656 (1,056) Mach 0.86 at sea level; 593 (954) Mach 0.90 at 40.0 (12.2)	4 x 30mm Aden cannon
Gloster P.279	57.5 (17.5)	61.0 (18.6)	1,100 (102.3)	10	32,000 (14,515)	2 x Sapphire (dev) 9,000 (40.0)	666 (1,072) Mach 0.87 at sea level; 599 (964) Mach 0.91 at 40.0 (12.2)	4 x 30mm Aden cannon
Gloster P.280	52.0 (15.8)	57.0 (17.4)	900 (83.7)	10	27,000 (12,247)	2 x Sapphire Sa.2 7,000 (31.1)	680 (1,094) Mach 0.89 at sea level; 605 (973) Mach 0.92 at 40.0 (12.2)	4 x 30mm Aden cannon
Gloster Javelin FAW Mk.1 (flown)	52.0 (15.8)	65.25 (19.9)	927 (86.2)	Range 8.9 to 10	31,580 (14,325)	2 x Sapphire Sa.6 8,150 (36.2)	Mach 0.94	4 x 30mm Aden cannon

Advanced Versions

Developments of the Standard Fighters: 1950 to 1956

The main subjects from the early chapters, Sea Vixen, Scimitar, Hunter, Swift and Javelin, were all proposed in supersonic form although none ever made it into the air. On 1st February 1954, in reply to a question about piloted supersonic fighters, Duncan Sandys, the Minister of Supply, informed the House of Commons that a number of supersonic service types were in the course of development, but he was not free to go into details. Some of the aircraft he referred to are described here, others are in Chapter 6.

De Havilland DH.110

Some published sources state that a thin-wing supersonic Sea Vixen was designed to the Thin Wing Javelin Specification F.153. In fact there were several studies for supersonic DH.110s, still under that project number, but apparently not to any particular specification. Much work was done on supersonic thin wing variants and the Air Staff was kept informed of progress, but no final layout was ever completed or a brochure prepared. In addition, other supersonic fighter concepts were studied by DH long before the DH.117 came together (Chapter 8); both straight and swept wings were assessed, one single-seater had a nose intake and resembled the F-86 Sabre or 1950s Soviet MiGs, but was a bit bigger.

Thin-wing DH.110 work ran from December 1953 to late summer 1954. Options were:

a: Convert to a delta increasing wing area to about 810ft² (75.3m²). It was thought this should have a satisfactory performance if wing thickness was a constant 7%, but a delta planform would have involved large structural changes and it would probably have been easier to design a new aircraft;

b: Cut wing thickness to 6% throughout from either just outboard of the boom (the fold position) or outboard of the intakes over the boom, combined with a tip chord increase of 1.5ft (0.46m) tapered out uniformly from the fold to take wing area up to 672ft² (62.5m²);

c: Extend the chord over the whole span – wing depth would be unchanged but the t/c would be lowered. A wing area increased to 794ft² (73.8m²) would markedly benefit landing and take-off.

It was desirable to cut fin and tail thickness also but there would be difficulty in finding more space for fuel since two Avon RA.24Rs would be fitted, reheated to 1,800K for 5,000lb (66.7kN) thrust.

Option 2 seemed to get most attention and in mid-June 1954 was estimated to have an all up weight with two Blue Jay, four Adens and ,030gal (4,683lit) of fuel (940gal [4,274lit] internal) of 37,170lb (16,860kg). With two Blue Jays, sea level rate of climb was 33,600ft/min 10,241m/min) with 3 minutes to get to 0,000ft (12,192m). In the clean condition Mach 1.0 could be reached at 36,000ft 10,973m). More advanced studies in April 954 of the basic DH.110 configuration included a 6% wing of either 450 or 500ft² (41.9 or 46.5m²) with a single Rolls RB.106 or de Havilland PS.26 Gyron and an estimated Mach 1.49 and 1.43 at 36,000ft (10,973m) respectively, or a 7% 750ft² (69.8m²) wing and two RB.106 for Mach 1.55.

On 7th November 1955, DH did complete a brochure for a high altitude DH.110 for the RAF which was really the standard production Sea Vixen with a Spectre rocket mounted in the top of the inter-jet fairing between the two Avons. This land-based aircraft could be supersonic on the level above 30,000ft 9,144m) and make interceptions up to 0,000ft (21,336m). It was particularly attractive since no serious aerodynamic difficulties were likely to be encountered. After more than 270 supersonic dives, a maximum Mach number of 1.25 had been reached with the DH.110 prototypes with aerodynamic and handling qualities proved up to Mach 1.2, the pull out at high 'g' and supersonic speed being quite free from buffet.

With the rocket turned on at 30,000ft, time to 50,000ft (15,240m) was 6.3 minutes and 70,000ft 9.3 minutes. A maximum 72,000ft 21,946m) at Mach 1.25 could be achieved before exhausting the rocket fuel. Sea level rate of climb was 13,200ft/min (4,023m/min); 16,800ft/min (5,121m/min) at 30,000ft with the rocket just switched on. The four guns were removed to make room for the rocket's hydrogen peroxide fuel but the existing AI.18 radar and two Blue Jay installation was retained with provision for carrying two more or the Mk.4 weapon (Red Top) when available. Various naval fittings such as hook and wing fold were omitted. With these modifications and using a production wing, prototype flight date would be November 1957 with service entry 1959.

For the interception of the targets expected in 1959, higher speeds up to Mach 1.8 (at 59,000ft [17,983m]) and shorter times to height were predicted by fitting two Spectre rockets. Mach 1.4 ceiling would be above 75,000ft (22,860m). There were also 1954 studies to fit reheated RA.24Rs to the standard

DH.110 but they were never tried. These were early days in the study of acoustic pressures on the tailplane, and the fatigue caused by it. The DH.110 Sea Vixen had a high tail with the jet pipes underneath and both reheat or rockets would have exposed the tail to high acoustic pressures. In short, the tail may well have failed from fatigue at some point so these supersonic projects might have needed considerable work to counter this. Extensive testing of the later DH.117 indicated that it too would suffer similar acoustic problems.

Supermarine Type 576

This was a supersonic project submitted in December 1958 to a new requirement for a naval fighter replacement, but at the time the Naval Staff decided an all-new aircraft was the direction to take. Hawker sent a brochure for the P.1127 vertical take-off aircraft, DH Airspeed sent thoughts on Sea Vixen developments, Vickers Supermarine also sent an addendum to its Type 571 strike project. The initial Type 576 was itself a strike aircraft in single or two-seat versions, the latter to the NR/A.39 Buccaneer requirement, but a fighter version soon followed. Power for the 576 came from two RB.146 engines (later the Series 300 Avon) developed from the RA.24 with an extra stage in the compressor. Blowing was extended over the outer as well as the inner wing and new dorsal fuel tanks feeding into the main fuselage tanks were introduced to provide an additional 450gal (2,046lit) of internal fuel. Another underwing station near each wing root was added.

The production Scimitar was limited to fair weather operation by its radar and sighting system. It had an operational ceiling of about 40,000ft (12,192m) at which a continuous manoeuvre 'g' of 1.5 was available. The Ferranti Airpass nose radar and Elliott auto pilot had been proposed for the strike role, but the fighter required the addition of a computer. On the 576, provision was made for four Firestreak weapons, or the later Red Top, carried on the inboard pylons. Red Top could attack from any direction except for a small area dead-ahead of the target. The air-to-air rocket battery used on the Scimitar was retained and 200gal (909lit) drop tanks could fit on the outer wing points. Consideration was given to modifying the current Scimitar on a retrofit basis.

From the performance aspect, studies were made in April 1959 of four alternatives:

a: The addition of two de Havilland Spectre rockets to the dry RB.146s using the dorsal tanks to carry enough HTP fuel for

at least 1.75 minutes operation. Continuous 2.2 'g' was available with half fuel for a Mach 1.4 interception at 55,000ft (16,764m). The rocket engines were located in the fuselage beneath but slightly inside the jet pipes and, according to the makers, gave greater noise levels than the Scimitar's Avon 202s. However, with usage confined to altitude it was probable there would be little noise generated structure damage. In order to balance the weight of the rockets which were aft of the centre of gravity, extended wingtips were needed which also improved the maximum patrol altitude. Mach 1.8 could be reached at 65,000ft (19,812m).

b: The use of wing tip nacelles containing rocket fuel and rockets in a simple self-contained installation. This idea reduced the noise problem but was not favoured by the designers because if the rockets did not have equal thrust, yawing moments would be large.

c: Alternative to the rockets, reheated RB.146s were studied, but to obtain a reasonable supersonic performance a thinner wing was essential which at this stage was confined to the portion of the wing outboard of the folding joint. This aeroplane had the advantage of a higher speed during the early part of an interception accelerating typically to

A composite drawing showing the possible alternatives to the DH.110 wingplan for making it supersonic. The starboard surface has the full delta wing; the port side two different ways of increasing wing area. Derek G Brown

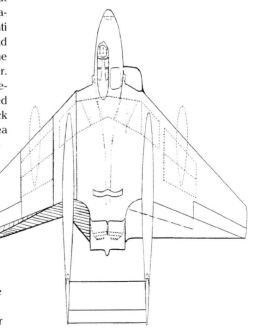

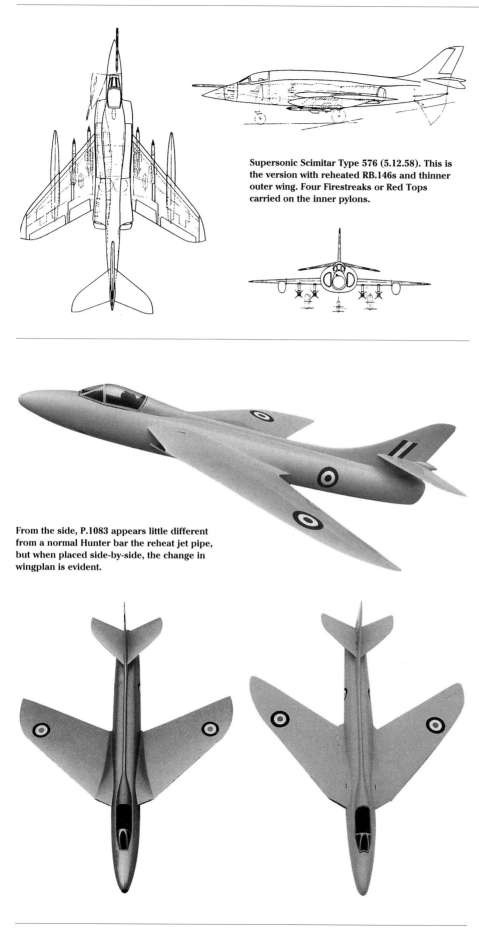

Supersonic Scimitar Type 576 (5.12.58). This is the version with reheated RB.146s and thinner outer wing. Four Firestreaks or Red Tops carried on the inner pylons.

From the side, P.1083 appears little different from a normal Hunter bar the reheat jet pipe, but when placed side-by-side, the change in wingplan is evident.

Mach 1.6 at 45,000ft (13,716m), but had less ability to gain altitude than the rocket variant.

d: The second reheated version had the wing thinned from the root outboard giving better speed and manoeuvrability at the expense of some loss in patrol time at a given weight.

The estimate for these proposals to enter service was 1962 for version (a) with (b) and (c) about six months later and the final project a further six months.

Hawker P.1083

An aircraft with 50° sweepback was first recommended for research purposes during discussions at RAE on 27th September 1949, preferably by modifying an existing machine. As a result, a brochure was sent by Supermarine in February 1950, but it was then suggested that Hawker should be asked to consider the idea by modifying the F.3/48. Sydney Camm's team had considered a project with a thinner wing and greater sweep in May 1950, writing an appraisal note on 28th June. This showed a conversion of the basic F.3/48 Hunter with a new set of wings on existing pick up points, the only fuselage modification being strengthening of the rear spar frame. The intakes were unaffected. At this time, the only aircraft planned with a 50° wing was the Short S.B.5 low speed aircraft to ER.100. The P.1083 was looked on as a possible research aircraft and for a while work proceeded to this end.

Things became more concrete when DMARD, A E Woodward Nutt, wrote to Sydney Camm on 7th March 1951, requesting an official brochure for military applications (he also wrote to Joe Smith at Supermarine for a similar Swift development proposal). The fourth Hunter prototype was due to be ordered and he said this airframe could be used. After discussion with RAE, a brochure followed on 31st May for an F.3/48 development 'Thin Wing Hunter' with 50° swept wing increased from 40° and thickness 7.5% down from 8.5%, two Aden cannon and reheated Sapphire 4 engine. The firm claimed the main purpose of this development was to ensure the aircraft did not have any dive speed restriction. Reduced drag combined with a substantial increase in thrust from a reheated Sa.4 increased top speed by 40mph (64km/h) at all altitudes making level speeds in the region of Mach 1 possible. Speed without reheat was Mach 0.95 to 0.97, still up about 30mph (48m/h) on the P.1067.

The Ministry felt these estimates were reasonable but reheat was required for the best climb and turn performance and that gave a oor range. With no internal space available, a jettisonable fuel tank was required – the success of the aircraft depended on the satisfactory development of reheat. Climb to 45,000ft (13,716m) with reheat was 4.4 minutes, without 10.0 minutes, compared to 6.0 and 12.5 on the present P.1067. Ceiling would be 53,700ft (16,368m) with reheat, 45,800ft (13,960m) without. The Ministry was happy the P.1083's undoubted research value also showed good military potential.

Serious work began in the Drawing and Stress Offices in mid-October and much of the new wing's design was completed inside a month. On 8th November, ACAS(OR), Air Vice-Marshal Geoffrey Tuttle, explained how he wanted to see development of both the Hawker and Supermarine day fighters and Camm requested a talk a few days later when he had one or two interesting delta designs to look at as well' (almost certainly the P.1091 delta wing Hunter and P.1092). The P.1083 aircraft was planned to be the fourth F.3/48 P.1067 prototype, but Camm suggested that when the second P.1067 flew, the modified wings should go on the first aircraft, WB188, to get them flying earlier. He also felt an Avon engine with increased thrust would be a better choice than the Sapphire.

Full go-ahead was given by the Ministry on 12th December when an order for Swift F Mk.1s was also placed and go-ahead for the Swift stage 2 (Type 545) given. No reduction in armament was to be made, i.e. the P.1083 would not be accepted without four 30mm cannon. Power was to come from an Sa.3 or Sa.4 Sapphire, but engine choice was later deferred. Camm's insistence for the Avon brought agreement to fit an RA.14 in January 1952 as this engine was expected to be ready first. The Ministry also requested additional internal fuel, but Camm felt this would be difficult. Fifteen months fabrication work was assumed with the P.1083, hopefully to be ready in July 1953. A new Specification, F.119D, was issued in April 1952 to cover design of the 'Hawker Interceptor Fighter' with a Rolls-Royce RA.14R reheated to 1,500K. (The system of numbering specifications was declared Secret at the end of 1949 and a new series starting at 100 introduced, which did not reveal the year of the specification. See page 166).

Air Commodore H V Satterly, DOR(A), queried whether there would be any extra risk in ordering production P.1083s off the drawing board as per the P.1067 to establish and retain a clear a lead as possible over enemy fighters; unfortunately there was. In March 1952 it was reported that the standard F.3/48 fuselage could take the RA.14 Avon instead of the RA.7, but the maximum diameter of the P.1067's

reheat pipe was 31in (79cm) against the 36in (91cm) required. The Sapphire Sa.4 needed a greater depth fuselage leading to a new design altogether. This created a dilemma as to which engine to use, reheated RA.7, unreheated RA.14 or reheated Sa.4 and ordering the new wing was deferred by six months to sort this out.

There was a feeling at this time to put more Sapphires into Hunters anyway to reduce pressure on the Avon, versions of which were also in the Canberra, Valiant, Swift and DH.110. But as there was anxiety to get the job moving, the RA.7R was chosen for the prototype and work started in the Hawker Experimental Shop to manufacture the wings in October 1952. Production models were to get the RA.14R of 14,500lb (64.4kN) reheated thrust or the even more powerful RA.19R at 17,750lb (78.9kN), the pipe size problem being solved by using the engine skin as the actual rear fuselage skin.

In early April 1953, well into manufacture, the Air Staff requested the P.1083 (and the Supermarine 545) to be rearmed with the Blue Jay missile as primary weapon which created problems in both machines from a lack of space for radars and the like. The P.1083 had been developed as an improved performance F.3/48 with guns only, it had not been intended as a guided weapon carrier. Hawker was officially informed that the Air Staff were now only interested if it could carry four Blue Jays and performance investigations suggested with the AAM, cannon and only 420gal (1,909lit) of internal fuel, it would have little cruising endurance. The P.1083 also lacked manoeuvrability with the missiles aboard.

Much of the cancelled P.1083's fuselage and tail found its way onto the P.1099 F Mk.6 prototype. This view, taken in 1960, shows a Hunter that has been modified from F Mk.6 to FGA Mk.9 standard, as evidenced by among other things, the tail parachute housing and 230-gallon drop tanks on the inboard pylons. Eric Morgan collection

Outboard wing tanks were a possibility, but a full redesign was the real solution and this needed two more prototypes for which there was no financial provision. ACAS(OR) subsequently stated he thought the Air Staff was unlikely to want the Hunter development. If this was confirmed, they needed to decide if it was worth continuing the prototype, a difficult situation because if completed it was expected to become a test bed for the RA.14R engine as well. The aircraft was due to fly by the end of the year.

Tuttle reported in a memo on 9th June that thanks to flight test problems with the F.3/48 Hunter coupled with the difficulty of fitting reheat and the lack of space for extra fuel and equipment, the P.1083 was to be cancelled and work was to cease forthwith. It was considered the Hunter made a less attractive project than the Swift. Hawker was officially informed on 13th July. Camm and Stanbury consulted with Rolls-Royce about fitting the RA.14 in the standard Hunter and on 12th August Tuttle agreed that the firm should proceed with the large engined non-reheat version of the aircraft. A brochure covering the P.1099 was sent on the 24th and work began in the Drawing Office.

The front and centre fuselage and the tail from the cancelled P.1083 prototype, WN470, were used to construct the P.1099 XF833 which became the prototype for the Hunter F Mk.6 series and flew on 23rd January 1954. The F Mk.6 eventually used the Avon 203 of 9,950lb (44.2kN) thrust. A revised P.1083 brochure was sent to Woodward Nutt on 23rd September with RA.19R and the wing leading edge extended forward progressively towards the tips to give a thinner aerofoil section and some degree of camber. The engine had an infinitely variable reheat installation so that any level of thrust between non and full reheat was available. Sea level climb rate was 50,000ft/min (15,240m/min); at 36,000ft (10,973m) this was 14,400ft/min (4,389m/min); time to

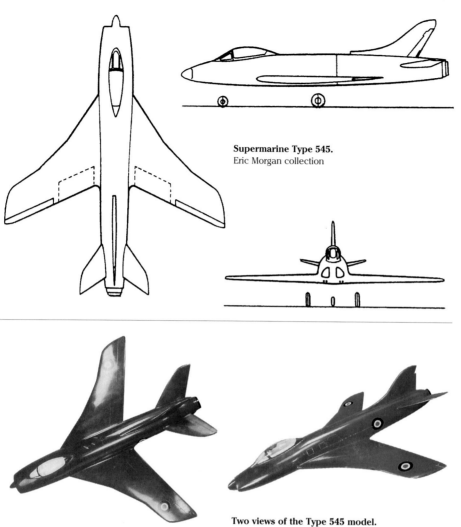

Supermarine Type 545.
Eric Morgan collection

Two views of the Type 545 model.

(13,716m), supersonic in a dive and absolute ceiling 55,600ft (16,947m). Compressibility effects would be both delayed and reduced by the greater sweep angle.

Stage 2 had the same fuselage, engine, inner wing including undercarriage and tail surfaces as Stage 1. The increased aspect ratio was obtained by adding new outer panels with 40° sweep in the middle section and 30° at the tip to prevent tip stalling and the instability normally associated with high aspect ratio swept wings. This increased area to 390ft² (36.3m²), span to 39.5ft (12.0m) and reduced the mean t/c ratio to about 7.5% (8.3% at the root, 6% at the tip) to give the same critical Mach number as the Stage 1 wing. Length remained 41.5ft (12.6m) and normal weight was 17,540lb (7,956). At 40,000ft (12,192m) top speed was 656mph (1,065m/h), 32mph (51km/h) more than the Swift F Mk.1.

–

The Ministry felt these were reasonable proposals with performance superior to the Swift, but it was clear if the Swift had an RA.12, Stage 1 would be only 20mph (32m/h) faster with better high speed characteristics but an inferior climb, turn and endurance capability. Hence, for all-round performance Stage 1 hardly seemed justified for operation at low or medium altitude. The reheated Stage 2 had the best performance meeting the requirements of OR.228 in almost all respects and its superiority over Stage 1 and the Swift became more marked as altitude increased thanks to the higher aspect ratio and lower wing loading.

Manoeuvrability considerations were likely to limit Stage 1 to about 44,000ft (13,411m) while Stage 2 at an even higher all-up-weight should be capable of combat at about 50,000ft (15,240m). Top speeds for both were re-estimated to be Mach 0.95 to 0.97 with reheat, Mach 0.94 to 0.95 without, both about 40mph (64km/h) higher than the Swift. Time to 45,000ft (13,716m) was 3.8 minutes for both reheated, 7.2 and 6.8 respectively without compared to 6.6 and 12.4 minutes for the Swift with only two guns. Ceilings with reheat were Stage 1 51,500ft (15,697m), Stage 2 56,800ft (17,313m), Swift 49,500ft (15,088m), without 46,800 (14,265), 50,000 (15,240) and 44,600 (13,594) respectively. Stage 2 had easily the best turn radius and it was concluded this aircraft was the most attractive and should make a good high altitude fighter.

RAE commented that at least a prototype of the higher performance aircraft should proceed as an insurance against possible future high performance enemy aircraft, besides having a useful research application. As stated, Geoffrey Tuttle was anxious to get both

45,000ft (13,716m) was 2.35 minutes and service ceiling 59,500ft (18,136m). Two months later the firm offered a P.1083 with all new 6% thick wing and 45° sweep but, by now, Sir Sydney Camm was in two minds whether to proceed with this or start again with a new project of the Mach 2 variety.

Supermarine Type 545
Joe Smith first submitted proposals for a 50° sweepback aircraft in February 1950 using a modified version of the Type 510 to E.41/46. DMARD requested in March 1951 that he reconsider it as a development of the Swift and this eventually comprised two versions under Type number 545. Stage 1 had a pure 50° swept wing and tail and was considered a big advance over the Swift at low and medium altitudes. If particular emphasis on high altitude was required, an appendix described Stage 2 with a new high aspect ratio cranked wing made by adding additional outer wing sections. The firm's investigations with a number of wing sweep angles and loadings, t/c and

aspect ratios had shown it was not possible to obtain appreciable increases in low altitude speed and at the same time greatly improve high altitude performance. Both developments were powered by an Avon RA.12 reheated to 1,500K.

The basic details of the brochure when submitted on 12th June 1951, were as follows:

Stage 1 had the existing Type 541 Swift wing swept a further 10° with the tip shape slightly modified and inboard flap end cut away to give clearance with the fuselage. Span was cut from 32.3 to 28.3ft (9.8 to 8.6m) and t/c ratio from 10% to 8.3%. Wing area was 314ft² (29.2m²), length 41.5ft (12.6m) and normal weight 17,490lb (7,933kg). The only major fuselage modification was adjustment to the air intakes for the bigger engine. Tail sweep was also 50° and variable incidence was incorporated similar to that developed for the Type 510. Armament was four 30mm cannon and internal fuel capacity 500gal (2,273lit). Estimated top speed at sea level was 734mph (1,181km/h), 645mph (1,038km/h) at 45,000ft

Hawker and Supermarine working on the next developments of Swift and Hunter once it was decided what form these should take. By November it was clear that ACAS(OR) favoured development of the Swift despite the original idea of a standard fuselage fitted with redesigned wings being dropped because of the bigger engine. Initial recommendations suggested ordering two prototypes, one with each set of wings, but on 22nd January 1952, Woodward Nutt gave the go-ahead for the Type 545 Stage 2 only.

Two fuselages were to be allocated off the Swift production line and suitably modified, the first a flying shell, the second incorporating provision for the Blue Jay missile. Specification F.105D.2 was raised to cover the new aircraft with an RA.14 reheated to 2,000K and issued on 14th October 1952, but without an individual Operational Requirement. Production aircraft were to be in service by 1957 and the mock-up was officially examined on 5th August 1953. Estimated flight dates in April 1953 were late 1953 and mid-1954 respectively, but by July 1954 these dates had been adjusted to November 1954 and August 1955.

When the Hawker P.1083 was cancelled, increased emphasis fell on the 545 and the Ministry confirmed carriage of Blue Jay as primary armament, the first prototype, XA181, becoming the cannon version and the second, XA186, the missile version. XA181 had a design Mach number of 1.3 but there were soon movements to improve this and other aspects. By July 1954 the Air Staff wished to revise their standards with consequent radical changes to the design of the fuselage. With several different versions of the Swift already, and now changes to the 545, George Edwards at Vickers (Supermarine's parent company) was prompted to write on 24th May to complain about the age old problem of when to standardise on a design and start production. These changes had assisted in the big 38% increase in estimated cost for the year April to April, 1952-53.

Modification of the 545 was first discussed during the Advisory Design Conference on 22nd January 1954, when an all weather capability with AI radar was mooted. At a St. Giles Court meeting on 12th July it was explained that a larger fuselage than that provided for the two prototypes would be needed and with an RA.19R engine, a maximum sea level speed of just over Mach 1 would be obtained. With the new RB.106 engine Mach 1.3 could be achieved at 40,000ft (12,192m) and with development of a thinner wing and modified intakes, and the RB.106 with convergent/divergent nozzle, a performance approaching Mach 2 could be possible. Joe Smith thought an RA.19 or RB.106 aircraft could be ready in 1958/59, and a Mach 2 machine in late 1960. Rolls-Royce reported that prototype RB.106s could be available by end 1956.

G Silyn Roberts, DMARD (RAF), felt that provision of the all weather capability put the aircraft so far ahead that the Air Staff should aim for a substantial improvement in performance. Therefore, it was recommended the RB.106 should be adopted to replace the RA.23/19 planned for production, and also the development batch scheme be introduced to accelerate development. This would enable a single-seat, single engine high altitude all weather Mach 1.3 interceptor capable of operating at heights up to 51,000ft (15,545m) to be in service in 1958/59 with possible development to Mach 1.7 or 2.0 and 60,000ft (18,288m) about two years later. The RB.106 version had a chin intake with an 18in (46cm) scanner radome above it rather like the F-86D Sabre. Joe Smith considered the two prototypes currently on order might be used for aerodynamic trials only with provision on the second machine to carry just dummy Blue Jays. Vickers-Supermarine also wished to consider the application of area rule.

Within a week, RAE expressed serious doubts about this programme, particularly getting an RB.106 flying in what would really be a new airframe within two and a half years. For Mach 2, the position was even more obscure because the latest Air Staff Requirement for such an aircraft specified a two-seat machine (what became OR.329/F.155T). RAE

The Type 545 prototype, XA181.
Eric Morgan collection

felt the jump to Mach 2 from 1.2 would turn out to be more difficult than by simply fitting a thinner wing to an already designed fuselage, the intake would need modification and area rule considerations would suggest a different fuselage shape. The Mach 2 aircraft should be considered a separate aeroplane and the first RB.106 machine, which they felt would achieve Mach 1.23, examined on its own in relation to other high altitude projects in this speed range.

The speed was approximately equal to that of the Thin Wing Javelin but Gloster's aircraft would have better altitude manoeuvrability. The F.23/49 (English Electric P.1) offered Mach 1.5 and a more direct development to speeds approaching Mach 2.2. The RAE felt the 545 had got out of phase with Air Staff requirements, had a quite inadequate high altitude performance even for 1957 and nothing outstanding to offer in view of its late time scale. Thus its position in the programme should be carefully re-considered.

In the meantime, work on the prototypes continued. Extensive tunnel testing at RAE found high instability occurred at moderate lift coefficients and tip stalling was dominant. Wing fences and eliminating the outer wing kink did not help, but lowering the tailplane had a much more powerful effect on stability. When placed below the wing chord plane, nose-up instability was near non-existent throughout the Mach range tested. In the event the tailplane was fitted above wing level and proved OK but, as related in Chapter 6, RAE was initially against the low tail position. It was also intended to use some titanium in the construction of the second prototype, the company's first aircraft to use this new material.

Presumably from the doubts raised by RAE, PDSR(A) suggested in August that the second prototype was not needed and was jeopardising the chance to step up ER.134D (Bristol 188) prototype numbers from two to four. Joe Smith was reluctant to scrap the machines at this late stage because of the bad effect it would have on moral at Hursley Park where they were already suffering from Swift cancellations. Nevertheless, Supermarine were informed on 8th October that the second prototype XA186 was no longer required. RAE was, however, still happy to have the first aircraft to provide useful experience in the upper transonic range filling a natural sequence in the family of Hunter, Swift and F.23 (P.1) and so work was to continue.

But on 16th August 1955, with XA181 near complete but still not ready to fly, R A Shaw recommended cancelling the aircraft because it was competing with the N.113 (Scimitar) and RAE no longer had a special interest in the wing. Supermarine was told to cease work on the 23rd. Both Smith and Edwards pushed hard for continuation stating flight trials could commence in four months, but abandonment was close. The 545 had seriously delayed work on the Scimitar and late version Swift F Mk.7, and was noted for inclusion in the cancellation programme on 3rd October the contract being terminated on 22nd December.

The Type 545, sometimes known as the 'Crescent Wing Swift', was finally cancelled largely to conserve funds as the research information it would supply would be of too little value and too late. A rough estimate suggested 500 man weeks were required to complete XA181 for flight test, about another year's work. The airframe was expected to go on loan to the College of Aeronautics, Cranfield for structural research (it did) while the test airframe, wings and tail went to RAE for various experiments including kinetic heat testing, the latter for application in the first place to the firm's Type 559 to F.155T. The crescent wing was, at the time, in fashion having been fitted to the Handley Page Victor bomber and the HP.88 research aircraft.

Gloster G.A.6 Thin Wing Javelin

This programme, also called the 'Super Javelin', was a direct development of the standard Javelin and began as an old fuselage with new engines and wings, but was to become an entirely new design, like the Type 545. At the start it was still a subsonic aircraft and draft specifications F.118D and P were issued around it, retaining the centre number 118 recently used for the photo reconnaissance P.350 variant. The Air Staff required the Javelin all-weather fighter to be developed to its maximum potential and to differ from the standard Javelin in particular with the equipment carried. The first project drawn to this end was the P.356 of July 1953.

Gloster P.356

At the Javelin Advisory Design Conference on 12th May 1953, the Air Staff requested a thin wing photo-recce version but emphasised that fighter development was to be regarded as the primary basis for the design; performance was not to be penalised on account of the PR provision. No definite performance requirements were laid down, but more thrust was certainly wanted and alternative missile armaments of two Red Dean, four Blue Jay, or two Red Dean and two Blue Jay together, plus the four Aden cannon and AI.18 radar, noted.

The P.356 brochure offered fairly reliable performance estimates in terms of climb, time to height etc, but less certain level speeds. Internal fuel was limited to 860gal (3,910lit) to keep down weight. The lower half of the fin was redesigned from the Javelin as per RAE suggestions and with the thinner wing, shallow dives to Mach 1.2 or 1.3 were possible at altitude. Main and rear spars were strengthened, and the all-moving tail and power controls then being developed for the standard Javelin were to be fitted. In clean condition ceiling was 61,700ft (18,806m), reduced to 59,200 (18,044m) with two Red Dean, two Blue Jay and two Aden. Time to 45,000ft (13,716m) clean was 6.3 minutes. Gloster stated the Red Dean and Blue Jay mix was the worst combination from a drag and weight point of view.

General discussions in mid-January 1954 confirmed the Bristol Olympus 6 at 16,000lb (71.1kN) thrust was a better choice for production aircraft than the Sa.10 of 14,000lb (62.2kN): the additional thrust was essential to deal with the weight of extra equipment. A programme schedule was drawn up in March but the specification took ages to prepare and was not ready until November having been renumbered F.153D during the summer to cover the 'Thin Wing Gloster All-Weather Fighter'. It was issued on 17th March 1955.

A prototype order was placed in March 1954. Allotted serial XG336, this was a clerical error since it duplicated one of the batch of 20 pre-production Lightning F Mk.1s. It was to have Sa.6 or Sa.7 Sapphires and it was hoped production deliveries could commence in early 1958. Provision was requested for flight refuelling and the specification wanted the best possible performance obtainable. Treasury Approval for a development batch of 18 aircraft was given in mid-January 1955, one of the first aircraft to be ordered in a 'pre-production' format. The order was placed on 5th April for XJ836-842 and XJ877-887.

When F.153D was first written, the main structural difference between the standard Javelin and the new TW variant lay in the wing itself, hence, structural test specimens

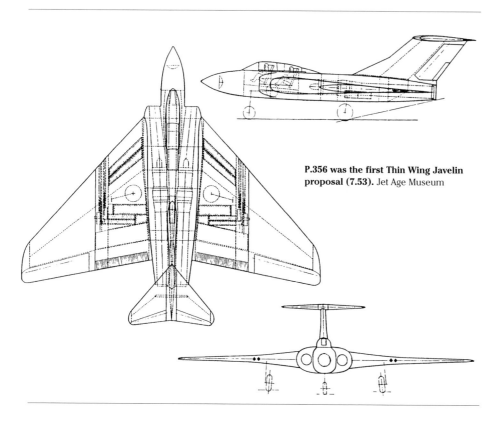

P.356 was the first Thin Wing Javelin proposal (7.53). Jet Age Museum

ere limited for tip to tip wing. Subsequently, the whole concept changed, larger engines were fitted, strength factors raised and the equipment so altered that F.153D no longer represented a Javelin but rather a new aircraft with the same general appearance. Structural testing was heavily increased as tip to tip now accommodated front fuselage, centre body structure and detail such as tailplane, aileron, elevator, rudder, fuel tank, intakes and radome, at a great increase in cost. Some money was paid, however, by the American Mutual Aid Programme along with cash for the Hunter F Mk.6. The next stage was the P.364 drawn in September 1953. It looked quite similar to the P.356, but the intakes were moved back slightly and Olympus engines introduced. Enlarged a bit more, this became P.370/ P.371/ P.372 in September 1954.

Gloster P.370 Series

These drawings covered the same aircraft but with different weapons (author's note: Gloster P-numbers represent drawing numbers, not projects and often showed different facets of the same design; for example P.373 showed fuel tanks and P.374 engine mountings. For convenience, however, the numbers are used for project identity throughout). P.370 had four wing mounted Adens while the missile versions had underwing pylons so P.371 could carry two Red Deans and P.372 four Blue Jay. A 57in (145cm) insert had been introduced in the front fuselage for CofG considerations and to accommodate guided weapon and AI.18 equipment.

A selection of more powerful Olympus engines was offered: the Ol.6 of 16,000lb (71.1kN), Ol.7 of 17,160lb (76.3kN) and Ol.7SR (simplified reheat) 20,550lb (91.3kN) with a possible full reheat version to follow. A range of performance estimates were available, but those for the Ol.7SR took the aircraft over Mach 1 on the level at height for the first time. With Adens only, all-up-weight was 58,200lb (26,400 kg) and maximum speed 742mph (1,194km/h) at sea level (Mach 0.975) and 705mph (1,134 km/h) at 40,000ft (12,192m) (Mach 1.07); sea level rate of climb was 22,600ft/min (6,888m/ min); time to 45,000ft (13,716m) 4.18 min. Ceiling was 67,000ft (20,422m). With two Red Deans and two Adens, these figures were a little inferior.

Richard Walker, Gloster's chief designer, wrote to G W H Gardner, DGTD(A), in early October 1954 to show his concern that combat weight had risen to 43,400lb (19,686kg), especially as further increases were expected. He doubted if the previously agreed strength factors would now be enough. On the P.370 with Olympus 6, it was possible to execute a

Wind tunnel model of the Gloster P.371 Thin Wing Javelin (9.54) as partially built with Olympus Ol.6/Ol.7 engines and two Red Dean missiles.
Ray Williams collection

2g level turn at Mach 0.9 and 45,000ft, raising this to 51,000ft (15,549m) with the Olympus 7, both with Red Dean and Blue Jay. Flight experience with the Javelin had verified that the aircraft behaved well at Mach numbers up to 1.06 with effective controls and it was expected that the Thin Wing F.153 would be controllable in dives to at least Mach 1.3. The mock-up was examined at Brockworth on 18th October 1955, the prototype and first two pre-production aircraft were to have the Ol.6, subsequent pre-production the Ol.7 with convergent/divergent nozzle. XG336 (built in the Experimental Shop) was to fly in July 1957, the last pre-production, XJ887, in June 1959.

During the late summer of 1955, the Air Staff examined the American McDonnell F-101 Vodoo, which had an all-up-weight roughly comparable to the F.153, but a speed of about Mach 1.6 at 35,000ft (10,668m), when the Gloster aircraft was barely supersonic. One reason was that the F.153 had about three times the wing area of the Voodoo and consequently its maximum operating altitude was much higher, but further investigation

showed the thin wing Javelin could be much improved by fitting full reheat. Estimates with Olympus 6 were top speed at Tropopause Mach 0.96, absolute ceiling 58,000ft (17,504 m), with Ol.7SR Mach 1.05 and 63,000ft (19,202m), and the Ol.7R with full 2,000K reheat Mach 1.4 and 66,000ft (20,117m), assuming the reheat could be kept alight and the aircraft did not lose trim. In comparison, the F-101's absolute ceiling was 51,000ft (15,545m) and the Air Staff recommended that Gloster should continue its work.

While visiting Washington on 12th December 1955, the Minister of Supply was shown secret papers on the Avro Canada CF-105 Arrow fighter then under evaluation by the USAF. He was highly impressed and cabled to Ministry to say so. In the new year, an evaluation team quickly departed to Canada to assess the project for possible use with the RAF. Its report was extensive and a full comparison to the Thin Wing Javelin was made.

It was realised that by about 1959 the standard Javelin would be marginal against improved versions of the Russian Myasishchev M-4 and Tupolev Tu-16 bombers due to limits in speed and height and the lack of a collision course missile. Unless the F.153 was brought into service with Red Dean, there would be a gap in the UK's all-weather air defences until

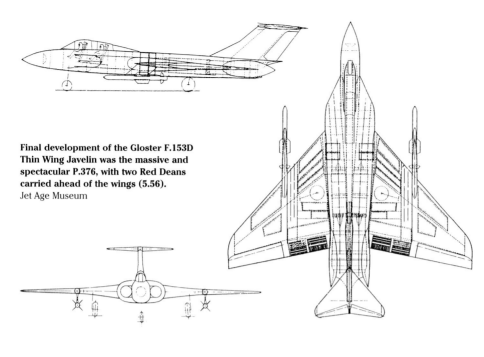

Final development of the Gloster F.153D Thin Wing Javelin was the massive and spectacular P.376, with two Red Deans carried ahead of the wings (5.56).
Jet Age Museum

the F.155 arrived in 1963. The English Electric P.1 was no substitute for it was not all-weather and again had just pursuit course weapons. But on Service entry in 1960-1961, the Thin Wing Javelin itself would be out of date thanks to a marginal performance against high altitude targets and effectively being useless against a Mach 2 bomber.

Assessment suggested a CF-105 with Hughes Falcon AAM could be in RAF service before a TW Javelin equipped with Red Dean and collision course computer, besides having a vastly superior performance which Avro claimed in August to be Mach 1.9 at 50,000ft (15,240m), 4.1 minutes to 50,000ft and ceiling 62,000ft+ (18,897m). Analysis moved on to assess if the Royal Canadian Air Force's weapon system could be introduced into the UK defence environment. A British CF-105 would have British engines – either Bristol Olympus, Rolls Conway or de Havilland Gyron.

Gloster P.376

In February 1956, Walker had been invited by E T Jones, DGTD(A), to examine the effects on the F.153D's timescale of the following modifications:

a: Using existing wings / tail unit but extend the fuselage fore and aft to improve area rule distribution (with redesigned intakes this would substantially reduce drag);

b: Or thin the wings to 5% (thereby greatly reducing fuel capacity, while the level of structural redesign gave a new aircraft, creating delay; it was not taken up.)

The result of a) was the ultimate Thin Wing

Javelin and a whopper of a fighter. Gloster described how the original F.153D conception had been for a subsonic/transonic aircraft associated with pursuit or collision course guided weapons using AI.18 radar, the Aden cannon being secondary armament. Speed was secondary to altitude performance.

Latterly, emphasis had been placed on a Red Dean combination where the existing aircraft's speed was judged adequate against targets capable of Mach 1.3 or for ahead collision course interception. But the service entry date plus further advances in target speeds made the present F.153D fall short of future requirements and the aircraft was now raised to the category of a truly supersonic fighter which would serve as a valuable interim type pending the introduction of more advanced aircraft.

Gloster claimed that this revision would not affect the timing of entry into service compared to the F.153D now in construction because the re-vamped design could be introduced from the fourth aircraft of the development batch; the predicted date for service entry was late 1960 or early 1961. On P.376, the Red Deans were moved forward relative to the wing, on pylons underslung from slim nacelles extending forward of the leading edge. With 1,800K reheat, estimated top speed at 45,000ft (13,716m) was Mach 1.63 increasing to Mach 1.79 with 2,000K. Fuel capacity was 2,960gal (13,456lit) with 2,200 (10,001) internal and 760 (3,455) in ventral drop tanks.

P.376's primary role was to intercept enemy bombers and an arbitrary figure of 50,500lb

(22,907kg) with two Red Deans plus 975ga (4,432lit) of fuel was described as an 'attack weight. At this weight it needed 8.4 minutes t reach 50,000ft (15,240m) at Mach 1.5; leve speed (2,000K reheat) Mach 1.82 at 36,000 (10,973m), Mach 1.66 at 54,000ft (16,459m climb rate at sea level 56,000ft/min (17,069n min), 16,000ft/min (4,877m/min) at 40,000f Hostile targets were expected to be destroy ed just 23 minutes from take-off, 230 mile (371km) from base while flying at 50,000f the prototype should now be ready to fly t December 1958. Bristol stated that Ol.21 pro totype flight engines with full reheat would b available by September 1958 with productio engines in early 1959. The Ministry querie the top speed as the wing was still thick for supersonic aircraft but there was little doul of the P.376's ability to accelerate to Mach 1 compared to the P.370's level Mach 1.

However the P.376 was too late. The pla had been to re-equip half of the thick win Javelin force with the F.153 but on 24th Fel ruary 1956, the Air Council was recommenc ed to cancel the TW Javelin and replace it wit the CF-105. The Defence Committee was ir vited to order the CF-105 in early April; it wa a desirable replacement for the F.153 and th RAF really wanted the machine to cover th gap until the F.155 arrived. From this point th Thin Wing Javelin was finished. At the sam meeting it was decided to cancel both th F.153 and Red Dean except the missile coul be used experimentally in connection wit the development of the new Red Hebe AAN Studies from mid-1955 had also looked at strike variant of the aircraft as a 'Canberra Re placement' but the draft OR.328 written for was abandoned on 20th March 1956.

The MoS's Walter Monkton wrote on 3r May: 'the sooner the Thin Wing Javelin i dropped the happier I shall be because ever week of further development is a waste c money'. The project was finally cancelled o 31st May and Gloster was instructed to ceas work in June when XG336 was believed to b 60-70% complete and the first of the XJs wer in the jigs. Some compensation had to b paid in addition to the money spent on th prototype and pre-production contracts. Th CF-105 was never bought either, principall because of the dollar cost but also the F.15 fighter was due in service in 1963 and, as th CF-105 was unlikely to be available until 196: it was not an aid to reinforcing the RAF durin the 1958-63 period. The solution was to spee up the F.155 and give high priority to the Sar SR.177 rocket fighter for high altitude wor (Chapter 10). But, as we shall see, neither c these aircraft were to fly as a result of the 195 White Paper.

When the Thin Wing Javelin was abandoned the whole of the Gloster Aircraft Company's resources was preparing to concentrate on its development and production. Following cancellation and a subsequent re-organisation period, practically the entire Gloster Project Office became engaged on high priority work such as OR.339 (Canberra replacement) and 'Project Guardian'; the latter being a development of the Thin Wing Javelin for submission to meet an Operational Requirement recently issued by NATO. Developments of the basic Javelin with aerodynamic refinements and improved radars were also suggested but the end for Gloster itself as a fighter firm was close.

Canada's Avro CF-105 Arrow, one of the world's finest ever fighter aircraft, whose presence killed the Thin Wing Javelin. Unfortunately, the cancellation disease that plagued British aircraft so much in the 1950s and 1960s also destroyed this machine in 1959. Ken Ellis collection

Supersonic Developments – Estimated Data

Project	Span ft (m)	Length ft (m)	Wing Area ft² (m²)	t/c %	All-Up-Weight lb (kg)	Powerplant Thrust lb (kN)	Max Speed / Height mph (km/h) / ft (m) x 1,000	Armament
de Havilland DH.110 (high altitude)	50.0 (15.2)	54.0 (16.5)	648 (60.3)	10	45,000 (20,412)	2 x Avon RA.24 11,250 (50.0) + 1 x Spectre 10,000 (44.4)	723 (1,164) Mach 0.95 at sea level Mach 1.43 at 61.0 (18.6)	2 (or 4) x Firestreak or Red Top
Supermarine 576 (fighter)	41.2 (12.6)	61.0 (18.6)	?	?	51,500 (23,360) typical take-off wt	2 x RB.146 13,220 (58.8) + 2 x Spectre 10,000 (44.4); or 2 x RB.146 c.15,000 (69.8) reheat	Spectre version: Mach 1.8 at 65.0 (19.8)	4 x Firestreak or 4 x Red Top
Hawker P.1083 (production aircraft)	34.33 (10.5)	45.9 (14.0)	358 (33.3)	7.5	20,000 (9,072)	1 x Avon RA.19R 12,500 (55.6) 17,750 (78.9) reheat	820 (1,319) Mach 1.08 at sea level; 790 (1,271) Mach 1.2 at 36.0 (11.0)	4 x 30mm Aden cannon
Supermarine 545 (1st prototype)	39.0 (11.9)	47.0 (14.3)	381 (35.4)	7.5 mean	20,147 (9,139)	1 x Avon RA.14R 9,500 (42.2) 14,500 (64.4) reheat	754 (1,213) at sea level 667 (1,073) at 45.0 (13.7)	4 x 30mm Aden cannon
Supermarine 545 (development)	39.0 (11.9)	46.25 (14.1)	381 (35.4)	7.5 mean	25,500 (11,567)	1 x RB.106 15,000 (66.7) 20,000+ (88.9) reheat	Mach 1.7+ (?)	2 x 30mm Aden + 4 x Blue Jay
Gloster P.356	60.0 (18.3)	54.75 (16.7)	1,220 (113.5)	11 root 5 tip	40,300 (18,280)	2 x Sapphire Sa.7 12,500 (55.6)	Clean: 746 (1,200) M 0.98 at s.l., 650 (1,046) M 0.985 at 45.0 (13.7). With 2BJ, 2RD, 2 Aden: 743 (1,195) M 0.975 at sea level, 646 (1,039) M 0.98 at 45.0 (13.7)	4 x 30mm Aden cannon or 2 x Blue Jay + 2 x Red Dean + 2 x 30mm Aden
Gloster P.371	60.7 (18.5)	62.0 (18.9)	1,235 (114.9)	11 root 5 tip	59,350 (26,921)	2 x Olympus Ol.7SR 20,550 (91.3) reheat	737 (1,186) M 0.97 at sea level, 667 (1,073) M 1.01 at 40.0 (12.2)	2 x Red Dean + 2 x 30mm Aden
Gloster P.376	60.6 (18.5)	72.0 (21.9)	1,235 (114.9)	11 root 5 tip	60,300 (27,352)	2 x Olympus Ol.21R 28,500 (126.7) reheat	Mach 1.82 at 36.0 (11.0) (50,500 lb / 22,907 kg wt)	2 x Red Dean

Chapter Six

Transonic Research

Breaking through the Sound Barrier: 1943 to 1957

The so-called 'Sound Barrier' first exerted its influence on fighter pilots during the Second World War when compressibility, the build up of compressed air ahead of an aircraft from about Mach 0.7 onwards, was experienced in high speed dives. The symptoms were distinct – sudden buffet or violent shaking of the aircraft and a strong tendency to either pitch up which was likely to rip the machine apart, or an ever steeper dive from which it was extremely difficult to pull out. Many pilots in their Spitfires, Typhoons, Mustangs and the like never managed to get out of that dive and were tragically killed without knowing what had really happened.

Due to the need to create lift, a wing is designed to have airflow passing over it at different speeds and, as a consequence, when it approaches the speed of sound, some airflow becomes supersonic before the rest. Hence there is a speed range where both subsonic and supersonic air is passing over the aircraft at the same time, before full supersonic flight is achieved. This is called the transonic range and the supersonic airflow produces localised and powerful pressure or shock waves which cause the buffeting. Those wartime pilots could never go fully supersonic in their piston engined machines, but they were approaching and entering a transonic condition. The development of the jet, an engine without a propeller, and modern wing shapes gave designers the tools to pass through this transonic range, through the

The first P.1, WG760; a well known view taken on 10th October 1954 showing the initially straight leading edge. North West Heritage Group

sound barrier, and into pure supersonic flight. A proper research aircraft was needed and Britain's first was called the Miles M.52.

Miles M.52

This somewhat controversial aeroplane does not really fall within the confines of this book but, as it was to influence much of what happened during the 1940s and '50s, including a full account is important. On 25th September 1943, an informal meeting was held at the Ministry of Aircraft Production (MAP) to discuss the future of gas turbine engines and aeroplanes. The full picture was assessed and agreement reached that future moves must include designing a very high speed research aeroplane and the engine to power it. Harold Roxbee Cox suggested ordering the research aeroplane from (say) Phillips & Powis Aircraft Limited while Power Jets adapted one of its current engines. The latter would throw a heavy load on Power Jets but there was the possibility of strengthening the team. Within a month, Phillips & Powis had become Miles Aircraft Limited.

Miles' project ideas were examined by Roxbee Cox in late October, the firm indicating it was to go into detail on the most conventional layout. N E Rowe, DTD, received the drawings and data for this Miles ultra-high speed aeroplane numbered M.52 on the 8th November, the firm labelling it the Gyrone Project. (The name Gyrone had been coined earlier by Sir Frank Whittle with the intention of marketing Power Jets' products under this generic title. De Havilland later perpetuated it without the 'e' for its Gyron engine). It was the opinion of all concerned that the design should be left fairly open at this stage but G H Miles, having already received verbal agreement to go ahead with two aircraft and obtain materials for a third, suggested they should plan for completion of the first aircraft one year from receiving instructions to proceed. An order was placed on 13th December to Specification E.24/43 for an aircraft with an estimated speed of 700mph (1,126km/h) at 40,000ft (12,192m) and a weight of 6,500lb (2,948kg).

On 28th December J E Serby, DD/ARD(S), wrote that work on the E.24/43 and the M.38 Messenger communications aircraft was delaying the Monitor (Miles' M.33 target tug to Q.9/42) so, to ease the position, he requested work should stop on the M.38 at once. Orders for the M.38 were cancelled except for two prototypes which were to drop behind the M.52 in priority. In April 1944 it was considered no longer necessary to keep the project in the Top Secret category and it was downgraded to Secret. The M.52 had a quite basic appearance with the fuselage shaped like a bullet and a very thin straight wing. To prove the basic aerodynamics of the wing and tail units, a Miles Falcon light aircraft was fitted with full-scale model horizontal surfaces made of wood and the craft was already at RAE for testing by late October 1943. The Falcon proved a good test vehicle albeit landing with an all-moving tail was a little more difficult than normal.

The all-moving, electrically controlled tailplane was a new feature and a Spitfire was the preferred vehicle for testing it at higher speeds rather than a Mustang. Serby wrote to Joe Smith at Supermarine on 11th April to explain why the MoS needed a Spit, thereby letting him into the secret. The same month the M.52's CofG was moved forward following RAE tunnel testing which brought an alteration to the general arrangement. Now the design was more settled, RAE was able to produce in July Technical Note Aero 1470 that reported on a much fuller tunnel testing programme which chiefly investigated the possibility of the aircraft travelling at supersonic speeds. The results showed that the maximum Mach number attainable in level flight was 0.95 and sonic speed could be reached by diving from 50,000ft (15,240m).

The growing information and experience of supersonics and compressibility from piston and early jet fighters prompted a series of informal discussions and committee meetings during 1945 and 1946 on the problems of supersonic flight. Over 30 such meetings were to take place and, when available after the War, they included new German knowledge on the subject. Representatives from all the aircraft and engine firms were invited to attend and submit information on flying their own products at high speed. For example the second meeting on 4th October 1945, was attended by 50 people including D L Bancroft (Miles), R E Bishop and R M Clarkson (de Havilland), Sydney Camm and A Lipfriend (Hawker), George Carter (Gloster), A N Clifton (Supermarine), H Constant (Power Jets), D L Ellis (English Electric), Stanley Hooker (Rolls-Royce), M B Morgan (RAE), F M Owner (Bristol Engines) and N E Rowe and J E Serby from MAP.

At this particular meeting, Flight Lieutenant W A Mair of RAE explained that the two outstanding items of German knowledge were the expected effectiveness of sweep-back postponing compressibility effects and the results of work done on aerofoil sections for use at high Mach numbers. It was noted that 25° of sweepback only gave a 10% rise in critical Mach number so that at least 35° should be used. However, the use of a very low aspect ratio would itself raise the critical Mach number (e.g. reducing an unswept wing's aspect ratio from 6.0 to 1.1 gave the same rise in critical Mach number as the introduction of 30° of sweep at the same aspect ratio) and the German Professor Alexander Lippisch thought that sweepback would make no further improvement. A number of unconventional shapes (square, triangle, semicircle) had been proposed in Germany and, on the whole, the triangular shape appeared best. E T Jones from A&AEE was impressed by the disadvantages of sweepback and thought it might be a very long time before piloted aircraft with this arrangement were developed.

Miles was able to report that tunnel testing models of its straight-wing M.52 indicated that some compressibility effects were present but, due to the thinness of the wings, the larger, more normal effects experienced on models with greater thickness/cord ratios were not obtained. Tailplane area, however, was increased slightly to compensate for a slight loss of stability at high speeds. Some

Wind tunnel model at RAE Farnborough, close to the Miles M.52 configuration. The photograph is dated 19th May 1947. Brian Kervell collection

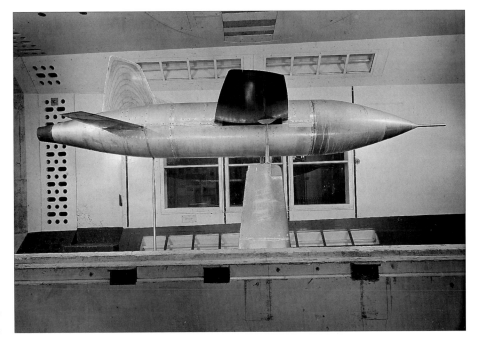

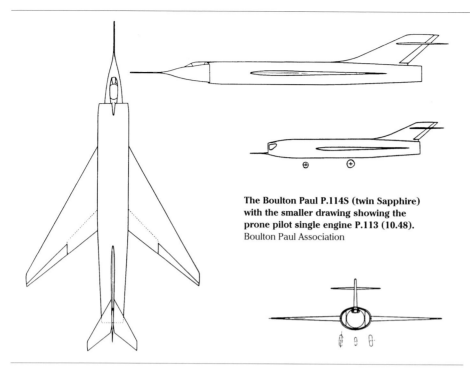

The Boulton Paul P.114S (twin Sapphire) with the smaller drawing showing the prone pilot single engine P.113 (10.48).
Boulton Paul Association

difficulty was experienced fitting the proposed split flaps so it was decided to substitute normal plain flaps. A later meeting on 9th October reported how tunnel testing had revealed that the pilot could only escape the M.52 safely if he could invert it, a fact equally true at low or high speeds. For the first time arguments for and against continuing the aircraft began.

Progress on the M.52 had certainly slowed down and weight growth was just one problem. Getting the pilot out in an emergency was another. The cockpit was inside a pointed nacelle which formed the intake centre-body and whether the cabin, to be ejected as a whole capsule, would be automatically ejected forwards in front of the aeroplane on release by the internal duct pressures, or whether rocket propulsion was necessary, was still undecided by September 1945. Miles was informed that the project was cancelled in 1946 by Ben Lockspeiser, MAP's Director General of Scientific Research (DGSR).

The official reason given was that it was too dangerous for test pilots to fly the M.52 and future research would use pilotless models released from other aircraft. Sir Peter Masefield has said that Lockspeiser, after visiting a German research laboratory at Munich, became convinced that highly swept wings were the only solution and the M.52 would be incapable of breaking the sound barrier with straight wings, despite the evidence discussed above. In fact, when the first indications of pronounced sweepback arrived from Germany, Miles wondered if the effect may be so far reaching as to justify embarking upon an entirely new layout for the E.24/43. Another factor was a doubt whether the M.52 would

actually reach supersonic speeds with the installed power and fuel. Certainly the shape was suitable because some pilotless models released from Mosquitos were small copies of the M.52 and one reached Mach 1.38 on 10th October 1948.

The author cannot add to the technical arguments about how successful the M.52 might have been, but the points listed would certainly have added to another problem, cost. A memo written on 22nd January 1946, stressed how, over two years before, the Miles contract was placed as a matter of urgency, but the progress so far made did not seem very rapid. By 30th November 1945, the firm had spent £73,000 and estimated it would cost another £250,000 to complete. Additional financial approval was therefore needed.

At DGSR's Supersonic Committee meeting on 12th February no firm decision was reached on whether to continue the M.52. It was unanimous that there was no case for continuing on the grounds of obtaining information at transonic or supersonic speeds (the reason for placing the contract), but a case was put forward to complete the aircraft for use as a test bed for Power Jet's W2/700 engine to supply useful information on ducted fans and afterburning. H F Vessey, ADARD (Res), suggested that past experience with Miles led the Ministry to regard the firm's new cost estimate to be an under-estimate and if flight tests on the engine were essential, designing and building a fresh aircraft on more conventional lines might be quicker.

Air Commodore G Silyn Roberts, DARD, wrote on the 15th advising that the contract should be cancelled. Since E.24/43 was writ-

ten, considerable additional information had been acquired and the technique of telemetering had developed into a practical proposition so that many problems of supersonic flight appeared capable of solution by model tests. These would be cheaper than full-scale testing and removed the risk of fatal accidents. H M Garner, DDGSR, added 'Although we had the best scientific advice in the country, we made two mistakes in the design…the square wings and the annular intake. We found from German information in 1945 of the great advantage of sweptback wings and recent experiments have shown the annular intake has low efficiency at high speeds. This information came to light nearly two years after the project was launched'.

On the 20th, Lockspeiser wrote (not typed but in his own hand) 'We must cut our losses and cancel the contract on this aircraft … I have discussed the matter with the firm. There will be no tears anywhere except perhaps at PJs [Power Jets] – but we are not paying £250,000 to test an engine. I believe the conception behind the decision to build this aircraft was to get supersonic information. We now know that was putting the cart before the horse. No more supersonic aircraft 'till our rocket propelled models and wind tunnels have given us enough information to proceed on a reliable basis'. In fact interest in the W2/700 was also waning. Group Captain G E Watt observed that to clear a new engine for flight 'we almost invariably spend more money than is spent on manufacture of the prototype aircraft' and he made a plea for careful planning in the future in order to 'husband our very slender resources'. In early March action was taken to cancel the contract and suspend Power Jet's W2/700 work.

One feels the comment on 'slender resources' reveals much about the situation behind the M.52's cancellation. Many have said it was a great mistake – technically, I cannot comment on that. But one must try and take in the complete picture. The Labour Government elected into power in July 1945 under Clement Attlee inherited a country that was financially, after six years of war, near bankrupt and there were many difficulties to contend with like bombed cities to rebuild and the restarting of non-military industries. The need to rebuild the civil aviation industry was a pressing need and had been one reason for the wartime Brabazon Committee. To many, a project such as the M.52 cannot have seemed very important, particularly when there was the possibility of getting the same information from cheap unmanned models (in fact the model programme was to prove very expensive).

It was left to the Americans to break the sound barrier with the experimental Bell X-1 on 14th October 1947, an aircraft not dissimilar to the M.52 though rocket powered which, in some respects, made it a less advanced aeroplane. With the demise of the M.52 and the switch to powered models, full-scale high speed research moved to de Havilland's DH.108 Swallow based on the Vampire and it became the first British aircraft to go supersonic (in a dive). Research into the high speed characteristics of swept wings followed with Hawker's P.1052 and Supermarine's Type 510, while the behaviour of delta wings was examined by two more experimental aircraft, the Boulton Paul P.111 to E.27/46 and the Fairey Delta I to E.10/47.

In 1949 full supersonic flight officially returned to the agenda in Specification E.16/49, but Ministry interest in supersonic flight was already wide awake.

A committee called The Advanced Fighter Project Group was established at RAE in early 1948 holding progress meetings between 1st March and 31st August. Stimulus must have come from America's achievement in breaking the sound barrier because once supersonic research aircraft are known to exist, supersonic fighters will not be far behind. The committee's report was issued in November 1948 which envisaged a level flight Mach number of 1.4.

On 16th March 1950, Emmanuel Shinwell, Minister of Defence, announced in the House of Commons that work had started on an aircraft capable of supersonic flight, but did not mention that it was already two years down the line. Many of the projects described below began from this work which sat outside the normal lines of requirement. The scale of study into dedicated transonic and supersonic aeroplanes at this time was undoubtedly larger than has been acknowledged.

Boulton Paul P.113 and P.114

The P.114 was the smallest possible design to satisfy an unofficial 700 knot (1,297km/h) at 45,000ft (13,716m) dual research/fighter requirement, the fighter part dictating its weight and size. It had two reheated Avons (P.114A) or Sapphires (P.114S), an all-flying tail and lower fuselage mounted Adens inside the intakes. P.114A and S were near identical except A's wings were clipped; 45,000ft (13,716m) was reached in six minutes.

The similar but smaller P.113, with an all-up-weight of 12,850lb (5,829kg), a reclined chest-down pilot's seat inside the intake and a single Avon or Sapphire with rocket boost, could satisfy the research element alone at an earlier date.

Gloster P.284 and P.285

Two further aircraft to compare prone pilot (P.284) and conventional (P.285) seating, in fact they were identical apart from the forward fuselage and were prepared to the unofficial transonic fighter specification. Power was supplied by a Sapphire Sa.2 for a top speed at 45,000ft (13,716m) of 835mph (1,344 km/h) Mach 1.25 for the P.284 and 806mph (1,297km/h) Mach 1.2 for the P.285. Absolute ceiling was 63,000ft (19,202m), sea level climb rate 35,000ft/min (10,668m/min) and internal fuel 280gal (1,273lit). To keep down size and weight and help performance, equipment was minimal but two 30mm Adens were sited in the wing roots.

The prone pilot position was taken seriously for a short period because it reduced frontal area and so eliminated the drag of the cockpit canopy, and enabled pilots to withstand up to 7g in relative comfort, a great improvement. A programme involving the RAF Institute of Aviation Medicine began in 1951 and used two test aircraft, the piston powered Reid and Sigrist RS.4 Bobsleigh and later a Meteor F Mk.8, both with a second prone cockpit in the nose. The disadvantages far outweighed any advantages; a restricted view, an unnatural posture and nowhere to put the instruments were just three reasons that brought abandonment after plenty of money had been spent.

Hawker P.1069, P.1070 and P.1071

Three similar 1948 research projects proposing a single Avon or Sapphire and a 50° sweep wing but the P.1070 added a 2,000lb (8.9kN) rocket motor in the rear fuselage between tail

and jet pipe. Each was an enlargement of the previous one – P.1069 span 25.75ft (7.8m), length 36.5ft (11.1m), area 235ft^2 (21.9m^2); P.1070 27.25ft (8.3m), 39.5ft (12.0m), 265ft^2 (24.6m^2). The P.1071 introduced two 30mm cannon and for the mixed powerplant carried 340gal (1,547lit) of fuel for the Avon and 190 gal (864lit) for the rocket.

E.16/49 (and OR.282)

This document was based on Armstrong Whitworth's project AW.58, the first draft dated May 1949. Power was to come from a Rolls-Royce AJ.65 and a maximum level speed at 36,000ft (10,973m) of at least 642kts (740mph/1,190km/h), Mach 1.12, was requested. With development, the full specification issued in September covered the design and construction of a Transonic Research Aircraft powered by one Sapphire engine with 1,500K reheat for investigating the problems associated with supersonic speeds. A maximum diving speed corresponding to Mach 1.5 was called for but there was no level speed limit, just that sonic speed had to be exceeded in level flight without reheat. As knowledge grew it was expected that extensive alterations to the lifting and control surfaces might be necessary and the design had to be adaptable to permit this. Although for research, the machine had to have the means to install two 30mm cannon and a 15in (38cm) scanner. Powered controls were requested.

Armstrong Whitworth AW.58

The project itself was first tendered in November 1948 in response to an August MoS contract and was drawn with a 60° swept wing

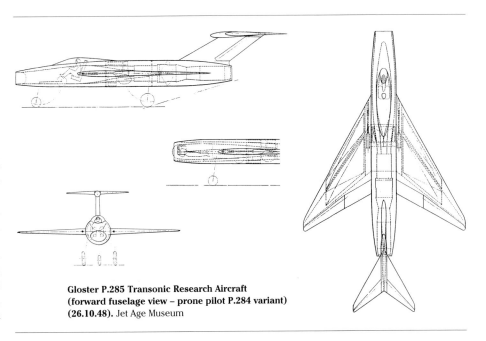

Gloster P.285 Transonic Research Aircraft (forward fuselage view – prone pilot P.284 variant) (26.10.48). Jet Age Museum

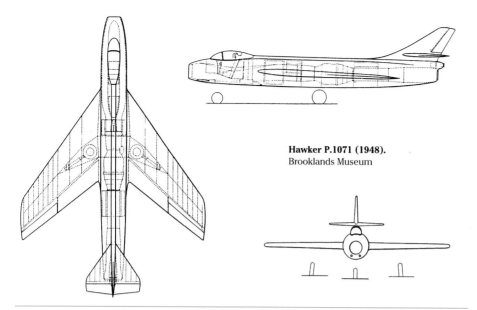

Hawker P.1071 (1948).
Brooklands Museum

and all-moving variable incidence tail mounted high on the fin. Development potential for fighter capability was requested, so well inside the nose intake was a housing to accommodate a radar scanner while any guns were likely to go in the wing roots where space was allocated for ammunition boxes (the fighter version was 51.2ft [15.6m] long and spanned 27.5ft [8.4m]). The wing had drooped leading edge slats and elevons. The main undercarriage retracted into the fuselage and fuel capacity was 217gal (986lit). A similar version with two engines was rejected by AWA before submission.

Contracts were approved in April 1949 for the AW.58 and for an English Electric supersonic research aircraft to F.23/49 called P.1 (below). Two AW.58s were ordered with serials WD466 and WD472, but by the Advisory Design Conference on 15th July AWA was expecting a maximum of only Mach 1.07 without reheat and it was here the decision was taken to go for a Sapphire reheated to 1,500K. Much work was done on the Sapphire intake system while the AW.58 mock-up was started on 1st October. Later, a cranked wing layout was examined with outer portion sweep reduced to 40° just beyond a mid-wing kink.

By now there were two other projects in the supersonic field, the P.1 and work by Fairey that would eventually lead to the Delta II. A meeting at RAE on 27th September chaired by H F Vessey, AD/ARD(Res), was called to choose between the cancellation of the AW.58 or the Fairey supersonic project, as cancellation of one was essential on financial grounds. The whole scene of high subsonic and supersonic flight research was examined and it was accepted that three main approaches needed exploration:

1: High sweepback, moderate aspect ratio – to be covered by the twin engine English Electric proposal (P.1) with 60° sweep.
2: Medium sweep, moderate aspect ratio – because of doubts about the behaviour of the high degree of sweepback in (i), a project to explore sweep intermediate between 60° and that of existing aircraft (up to 40°) was highly desirable. Modification of an existing aircraft was a possibility (thus opening the course of events that led to the Supermarine 545 Swift and Hawker P.1083 Hunter).
3: High sweep delta, low aspect ratio – it was realised this area must not be neglected. Early research data on medium sweep deltas was reassuring and the wing's structural advantages were considerable.

In summary, the original AWA E.16/49 was a 60° sweep aircraft, but the firm was pressed to provide information on medium sweep angles by reducing to 50°. This proved impossible on CofG and performance grounds. Sweeping the tips forward (the kinked wing) was designed to improve control effectiveness at high speeds as, in effect, an alternative to the English Electric device of placing controls normal to the aircraft axis. As it was, the AW.58 was considered to be a close approach to the P.1 and the case for continuing was not strong as it tended to duplicate the English Electric machine. In addition, the single engine performance margin was small (reduced still more by sweeping forward the tips) while AWA itself was a slow moving firm.

It was agreed that the Fairey delta proposal showed considerable promise and should

proceed, and recommended that a 50° sweep aircraft be constructed for research purposes. The AW.58 contract was to be cancelled. It was noted that using reduced sweep at the tips was an alternative to the English Electric project with square controls and it might be desirable to interest the firm in investigating this layout (the English Electric P.1 was actually refitted in January 1957 with a kinked leading edge to reduce sweep angle at the tip).

A further meeting at Shell-Mex House on 8th November reported how design contracts had been originally placed with a number of firms for high speed projects within a supersonic research programme. Two designs from English Electric and AWA were selected as a basis for ordering aircraft while a Fairey design was referred back for further investigation of a single engine version (which generated Schemes 3, 4 and 5 below). It was these revised Fairey proposals introducing a delta wing that brought the recommendation to cancel the swept AW.58.

However, this caused a problem, for whilst there might be good technical reasons for placing the order with Fairey, it already had the GR.17/45 (later the Gannet) and was to receive a contract for the N.14/49 naval fighter. On the other hand, AWA would be left with only the Meteor night fighter and no prospect of adequate work to employ their design staff. H F Vessey was loath to see the work go to AWA as neither he nor the RAE were favourable towards the firm's technical ability to handle such an advanced project. Fairey also had problems but it was better suited to deal with the difficulties that would arise.

It was argued that AWA should be given a similar opportunity to Fairey to review its proposal and put forward a delta design. S Scott Hall, PDTD(A), asked if there was justification in placing so much confidence in delta wing projects but it was emphasised that the Americans had flown them successfully. It was finally agreed that DMARD, J E Serby, should approach AWA and seek proposals for a delta wing design based on the Sapphire engine; work on its present E.16/49 aircraft was to be stopped 'temporarily' and its deficiencies examined.

Four days later Serby wrote requesting the suspension of work and a new single engine delta design study to compete with the Fairey project but still to E.16/49 requirements. A full brochure was submitted on 23rd January 1950 but a provisional rework was ready nearly two months earlier. AWA looked at tailed and tail-less deltas with speeds and weights similar to the original swept version while a meeting at RAE on 19th December debated the fitting of a tail; would the plane work subsonically without one? Tunnel testing on high tails had shown instability at certain lift coefficients. The Gloster F.4/48 had a similar arrangement to the delta AW.58 but it was felt that this worked because leading edge sweep was 48°, less than AWA's machine.

It seemed the only workable position was beneath the body, but H Davies of RAE felt there would be problems with ground effect on the tail at take-off and landing. AWA were asked to look into a forward (canard) position as this might be better, but in the event the AW.58 got a T-tail. The firm had itself emphasised the need for a tail to ensure adequate manoeuvrability should the AW.58 be turned into a fighter. The new layout retained elements of the swept wing's fuselage, but was an altogether more solid looking aircraft. The wing was placed high on the fuselage and fuel capacity was now 340gal (1,546lit). Plans included a 3/8th flying scale model with Armstrong Siddeley Adder engine to start building before end 1949.

The RAE's drag estimate differed widely from AWA's and the firm acknowledged its own figure was probably incorrect. AWA explained that the figure could be reduced to 90% of the RAE estimate to give Mach 1.1 at 36,000ft (10,973m) and that this brochure was more realistic than was normal at this stage as the cockpit was based on the swept wing mock-up and the undercarriage on agreed wheel sizes. Further comparison of the AW.58 and Fairey deltas was made at Thames House on 21st March when it was clear the latter was lighter, faster and superior. Comparing the two with the same engine (i.e. putting an RA.7 Avon in the AW.58), AWA's project had a big drag penalty and, with 1,500K reheat, gave a best estimate of Mach 1.0 compared to 1.25 for Fairey. Climb to 40,000ft (12,192m) was 8 and 5 minutes respectively.

The AW.58 had a tail to cope with a wing loading of 42lb/ft² (205kg/m²) when Fairey's 33lb/ft² (161kg/m²) could do without. Design of the nose intake was easier than wing root alternatives but, after thorough tunnel testing, the latter on the American Douglas X-3 had given 85% efficiency up to Mach 1.8, so this was not a problem. Finally, Fairey were considered a stronger design team and likely to have their machine ready three months earlier. On 16th May A E Woodward Nutt informed AWA that the Fairey project was the favoured design and the suspended AW.58 construction contract was finally cancelled. The firm was very disappointed and disposed of its cockpit mock-up and three-fifths scale intake model in August.

Fairey Supersonic Projects

Back on 3rd August 1948, Fairey Aviation had received an unofficial requirement from Sir Harry Garner, PDSR(A), for an aircraft with a sufficient ratio of excess thrust to weight to enable flight characteristics at sonic speeds to be explored together with adequate stability and control and accomplished as far as possible by orthodox means. The firm's proposal in September concluded that these requirements were best met by an aircraft employing very high sweepback on the wing and tail and powered by two stacked and reheated Rolls-Royce Avons. Fairey calculated its design would be capable of accelerating in level flight to Mach 1.5 and could sustain the speed long enough for accurate measuring.

The design had removable wing tips which reduced span to 31.5ft (9.6m) and maximum internal fuel totalled 500gal (2,273lit). Split flaps were fitted and the stacked engines were fed by a nose intake. Around Mach 1.35 could be achieved at the absolute ceiling of 61,000ft (18,593m). A second design, Scheme 2, was sent in November for a Military Piloted Transonic Aircraft while, in parallel with this investigation, the Hayes team was also working under contract on a series of ground launched pilotless research models of identical basic configuration.

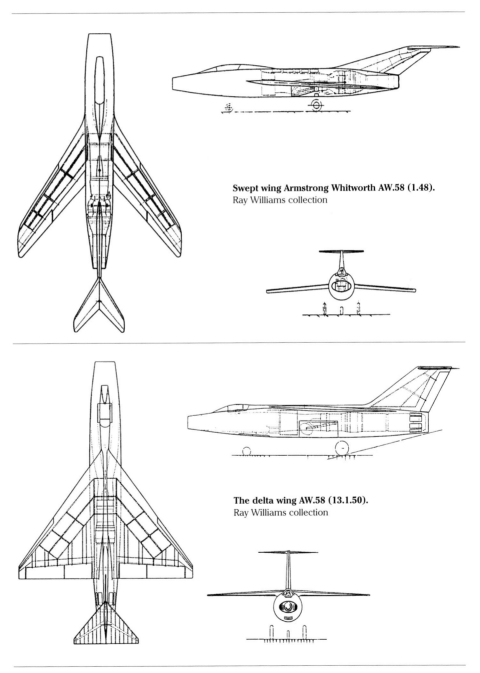

Swept wing Armstrong Whitworth AW.58 (1.48).
Ray Williams collection

The delta wing AW.58 (13.1.50).
Ray Williams collection

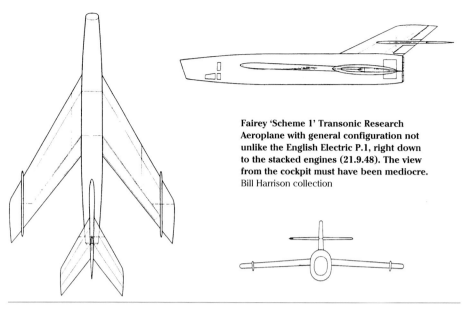

Fairey 'Scheme 1' Transonic Research Aeroplane with general configuration not unlike the English Electric P.1, right down to the stacked engines (21.9.48). The view from the cockpit must have been mediocre. Bill Harrison collection

Fairey Delta II second prototype WG777 photographed 2nd March 1959 on test at RAE Bedford (Thurleigh). Eric Morgan collection

The French Dassault Mirage III-001 prototype which first flew on 17th November 1956, having benefited from Delta II experience.

Schemes 3, 4 and 5 of April 1949 followed in reply to another PDSR(A) request for an aircraft to meet the purely research requirements of the same specification and introduced tail-less layouts with low aspect ratio delta wings but different intakes. The advantages over the highly swept wing with tail arrangement were low structure weight, possible use of conventional control surfaces, better fuel and undercarriage accommodation and elimination of early longitudinal instability. Limited knowledge of delta wings was recognised, but the ideas were sufficiently promising to be continued.

Both single and twin engine studies were included. All used the RA.3 Avon reheated to 1,500K housed within the fuselage and had the complete wing trailing edge hinged and

split spanwise to provide one inboard and one outboard controller per wing, the inboards were used as trimmers, the outboards as elevons for both longitudinal and lateral control. All metal construction and power operated controls were employed. Respective sea level climb rates were 27,400, 30,000 and 38,250ft/min (8,350, 9,144 and 11,660m/min) in full reheat at Mach 0.9; 2.80, 3,00 and 2.20 minutes to 45,000ft (13,716m); ceilings 56,000, 53,600 and 58,600 ft (17,070, 16,337 and 17,860m); internal fuel 220, 220 and 420gal (1,000 and 1,910lit).

Four more schemes, numbers 6 to 9, were forwarded in early July. Scheme 6 had a nose intake and single Avon very like 3, 8 had split underfuselage intakes, Schemes 7 and 9 used the wing root position and were gradually

moving towards the eventual Fairey Delta II. The performance of these projects generally met the requirement and the nose intake was preferred by Fairey, but the high pressures developed involved serious structural problems. Wing root intakes suffered from the uncertainty of boundary layer separation behind the nose shock wave.

All these proposals were appraised during a meeting of representatives from Fairey, RAE and the MoS on 11th July 1949. There was still support for a nose intake but this gave a weight penalty. Wing root entries would be difficult but armament would ultimately make them a necessity. Degree of sweep was assessed and the meeting concluded that the design study for a single engine delta of approximate aspect ratio 2.0 and 60° sweep was sound and formed a logical extension of the firm's E.10/47 work (the Delta I). An improved design followed on 31st January 1950, and a recommendation in March to order two prototypes. Go-ahead was given on 16th May the same day AWA was informed its project was dropped, but the prototype contract was not placed until October. Fairey's design team would have to be strengthened. Specification ER.103 was written around the aircraft having originally been called ER.100D under the new specification system. ER.100 was the first number in the series and was next allotted to a Boulton Paul project, and then transferred to Short Brothers & Harland for its S.B.5.

Fairey ER.103 Delta II

The Fairey delta wing research project was to investigate problems associated with flight at transonic and supersonic speeds up to Mach 1.5 and at least 45,000ft (13,716m). Top speed in level flight was to be substantially supersonic and the engine installation was to be a modified Avon RA.3 engine of 8,300lb (36.9 kN) thrust reheated to 1,500K and fitted with a variable nozzle. The aircraft was to be a single-seater and no armament was needed. Two aircraft were ordered, serialled WG774 and WG777. (Note: several published sources suggest ER.103 also covered English Electric's P.1, but no official document states this. P.1's real specification was F.23/49 which included armament).

By early January 1951 the project was close to that eventually built but had an all-moving T-tail with a weight penalty of 200lb (91kg). Estimates expected level speed to be Mach 1.3 with a design diving speed of Mach 1.7. Fairey reported that the tail introduced a serious stiffness problem for the fin's structure design difficulties in its movement plus an unknown but large drag effect. The weight penalty was not prohibitive but it was vitally important to save weight on this aircraft. The call for a tail was dropped in mid-May. The Mock-up conference was held on 27th June and in early January 1952, ER.103 was altered to raise maximum undercarriage retraction speed to 230mph (370km/h), a necessary step after pilots found that the Boulton Paul P.111 research aircraft's 185mph (298km/h) limit made retraction difficult to complete in the short time available. At this point, estimated first flight was October 1953, but Fairey became heavily involved in the Gannet 'Superpriority' programme which delayed work so much that construction did not start until summer 1952. Ram jets were considered as supplementary power units in July 1955.

The two Fairey Delta IIs were to experience long and immensely successful careers. The first prototype was completed in mid-1954 and flew for the first time on 6th October. Its maiden supersonic flight was achieved on 28th October 1955 without problems nor use of afterburner. Fairey realised the aircraft had a much greater speed potential than previously thought and on 10th March 1956, it regained the World Speed Record for Great Britain with an average 1,132mph (1,821m/h) at 38,000ft (11,582m), equating to Mach 1.73. The aircraft could go still faster but was limited by fuel, so often a problem with British aircraft. Because of the large number of investigations planned there were often suggestions for a third prototype, one of the last described having a more powerful engine and sets of interchangeable wings swept at 60 and 70° to allow direct comparison.

Tremendous supersonic knowledge was gathered but the firm never flew its baby as a fighter, a great frustration and particularly so when Dassault of France produced its Mirage III fighter that was similar in size and shape to the Delta II and sold in big numbers all over the world. What WG774 was converted into was a high speed research aircraft for the Concorde supersonic airliner, the machine being rebuilt with an 'ogee' wing in the early 1960s as the BAC Type 221.

Fairey ER.103 Fighters
Of course, Fairey did offer some supersonic fighters based on the Delta II. The first project was called ER.103B and offered a modified fuselage to house a single Gyron or RB.122 engine reheated to 2,000K, but with the same wing. All-up-weight with 200gal (909lit) fuel in external tanks was 20,650lb (9,367g), span was 28ft (8.5m), length 54.67ft (16.7m) and the aircraft was expected to fly 18 months from go-ahead. The ER.103C had the bigger engine but introduced a Ferranti radar and two Firestreaks mounted on the wing tips.

Wing area was much increased and of cranked delta form similar to the firm's F.124T rocket fighter. All-up-weight was quoted as 27,300lb (12,383kg), time to 45,000ft (13,716m) 1.9 minutes and top speed Mach 2.26 at 55,000ft (16,764m). First flight would take 30 months.

–

English Electric's P.1 was the only project from this programme to lead to a production aircraft, but development took a long time. The result, of course, was the superb Lightning. The Warton based company became famous in the late 1940s with its Canberra bomber to B.3/45 which set the standard for others to beat, was built in large numbers and is still in service today. Well before it flew in May 1949, Chief Designer Teddy Petter turned his thoughts towards fighters and particularly supersonic machines.

English Electric P.1
In the late 1940s, supersonic fighter design was undertaken using slide-rules, desk-top calculators and a limited amount of theoretical fluid mechanics information on wing shapes. There were few wind tunnels and no computers. When the P.1 (later P.1A) was turned into the P.1B Lightning in the mid-50s, it made use of several technological firsts including a new supersonic tunnel at Warton, the first such tunnel built in Europe and in use from July 1950. Petter tendered the first brochure for his firm's Project 1 (P.1) in November 1948 and on 1st March 1949, completed a detailed investigation of the intake and exhaust arrangement. This, and discussions with Rolls-Royce Hucknall, prompted a major revision to the original brochure's ducting which led to some marked improvements.

Extensive tunnel testing and the construction of a mock-up were approved by the MoS in early April when Petter submitted the latest

general arrangement, dated 25th February 1949, of what he called the Transonic Fighter. This showed an early form of leading edge root extension (LERX), wing sweep angles of 75° and 60° and tail near the base of the fin replacing the original T-tail. Span was 34.8ft (10.6m), length 47.33ft (14.4m) and the wings had 4° of anhedral. Provision for afterburning with circular jet pipes on both engines had also been made. Petter explained they were still carefully studying the question of sweepback and the pros and cons of 60° compared to 45-50°, but he felt there may be good reasons for sticking to the present proposal. The Ministry had already stated that, provided the preliminary tests were satisfactory, they expected to issue full cover for the design and construction of prototypes in about six months.

Engine choice at this time was a supersonic version of the Avon called RA.4 which, for a period, was known as the Tyne. However, the compressor problems of the original RA.1 had surfaced and E W Hives, Managing Director of Rolls-Royce, stopped work on supersonic engines until the firm's knowledge of compressor design was good enough, a decision that killed the Tyne. English Electric and Rolls-Royce worked together on the shape of the P.1's fuselage and the stacked twin engine layout was changed from upper engine forward/lower aft to upper aft/lower forward.

The stacked engine arrangement idea on the P.1 was solely to reduce frontal area and thus supersonic drag but, apart from the French Nene-powered Sud-Est SE.2410 Grognard prototypes in 1950-1, it was never flown on another aircraft. A number of British designers, however, did use it on projects that were never built – Blackburn and General's 'Mark 3' Transonic Swing Wing project of June 1950, the Bristol 177A, Fairey's first Transonic Research Aircraft mentioned above,

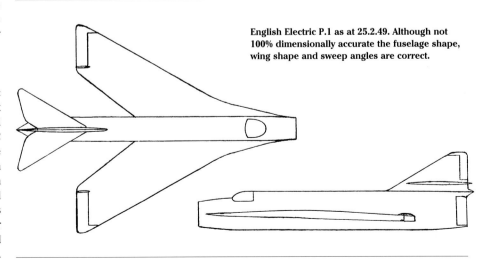

English Electric P.1 as at 25.2.49. Although not 100% dimensionally accurate the fuselage shape, wing shape and sweep angles are correct.

Hawker with its P.1077, Saro with an early version of the swing-wing P.149 to ER.110T, the Supermarine Type 559 to F.155T and Westland's N.40/46. Abandonment of the Tyne was not well received by Petter and the only other suitable engine was the Sapphire. Petter left English Electric soon afterwards and was replaced by F W Page who reported to the MoS on 6th April 1950, that there was no alternative but to use the Sapphire on the prototype. Two Sa.5s were fitted for initial flight test.

F.23/49 (and OR.268)

This was the specification written around the project for an *Interceptor Fighter with Supersonic Performance*; for some years the P.1 and its successor the P.1B, were called the F.23 in Ministry papers. The first draft OR.268 had been prepared in May 1949, but the full specification was not issued until April 1950 for a twin-engine single-seat supersonic fighter to operate in Europe and desirably any part of the world. Design requirements at this stage were not too rigid, but a minimum top speed of Mach 1.2 or higher was called for with climb to 50,000ft (15,240m) from start up no more than 6 minutes. Climb rate at 55,000ft (16,764m) had to be at least 1,000ft/min (305m/min) and minimum endurance from take-off to landing one hour. At least two 30mm Aden cannon were to be carried.

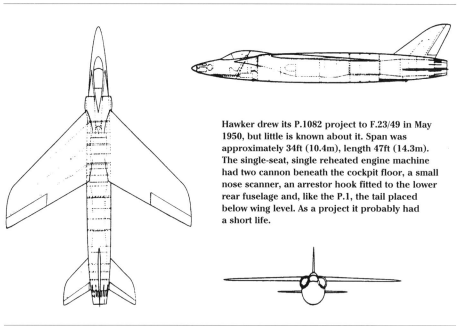

Hawker drew its P.1082 project to F.23/49 in May 1950, but little is known about it. Span was approximately 34ft (10.4m), length 47ft (14.3m). The single-seat, single reheated engine machine had two cannon beneath the cockpit floor, a small nose scanner, an arrestor hook fitted to the lower rear fuselage and, like the P.1, the tail placed below wing level. As a project it probably had a short life.

The P.1 was built with a distinct and very individual nose intake, but in July 1951 English Electric reported to the MoS that they were investigating the possibilities of using suppressed or semi-suppressed side air intakes instead of the present nose entry with a view to leaving more space in the nose for operational equipment (author's note: possibly under designation P.3). Tunnel testing through the second half of 1951 intended to explore if side intakes could be designed to give a reasonable efficiency and avoid a tendency for unstable flow. The firm hoped to have the answer by year's end. One big problem was what equipment would be fitted as the aircraft's role was yet to be settled. A return to tunnel testing a solid nose was made in January 1954 but, in the event, English Electric chose the P.1B configuration described shortly.

Top: **Early wind tunnel model of the English Electric P1.**

Left: The **Short S.B.5, WG768, low speed research aircraft, with original T-tail.** Shorts

British Secret Projects: Jet Fighters

A big dispute centred on another design feature, the low position of the tail. Forty-eight tunnel models had been tested and the P.1 was found to suffer from pitch-up. This was cured by removing the guns from an innocent looking fillet at the wing/fuselage join, lowering the tail, raising the wing and completely re-arranging the fuselage. The P.1's design did not settle until the beginning of 1950. English Electric was convinced that the low tail would cure the problem of transonic pitch-up and based its theories on the tunnel figures, but the MoS requested a T-tail after the aerodynamicists at RAE had predicted stability and control problems. This led to a head-on controversy and to prove its facts the Ministry funded a low powered ⅞th scale research vehicle built by Short Bros.

Short S.B.5

Specification ER.100 dated 28th October 1950 was prepared for a *Research Aircraft for Exploration of the Low-Speed Characteristics of Highly Swept Wings*, especially their take-off and landing behaviour. The aircraft was to have a similar ground angle, wing planform, wing section, vertical tail position, cockpit layout and instrument panel as the English Electric F.23/49. The wings could be detached to assess different sweep angles of 50, 60 and 70°, together with a mix of 'T' and low tails. In effect this was one of the world's first variable sweep aircraft but it could not change the sweep angle in flight. One Rolls-Royce Derwent 8 (RD.7) centrifugal jet of 3,500lb (15.6kN) was fitted and the undercarriage was not retractable.

A mock-up was completed in February 1951 and to illustrate how much the Ministry wanted to get its test aircraft 'right', there were at least 12 Design Conferences. The solitary S.B.5, serialled WG768, first flew on 2nd December 1952, with the T-tail and 50° wing, on 29th July 1953, with the wing set at 60° and on 10th January 1954, with the low tail. The third configuration gave some of the best low speed handling results so proving English Electric's theories conclusively and contradicting RAE and Ministry opinion, but in all formats the machine was under-powered. The relevant Ministry meetings in 1954 during what had become a most embarrassing situation must have been highly entertaining for a neutral observer and the outcome was a great success for English Electric. The S.B.5 had a maximum speed of 400mph (644m/h) and a ceiling of 10,000ft (3,048m).

English Electric considered the S.B.5 a complete waste of money and initially this was true for the lack of power controls and all-moving tailplane made low speed handling still less than satisfactory while offering no experience of transonic or supersonic speeds, but it did give Test Pilot 'Bee' Beamont some advance practice and confidence in flying a highly swept wing at low speeds. Fortunately, the S.B.5 could be used for other research and in 1957 was re-engined with a Bristol Siddeley Orpheus axial turbojet of 4,850lb (21.6kN). On 18th October 1960, WG768 flew with the 69° wing and continued experimental flying for another seven years.

The first P.1B, XA847, displays that famous wing shape. North West Heritage Group

–

The first P.1, WG760, made its maiden flight on 4th August 1954 and a week later, on flight three, became the first British aircraft to exceed the speed of sound in level flight and with reheat still to be fitted. The machine was to prove a great success but speed was never allowed to exceed Mach 1.51 thanks to a directional stability limit caused by the lack of fin area. It was a lovely aeroplane to fly but suffered from a small fuel capacity, rectified a little by the underbelly tank fitted to the second machine WG763.

Towards the end of 1955 WG760 received rudimentary afterburners which seriously cut available dry thrust but pushed the maximum up to 9,200lb (40.9kN). This gave such as vast improvement in climb rate that 40,000ft (12,192m) could now be reached in 3.5 minutes. The first prototype was also to receive a modified wing with a kinked leading edge and expanded tip chord which reduced subsonic drag by up to 20%. This was later used on production aircraft.

The P.1 failed to meet the specified endurance through using Sa.5s without variable nozzles. Back in January 1951, Rolls-Royce had commenced detail design of the RA.8 Avon, the first version to use the compressor modifications gleaned from the Sapphire, and this began running on the test bed in November. Development moved onto the RA.14 and Peter Ward at Rolls drew a scheme for installing the engine in the P.1, a team visiting Warton to offer opinions on refitting the Avon into the fighter. Warton considered the idea feasible provided it was furnished with a fully variable reheat nozzle. In the meantime, English Electric designed a new 2 shock conical centre body intake and front fuselage replacing the P.1's pitot intake to make the machine viable for Mach 2. These proposals were not based upon any official MoS specification or Air Ministry OR, but initially arose out of a meeting at the Ministry on 11th July 1951. Brochures followed for the new project entitled P.1B and from now on WG760 and WG763 were referred to as P.1As. On 9th June 1952, it was decided to order additional F.23/49 prototypes with the modified front fuselage, instructions arriving at English Electric in July to proceed with three P.1Bs.

In the event, the P.1B received the RA.24, the firm claiming this powerplant would make a speed of Mach 2 possible. A sixth prototype (i.e. a fourth P.1B) was suggested in October 1953 as an RA.24 test bed, but to the Ministry this was a doubtful starter as there were no spare funds. Specification F.23/49 was revised to accommodate the new aircraft and re-issued on 3rd June 1953. Alternative armaments were at least two and possibly four Blue Jay AAMs plus two 30mm

Lightning XN725 was an F Mk.2 rebuilt as the F Mk.3 prototype with Avon 301s and larger fin.
Brian Kervell collection

Aden cannon, two Aden plus 60 2in (5.1cm) air-to-air rockets or four Adens only.

The first P.1B, XA847, flew on 4th April 1957 and during flight 282 on 25th November 1958, became the first British aircraft to achieve sustained flight at Mach 2.0. Another 20 pre-production aircraft were ordered prior to production of the F Mk.1. Including the three P.1Bs, a total of 337 aircraft were to be built. The Lightning became one of the most popular and loved of all RAF aircraft and possessed a phenomenal rate of climb for interception purposes thanks to the high thrust to weight ratio, the vertical climb direct from take-off being a favourite display item at air shows and virtually unique until the arrival of the American F-15 and F-16. All through its career, however, it suffered from low endurance and as a fighter did lack some agility. Final withdrawal from RAF service was in 1988 and the author misses seeing and hearing them tearing about the sky.

Suggestions for naming the aircraft were made at the MoS over a two year period before Lightning was chosen in May 1956, but this was not revealed publicly until production orders were placed during 1958. Names rejected included Flash and Defender (both suggested by English Electric), Arrow, Eagle, Electra, Lancer, Rapier and Scimitar. The criterion was that fighter names had to suggest speed and aggressiveness, but on this occasion the MoS considered it even more than usually important that an apt and compelling name be given for what was to be the RAF's first truly supersonic aircraft. At one point in June 1954, the CAS had pointed out 'that no currency should be given to the fact that Lightning had been the name recommended by DCAS'. He doubted whether, in fact, the name would have been chosen.

In 1958 English Electric looked at fitting the RB.133 engine for comparison with the RA.24 to give more thrust, but the F.3 version even-

tually introduced the Avon 301 of 13,220lb (58.8kN) dry thrust and 16,300lb (72.4kN) reheat giving speeds up to Mach 2.1 at height. The F.6 had a sea level climb rate of 50,000 ft/min (15,240 m/min). EE also suggested in June 1954 the fitting of a twin 2,250lb (10kN) Napier Scorpion rocket pack in the rear ventral slipper tank to boost altitude performance and increase flexibility, the firm stating this would be essential if the MoS wanted an interceptor to work above 45,000 to 50,000ft (13,716 to 15,240m). The idea was taken up but then cancelled on 8th July 1958 without being flown, since by then it was felt an advanced RA.24 would give greater thrust, the development of new versions of the engine being accelerated. The cost of fitting the rocket motors had also increased by a factor of 4.

The manufacturers looked at applying alternative horizontal surfaces such as a V-tail unit, which was found to be destabilising both longitudinally and laterally compared to the normal tail. A delta wing increasing area by about 25% was tunnel tested in the early 1950s and showed a rearward shift of aerodynamic centre while reducing the tailplane's contribution to stability. There was little effect on induced drag.

The idea of fitting a delta to the P.1 (and to the Hawker Hunter as Kingston project P.1091) matched similar work in the Soviet Union where both Mikoyan and Sukhoi built and flew swept and tailed versions of their new fighters. The Ye-2 and Ye-4 flew in 1955, the latter becoming the production MiG-21; both Sukhoi machines were to enter service as the Su-7 (swept) and Su-9 (delta).

In the 1953 P.6 brochure to ER.134T (Chapter 7), an appendix re-examined a delta version, the resulting 60° delta being very near the optimum for a high speed delta that could operate successfully at low speeds. Drag coefficient was reduced but skin friction was increased due to the extra wetted area and preliminary assessment suggested a 250lb (113kg) increase in structure weight. Absolute shift of aerodynamic centre from low to high Mach numbers was much greater than on the F.23/49 at transonic speeds leading to a more difficult trim problem. The overall effect was a small but definite loss in level speed, ceiling and climb, but take-off, landing and manoeuvrability were little changed.

Another serious point was interaction of the trailing edge flaps over the low tail, but raising the tail was unacceptable to English Electric while not having one at all greatly magnified the trim problem and associated drag. A powerful tailplane was the only method of ensuring adequate control and freedom from pitching oscillations. Development of a tail-less machine would be preoccupied with stability and control problems over a wide speed range instead of researching the engineering and structural limitations near Mach 2. A powerful tailplane would be the big safety factor in such research making the P.1's semi-delta the more desirable. Tail-less designs would not be considered until more flight experience was obtained at these high speeds. Considerable time had been spent on a delta project and English Electric concluded that though there was little change in performance characteristics, the data showed a serious deterioration in high speed handling. Tunnel tests would continue before a decision was made on the case for flight research. Sadly the latter never took place.

Throughout its long service career, the Lightning never carried more than two missiles, initially Firestreak (Blue Jay) and later the development called Red Top. Tunnel testing examined wing tip Blue Jay carriage which increased span by 15% and improved aircraft stability but gave a large drag penalty. It was hoped induced drag might be reduced by the increased aspect ratio but the figure actually went up by 35.8%. A four missile armament of two wing tip missiles together with two more on the fuselage sides was tunnel tested in November 1953. The tip results repeated the earlier work but the fuselage mounts had little effect on stability and became the favoured position for missile carriage. In response to a Ministry request, studies were also made in early 1958 for fitting the American Falcon, Sparrow and Sidewinder

British Secret Projects: Jet Fighters

AAMs instead of Blue Jay, but the first pair needed a new fire control system while four Sidewinders gave higher aircraft limitations than two Blue Jays.

–

The Fairey Delta II and English Electric Lightning introduced the prospect of speeds up to Mach 2 a mere 15 years or so after the maiden flight of Britain's first jet aircraft, the Gloster E.28/39. Big technological advances in many areas were essential to achieve this and some examples are described below. One of the most important, but most neglected, were the materials used in manufacture, a subject close to the author's heart.

Increases in aircraft speed and weight, and jet engine power, brought the need for new materials to cope with the extra stresses, the effects of kinetic heating on the airframe and higher operating temperatures inside the engine. The need was not just for more strength, but for resistance to corrosion, temperature and fatigue cracking. For many critical fuselage structural parts and aircraft skins, aluminium 'light' alloys remained supreme and developments kept them ahead until the arrival of carbon fibre composites. It has been acknowledged that Britain's wartime jet engines were superior to Germany's in terms of life and reliability and the development of a nickel-chrome alloy called Nimonic was a big factor. The alloy's resistance to oxidation at elevated temperature prevented the deterioration suffered by the steel alloys used in German engines and Henry Wiggin & Co moved on to produce a series of Nimonic alloys with even better properties.

Early jets had used aluminium discs and blades in their compressors but as temperatures increased, these were no longer suitable. However, a 'new' metal, titanium, was able to fill the gap. In nature titanium is widely distributed and of the structural metals is the fourth most abundant. The problem is that it doesn't occur naturally in pure form and electrolytic separation from the ore in an inert atmosphere is an extremely expensive process. Only when adopted by the aircraft industry was the cost felt acceptable for the metal's excellent strength to weight ratio gave weight savings that converted directly into savings in fuel etc.

Titanium has a density just over half that of steel while its specific strength is superior to most other structural metals and its corrosion resistance outstanding. It was this high-strength low density characteristic, which is maintained at elevated temperatures, that resulted in its swift adoption by the aircraft industry. For equal strength, weight savings approaching 40% were possible by replacing steel or

Contemporary of the Lightning and a not that dissimilar layout except for the single engine; a Sukhoi Su-7BKL at Prerov airbase on 21st September 1991. Ken Ellis collection

nickel with titanium alloy parts. The first British commercial titanium alloy was used to make compressor blades for the Avon engine and from then on the titanium and jet engine industries grew up side-by-side, each nurturing the other. Other new alloys quickly found their way into critical airframe parts on such as the Sea Vixen and Scimitar before the Lightning used it quite extensively. Titanium has proved an immensely successful aircraft material.

Another vital point was the setting up of dedicated blade manufacturing facilities and heavy forging plant for large components, particularly once the axial jet was established. The author's former employer, High Duty Alloys (HDA), already famous within the industry for its 'Hiduminium' range of aluminium alloys, was just one firm to invest a great deal of money and effort into this business. Under a Ministry sponsored 'Scheme 100', its Blade Forge began production of precision forged blades in 1950 and in the first 15 years of operation produced over 25 million. In addition a press capable of 12,000 tons (12,193t) maximum pressure was put into service in February 1953 as part of the 'Super-priority' programme to produce undercarriage legs, compressor discs and other heavy forgings. Happily, both are still busy today.

During the Second World War, HDA was responsible for vast quantities of aircraft stampings and pressings, particularly pistons, in a contribution made with other forges to the war effort, one which has been largely ignored by historians.

During the Korean War the UK was incapable of producing large numbers of axial jet engines because of the huge need for blades but there is an opinion that centrifugal engine

development was discarded too quickly. The Rolls-Royce Nene was turned into a fine 6,250lb (27.8kN) engine called the Tay but this never found its way into a British production aircraft, whereas the Americans used it as the J48 and France as the Verdon. If Rolls had produced a reheated 10,000lb (44.4kN) thrust centrifugal engine, it could have proved of great benefit during the early 1950s, although Stanley Hooker has stated that the Nene centrifugal compressor diameter was the maximum possible size of the Whittle type and they could go no further.

Pushing these new fighters up to Mach 2 needed ever more powerful engines. The Avon was turned into the RB.146-300 Series for later marks of Lightning, but new engines also appeared. The Bristol Olympus began as the BE.10 in 1946 and was developed into a range of engines and thrust ratings right up to Concorde's 593. Work started in 1950 on de Havilland's Gyron as the H.4 in a concept to double contemporary engine power and this first ran on 5th January 1953, quickly achieving the planned 15,000lb (66.7kN) dry, 20,000lb (88.9kN) reheated thrust. At the time, this made it the most powerful engine in the world. Uprated to 20,000lb dry, 25,000lb (111.1 kN) reheated, it was tested in the Short Sperrin bomber from 7th July 1955, but, despite being planned for the Hawker P.1121 interceptor, never flew in a production aircraft.

The RB.90 is believed to have been a larger Avon, but Rolls-Royce's big development was the RB.106 first proposed in January 1953 and intended specifically for supersonic aircraft up to Mach 2. It was a two spool engine reheated to 2,000K that was possibly to be called the Thames. Basic rating was 15,000lb (66.7kN) static and the external dimensions were set to provide interchangeability with the Avon RA.14 but, when reheated to 21,750 lb (96.7kN), with about twice the thrust. The complete compressor was rig tested in 1956,

but the RB.106 became a victim of the 1957 White Paper. Much of its technology, however, found its way onto the Orenda Iroquois for Canada's Avro Arrow.

By autumn 1953 there were three proposed engines in the 15,000 to 20,000lb thrust class – the Gyron, RB.106 and Armstrong Siddeley Project X, each of which offered a different approach to the design of new engines. Both Gyron and RB.106 received MoS sponsorship. Gyron was a single shaft axial and to the MoS represented the extension of conventional gas turbine technology to a design and thrust range suitable for sustained supersonic flight up to Mach 2. On the other hand the RB.106 was much more complex but gave a real technological advance since it was to be a two speed design with two separate axial flow compressors each driven independently by single stage turbines. Jet pipe reheat was designed into it with a new automatically controlled convergent/divergent propelling nozzle. With a variable intake, this would increase net engine thrust at high flight speeds.

RB.106 would take longer to develop than the more conventional Gyron and was about two years behind, but when fully developed was expected by the MoS to possess greater flexibility and lower specific weight and fuel consumption. Ministry support for the Gyron stopped in February 1956 but de Havilland Engines decided to complete further tests at its own expense having seen prospects for overseas sales. However, in October 1957 the firm acknowledged that, with no backing for the P.1121, development should discontinue and the engine was abandoned despite demonstrating 29,300lb (130.2kN) of thrust. A scaled down version called Gyron Junior did enter service in the Buccaneer S Mk.1.

The 'Area Rule' was to prove of great benefit in helping jet fighters reach these high speeds without big increases in drag. It states that an aircraft moving at transonic speed possesses minimum drag if the total cross-sectional area varies in a smooth and regular way from nose to tail. The theory behind this

went back several years to a patent by the German firm Junkers of March 1944, but was confirmed in early 1952 by NACA's Richard T Whitcomb. To explain the rule, imagine an aeroplane cut into transverse slices. If a graph is made for the total area of each slice, the resulting plot should give a smooth curve, any sharp departure from the curve means a sudden change in area and increased drag. Consequently when the plot starts to take in the wing, area must be reduced somewhere else and on early applications this resulted in a slimmed or 'waisted' fuselage.

Another important introduction was powered flying controls. Finely balanced manual controls proved quite unsuited for flight at near sonic speeds and the situation called for a more rigid power-operated method. The possible use of mechanical or electrical devices generated great debate culminating in a near conference size meeting at RAE on 27th August 1947, the biggest point of contention being the need for emergency manual control should the power controls fail. Powered controls were the way ahead and were swiftly adopted, but it was some time before a system of manual reversion could be left out.

One control surface that really needed power operation was the tail and a further step forward was the all-moving or slab tailplane; the 'flying tail'. The first generation of jet fighters such as the Meteor had fixed tailplanes with manually operated elevators but as they approached the speed of sound, shock wave build up on these surfaces could seriously curtail the elevator's effectiveness. Fighters that passed through the sound barrier into true supersonic flight needed something better and a powered all-moving tail was the answer accepted almost universally. A bigger elevator surface area was made available for the entire horizontal surface could change its angle of incidence relative to the fuselage.

The accommodation of more sophisticated radars and electronics as part of a weapon system added to the pressure for space within fighters, while air-to-air missile development proceeded at a rate comparable to the fighters themselves.

The Vickers Red Dean was an active homing all-weather weapon and required a powerful radar on the interceptor aircraft. Red Dean was split from the original Red Hawk (Chapter 3) in 1951 and was initially to be a 670lb (304kg) X-band active homer designed by Folland Aircraft. However Folland could not complete the work and development passed to Vickers.

A development contract to OR.1105 was awarded to Vickers on 26th March 1953 under the 'Superpriority' programme and in due course the firm turned it into a huge missile 16.1ft (4.9m) long and 1,330lb (603kg) in weight. Intended to be an all angle attack Mach 2.2 weapon operational at heights from 5,000 to 50,000ft (1,524 to 15,240m), Red Dean's main carrier was to be the Thin Wing Javelin, aircraft and missile entering service together, but Red Dean was cancelled along with that fighter in 1956. Sample rounds were taken aboard a test Canberra but no firing trials were made.

During 1955-6 Vickers advanced its missile into Red Hebe to OR.1131 for the fighter to F.155T (Chapter 8). Whereas the earliest weapons could only be used for tail attacks these semi-active radar homing missiles introduced a collision course interception capability, but with a weight penalty. Blue Jay weighed just 300lb (136kg) but was limited to attack from the rear; the bulky Red Hebe could be released head-on but it and its systems increased total aircraft weight by around 2,000lb (907kg), besides increasing drag. Red Hebe illuminated its target by AI radar, could be launched up to 7,400ft (2,256m) below it and from between Mach 1.2 and 2.5+ at 60,000ft (18,288), and could operate at a height between 30,000 and 70,000ft (9,144 and 21,336m).

The Weybridge firm considered Red Hebe and Blue Jay were effectively a complimentary pair for its Type 559 project to F.155T. Red Hebe took longer to climb but was ideal for dealing with a Mach 2 attacker, Blue Jay could be used for a Mach 1.3 target. From the late 1950s, Blue Jay (Firestreak) was turned into a more capable missile called Red Top (originally Firestreak 4) to later issues of OR.1117 and went on to arm the final versions of Lightning and Sea Vixen. It could reach Mach 3 when attacking a target up to seven miles away, had a more sensitive seeker and a larger warhead.

Lightning XR754 first flew as an F Mk.3 in July 1965, but is seen here just after conversion to F Mk.6 standard in early 1967.
North West Heritage Group

Transonic and Supersonic Project Data

Project	Span ft (m)	Length ft (m)	Wing Area ft² (m²)	t/c %	All-Up-Weight lb (kg)	Powerplant Thrust lb (kN)	Max Speed / Height mph (km/h) / ft (m) x1,000	Armament
Miles M.52	26.9 (8.2)	39.0 (11.9) max.	141 (13.1)	7.5 root 4.9 tip	7,754 (3,517)	1 x W2/700 3,175 (14.1)	Mach 0.95	None fitted
Boulton Paul P.114A	41.0 (12.5)	88.0 (26.8)	670 (62.3)	5.5	28,728 (13,031)	2 x Avon (reheat)	c.M 1.5 at 45.0 (13.7)	2 x 30mm Aden
Boulton Paul P.114S	46.33 (14.1)	88.0 (26.8)	700 (65.1)	5.5	30,360 (13,771)	2 x Sapphire (reheat)	c.M 1.5 at 45.0 (13.7)	2 x 30mm Aden
Gloster P.285	28.0 (8.5)	46.5 (14.2)	290 (27.0)	6 root 10 tip	13,000 (5,897)	1 x Sapphire Sa.2 7,500 (33.3), 9,450 (42) re-ht	806 (1,297), M 1.2 at 45.0 (13.7)	2 x 30mm Aden
Hawker P.1071	30.25 (9.2)	43.5 (13.3)	330 (30.7)	?	?	1 x Avon: 7,800 (34.7) +1 x 2,000 (8.9) rocket	Mach 1 (?)	2 x 30mm Aden
Armstrong Whitworth AW.58 (Swept)	24 (7.3)	45.2 (13.8)	190 (17.7)	8	c.12,000 (5,443)	1 x AJ.65 6,500 (28.9)	Mach 1.07	None fitted
Armstrong Whitworth AW.58 (Delta)	27.0 (8.2)	44.67 (13.6)	315 (29.3)	4 root 8 tip	12,300 (5,579)	1 x Sapphire 10,000 (44.4)	Up to Mach 1.5	None fitted
Fairey 'Scheme 1' (Swept wing)	32.33 (9.9)	54.67 (16.7)	434 (40.4)	8	16,500 (7,484)	2 x Avon 6,500 (28.9)	Mach 1.5 at 36.0 (11.0)	None fitted
Fairey Scheme 3	23.3 (7.1)	43.0 (13.1)	360 (33.5)	4	8,800 (3,992)	1 x Avon RA.3 6,500 (28.9) dry	Mach 1.646 at 36.0 (11.0)	None fitted
Fairey Scheme 4	19.0 (5.8)	46.25 (14.1)	361 (33.6)	4	8,700 (3,946)	1 x Avon RA.3 6,500 (28.9) dry	Mach 1.719 at 36.0 (11.0)	None fitted
Fairey Scheme 5	32.0 (9.6)	53.0 (16.2)	680 (63.2)	4	15,850 (7,190)	2 x Avon RA.3 6,500 (28.9) dry	Mach 1.745 at 36.0 (11.0)	None fitted
Fairey Delta II (flown)	26.8 (8.2)	51.6 (15.7)	360 (33.5)	4	14,532 (6,592)	1 x Avon RA.14R 9,500 (42.2), 14,500 (64.4) reheat	Mach 1.73	None fitted
English Electric P.1A (flown)	34.8 (10.6)	50.9 (15.5)	458 (42.6)	6.5 root 5 tip	27,100 (12,293)	2 x Sapphire Sa.5: 7,200 (32.0); Later Sa.5R: 4,200 (18.7), 9,200 (40.9) reheat	Mach 1.51	2 x 30mm Aden (2nd prototype only)
English Electric P.1B (flown)	34.9 (10.6)	55.25 (16.8)	458 (42.6)	5	c.28,000 (12,701)	2 x Avon RA.24R 11,250 (50.0) reheat; later developed to 14,350 (63.8) reheat	Mach 2.0+ at height	2 x 30mm Aden, 2 x Firestreak AAM

Chapter Seven

Progression to Mach 2

High Speed Research: 1952 to 1962

In 1952, the Ministry of Supply, having accepted transonic and supersonic fighters as the way forward, began to consider even higher speeds. The feeling grew that research into supersonic flight should be in advance of current designs and in December an experimental specification, ER.134T for *Research Aircraft for Mach Number 2*, was issued. A big stimulant was RAE report Aero 2462 entitled *An Investigation into an Aircraft to Fly at a Mach No of 2*, written the previous June by Warren, Poole and Appleyard. This suggested some directions for future supersonic research and outlined two basic airframes, the first having a pencil slim fuselage, straight tapered wings and engines fitted mid-wing; the second with straight wings and engines buried in the fuselage. It was hoped research and development would take speeds up to at least Mach 2.5, well ahead of current military requirements. From June 1952, ACAS(OR) began to press the MoS for a Mach 2 research aircraft.

ER.134T

This aircraft was to undertake practical research into the problems of aircraft design, manufacture and flight at speeds up to Mach 2, preliminary investigations (Aero 2462 and others) indicating this could be achieved with new engines expected to be available while it was high enough to provide a new set of problems from those encountered at lower speeds. Although intended for research the aircraft was to provide information for military aircraft of comparable performance and size and, thus, was to be of the fighter type capable of carrying 1,500lb (680kg) of 'special instrumentation'. Where possible the aircraft had to use proven equipment and systems to reduce the unknowns and get it ready earlier. Minimum top speed was Mach 2 in level flight but at whatever optimum altitude the designer chose. Required Mach 2 soak time was ten minutes minimum. Structural provision for Mach 2 at sea level was to be made and the drag limit had to give a reasonable margin for covering shallow dives through the maximum Mach number achieved in level flight. The following were tendered:

This view of the second Bristol 188, XF926, was taken on 31st July 1963. Today we would call the Type 188 a technology demonstrator. BAe

Armstrong Whitworth AW.166

AWA had already undertaken much exploratory research along similar lines to the RAE study and in its view no single engine was likely to be available in the near future with sufficient power to attain Mach 2. Aero 2462 was largely aerodynamic and AWA felt it gave little evidence as to whether the mechanical and structural engineering problems were likely to prove practicable with the then state of knowledge. This would be the deciding factor as to whether the whole project was feasible. A layout with two engines in the fuselage was impractical as the desired wing thickness was quite useless as a hollow container and all the necessary fuel, equipment, undercarriage, etc would also be in the fuselage. Therefore the unswept layout with engines in wing nacelles was considered the most likely to succeed and became the chosen route.

Light alloy was used for the wing although AWA stated a steel wing would be lighter because of the substantial loss in effective depth of the spar box when using very thick light alloy flanges. As designed, the wing was suitable for Mach 1.5 only at sea level unless it was made entirely of steel. AWA preferred to base its proposals on the more familiar design and fabrication of light alloy to reduce rivetting and stiffening, but steel was used in parts of the all-moving tail for stiffness.

ER.134T asked for a top speed about twice that of current fighter prototypes with a wing around half the present thickness/chord ratio. AWA's 4% wing needed moving surfaces on both the leading and trailing edges and the high wing loading, 72lb/ft² (352kg/m²), was felt to be an advantage in obtaining very high speed at moderate altitude, but also meant a relatively low standard of manoeuvrability had to be accepted. The wing as originally drawn was tapered 10° on both edges. A later proposal made the inner wing straight but the portion beyond the engine was swept 55° (trailing edge straight) increasing span to 40ft (12.2m) and wing area to 417ft² (38.8m²). Two reheated Sapphire Sa.7s were mounted in underslung mid-wing nacelles with two position nozzles and variable centrebody intakes, reheat providing 25% static thrust augmentation.

The AW.166 had a bicycle undercarriage, the outriggers folding into the engine nacelles, and all 900gal (4,091lit) of fuel was carried in the fuselage, the firm considering rather more was required than that specified. The machine could reach Mach 2 between 36,000 and 50,000ft (10,973 to 15,240m) for the required 10 minutes. Time to 45,000ft (13,716m) and Mach 2 was 10.1 minutes. Structurally AWA considered Mach 2 at sea level presented little extra difficulty apart from cockpit cooling and conversion to all steel and, in spite of the difficulties in meeting ER.134T, AWA was satisfied the AW.166 could attain speeds well in excess of Mach 2.

Later a small unsolicited brochure was prepared for an AW.166 fighter for Australia with Sa.10s, AI.18 collision course interception radar, a fatter more rounded nose and unspecified wing tip missiles. Span with missiles was 39.0ft (11.9m), length 73.0ft (22.3m) and gross weight 31,000lb (14,062kg). The Sa.10s with 30% reheat so enhanced the AW.166's performance that a fighter development had become practicable; the firm had not previously noticed the machine's remarkable climbing performance at Mach 2 which made interceptions up to at least 65,000ft (19,812m) quite feasible.

Boulton Paul P.128

BP dismissed the use of steel since it was impractical to machine the surface, so P.128 was designed in aluminium. A constant chord and very thin wing, made as one unit across the fuselage, resulted in a simplified, economic and easy to produce design. Full reference to P.126 thin wing work was made. Two Sapphire 7 engines in wing tip nacelles offered, in theory, perfect air intake conditions with the efflux well clear of the tail and substitution of alternative engines a fairly simple option. An aerodynamic 'end-plate' effect made a nose flap for landing unnecessary, drooped aileron type trailing edge flaps providing the desired lift. The thin wing made it imperative a bicycle undercarriage with nacelle outriggers was used. A centrally disposed engine was rejected because of the intake problems it created.

Careful use of variable centrebody intakes and convergent-divergent nozzles removed the need for the severe weight penalty of reheat and so P.128's performance was based on the thrust of a 'straight' engine. Fuel was carried in the fuselage above and below the wing. To reach 36,000ft (10,973m) needed 2.4 minutes, not including take-off or acceleration to Mach 2; the height band for Mach 2 was 36,000ft+. The maximum attainable 'soak' at this speed

with 1,500lb (680kg) of equipment was 7.5 minutes, 10 minutes was possible only when this was cut to 1,000lb (454kg). BP had concentrated on the research aspect of this aircraft but because of the simple fuselage included a fighter application that substituted a special forward fuselage unit with the necessary armament and radar.

Bristol Type 188

A project of predominantly steel primary structure but conventional with skin, stringers and frames. Bristol claimed the change from aluminium to steel cost little in weight, while surface machining would not be required as the skin was sufficiently thin for rolled sheet to be used. The layout was chosen after investigations showed general agreement to Aero 2462 but the inner wing leading edge had altered by the time the aircraft flew. Drooped leading edges were to work in conjunction with plain trailing edge flaps and the ailerons extended from nacelles to wing tips. It was felt such a planform would combine low wave drag at supersonic speeds with good transonic characteristics. Again in steel, the all-moving tail was initially placed quite low on the fin, but fin area was eventually increased with the horizontal surfaces hinged at the top.

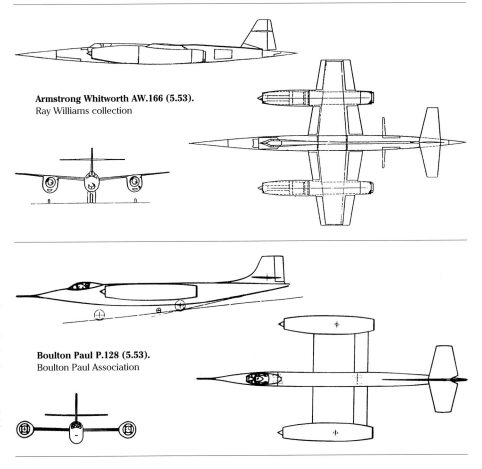

Armstrong Whitworth AW.166 (5.53).
Ray Williams collection

Boulton Paul P.128 (5.53).
Boulton Paul Association

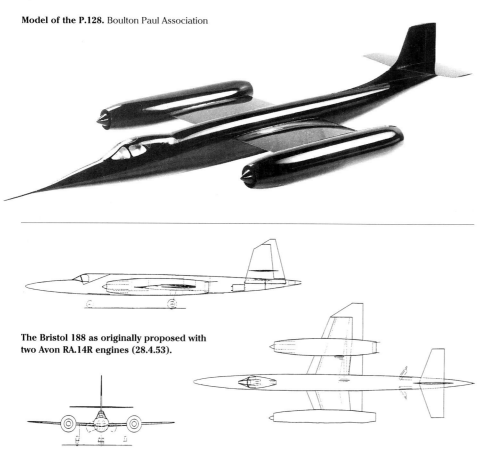

Model of the P.128. Boulton Paul Association

The Bristol 188 as originally proposed with two Avon RA.14R engines (28.4.53).

As proposed, the forward and aft portions of the body were to be conventional light alloy with a steel centre section embodying the wing-body joint (the finished article used steel throughout). All fuel (1,097gal [4,988lit]) and major equipment was housed within the fuselage. The engines, two RA.14R Avons reheated to 1,500K, were mounted in mid-wing nacelles symmetrical about the wing with variable centre body intakes.

Once Bristol was awarded the 188 build contract, suppliers of high alloy steels were consulted before the Firth-Vickers ferritic stainless REX.448 was chosen for manufacture. This alloy was available in 1953 in forging and sheet form for turbojets but needed further development for airframe structures. As construction of the first 188 got underway it was proposed to fit RA.24 engines for initial flight development with performance improved later on by substituting 'lightweight medium thrust engines of advanced design', and from March 1954 eight different turbojets were studied as replacements. Advanced preparations were made to use Armstrong Siddeley's P.176 supersonic bomber engine prior to that engine's cancellation.

With RA.14Rs, the aircraft was fully expected to meet the required 10 minutes level flight at Mach 2. At that speed a margin of thrust over drag was indicated up to 56,000ft (17,069m) but, for economy, level speed testing was to be made at 50,000ft (15,240m). However, acceleration to Mach 2 was best carried out at 36,000ft (10,973m) because of the higher excess thrust available at this altitude; the subsequent climb of just over one minute from 36,000 to 50,000ft at Mach 2 was not included in the 10 minute duration meaning additional high speed flight above the bare requirement was available. Level speeds in excess of Mach 2 were possible in the band 28,000ft (8,534m) to 56,000ft. Time to 50,000ft (15,240m) at Mach 2 was 10.9 minutes. At the cruise Mach number of 0.8 (no reheat), the ceiling was about 40,000ft (12,192m).

Reheat was necessary for acceleration from subsonic to supersonic flight and to maintain supersonic speed thereafter. Take-off could be made without reheat but, since this was required to complete a take-off if an engine failed, it would normally be used. Bristol stated complete design of a prototype would take two years from ITP. Specification ER.134D, written around the Type 188 after selection, increased required maximum speed to Mach 2.5 and in June 1957 the de Havilland PS.50 Gyron Junior was chosen to power the

aircraft, after cancellation of the P.176.

Fighter adaptations were kept in mind for the whole nose section ahead of the cockpit was available for the installation of military equipment and in September 1953 an addendum to the original brochure was submitted for a version called Type 188F. Changes included engine nacelles of near constant section (like those eventually flown), a 21in (53cm) radar dish and twin 30mm Aden cannon. The 188F's 8,000lb (35.8kN) thrust engines with variable reheat were of a new type based on the RB.106. The original RB.106 rated at 15,000lb (67.2kN) was designed for single engined fighters, but Rolls was prepared to offer the smaller variant for a twin engined aircraft. Ratio of frontal area to thrust was 70% of the RA.14 figure which considerably reduced nacelle drag. Length became 61.5ft (18.7m), span 32.67ft (9.9m) which, together with the new powerplant, reduced weight by 5,000lb (2,268kg) although the fuselage was essentially unchanged. Compared to the RA.14's, acceleration time from Mach 0.8 to 2.0 was halved to 1.7 minutes and ceiling increased from 57,000 to 69,000ft (17,373 to 21,031m). Top speed was unchanged and prolonged flight at Mach 2.25 now permissible.

English Electric P.6

The biggest problem alongside the already severe structural and engineering aspects in developing supersonic aircraft was kinetic heating. To counter this, English Electric began a research project examining the manufacturing problems and weight penalties through using titanium in primary structure. But for ER.134T, English Electric based much of its proposal on work already done for the F.23/49 (P.1) fighter, the P.6 brochure embracing four different designs after investigations into straight, swept and delta arrangements.

English Electric most favoured an RB.106 development of the F.23/49 called P.6/1 and most of the brochure was devoted to it. The chevron wing planform, fin and rudder arrangement were identical to the P.1 but the single engine reduced fuselage depth. The tail was all-moving, the ailerons and rudder conventional flap type controls and, to ensure successful transonic handling characteristics, the P.6/1 was fitted with irreversible power controls on all surfaces. The new powerplant was an RB.106R with 2,000K reheat, adjustable conical centre-body intake and fully variable convergent-divergent nozzle. P.6/1 top speed was over Mach 2, taking 9.5 minutes to reach it at 45,000ft (13,716m), and supersonic endurance was more than adequate to complete the specified 10 minutes. The air craft could still accelerate at Mach 2 at all altitudes between 36,000ft and its ceiling of 64,000ft (19,507m), but transonic ceiling was rather below 60,000ft (18,288m). Cockpit layout was very close to the F.23/49 third prototype (P.1B) with the canopy raised above the body for better all-round vision. English Electric assumed a simple search radar would be available to fit inside the intake bullet. Internal fuel totalled 800gal (3,638lit).

The firm usually viewed research aircraft in terms of their value to fighter design and the P.6/1 was prepared on that basis with armament and combat equipment replaced by the research instrumentation. Provision was made for either two 30mm Aden cannon and two or four Blue Jay AAMs, or four Adens only. The missiles were to be wing tip mounted, final decision on two or four dependent on their effect on performance and handling, and the guns were fitted in the upper fuselage with the barrels alongside the cockpit. English Electric concluded the highly swept wing was likely to prove the most satisfactory and such an aircraft would be suitable not only for research purposes, but as a practical fighter of outstanding performance. The firm hoped its F.23/49 experience would reduce design and build time by such a degree that it would win the competition on these grounds alone.

English Electric also suggested a comparatively simple adaptation of the F.23/49/P.1 aircraft using the existing 8,900lb (39.8kN) reheated Sapphire Sa.5 engines and jet pipes but with the fixed convergent nozzles replaced by a convergent-divergent arrangement. This would achieve Mach 2 between 36,000 and 57,000ft (10,973 and 17,374m) with an adequate research endurance of just over 5 minutes at that speed using drop tanks. All up weight was 27,360lb (12,410kg). In view of the new problems for producing aircraft to fly at Mach 2, it was suggested that development of this type would prove a valuable intermediate step enabling knowledge to be gained much earlier than by other means. Moreover it would be independent of new engine developments.

Appendix 1 covered a further modification of the F.23/49 called P.6/2. General configuration, wing structure and engine layout followed the P.1 closely except the deeper body allowed a slight increase in vertical clearance between wing and tail. The engines were two more powerful Sapphire Sa.7s; an alternative was the RA.18. P.6/2's armament was the same as P.6/1 but with the extra option of two 30mm Aden and two batteries of 2in (5.1cm) air-to-air rockets. Mach 2 ceiling was 70,000ft (21,336m) with 10 minutes at Mach 2 possible and 9 minutes needed to reach this at 50,000ft

(15,240m). Fuel load was 770gal (3,501lit).

Appendix 2 departed from the F.23/49 in discussing an unnumbered straight wing project, identified in published references as P.6B. English Electric had studied Aero 2462 with great interest and 'P.6B' general layout was initially based on the design suggested in the RAE report, although it was soon apparent that to meet ER.134T a larger aeroplane was needed. Two versions comprised a research and an operational aircraft, the latter about 2,000lb (907kg) heavier. Construction was light alloy. The design showed a straight taper wing, all-moving tail well up on the fin to avoid wing leading edge turbulence, and a bicycle undercarriage with outriggers. All the fuel and equipment was housed in the fuselage. The Sapphire Sa.7 engines proposed for the P.6/2 were used, here mounted in symmetrical mid-wing nacelles each with a variable centre body intake and convergent-divergent nozzle. 'P.6/B' could reach Mach 2 within a height band of 36,000 to 65,000ft (10,973 to 19,812m) but no figures for endurance were quoted. The operational version carried the same military equipment and gun armament as the P.6/1 and P.6/2 with cannon forward of the cockpit and a nose re-

shaped for radar, cutting length by 2ft (0.61m).

Once a detailed drag analysis and the fuel assessment for supersonic endurance was complete, the straight wing 'P.6B' appeared less attractive than the swept wing studies. The thrust margin at transonic speed was small due to heavy drag from the wing and nacelles.

Other disadvantages included the effects on manoeuvrability between subsonic and supersonic speed from large movements of the aerodynamic centre, complete lack of control in the event of engine failure at take-off and the extra drag produced by a tail placed high on the fin. The favoured low tail from the swept designs was discounted by the powerful wing jet efflux. Finally, using normal ailerons for lateral control, aileron reversal was expected to occur at about 635 mph (1,019km/h) EAS which was unacceptable since Mach 2 was best obtained at 36,000ft (10,973m) where the EAS was already 720mph (1,158km/h) and would increase considerably in shallow dives. This would necessitate using spoilers which had doubtful aeroelastic effects on a straight wing at supersonic speeds, with an attendant drag penalty in manoeuvres.

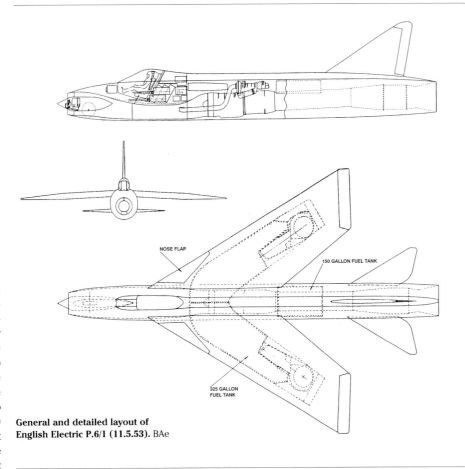

General and detailed layout of English Electric P.6/1 (11.5.53). BAe

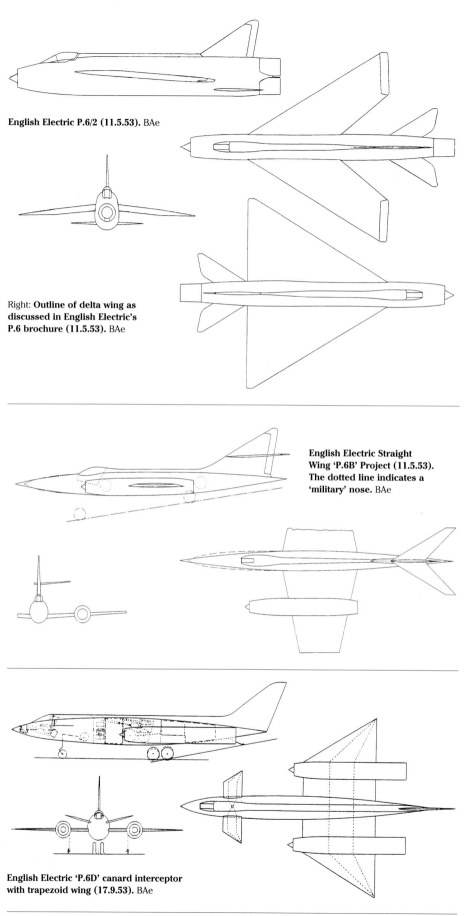

English Electric P.6/2 (11.5.53). BAe

Right: **Outline of delta wing as discussed in English Electric's P.6 brochure (11.5.53).** BAe

English Electric Straight Wing 'P.6B' Project (11.5.53). The dotted line indicates a 'military' nose. BAe

English Electric 'P.6D' canard interceptor with trapezoid wing (17.9.53). BAe

English Electric agreed that the straight wing design may be as good as any at Mach 2 but a practical design proved very large and expensive, had poor transonic and altitude performance and a number of severe stability, control and aeroelastic problems that needed considerable investigation. Indeed, transonic performance was so marginal that the operational version had to dive to reach supersonic speeds in high air temperature conditions. In a third appendix, the prospect of fitting the F.23/49 with a full delta wing was examined briefly as a continuation of previous research (described in Chapter 6).

A summary examined current engine development and its influence on these projects, but which makes valuable reading in relation to the overall picture. The F.23/49/P.1 was designed at a time when level supersonic performance could be envisaged by English Electric only by staggering two Sapphire engines in the fuselage. Engine thrust per frontal area had continued to improve since then and the Sa.4 had been bench tested at over 10,000lb (44.4kN) thrust. Rolls' RA.18 was of similar size and thrust whilst applying reheat to engines on the test-bed had raised thrust levels by over 40%. Convergent-divergent nozzles had also been bench operated while English Electric had filled some of the gaps in supersonic centre-body intake knowledge in its high speed tunnel. With these improvements, the current F.23/49 arrangement was now capable of performance well in excess of Mach 2 at altitudes up to 70,000ft (21,336m) and it was the P.6/2 that utilised the new intakes and jet pipes in a larger fuselage with new engines and more fuel.

P.6/2 gave considerable performance margins but a search had been made for a simpler and cheaper solution. The next radical improvement in fighter propulsion was to be the single supersonic engine, as represented by the RB.106, and to allow this development, English Electric considered the power plant should remain in the fuselage. It was noted that the straight wing proved even more disappointing at transonic speeds where its drag was relatively high since full advantage from the RB.106 was forthcoming only at much higher speeds. Primary emphasis was, therefore, given to the single-engine fighter, English Electric stressing that since the RB.106 had sufficient thrust to give a maximum speed in excess of Mach 2 with a thin wing of almost any planform, the *swept-back wing* was critical to improving the transonic performance where the RB.106 showed smaller gains over existing engines.

As the F.23/49 wing and tail arrangement was selected at optimum performance, it had been re-considered in relation to a single RB.106 as the P.6/1 and shown to make a much cheaper fighter capable of high performance at all transonic and supersonic speeds. Use was made of existing wings, tail surfaces, undercarriage, controls and systems so that the additional cost of developing this version was estimated to be substantially less than an all-new machine. Take-off weight was less than that of the present F.23/49, but flying characteristics were much better than the straight wing 'P.6/B' and delta wing considered in the Appendices.

As described in the Tender Assessment, the straight wing 'P.6B' was one of the projects favoured by the Ministry and RAE and a deeper investigation was requested. This resulted in a thorough revision to a canard trapezoidal layout officially unnumbered by English Electric but dubbed 'P.6D' in published accounts. It was based on the availability of the RB.106 plus previous work on a 'Canberra replacement' designed to give a burst of supersonic speed near a target. For a fighter version, the RB.106 could be scaled down to about 2/3rd size for an all up weight around 30,000lb (13,608kg). Much fighter equipment and the radar had to be situated near the nose and so to prevent the CofG from moving too far forward, four upward facing Adens were placed in the centre fuselage.

Use of a trapezoid wing was expected to prevent the large forward movement of aerodynamic centre at high subsonic Mach numbers inherent in the straight wing 'P.6B'. The canard, although creating problems with trim, avoided the mechanical difficulties of a fin-mounted tail and permitted use of a higher wing loading. The engines were combined with a variable conical intake and boat-tailing was almost eliminated by the variable nozzles in the reheat position. Maximum speed and ceiling were very similar to the swept P.6/1, the canard having lower transonic performance but, at 69,000ft (21,031m), a higher ceiling for Mach 2. Although transonic characteristics were improved over the 'P.6B', it was considered they would still not compare with the F.23/49 developments and again it was stated the P.6/1 was still the cheapest and most flexible arrangement for a fighter, with relatively little development needed.

The canard arrangement did have distinct possibilities for a 'Canberra replacement' using the current RB.106 with wing area scaled up proportionally. Dependent on mission, fuselage size and weight could also be scaled up to all-up-weights well over 50,000lb (22,680kg). Freddie Page confirmed English Electric were not particularly interested in building an aircraft of this size specifically for research purposes. The Warton team was convinced that a straightforward Mach 2 development of the F.23/49 could be produced as a fully operational day/night fighter, Page stating that 'when you go into this it is surprising how little development is required'. Eventually, the Lightning proved this opinion correct.

Hawker P.1096 and P.1097

Two projects of essentially light alloy construction and sharing a similar fuselage, the similarity ending with wing and tail. P.1096 had a 'rather daring' high and near complete delta wing and a low tail; P.1097 had wings based on those of the P.1083 supersonic Hunter with a T-tail. Respective fuel capacities were 650 and 800gal (2,955 and 3,637lit).

Each had a fuselage mounted RB.106R reheated to 1,800K and fed by split wing root intakes; a natural development of the Sea Hawk and Hunter's. The wing form made for considerable differences in the supersonic performance of the two aircraft and their ability to reach the specified requirements. P.1096 could reach Mach 2 in a height band of 20,000 to 68,000ft (6,096 to 20,726m) and achieved the 10 minutes at Mach 2 using 1,500K reheat, the speed was reached in 5.35 minutes at 60,000ft (18,288m). Somewhat inferior, the P.1097 could only reach a maximum Mach 1.9 at 36,000ft (10,973m) with a best supersonic endurance of 5 minutes at Mach 1.77 and 1,725K, the time to reach this speed at 45,000ft (13,716m) being 10.44 minutes.

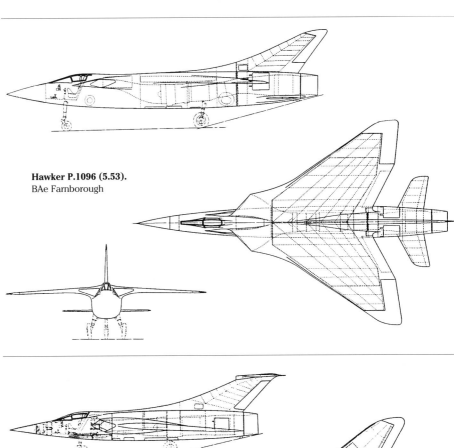

Hawker P.1096 (5.53).
BAe Farnborough

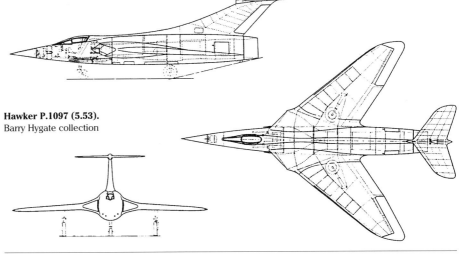

Hawker P.1097 (5.53).
Barry Hygate collection

Like other fighter firms, Hawker was not really interested in projects purely for research but rather more for production and, therefore, these proposals were looked at solely in regard to their fighter potential. To this end, the P.1097 was drawn with four Aden cannon beneath the cockpit.

The P.1097's performance appears quite inferior to other ER.134T projects, but was still pretty good for 1953.

Saunders-Roe P.163

An early version of this project showed a slim fuselage and two Olympus or Avon RA.14 engines tip nacelle mounted on a straight, tapered short span wing. This final configuration settled on a clipped delta wing and an all-moving tail on top of the fin. The aircraft was designed to be as straightforward and simple as possible drawing on experience from the SR.53 supersonic and SR/A.1 flying-boat fighters. The P.163 was designed for easy production in small numbers using minimum tooling and yet be capable of mass production if required. Ailerons and flaps were conventional and wing droop leading edges were employed, all controls being power operated. Conventional light alloy semi-monocoque construction was used for the main fuselage and the wing consisted of a thick-skin multi-web aluminium box beam. The effects of kinetic heating on the structure had been investigated and found to be insignificant, Saro's only concession being a cockpit screen consisting of two sheets of toughened glass in the form of a Vee.

This was the only ER.134T submission to use a mixed powerplant, not surprising considering Saro's experience in the field and especially as the SR.53 interceptor had just been ordered. In the lower front fuselage, behind a variable centrebody inlet was a Gyron turbojet with 1,775K reheat, further aft a Spectre rocket. This was a bi-fuel motor using concentrated hydrogen peroxide (HTP) and kerosene in the ratio 9:1 and P.163 carried 390 gal of HTP and 1,070 of kerosene (1,773 and 4,864lit). The fuselage shape and powerplant disposition avoided the need for a long jet pipe for the Gyron. Choosing such a large turbojet enabled the P.163 to fly at Mach 2 without the aid of the rocket, the latter being used for the upper stages of climb, acceleration and also high speed high altitude manoeuvres.

In addition, using the rocket motor together with the jet greatly reduced time to a given height and acceleration to a given Mach number at altitudes between 36,000 and 60,000ft (10,973 and 18,288m). Mach 2 could be reached over 31,000ft (9,449m) with a 1 minute soak at this speed possible using jet plus reheat only. Time to Mach 2 at 60,000ft was quoted as 9.6 minutes; for 60,000ft alone using reheat above 36,000ft and the rocket above 45,000ft (13,716m) 8.3 minutes. Sea level climb rate with reheat on but no rocket was 35,500ft/min (10,820m/min).

Saro appreciated the specification could be met by an aircraft powered by one or more turbojets only, but believed this mixed power proposal gave greatly superior performance at the expense of only a small increase in weight and size. It was felt adding the rocket made the machine a far better research instrument by extending the range of altitude at Mach 2 and permitting high speed manoeuvres at all heights. Should the P.163 be considered as a high altitude interceptor, this added flexibility greatly enhanced its fighter potential and, in fact, would be essential to achieve the necessary time to height and manoeuvrability.

Vickers (Supermarine) Type 553

The 553's planform lay between three alternatives: a straight wing, a swept wing or a delta wing aircraft. It was accepted the straight wing would achieve the highest speed but drag peaked at about Mach 1.1 and the margin of thrust over drag between Mach 1.0 and 1.5 was such that time and fuel would be wasted when accelerating to top speed. It was also unsuitable for military applications. The swept wing was very much better in this respect, the need for a stiffer and thicker wing being offset by the wing's advantage at transonic speed without sacrificing too much super

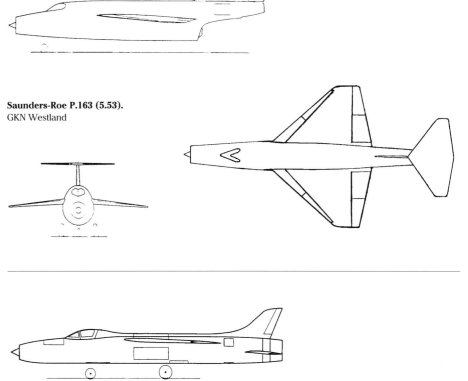

Saunders-Roe P.163 (5.53).
GKN Westland

Vickers (Supermarine) Type 553 (9.4.53).
Eric Morgan collection

sonic speed. The delta exploited this feature even more but suffered a reduced lift coefficient making it necessary to increase gross area by 50%. It also had high drag in certain manoeuvres again rendering the aircraft unsuited for military adaptation. By and large, the moderately swept wing held the advantage.

An aluminium alloy structure was preferred to steel, the choice forcing a slight restriction to maximum performance. Light alloy was satisfactory for the aerodynamic heat generated at Mach 2 at upwards of 30,000ft (9,144m), but the 553 was capable of higher speeds and maximum performance would need steel. The choice was marginal and subject to further study for steel would present a weight penalty, particularly if used to skin the fuselage, and presented new problems in fabrication.

The highest skin temperature attained would be 272°C at 12,000ft (3,658m) and Mach 2.0, but at Mach 1.2 it would stay at 150°C from 25,000 to 50,000ft (7,620 to 15,240m) when it would start decreasing and come within the then present knowledge of light alloys. Even in a dive the temperature would rise from 115 to 210°C in 35 seconds, so care would have to be taken. Titanium or steel would shield the engine. Engine choice lay between an RA.14 and the proposed RB.106, their dimensions were similar. The latter was chosen with reheat to 2,000K, a long reheat jet pipe with convergent/divergent nozzle and an annular nose entry with adjustable centre body. This installation gave about 20% more thrust than a pitot entry; scoop intakes were rejected.

Supermarine felt the 553's orthodox form would provide the best performance and could be produced quickly as there were no great departures from current manufacturing practice. The wing was shoulder mounted with a power operated low all-moving tail, this combination being favoured aerodynamically to alleviate pitch-up problems which were just being recognised at the time. Alternative tail positions were either well above the main plane chord line or below it. A leading edge flap, sometimes called a 'drooped snoot', was fitted over the entire span having been proved in flight on the Type 508. Inboard and outboard ailerons were proposed, the inboard pair acting as ailerons at high speeds and as trailing edge flaps for take-off and landing. The thin wing made it difficult to achieve sufficient stiffness.

Sea level rate of climb was 53,000ft/min (16,154m/min) at a climbing Mach number of 0.9, the speed for climb to 36,090ft (11,000m). The rest of the climb to an operating height of 50,000ft (15,240m) was made after acceleration to Mach 2. The maximum level speed ignoring temperature limitations was given as

Mach 2.4 (1,590mph [2,557km/h]) at 36,090ft, a figure reduced to 2.3 due to kinetic heat; at sea level these figures were Mach 1.35 and 1.22. The 553 without reheat was just supersonic at all heights up to at least 34,000ft (10,363m) and capable of Mach 2 between 26,000 and 60,000ft (7,925 and 18,288m), but it could only soak at this speed for 5 mins, half the required time. 6.87 minutes was the time stated to reach Mach 2 at 50,000ft (15,240m). Ceiling was 60,000ft.

Internal fuel totalled 780gal (3,547lit) and a reference to 1,500lb (680kg) of 'special instrumentation' was interpreted to mean the aircraft should be adapted to military work without appreciable modification, the 1,500lb being replaced by armour and armament. The gun battery would lie in the top of the fuselage forward of the windscreen with Radar Ranging Mk.1 or Mk.2 housed with ease in the intake centre body. The firm quoted an all-up 'combat' weight of 26,000lb (11,794kg) and, armed, felt this aircraft would be a very formidable defender indeed.

Test pilot Dave Morgan felt sure the 553 would have been a superb aircraft to fly and considered the nose intake to be a good feature for a research machine, albeit not so for a fighter with radar.

–

Two Tender Design Conferences were held at the MoS on the 8th June and 28th August 1953. After the first a working party was established to further assess the three finalists, submitting their report on 24th August.

Throughout, RAE favoured designs of straight wing layout with two engines buried in wing nacelles, although the strong trend towards swept wings in current aircraft for moderate supersonic speeds was reviewed. At the first meeting deep discussion centred on the favoured straight wing planform which some felt gave high transonic drag, but this was countered by the argument of fitting exceptionally thin wings. A E Woodward Nutt, PDRD(A), felt attention should concentrate on designs using engines known to be available which, combined with the wing nacelle configuration, allowed comparatively easy engine changes when newer powerplants appeared. A statement on forthcoming engines gave the following progress reports:

– RB.106: at design stage and expected to be complete by end 1953. First test-bed run planned mid-1954, available for installation in airframe without reheat at end 1956 and with reheat end 1957. The dates quoted were agreed between MoS and Rolls-Royce.

– RA.14: would be available with reheat earlier than the RB.106 but no date was given.

– Gyron: already at test-bed development stage and expected that an engine would be ready for installation without reheat by mid-1955, with reheat by mid-1956.

– Sa.7: would be ready in a few months with expected availability for flight early 1954. 25% reheat, proposed by AWA for the AW.166, had been obtained with 40% due soon.

Artist's impression of the Type 553. via Eric Morgan

Model of the Type 553.

It was decided that the dates quoted for the RB.106 and to a lesser extent the Gyron, even if achieved, would delay the availability of the aircraft unnecessarily, and it was agreed the object should be to get an aircraft capable of Mach 2 as soon as possible rather than delaying matters by striving for even better performance.

Regarding the tenders, English Electric's swept wing designs were ruled out on grounds of planform adopted. Supermarine's 553 did not meet the endurance requirements and was powered by the RB.106, the use of which seemed to preclude any submission. The ten minute endurance at Mach 2 laid down in ER.134T was considered essential as an extensive research programme would be required on the aircraft and restricted endurance would be very detrimental. Both the Hawker projects relied on the RB.106 and also used wing root intakes, an uncertain quantity on an aircraft of this nature, so neither was considered acceptable. Saunders-Roe was an organisation new in the field of high speed aircraft and it was decided to wait until they had proved themselves with the rocket interceptor (SR.53) before entrusting them with another major design. For this reason, and through doubts as to the availability of the Gyron, it was decided not to consider the P.163 further, although it was considered quite an attractive design with the combination of rocket and gas turbine allowing great flexibility in the flight plan. Rockets could, however, be fitted to other designs, the wing engined proposals were particularly suited for their installation.

All swept and delta submissions showed no performance superiority over the favoured straight wing with engine pods. Boulton Paul's P.128 was not assessed in detail. It made no use of reheat, fell short of the required endurance and had no margin for acceleration.

This was assuming that the endplate effect of the tip-nacelles was valid at supersonic speeds, a factor which itself was quite uncertain. Doubts were expressed as to whether the BP design team was strong enough to undertake a project of this nature. Three straight winged designs remained, the AW.166, Bristol 188 and English Electric 'P.6B'. H F Vessey remarked that if the Bristol 178 rocket propelled fighter to F.124T was built, information appertaining to the straight wing configuration would be obtained independently which weakened the case for this Mach 2 aircraft, but it was concluded that financial approval was not forthcoming for both the rocket fighter and ER.134 aircraft.

As stated, English Electric felt its straight wing design was inferior to the swept P.6 layouts through high drag and weight, and the firm queried the wisdom of considering it. The list of disadvantages for the 'P.6B' were considered worthy of discussion at the conference and, if showing substance, the policy for straight wings might need to be reconsidered. But the reasons for the layout's rejection by the firm were not absolutely clear and it was felt, therefore, the design should be reassessed with more data. Based on NACA research, the assessors felt English Electric's project suffered from several unjustified assumptions which spoilt the design and further work was requested from the firm. Finally, the use of steel was examined, Bristol being the only firm to employ it. RAE's opinion was that dural (aluminium) could not be extensively used much further in the Mach number range.

For the final trio, the time for independent assessment would be too long so a small working party from Farnborough's Aero and Research and Development departments visited each firm. After full consideration its report was submitted in time for the second

conference. On 17th September English Electric submitted its brief addendum to the P.6 brochure detailing the trapezoidal canard of reduced weight and including modifications based on the two rival designs to give similar capabilities. However the most favourable solutions were considered to be the AW.166 and Bristol 188, the former having a slight edge. It had been agreed at the 28th August Conference that a contract should go to AWA for a first prototype built in light alloy but with a steel wing fitted on the second. However, the firm was full with Javelin work so a contract was awarded to Bristol in mid-December for the all-steel 188 but several major parts, including tailplane, fin and outer rudder, were in fact sub-contracted for manufacture by AWA.

The first contract covered two flying airframes. Serials XF923 and XF926 were assigned on 4th January 1954, and built around Specification ER.134D of 11th March 1954 which now called for a maximum Mach 2.5. In 1955 a contract was awarded to Avro for its Type 730 high altitude supersonic reconnaissance bomber to OR.330 while a supersonic interceptor to OR.329 (next chapter) was also under consideration, so a second order for three more Bristol 188s followed, (with serials XK429, XK434 and XK436) to assist these developments. This decision was taken in September but the second group was cancelled in 1957 for economy after both OR.329 and OR.330 were abandoned by the new all-missile defence policy. After an extensive review of research needs and costs, it was decided that the Bristol 188 project should continue but with the two original aircraft only and in June 1957 the engines were changed to de Havilland Gyron Juniors. Back in October 1954 a total of six aircraft had been considered as the final number needed.

Completion was very late because the stainless steel construction technique proved exceptionally troublesome, yet throughout there was a continual trend toward exploiting the airframe for even higher Mach numbers and, late in manufacture, Mach 3 seemed possible with improvements in propulsion. The finished article featured a built in and very extensive instrumentation system, comprising paper and magnetic tape recorders and continuous telemetry, to facilitate rapid acquisition of test data on aerodynamics, structural loads, kinetic heating, etc. The Type 188 was the world's first stainless steel aircraft.

Once in the air (first flight 14th April 1962) performance disappointed with maximum speed achieved only Mach 1.88 and soak time limited to two minutes by the unexpected thirst of the Gyron Juniors, a period insufficient to enable the airframe to become soaked by kinetic heating. These engines just did not have enough power. Problems with engine surge at supersonic speed also caused severe difficulties in both pitch and yaw. The two airframes flew until 1964 before the programme was closed. The Bristol 188 brought new knowledge of airframe manufacture; to quote BAC's George Edwards 'we learnt not to make aeroplanes that way'. In truth, the aircraft was an expensive failure and the author has never heard any praise given to it, a pity because it very much looked the part. Might one of the other proposals

such as the P.6/1 or Type 553 have been a better choice?

In early August 1958, the American Mutual Weapons Development Program (MWDP) team of General Boyd, John Stack, Colonel Klein and Colonel Chapman examined several British projects including the Hawker P.1127 V/STOL aircraft (which was highly regarded) and the Bristol 188. They were not impressed with the 188's design or purpose saying 'all it will give is experience about steel fabrication. If all the available information were pooled it would be seen that little new could come out of ER.134'. The DDGSR(A) agreed but pointed out that the machine would be

the only Mach 2.5 engine test bed that the UK had. The Americans would not recommend it for MWDP aid.

It is interesting to note that Saab in Sweden examined a 188-type layout amid numerous 1950s studies originally aimed at an attack aircraft under project Saab 36, but eventually went for the Viggen multi-role aircraft programme. Perhaps the nearest was Project 1371 of January 1956 but a sister design, the 1357 (July 1955), dispensed with the tail and introduced a canard. It suggested most strongly a canard Type 188.

Mach 2 Research Aircraft to ER.134T – Estimated Data

Project	Span ft (m)	Length ft (m)	Wing Area ft² (m²)	t/c %	All-Up-Weight lb (kg)	Powerplant Thrust lb (kN)	Max Speed / Height mph (km/h) / ft (m) x 1,000	Armament
Armstrong Whitworth AW.166	36.75 (11.2)	66.67 (20.3)	386 (35.8)	4	28,000 (12,700)	2 x Sapphire Sa.7 11,000 (48.9), 13,750 (61.1) reheat	Mach 2.3 at 45.0 (13.7)	–
Boulton Paul P.128	28.67 (8.7)	63.67 (19.4)	312 (28.9)	4	26,493 (12,017)	2 x Sapphire Sa.7 11,000 (48.9) dry	Mach 2 at 36.0 (11.0)	–
Bristol Type 188	35.67 (10.9)	68.0 (20.7)	358 (33.2)	4	30,000 (13,608)	2 x Avon RA.14R 8,850 (39.3), 11,300 (48.9) reheat	Mach 2.25 at 36.0 (11.0)	–
English Electric P.6/1	34.8 (10.6)	52.15 (15.9)	460 (42.7)	6.2	26,978 (12,237)	1 x RB.106R 15,000 (66.7), 20,750 (92.2) reheat	Mach 2	–
English Electric P.6/2	35.5 (10.8)	54.5 (16.6)	473 (43.9)	6.2	29,993 (13,604)	2 x Sapphire Sa.7 11,000 (48.9), 15,400 (68.4) reheat	Mach 2+	–
English Electric 'P.6B' (Straight Wing)	40.0 (12.2)	62.67 (19.1)	550 (51.0)	4	35,900 (16,284)	2 x Sapphire Sa.7 11,000 (48.9), 15,400 (68.4) reheat	Mach 2	–
English Electric 'P.6D' (Trapezoid)	34.5 (10.5)	56.7 (17.3)	?	?	30,000 (13,608)	2 derated RB.106R 10,000 (44.4), 13,800 (61.3) reheat	Mach 2	–
Hawker P.1096	33.0 (10.1)	53.67 (16.4)	469 (43.5)	4	20,000 (9,072)	1 x RB.106R 15,000 (66.7), 20,750 (92.2) reheat	Mach 2.35 at 36.0 (11.0)	–
Hawker P.1097	35.0 (10.7)	49.33 (15.0)	380 (35.3)	7.5	22,200 (10,069)	1 x RB.106R 15,000 (66.7), 20,750 (92.2) reheat	Mach 1.9 at 36.0 (11.0)	–
Saro P.163	30.0 (9.1)	57.85 (18.1)	450 (41.8)	4	34,500 (15,649)	1 x Gyron 25,000 (111.1) reheat + 1 x Spectre rocket 8,000 (35.6)	Mach 2.5 at 40.0 (12.2)	–
Supermarine Type 553	30.8 (9.4)	58.0 (17.7)	330 (30.6)	5	27,000 (12,247)	1 x RB.106R 15,000 (66.7), 22,600 (100.4) reheat	Mach 1.22 at sea level Mach 2.3, 1,523 (2,450) at 36.1 (11.0)	–
Bristol Type 188 (flown)	35.1 (10.7)	77.67 (23.7)	396 (36.8)	4	?	2 x Gyron Junior PS.50/DG.J.10R 10,000 (44.4), 14,000 (62.2) reheat	Mach 1.88 (highest achieved)	–

Chapter Eight

The Ultimate Interceptor

High Altitude Fighters: 1953 to 1959

As the ER.134T work rolled on, RAE and TRE opinion turned towards a Mach 2 fighter and a working party under Sir Arnold Hall was organised to assess what could be done. It met throughout 1954 and its reports included *Layout and Performance of an Operational Supersonic Aircraft* that offered some twin engine 'working' designs based on the Bristol 188. These were evaluated against English Electric's P.6/1 single engine swept wing aircraft to ER.134T to compare planforms. Subsequently a requirement was drafted and possible contractors examined. AWA would have to be omitted if it won the M.148T competition (the Blackburn Buccaneer was the successful tender) and de Havilland could not take on a fighter and the supersonic OR.330 reconnaissance aircraft (won by the Avro 730). Some firms were yet to show much

appreciation for the 'weapon system' concept. On 15th January 1955, F.155T was issued for a *Day-Night High Altitude Fighter Aircraft*.

F.155T (and OR.329)

This requested a highly advanced all-weather interception system capable of destroying very high altitude enemy raiders operating at 60,000ft (18,288m) and Mach 1.3. The weapon system concept was to be employed where aircraft and systems were treated as a single entity. Entry into service must be as soon as possible but not later than January 1962, which implied flight and weapons development completed in 1961 (it had been estimated that the threat to Britain could be met by the F.23 [Lightning] and Thin Wing Javelin until about 1963). The aircraft was to be capable of both collision and pursuit types of attack and carry guided weapons only, coupled with an advanced intercept radar called AI.18 capable of long range and wide coverage. To cover the workload a crew of two was essential.

An in-house artist's impression of Fairey's huge 'Delta III' fighter to F.155T. The missiles are Red Hebe, a development of Red Dean, which would, had the weapon entered service, have received a more rounded nose.

A Normal Warning Time Sortie (45 minutes) and an Extended Warning Time Sortie (76 minutes) were specified but from start up the fighter was to reach 60,000ft, 70 nautical miles (nm) (130km) from base in six minutes at a speed not less than Mach 2, with a further minute to reach an attack position. The aircraft was to be as small as possible and able to turn supersonically through large angles. Minimum ceiling was 65,000ft (19,800m) at Mach 1.5, but the machine must also be able to cruise on atmospherically aspirated engines at 45,000ft (13,716m).

OR.1131 covered two different air-to-air missiles for the F.155T fighter – one infra-red guided for rear or beam attacks, the other by radar for attack from all angles. Both had to be operable from 70,000ft (21,336m). The first, to

e developed by de Havilland, was called Blue
Vesta, the second from Vickers, the Red Dean
development called Red Hebe. Over 40 years
on, there is some confusion over the missile
armament for the brochures refer to Red
Dean and Blue Jay Mk.4 as well. Blue Vesta
weighed 340lb (154kg) and was short-lived,
DH only releasing tentative details to satisfy
the aircraft designers immediate needs and
there was much criticism that Red Hebe, at
approx 1,300lb (590kg), was too heavy. Consequently a 'small Vickers missile', actually a
scaled down Red Hebe weighing 675lb (306
kg), also received attention. De Havilland Propellers began work on Blue Jay Mk.4 at this
time, the weapon becoming Red Top.

F.155T Issue 2 of 5th July cut the time to
60,000ft and Mach 2 to four minutes; acceleration in level flight at 60,000ft from Mach 1.3
to Mach 2.0 was to take approximately one
minute. Firms invited to tender were to have
their submissions in by 12th October. Bristol
was omitted through its pre-occupation with
the Type 188 which was regarded as a vital
forerunner to this operational aeroplane.
Completion of the ER.134 aircraft was extremely important and a fighter order would
be a serious distraction from the task.

Armstrong Whitworth AW.169

This submission, as one might expect, was
based on work done for the AW.166. Its construction was to be of conventional light alloy
materials which allowed an adequate strength
and stiffness margin up to a specified 'design
dive speed' of Mach 2.55. Detailed study had
been given to the structural design problems
arising from the high altitude, high speed and
high manoeuvrability requirements coupled
with the large thrust and stringent fuel demands, all of which combined to give a high
gross weight. AWA established that the actual weight growth factor rose quite rapidly with
increased military load and devoted much
time to the restriction of this item which prevented the aircraft from being excessively
large, gross take-off weight finishing in the region of 54,000lb (24,494kg).

At sea level the maximum performance was
restricted to an engine limitation of Mach 1 to
maintain a reasonable structure and power
plant weight in an aircraft intended primarily
for high altitude operations. From a performance standpoint the aircraft could exceed
the speed limitations at all heights and given
an adequate margin of fuel with the rocket
switched off, predicted speeds varied from
about Mach 2 at sea level to 2.7 at height. Maximum sea level rate of climb with 2,000K reheat
was 55,000ft/min (16,764m/min) reducing to
32,000ft/min (9,754m/min) with the reheat off.

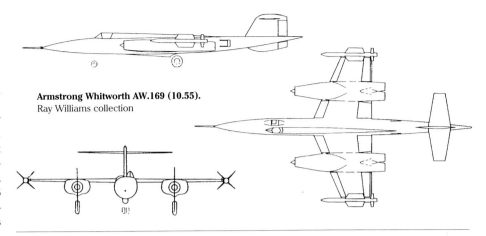

Armstrong Whitworth AW.169 (10.55).
Ray Williams collection

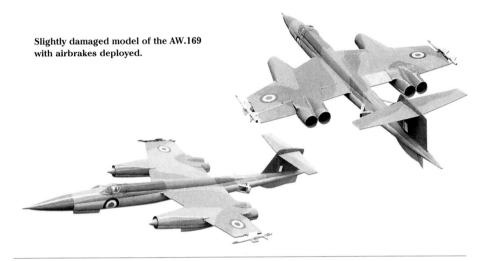

**Slightly damaged model of the AW.169
with airbrakes deployed.**

The wings were very thin preventing any
substantial storage of fuel and equipment, all
of which were carried in the fuselage. The
four Gyron Juniors were to be slung in paired
nacelles under the wings to maintain complete continuity of the main spar structure.
Choosing this particular four engine layout
gave a convenient location for the main undercarriage wheels between the air intake
ducts keeping drag to a minimum. The air
intakes had moving centre-bodies with variable convergent-divergent nozzles. A Spectre
rocket motor with variable thrust control was
installed under the fuselage to provide the
thrust required for high altitude acceleration
and manoeuvrability and the all-moving tail
was located high on the fin. Normally some
11,600lb (5,262g) of kerosene and 4,500lb
(2,041kg) of HTP were carried.

An extensive wind tunnel programme was
carried out and a cockpit mock-up prepared
at Baginton. The crew sat side by side with
the pilot given a conventional hood offset to
port and the radar operator placed slightly
lower under a blister type transparency. The
main 33in (84cm) radar dish was in the nose,
an X band AI system of 20 miles (32km) range

fitted in co-operation with GEC plus an additional Q band installation in one of the nacelle
centre-bodies to give range information on a
jamming target up to about 8 miles (13km)
range. A maximum of two missiles only were
to be carried and these fitted on the wing tips
which AWA considered the best stowage position for minimum all-up drag.

The firm considered the proposal was as
much as could be accomplished by the requested in service date of 1962 but further developments were envisaged beyond that
time. From a January 1956 ITP, first flight was
predicted to be June 1959 with squadron service in April 1962. More powerful engines and
the use of stainless steel would allow higher
limiting speeds up to Mach 3.0 and consideration was being given to the unstable aircraft
concept.

De Havilland DH.117

This project was to be built in light alloy with
its fully proven methods of design and construction to help keep development time to a
minimum and allow operation up Mach 2.35.
Much use was to be made however of titanium
forgings and sheet, based on experience

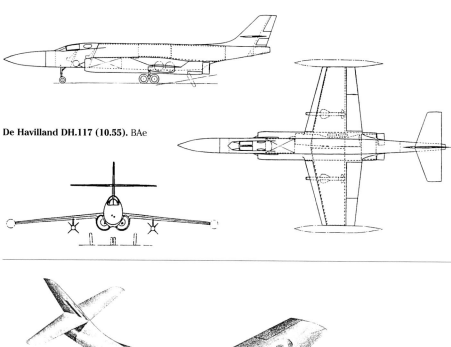

De Havilland DH.117 (10.55). BAe

Impression of the DH.117 with Red Top missiles.

gained with the DH.110. The fighter could make the specified Normal Warning Sortie (60,000ft [18,288m], Mach 2.0 in 6 minutes) and was capable of interceptions at Mach 2.35 in an area 100nm (185km) from base (slightly less at lower altitudes) within 10 minutes of take-off.

Total fuel capacity (kerosene and HTP) with 400gal (1,818lit) in wing tip drop tanks was 2,635gal (11,980lit). With the rocket fuel aboard for combat in the Extended Range Sortie and full internal fuel with drop tanks, radius of operation and patrol time were considerably increased over Specification. Mach 2.0 interceptions were now possible 275nm (510km) from base after a patrol time of 40 minutes compared to 15 minutes for F.155T. The ability to operate over an extensive range of supersonic speed did not compromise low speed characteristics which were of similar standard to aircraft in service. The DH.117 had a high wing loading of up to 120lb/ft² (586kg/m²) compared to aircraft of the time,

but on take-off with full reheat and full rocket thrust the thrust/weight ratio prevented any increase in take off distance on current aircraft. The Spectre rocket was housed in the fuselage rear end.

DH felt development and full service trials of an aircraft fully meeting the specification could not be achieved within the time limit and the need to carry alternative weapon systems and their equipment for full automatic interception would entail a very much larger and more complex design in a longer time-scale. Therefore the Blue Jay Mk.4 had been selected as armament with the resulting system, although not fully automatic, enabling interception and attack to be made on a beam collision course with a high chance of success. Sufficient rocket fuel was available to follow up with a stern chase. At take-off weight 51,175lb (23,213kg), sea level climb rate with reheat and rocket was 36,800ft/min (11,217m/min). The brochure also made reference to Blue Vesta.

It was thought that two prototypes produced by hand methods in the Experimental Department and without equipment could be in the air in December 1958 and June 195 respectively. These were to be followed by pre-production machines from the Production Department using a relatively lower standard of jigging than in the final production model and flying between October 1959 and June 1961, the fifth machine onwards being more representative of production standards. The first production machine would be delivered in January 1962 for squadron service later in the year. The aircraft was considered the most effective interceptor that could be designed and developed in the time available, some pruning of equipment having been necessary.

To assist development, DH suggested flying a Hunter with a new set of wings. The wings on Hawker's P.1118 were similar to the DH.117's, so it is possible the Kingston project was stimulated by this idea. In fact the DH.11 did get as far as the detailed mock-up stage at Hatfield and this apparently survived until the early 1960's. Because the design had been to a large extent dictated by the January 196 deadline, details were included of possible future developments and comprised a full standard of automatic attack, improved weapons and radar, higher powered engines catapult take-off and arrested landing and the introduction of a steel airframe to take full advantage of the performance capabilities. It was felt the design of the steel structure could begin well before the light alloy version entered service. The DH.117 fulfilled R E Bishop's desire to do an F-104 Starfighter type of aircraft and work on it continued for about a year.

English Electric P.8

A P.1B development. Wing structure comprised five aluminium alloy spars forming a box covered by alloy skins, the fuselage contained closely spaced frames reinforced with stringers. The P.8 had a new cambered wing (tested on the first P.1A WG760) and an all moving tail. The most favoured engines from several alternatives were a pair of RB.126s planned as a straightforward development of the RA.24 Avon, fitted one above the other and staggered to keep fuselage depth to a minimum as in the P.1. The conical centre bullet was retained and either variable convergent-divergent nozzles or an exhaust ejector system would be fitted with reheat to 1,575K. Unlike the P1, both nose and main gears were contained within the fuselage allowing the wings to be used for fuel for a much greater capacity than before, without he need for external tanks; 1,050gal (4,774lit) were carried at overload.

Mach 2 could be reached at 46,000ft (14,021m) without reheat and 60,000ft (18,288m) with both afterburners, but below 36,000ft (10,973m) speed was limited near to the structural limit of 806mph (1,297km/h), Mach 1.06 at sea level. To English Electric, the use of reheat made level speed meaningless since the aircraft could climb rapidly at 800mph (1,287m/h) and then up to Mach 2 to over 60,000ft. The AI.23 radar was to be used initially without changes except scanner diameter was raised from 24 to 27in (60 to 68cm). English Electric accepted the requirement of air-to-air missiles as the primary weapon but could not reconcile the carriage of infra-red and radar operated weapons, the firm considering it impossible to carry both together and, therefore, that development of the former was most important. The choice was a pair of Blue Jay Mk.4s which could be changed for two packs of 24 x 2in (5cm) rockets.

P.8 was considered a logical sequel to the F.23/49 development programme and the Experimental Manufacturing Department was expected to be clear of the P.1 prototypes in late 1956 giving good continuity. This development of the F.23/49 had been given extreme area rule analysis and showed no performance inferiority up to Mach 2 provided there was some alteration in fuselage shape. That gave some local bulges useful for stowing the undercarriage and equipment while the canopy had a more efficient shape seating the two man crew in tandem. The wing leading edge and tip was altered to take tip mounted weapons, tunnel testing showing this position reduced drag. The structure had been redesigned to cut weight.

The level of redesign from the P.1B was kept to a minimum yet the first prototype would be more complete equipment wise than that aircraft. However, since redesign was minimal it was felt the full design effort on the P.8 should wait as later production aircraft would become too far advanced for flight experience modifications to be incorporated economically. Hence the brochure suggested a 'short step' development from the existing F.23/49 system using RA.24s, though English Electric still accepted flight development must be complete in 1961 with service entry in January 1962. To achieve this the P.8 differed from the specification in some respects. From a January 1956 ITP, first flight of the first development aircraft would be late April 1959. Test pilot 'Bee' Beamont was adamant the P.8 would need 50% more fin area and improved rear vision.

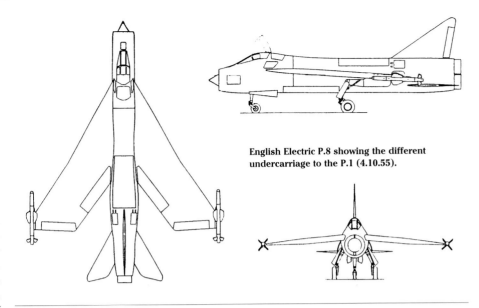

English Electric P.8 showing the different undercarriage to the P.1 (4.10.55).

English Electric P.8 model displaying area ruling.

Fairey F.155

Fairey studied F.155T closely and concluded that while it was possible technically to meet the complete OR, the weapon system was unlikely to be fully developed by 1962 because of the new equipment and methods of construction in the design. Hence they had studied an alternative simpler aircraft which would have the performance to meet the threat, but by using present construction methods and equipment could be available by or before 1960 due to the relative ease of manufacture. This was complemented by a much more substantial design fully meeting the specification but available rather later.

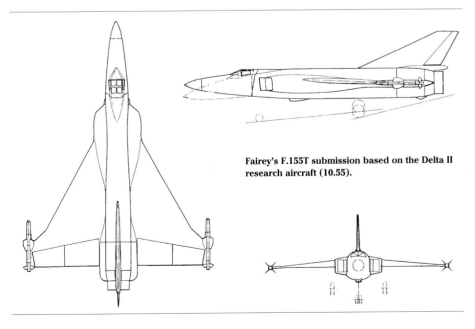

Fairey's F.155T submission based on the Delta II research aircraft (10.55).

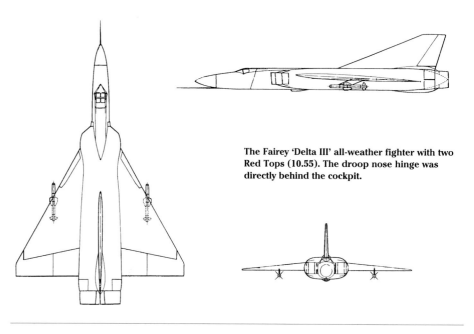

The Fairey 'Delta III' all-weather fighter with two Red Tops (10.55). The droop nose hinge was directly behind the cockpit.

Model of Fairey's F.155T cranked delta project based on the Delta II with wing-tip Red Top air-to-air missiles and bogus serial ZA435. Peter Green

Fairey Delta II development

This was the lightest and simplest aircraft possible having the requisite performance. As construction was based on standard practice, it was easy to manufacture and used considerable background knowledge available from the ER.103 Delta II. Power came from a reheated Gyron, plus a Spectre rocket motor on each side of the area-ruled fuselage. Fairey used its own fully duplicated power controls and the complete cockpit and nose section folded down for take-off and landing as per Delta II practice. Two Blue Jay Mk.4s were carried, one per wing tip, which combined with Ferranti's AI.23 radar gave what Fairey considered to be the best combination available in 1960 and capable of much development. Mach 2.5 could be reached at 59,000ft (17,983m) using reheat only whilst, according to the brochure, adding the rocket

power increased altitude for this speed to over 90,000ft (27,432m). It was felt a prototype could be flown in 30 months with eleven more airborne after another 18 months. After this project had been rejected, Fairey adapted it to take two underwing Red Hebe.

Fairey F.155 (all-weather)

The second design was much larger which Fairey stated was capable of considerable development as a 'weapon system' and able to meet any likely threat. During preliminary studies, both single and twin engine layouts of various size and planform had been assessed with the conclusion that the specification was best met by a twin engine delta with

rocket assistance. The delta gave excellent manoeuvrability at high altitude, the best landing and take-off characteristics, and the lightest structure weight.

For the wing, centre fuselage and fin a high tensile stainless steel similar to the American 17.7PH (and the subject of a current development programme at Fairey for large helicopter blades) was chosen while other parts of the aircraft, where heat resistance had greater importance than strength and stiffness, were to be fabricated in titanium. The minimum required performance could be met using a light alloy structure, but the powerplant gave an actual performance far greater than this and with room for development so, as a consequence, Fairey had chosen materials that would make full use of the considerable potential of this aircraft.

The choice of two jet engines stemmed from the need to have development potential in the aircraft while adding rockets gave the best operational characteristics. The most suitable combination was felt to be a pair of RB.122s with two Spectre Juniors. An alternative powerplant was the use of smaller jets and larger rockets but this gave just a small reduction in weight and provided far less flexibility of operation. In fact, Fairey considered that many missions were possible without the rockets altogether which gave a longer range by substituting the HTP with more kerosene. The brochure figures were based solely on the RB.122 but full interchangeability with the Gyron was provided because in the early development period the latter would probably be the only suitable engine available. Maximum level speed with reheat was well above Mach 2 and when unlit this dropped to Mach 1.90 (with Blue Jay Mk.4 aboard) or Mach 1.57 (Red Dean) at 36,000ft (10,973m). Maximum ceiling was 70,000ft (21,336m).

The droop nose was retained. On the advice of RRE (TRE as was) and GEC the radar installation was based on a developed and lightened AI.18, though full details were as yet unavailable. The weapons varied a great deal in overall weight and complexity which gave difficulty in integration with the aircraft, compounded by not knowing when the weapons would be ready. As Blue Jay would be available first the main submission was based on this, but full provision was made for Red Dean with switch from one to the other straightforward. All-up-weights would not vary by much as the heavier collision course weapon needed less fuel to get a 'kill' at a given distance but Fairey suggested the larger missile was too heavy and elaborate and asked for some simplification before it was too late. Various carriage positions were investigated before concluding that the underwing position gave the best compromise between drag, weight and field of view for the weapon radar. Four Blue Jay could be carried as an overload if called for.

The company felt experience gained in producing the Delta I and Delta II would still carry over to this aircraft, saving many months in design and development. While a light alloy structure would have been capable of successful operation up to the minimum required performance, the chosen aerodynamic and powerplant parameters gave an actual performance far greater than this and still with room for development. The materials selected enabled full exploitation of the considerable potential of this aircraft and indeed, with engine developments only, speeds up to Mach 3.0 at 36,000ft (10,973m) were possible without airframe redesign. This structure limit was reduced to Mach 2.27 by the current engine limits and 1.905 when reheat was not employed. With Blue Jay, 91,800ft (27,981m) could be reached in 2.5 minutes using reheat and rockets, 75,000ft (22,860m) in 1.5 minutes reheat only. As well as high altitude interception, the aircraft was capable of medium low level interception, strike and photo reconnaissance operations. Delivery of the first aircraft would take three years; the first 24 six years.

Hawker P.1103

From its appearance, clearly a product of the Sidney Camm line, this was another project to be built conventionally in light alloy and was an attempt to meet F.155T with the smallest possible aircraft. The layout used a 40° swept wing, chosen because of its good transonic characteristics, load relieving ability and structural suitability for the single engine arrangement. A high tail was incorporated which, in Hawker's opinion with the aid of wind tunnel experimentation, could be developed satisfactorily against pitch-up and was strongly preferred from all other aspects. An alternative version with a low tail just below wing level had also been investigated in detail and included in the brochure. This had the fin height reduced by 6in (15cm) and no wing rocket boosters, but the low tail gave less subsonic stability at low incidence and was more prone to ground effect.

The single engined design was considered the cleanest aerodynamically and with the highest thrust/weight ratio, and used the most powerful engine available in the Gyron. At the time this engine's development programme was well advanced and it was expected to deliver a thrust of about 25,000lb (111.1kN).

Other engines studied in this thrust category were Armstrong Siddeley's P.173, Rolls' RB.122 and the Canadian Orenda PS.13. To improve high altitude manoeuvrability and acceleration, a pair of detachable and completely self-contained rocket motor boosters were carried in the mid-wing position holding sufficient oxidant and fuel for 3.7 minutes operation.

A maximum level speed of Mach 2.0 would be achievable within the range 30,000 to 65,000ft (9,144 to 19,812m) and acceleration from Mach 1.3 to 2.0 at 60,000ft would take just over two minutes when using the rockets. Design dive speed above 36,000ft (10,973m) was limited to Mach 2.3 because of the light alloy structure and at low altitudes 864mph (1390km/h). All-up overload weight at take-off with rockets attached was 40,000lb (18,144kg) with Blue Jays aboard, 41,850lb (18,983g) with Red Hebes. Ceiling was at least 68,000ft (20,726m) and sea level rate of climb 61,000ft/min (18,953m). Internal fuel capacity was 1,100gal (5,002lit).

P.1103 had a radar dish at least 30in (76cm) in diameter. Armament was a pair of Blue Jay Mk.4s or two of the Vickers small radar missiles carried externally because of the impossibility of stowing such irregularly-shaped articles within the small compact airframe. Further, it afforded the best possible field of view for the weapon sensing heads. Hawker stated that Red Hebe was at present still too large, aerodynamically dirty and completely out of harmony with this aircraft and indeed on any other where it would be mounted externally. The alternative, mounting internally or semi-internally, implied a fuselage that would be too large and the firm urged that all efforts should concentrate on developing

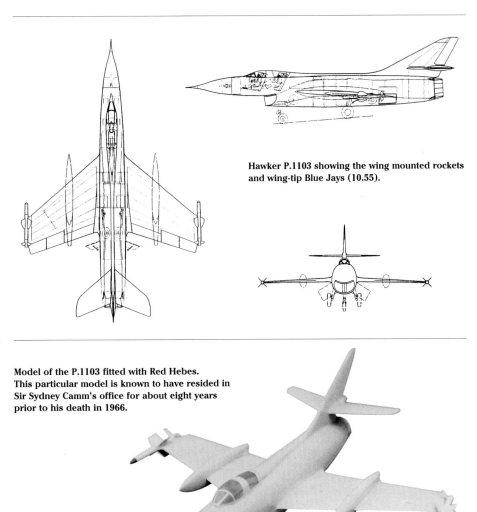

Hawker P.1103 showing the wing mounted rockets and wing-tip Blue Jays (10.55).

Model of the P.1103 fitted with Red Hebes. This particular model is known to have resided in Sir Sydney Camm's office for about eight years prior to his death in 1966.

Blue Jay and/or the Vickers small radar missile to perform the Red Dean mission. However, Red Hebe's weight was not excessive and it was considered that carrying a pair of such weapons on P.1103 was possible if the performance loss from their drag could be justified. All P.1103 illustrations showed wing tip Blue Jay's but the 1/24th scale model kit contained sets of both missiles.

Saunders-Roe P.187

This followed a long line of Saro rocket or rocket plus jet fighter projects, including the SR.53 and SR.177; the resemblance and outgrowth from the latter apparent. The extensive design work undertaken on these fighters had been fully drawn upon in preparing the P.187 which in principle was a scaled

version of the earlier aircraft. Saro began studies for F.155T with schemes based on a straight tapered wing but eventually the clipped delta evolved. Proven manufacturing techniques were used and the aircraft was designed to allow detailed engineering and construction to be undertaken in the shortest possible time. The wing had a droop leading edge and blown flaps and spanned 48ft (14.6m) without weapons. The tail was all-moving and the fuselage area ruled. A sliding nose cone gave exceptionally good vision during approach and landing but when raised became highly faired for flight. This was not a droop nose as employed on the Fairey Delta II but the entire nose with its radar slid downwards like a lift, the shape of the 'join' such that the air intake flow was not disturbed.

Saro P.187 model (displaying some damage to the missile fins.

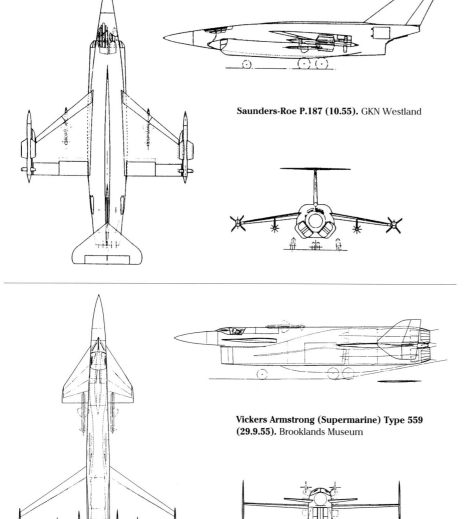

Saunders-Roe P.187 (10.55). GKN Westland

Vickers Armstrong (Supermarine) Type 559 (29.9.55). Brooklands Museum

Two PS.52 engines, a projected development of the Gyron with an additional front compressor stage to increase pressure ratio to 7:1 and 40% reheat for 35,000lb (155.6kN) thrust, were to be fitted while above the jet pipes a battery of four Spectre rockets were mounted side by side exhausting below the fin. These gave maximum level speeds of Mach 2.5 (structure limit) and 3.0 (fuel limit) with an ultimate ceiling of 76,000ft (23,165m). The maximum altitude for Mach 2 cruise on turbojet power only was 57,000ft (17,374m) and total time at Mach 2 was put at 6.6 minutes. Saro felt its experience in designing fuel systems involving the segregation of HTP and kerosene had been utilised to great advantage. A pair of Red Deans were carried on the wingtips plus two Blue Jay Mk.4s on underwing pylons. Both Normal and Extended Warning Sortie times were exceeded, by 3.5 and 13.2 minutes respectively.

The brochure stated that prototype first flight would be 200 weeks after ITP. Saro explained how certain features would be subject to detailed modification after further investigation. For example the fairing ahead of the air intakes when the nose was depressed and the arrangement of the rocket engines would be subjected to tunnel testing to determine the optimum design. The side by side rockets gave a flat-topped fuselage providing the fin with end plate effect. Although accepting the challenging requirements of F.155T, in formulating the design the firm was aware that a much reduced all-up weight could be obtained by carrying the infra-red and radar weapons separately. Saro also felt that the armament and equipment equirements of F.155T could be eased and, with experience from this and other investigations, it could quickly prepare an alternative design for a smaller aircraft with Gyron or Gyron Junior engines. The SR.177 was considered a realistic alternative to the requirement, certainly for carrying Blue Jay.

Vickers (Supermarine) Type 559

This unusual canard configuration employed wing geometry described as 'lobster-claw' and was selected from numerous alternative layouts. Recent experience suggested that airframe structure and equipment adjacent to the jet nozzles might suffer damage from noise and high frequency vibration and the engines considered for F.155T were estimated to have a much higher noise level than previously. Consequently the layouts were examined very much with the view that the propelling nozzles should be at the extreme aft end of the aeroplane.

Orthodox designs with this feature tended to be tail-heavy (and very heavy overall) unless the engines themselves were separated from the nozzle and reheat sections and moved forward to about amidships, in which case the whole afterbody of the fuselage became 'hot' and practically useless for fuel and equipment. This was avoided by the adoption of the canard layout resulting in a compact powerplant installation and a relatively light airframe, helped by the substantial contribution to lift from the foreplane. Comparisons were also made, on the 'canard' layout, to assess the relative merits of fuselage or wing-mounted engines; the latter had some attractive features but was rejected as the intakes needed to be clear of the foreplane wake while an engine failure produced uncontrollable swing. Refining the design would continue.

The method of manufacture would not differ much from previous experience except for a growing trend to use parts machined from large slabs of aluminium alloy. The major portion of the fuselage would be constructed of light alloy, but the hot section, from the compressor face aft, would be largely in titanium ICI.314A alloy sheet and structural steel. The foreplane and parts of the wing leading edge were also given titanium skins. The foreplane, which had a span of 19.2ft (5.8m), area 202ft^2 (18.7m^2) and t/c 4%, had cropped tips to prevent buffet and the vertical fins on the mainplane were in fact wing tip endplates so that they would be unaffected by vortices from the foreplanes.

Much of the fuel was housed within the mainplane where the torsion box was employed as a kerosene tank; the remainder

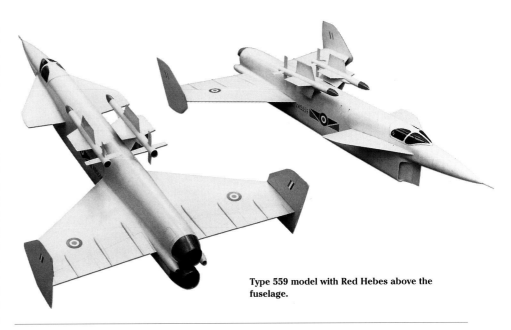

Type 559 model with Red Hebes above the fuselage.

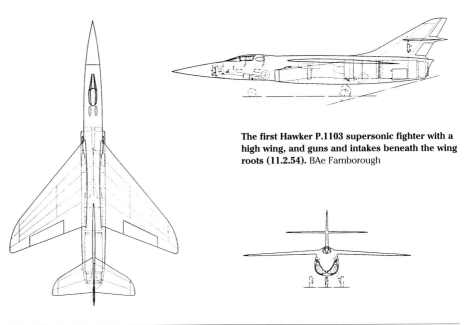

The first Hawker P.1103 supersonic fighter with a high wing, and guns and intakes beneath the wing roots (11.2.54). BAe Farnborough

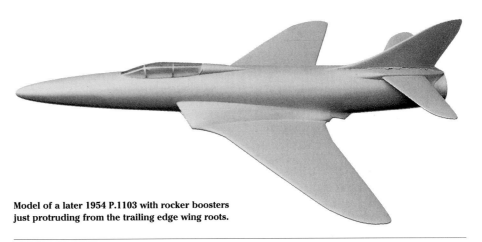

Model of a later 1954 P.1103 with rocker boosters just protruding from the trailing edge wing roots.

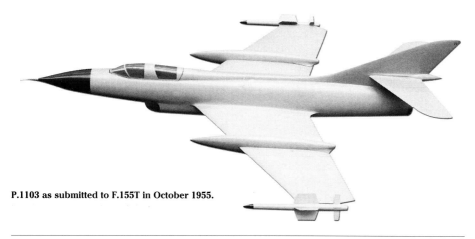

P.1103 as submitted to F.155T in October 1955.

was in the fuselage. Internal capacity was 1,870gal (8,500lit) of kerosene and 145gal (659lit) of HTP, another 519gal (2,360lit) of either available externally in a fuselage ventral tank. The two Gyron engines reheated to 1,950K were placed unusually one above the other, in part to reduce frontal area as with English Electric's Lightning, after comparison with a side-by-side format. The Gyron was selected because it appeared suitable and already existed but alternatives such as the RB.122 could be employed. The pair of Spectre Junior rockets were situated either side of the jets at wing level, this mixed powerplant ensuring that the performance requirements of the specification were met substantially, the top speed of Mach 2.5 being a structural heating limitation.

Weapon load was either two Blue Jay Mk.4 or two Red Hebe carried alternatively and unusually atop the fuselage, but Red Hebe would have given a major drag problem to the 559. Sea level rate of climb with Blue Jay was 51,500ft/min (15,697m/min), with Red Hebe 50,000ft/min (15,240m/min). Development of the fully-automatic control and guidance system was planned to occur in step-by-step stages along with development of the aeroplane, though basic control installations would be needed for first flight. It was estimated that design of the first flying shell/minimum equipment prototype would be complete in 134 weeks from date of order with design of the third (complete) prototype in 170 weeks, the corresponding first flight dates were 160 and 208 weeks from order date. The engineering staff necessary to deal with detail design and manufacture of the aeroplane would have been released from existing commitments by early 1956.

Avro 729

Avro also made some suggestions towards F.155T in a project developed from the Avro 720 rocket fighter to F.137D and fitted with a Gyron Junior engine and enlarged cockpit to accommodate the extra crewman. Little material on the project survives, it was just a private study and not tendered.

–

Following the usual procedure with all design competitions, the seven brochures were studied closely by departments and establishments specialising in a particular aspect of the requirement. Generally speaking they suggested that most companies had not yet grasped effectively the concept of a weapon system. Avro Canada was invited to comment on F.155T, particularly in relation to its CF.105 Arrow which, at the time, had just about seen off the Gloster Thin Wing Javelin. However, the Arrow was designed to meet a threat flying at 50,000ft (15,240m) and Mach 0.9 and, despite the addition of collision course weapons to deal with greater threats, in its present form it did not meet F.155T.

On 28th November 1955, the Fairey 'Small' Delta II development and Saro's P.187 were eliminated from the competition, the former because it was not designed to carry Red Hebe (but a later version received the missile), the latter was just too big, too heavy and too expensive. Three days earlier, English Electric had suggested two versions of its P.8 – a single-seater to carry the Blue Vesta AAM and a two-seater with a possible alternative semi-active collision course weapon. But the Air Staff indicated that its requirement for a radar weapon was firm and this led to a recommendation on 28th February 1956, that the P.8 and Hawker's P.1103 should also be rejected. Neither had a chance of meeting the specification, but this was not to rule them out of further consideration in a different context to OR.329/F.155T. The P.8 had been by far the best effort towards the overall weapon system, but was out of date as regards the airframe.

A full Tender Design Conference was held in Room 358, St Giles Court, Ministry of Supply, on 27th March, to discuss the four survivors.

Technical aspects were discussed first which produced the following order of merit, the top three being capable of development into capable fighters from the AI viewpoint. There was little to choose between AWA and Fairey, but the Vickers submission was markedly inferior to both whilst the DH.117 was unacceptable.

1st Equal: Armstrong Whitworth. An attractive design that generally met the performance and handling requirements. The wing engines were convenient for servicing but a possible difficulty might be the noise effect of the jet efflux on the structure, which might lead to a redesign and strengthening of the rear fuselage and tail.

1st Equal: Fairey. This had shortcomings in high altitude manoeuvrability and endurance but it was believed these could be overcome by detail redesign. Drag would be appreciably reduced through a change of afterbody shape while some weight could be saved by cutting the very high design diving speed chosen. It had good development potential and used steel and titanium to avoid possible heat problems from any future speed increase. Morien Morgan of RAE pointed out how some firms were just able to meet the requirements using light alloy but major structural changes would be necessary if any marked performance increase were to be achieved when, on the other hand, Fairey had thought it unreasonable to design an aircraft that would be halted in development due to heat problems. The firm also had its ER.103 experience to draw from and was praised for a very great achievement in producing the Delta II, an aeroplane that had flown at progressively greater speeds during development flying. This work was assumed to have given Fairey a substantial background of experience not available anywhere else.

3rd: Vickers. On performance and handling alone this project was rated above Fairey's but lateral control was complicated and there were serious doubts about the wisdom of adopting the aerodynamic unknowns of the canard layout. The weapon position was also declared unsatisfactory. (Later experience was to show mounting missiles above the wings or fuselage was very 'draggy').

4th: de Havilland. This did not meet the performance and its 5% thick wing was considered too much and very out of date for a fighter entering service in 1962, but fitting a 4% wing would increase structure weight. DH had designed primarily for carriage of Blue Vesta and installing Red Hebe, a firm Air Staff requirement, would seriously cut performance. It was a logical development of the firm's experience and family of all-weather ighters but a bad fourth technically and well below the others. The firm had made an alternative submission at the last moment (on 12th March) but it was felt this should not be seriously considered as, given the opportunity, the other firms could have used later knowledge to do likewise. Saro had, in fact, been refused permission to do this.

The firms' ability to tackle such a sophisticated weapon system, their facilities and their current and likely future workload were now examined. Armstrong Whitworth was part of the Hawker Siddeley Group who at the time was very busy with military work including the RB.156D bomber (Avro 730), Vulcan developments and the Thin Wing Javelin, giving doubts as to their capacity to take on such a large new project. In addition, AWA had a relatively small team and the wisdom of encouraging the firm to enlarge into a fully fledged design team for fighters was questioned. Research aircraft were likely to become more and more complex in the future and the present AWA set up was considered ideal for undertaking such tasks.

De Havilland had proposed that all work on the DH.110 be transferred to Christchurch should it be successful, to ensure the full facilities of the group would be available for this project. However its expanding work in missiles, particularly the Blue Streak ballistic missile, influenced the picture so it was agreed the DH.117 should not be considered further. Vickers Armstrong (Supermarine) was felt to be well able to undertake the work, but if the organisation were asked to take on the new Wallis project (which was quite likely) it would be heavily loaded and might not meet the required dates. Thus, since the Type 559 submission was technically a poor third, it was declared unsuccessful.

Fairey had few up-to-date facilities and a not very strong design team in respect of well known people. It had, however, built up a guided weapon element at Heston and part of the 'Green Cheese' team had become available after cancellation of that project. With recruitment the firm could undertake F.155T on the assumption that the Gannet would go ahead but the Rotodyne would peter out. It was considered that Fairey had now finally grasped the importance of the weapon system approach and was confident it could undertake the task with the help of Heston, so a recommendation was made to Controller Aircraft that the large Fairey project should be ordered. Attention was drawn to the striking fact that the submissions by the most experienced fighter firms showed the least probability of meeting F.155T whilst those with 'least knowledge' were the most optimistic.

In the light of cancellation of the Thin Wing Javelin and no order being placed for the CF-105 Arrow – decisions that placed greater emphasis on early Service entry for the F.155T, the Air Council agreed in April to continue wind tunnel work for about a year on both the Fairey and AW.169 to allow the situation to be placed in a clearer perspective for final selection, Fairey being the first choice with AWA a reserve. On 25th October 1956, the first model of its fighter was successfully fired by Fairey on the Larkhill test range reaching a speed between Mach 1.4 and 1.8 while in November AWA was informed that the AW.169 had been cancelled, the Fairey becoming the Air Ministry requirement.

On 4th April 1957, the Minister of Defence published his White Paper cancelling development of manned fighters which, of course, included F.155T. The period from issue of specification to Tender Conference had seen events move swiftly, but a year later no orders were forthcoming. In fact the aeronautical press reported that Fairey was informed in late 1956 that no order was likely suggesting then a change in policy. The Minister responsible, Duncan Sandys, cancelled F.155 on 29th March and Fairey's desire to see a fighter created from its so successful Delta II, died with it. Had an order been placed a new specification, F.155D, would presumably have been written around the aircraft.

There were strong opinions within the Air Staff that this was the right aeroplane to build. Wg Cdr Harold Bird-Wilson, DD.OPS (Fighter), wrote on 27th August 1956, under the title *Recommendations* that, in his view, 'if the RAF is to have an adequate fighter force for the 1960 era, then a decision must now be given to Fairey to proceed as quickly as possible into the material phase of producing an aircraft that will have the desired all-round performance to meet the threat for this period. Surely, Fairey has proved to everyone, by its Delta II, that it has the technical know-how and the engineering skill to produce the next breed of fighter for the Royal Air Force. Unless this firm is given the go-ahead immediately, it will be another case once again of *too little – too late'*.

The Fairey F.155T was the cutting edge of technology in the 1950s and at the designers was unofficially known as the Fairey Delta III. Although none of the firm's archives or any Ministry documents used the title, there is every chance that this is what the machine would have been called. At the time of cancellation, Fairey was due to test a wing mock-up for overwing air-to-air missile launchers and had also brochured an offensive version that carried a single 'special weapon' on one Red Dean pylon with a drop tank on the other.

The F.155T designs were some of the most monstrous and exciting combat aircraft ever drawn; their brute power is very evident and in most cases maximum speed was a kinetic heat structure limit, not a power limit. But one senses that, had it been built, the 'Delta III' might have flown in prototype form only because of its massive size and complexity. It would have been a very expensive aircraft to develop.

–

Not all the F.155 projects died with the White Paper as, for a short period, one of the early casualties was to move on and illustrate how much, and for how long, a project can evolve. Work on Hawker's P.1103 had begun in early 1954 as a supersonic two-seat fighter with Gyron engine reheated to 1,775K and 4% wing. Numerous layouts passed between the Project Office and Experimental Drawing Office, one (model pictured) had rocket boost and was armed with two Blue Jay. By July, Hawker had examined three different arrangements: a low wing with leading edge intakes, a mid-wing arrangement with leading edge intakes and a medium-low wing with under-fuselage scoop intake. The first pair suffered from balancing problems and insufficient fuel.

As Hawker continued with its 'new fighter', so did discussions with Rolls-Royce on future supersonic engines. On 14th October the firms agreed to continue with the RB.106 engine but with diameter increased from 37in to 41in (94 to 104cm), a version subsequently called the RB.122, and that the 'new fighter' should be single-engined with a single intake under the fuselage. In December, work encompassed a two-seat large radar version and, by year's end, another smaller variant incorporating one seat, a small radar and a Gyron Junior engine. It was decided to proceed with the larger version on 11th January 1955, when the layout was not too far off that described to F.155T, and four days later the first issue of that document made its appearance.

RRE suggested fitting a 40in (102cm) scanner in June and on 16th August de Havilland Propellers unveiled the Mk.4 development of Blue Jay. De Havilland Engines discussed the Gyron thrust rated at 25,000lb (111.1kN) and, at the end of the month, High Duty Alloys visited and agreed that light alloy manufacture would be suitable for the P.1103. This aircraft was submitted to F.155T on 5th October. Hawker continued development and briefly examined fitting American Falcon and Sidewinder AAMs in mid-January 1956 but, on 24th April came the news its Tender had been unsuccessful. However, it was decided not to stop work on P.1103 design and construction.

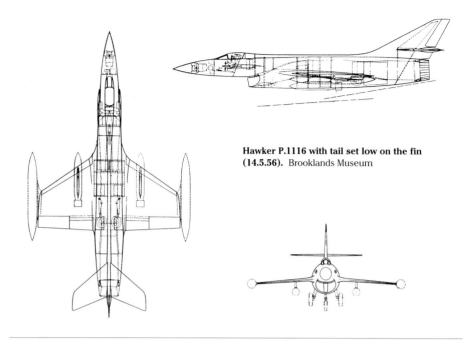

Hawker P.1116 with tail set low on the fin **(14.5.56).** Brooklands Museum

Two views of the Hawker P.1121 scale model (6.56).

phasis was placed on fighter characteristics at the expense of strike. Camm took the criticism to heart having based the P.1116 partly on Air Staff advice. He rewrote the brochure in early June after launching another design study on 28th May for a single-seat strike version designated P.1121.

Hawker P.1121

This concentrated a little more on the low-level ground attack role. It retained the P.1103's 5% thick wing rather than the P.1116's 4%; had greater sweep than P.1103 and an altitude performance slightly better than P.1116 at nearly Mach 2.3. The brochure was submitted on 12th June and the delivery dates for an imaginary 60 aircraft order, given a start date of 1st August 1956, were: prototype first flight April 1958, first delivery December 1958, 60th delivery June 1961. Air Marshal Tuttle encouraged Camm to continue with the investigation but warned of the financial squeeze following OR.329 go ahead, suggesting that the country would not be in a position to afford a specialised ground attack aircraft as well.

At the end of August, Hawker decided to press ahead with the P.1121 in its original general purpose strike fighter configuration with priority given to interceptor performance but the low altitude ground attack role a strong second.

Not everyone offered support. The Air Staff's Group Captain J F Roulston was amazed the project had been reconsidered, even for fair weather operation. He was convinced that Hawker had yet to grasp the weapon system concept and was just producing an airframe of high performance. As a weapons system the P.1121 was useless and if accepted, made the Air Staff guilty of perpetuating a method which it so roundly condemned, of looking at the airframe and equipment in isolation.

Group Captain H N Wheeler made a fuller assessment against OR.329/F.155T on 31st August. The P.1103 had been criticised for its very poor altitude performance despite having rocket motors to augment it. P.1121 had no rocket and its acceleration and climb figures were well down on OR.329's. For example, time to 55,000ft (16,764m) for P.1121 from wheels rolling was about 8 minutes when OR.329 called for take-off to 60,000ft (18,288m) in 4 minutes.

Acceleration from Mach 0.9 to 2.0 at the tropopause was 3.5 minutes, again below specified and, for the timescale 1960-1965, an armament of two Firestreaks was ineffective. The provision of a 'navigational aid' without detailed information to back it up was highly criticised.

Hawker P.1116

Sydney Camm met Sir Tom Pike, DCAS, on 3rd May to seek advice on what direction to take the project and was informed of a likely Air Staff requirement for a long range interceptor with ground attack capability. Since the OR.329 fighter was unlikely to fulfil this general purpose role, DCAS suggested that Hawker could profitably adapt the P.1103 to it. A full study began on 8th May designated P.1116 and the optimum design indicated a smaller wing of less sweepback coupled with the same basic Gyron from the F.155T work; brochures were presented on the 16th.

P.1116 had 1,360gal (6,183lit) of internal fuel plus another 500 (2,273lit) in wing tip tanks. The Air Staff felt the P.1116 was inferior to OR.329 from an intercept point of view, even without the second crew member and collision course facilities, and felt too much em-

Wheeler found it difficult to believe the aircraft could be ready by 1961 suggesting 1963 was more likely. The P.1121 was clearly inadequate as an interceptor and no further consideration should be given to it in this role.

Air Marshal Satterly, ACAS(OR), informed Hawker on 2nd October about the possibility of the P.1121 being adapted to suit the Operational Requirement now being prepared for a Canberra replacement (later OR.339). The firm was officially informed later that month that the financial situation dictated the RAF would be equipped with English Electric P.1Bs and possibly Saro 177s until 1964/65 when a new fighter to at least OR.329 requirements was expected. Any other fighter in this period not satisfying OR.329 would have very little chance of support and Hawker was told not to proceed unless there were foreign sales in mind (author's note – the P.1B Lightning lasted until 1988, the SR.177 just over another year; so much for in-depth evaluation).

Work did continue with Air Ministry advice and on 29th October Reginald Maudling, the Minister of Supply, announced to the House of Commons that the Hawker Siddeley Group was developing a new fighter as a Private Venture. Neville Spriggs, Hawker Managing Director, told the press that the project was going very well and to remember that before the War the firm built the Hurricane as a similar Private Venture which 'proved to be wise'.

Hawker was constantly pushed to offer a complete weapon system rather than a flying machine capable of being evolved into a system. Consequently, in November, a two stage interceptor was proposed; firstly with underwing Blue Jay Mk.4 (Red Top) infra-red AAMs and 'J' band AI.23 radar to be available in 1961 -62, secondly with the semi-active radar missile being investigated by Fairey's Weapons Division around OR.1131 (of a size and weight that did not unduly penalise performance), 'J' band AI.23 and, possibly, an additional 'Q' band for target illumination. S Scott-Hall, who had just become Scientific Advisor to the Air Ministry, visited Hawker on 19th December and appeared worried that he had apparently inherited an office full of highly qualified pure mathematicians with no practical experience of aircraft, and wondering if they were suitable to advise on future requirements.

On 7th January 1957, Camm visited Maudling to be politely told that the Minister could not interest himself in ordering P.1121, but an impending change of Cabinet may have accounted for his lack of interest. A full scale mock-up was completed two weeks later. The Ministry now suggested the machine could fill the proposed OR.339 strike role as a two-seat air superiority strike aircraft. The

P.1121 Air Superiority Strike Aircraft brochure was submitted in March with the Rolls Conway Co.11R favoured rather than the Gyron. Normal take-off weight was 43,700lb (19,822 kg) with 1,500gal (6,820lit) of internal fuel and another 450 (2,046) in drop tanks. The main weapon was a nuclear Target Marker Bomb and top speed was just under Mach 2.1 at the tropopause. As it was still a single-seater carrying stores externally, and had an inadequate radius of action, the P.1121 was declared as unacceptable as a strike/reconnaissance aircraft for the RAF on 30th May.

A change of Prime Minster from Sir Anthony Eden to Harold Macmillan occurred bringing a new Defence Minister, Duncan Sandys, and a cold chill throughout the British military aviation industry as the press expressed the view that the fighter was obsolete. Camm found Tuttle, DCAS, very depressed regarding the future of manned aircraft in the RAF and confirming that the Avro 730 supersonic bomber had been cancelled. The White Paper was issued on 4th April and the public press also referred to the P.1121 as a fighter that now had little hope of official backing. During July, de Havilland began running the Gyron engine behind a full scale P.1121 intake model to measure the losses under static conditions, but surging began well before full rpm (and hence thrust) was reached, a problem that was to persist. Dr Stanley Hooker of Bristol engines expressed interest in fitting the Olympus and the firm was loaned the full scale intake. A full throttle run was achieved with this combination on 8th October.

On 25th September 1957, the Hawker board agreed to continue with the P.1121 but at a much reduced rate of expenditure. Two months later the Experimental Drawing Office began an investigation into how far a two-seat P.1121 could be made to satisfy OR.339, the work being completed in a month. Design and construction work continued into April 1958 but at a slow rate, despite the preliminary high speed tunnel drag results from AWA proving very encouraging. Work fizzled out soon afterwards although the odd brochure was prepared during 1959 for possible overseas sales. The prototype was about half complete when work closed. It was to have been powered by a Gyron PS.26-6 reheated to 1,800K with a variable convergent final nozzle. The thrust limit ceiling was 58,000ft (17,678m), although the zoom ceiling was 70,000ft (21,336m). The last two-seat 'P.1121' was a development called P.1123 for a Mach 2 tactical bomber which had four-wheel main gears, very like France's Mirage IV.

One wonders why Camm persevered with the P.1121 when so little official support was forthcoming. Maybe he could see Fairey's 'Delta III' was much too big a step to take in one go and a P.1121 type was a better option, hoping perhaps it would prove the point and gain the support it deserved once it had flown. But the documents examined by the author suggest that the Air Staff and Ministry were so keen on F.155T and its requirements that they just did not like Hawker's more conservative project, despite the fact it might have proved severe competition to American

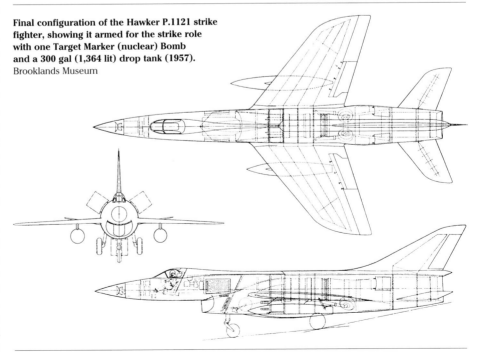

Final configuration of the Hawker P.1121 strike fighter, showing it armed for the strike role with one Target Marker (nuclear) Bomb and a 300 gal (1,364 lit) drop tank (1957).
Brooklands Museum

Phantom and Starfighter sales campaigns, particularly so in Europe where there were already many users of the Hunter. Neither the P.1121 nor Fairey's giant flew, another 'might of been' from this period of aviation history. The author wishes both could have flown at least as prototypes.

The key element of fighter design throughout the late 1950s was the perceived threat of bombers attacking at 60, 70 or 80,000ft and ever higher speeds. However, the threat of interception by high altitude fighters and/or surface-to-air missiles, backed up by ever more sophisticated radar, brought a world-wide change to low level bombing. The enemy bomber's speed proved to be rather less than predicted while at most its height became around 200ft (60m) which brought a pile of new problems but only repeated the steps taken in Britain with the Buccaneer and later TSR.2. Would the validity of a dedicated and highly expensive high altitude interceptor have been questioned before the machine entered service? After this period, the chase for ever more speed fell away and few Mach 3 projects have been proposed in Britain since the early 1960s.

Mach 2 Interceptors to Specification F.155T – Estimated Data

Project	Span ft (m)	Length ft (m)	Wing Area ft² (m²)	t/c %	All-Up-Weight lb (kg)	Powerplant Thrust lb (kN)	Max Speed / Height mph (km/h) / ft (m)	Armament
Armstrong Whitworth AW.169	51.67 (15.7)	84.0 (25.6)	680 (63)	4	53,520 (24,276) Red Dean, 54,000 (24,494) DH passive AAM	4 x Gyron Jnr. PS.53 + 1 x Spectre rocket 15,000 (66.7)	Mach 2.0+ at height	2 x Red Dean or 2 x de Havilland passive weapons
de Havilland DH.117	38.0 (11.6)	66.8 (20.3)	450 (41.8)	5	54,775 (24,845)	2 x Gyron Junior (dev) 12,000 (53.3) + 1 x Spectre Spe.5 rocket 10,000 (44.4)	Mach 2.35 at height	2 x Blue Jay Mk.4
English Electric P.8	38.36 (11.7)	50.4 (15.3)	471 (43.8)	5.3 root 2.4 tip	31,768 (14,409)	2 x RB.126 13,400 (59.6)	Mach 2.0-2.5 at height	2 Blue Jay Mk.4 or 2 packs 24 x 2in RP
Fairey Delta II derivative	37.6 (11.4)	56.25 (17.1)	600 (55.7)	4	30,100 (13,653)	1 x Gyron + 2 x Spectre	Mach 2.5 at height	2 x Blue Jay Mk.4
Fairey 'Delta III'	46.8 (14.2)	74.3 (22.6)	1,100 (102)	4	BJ: 48,000 (21,772) RD: 50,460 (22,888)	2 x RB.122 + 2 x Spectre Junior	Mach 2.27 at 36,000 (10,973)	2 x Blue Jay Mk.4 or 2 x Red Dean
Hawker P.1103	39.0 (11.9)	63.0 (19.2)	500 (46.4)	5 root 3.5 tip	41,850 (18,983)	1 x Gyron 25,000 (111.1) + 2 x booster rockets 2,000 (8.9)	Mach 2.0 at height	2 x Blue Jay Mk.4 or 2 x Red Hebe
Saro P.187	51.6 (15.7)	83.5 (25.4)	870 (80.8)	5	97,000 (43,999)	2 x Gyron PS.52 25,000 (111.1), 35,000 (155.6) reheat + 4 x Spectre rockets 10,000 (44.4)	Mach 2.5 at height	2 x Blue Jay Mk.4 and 2 x Red Dean
Vickers (Supermarine) Type 559	42.0 (12.8)	68.25 (20.8)	615 (57.1)	4	62,190 (28,209) Red Hebe	2 x Gyron PS.26/1 20,000 (88.9), 27,000 (120) reheat + 4 x Spectre Junior 5,000 (22.2)	Mach 2.5 at height	2 x Blue Jay Mk.4 or 2 x Red Hebe

Hawker P.1121 Evolution

P.1103 (First drawing 11.2.54)	37.0 (11.3)	62.0 (18.9)	470 (43.7)	?	?	1 x Gyron	Supersonic	2 x 30mm Aden + AAMs
P.1103 (to F.155T)	39.0 (11.9)	63.0 (19.2)	500 (46.4)	5	41,850 (18,983)	1 x Gyron + 2 x Booster rockets	Mach 2.0	2 x Blue Jay Mk.4 or 2 x Red Hebe
P.1116	32.0 (9.8)	63.4 (19.3)	422 (39.2)	4	?	1 x Gyron 25,000 (111.1)	Mach 2	2 x 30mm Aden + bombs or AAMs
P.1121 (Prototype - fighter role)	37.0 (11.3)	69.1 (21.1) (with probe)	474 (44.1)	5.1 root 3.8 tip	42,000 (19,051)	1 x Gyron PS.26/6 17,400 (77.3), 23,800 (105.8) reheat	Mach 1.3 at sea level, Mach 2.35 at 36,000 (10,973) (design limit)	2 x Red Top + 50 x 2in (5cm) RP or 2 x 30mm Aden (prototype unarmed)

Chapter Nine

First Steps to Tornado

Prototype of the Panavia Tornado Air Defence Variant. From a British point of view, this aircraft can be considered as the final word in variable geometry.

The First Fighters with Variable Sweepback: 1948 to 1952

On 7th February 1948, General Aircraft Ltd submitted what was probably the first ever British proposal for a manned supersonic variable sweep aircraft. GAL was working in conjunction with Professor G T R Hill who had been the main inspiration behind the famous pre-war Westland Pterodactyl series of experimental prototypes and fighters and this project was based on his ideas. Hill was seconded to the Air Ministry in 1939 and later the Ministry of Aircraft Production, but his interest and inventiveness in aircraft wing design continued alongside studies into supersonic flight. After the war he became a consultant to Short Brothers where he conceived the 'aero-isoclinic' wing and, for the period 1947 to 1950, to General Aircraft.

General Aircraft 'Transformable Delta' Supersonic Aircraft

This landmark and unsolicited project from GAL was submitted to PDSR(A) as a research aircraft. Of basic appearance, the machine was designed with speed in mind. The chief objective was not only to produce a wing layout with drag reduced sufficiently to allow flight well into the sonic range, but to combine the differing needs of low and high speed flight in one airframe. Main and subsidiary wings were mounted on the fuselage in such a way that the main wing (hinged at the root) swung back to form a continuous lifting surface of delta shape. When spread, the main surface was separated from the subsidiary to become essentially a conventional straight-wing with its own control surfaces, whilst the subsidiary became the tail. When swept, the main wing ailerons were locked and inoperative, lateral control now coming from deflectable surfaces at the wingtips.

At no point did any part of the wing protrude into the fuselage.

The fuselage was circular along its full length, excepting the single-seat nose cockpit built as a jettisonable capsule. The machine had no undercarriage, instead utilising a skid. Fuel was transferred fore and aft to reduce centre of pressure/centre of gravity movement effects and give adequate longitudinal trim and stability. A later modified proposal dated 23rd June swept the trailing edge 16.5° and the fully swept leading edge 66.5° and was expected to raise top speed to Mach 1.38 at 36,000ft (11,000m) by reducing wave drag. GAL stated its proposals were for research only but the solution was considered a stepping stone towards the realisation of a potential

Professor Hill's General Aircraft 'Transformable Delta' showing both 'High Speed Configuration' (swept) and 'Low Speed Configuration' (7.2.48). BAe

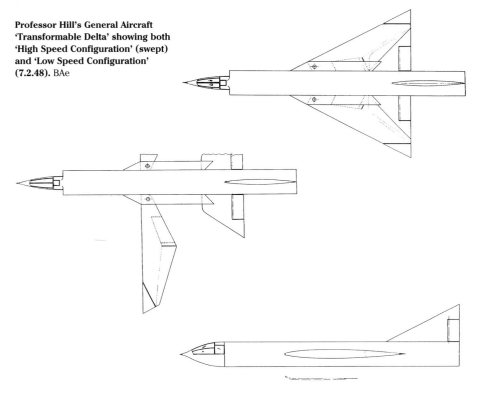

aeroplane for operational use by normal pilots (which presumably meant Service pilots). These initial projects received severe criticism from PDSR(A) and was disliked by H F Vessey, AD/ARD, who felt the performance figures were optimistic. Hill eventually patented his 'Transformable Delta'.

Blackburn and General Transonic Aircraft
Another proposal followed in February 1949. GAL had now become part of Blackburn and General Aircraft (BGA) and was effectively under the full control of Blackburn. This layout looked more conventional than the earlier rather crude deltas and BGA felt a practical solution to the mechanical problem of folding and spreading wings in flight was perfectly feasible. In its new form, the design was closely related to the requirements sent to the company by PDSR(A) on 8th October 1948 for a Transonic Aircraft Design Study (presumably under the programme examined in Chapter 6) but still attempted to deal with the need for a small span for very high speeds and a large span for the much lower speeds at take-off and landing.

Several designs aimed at reaching and passing sonic speed and incorporating a delta wing were currently under development, but all suffered from the compromise in shape forced by the conflicting needs of high and slow speed. In order to reach the highest possible speed, wings with a high degree of sweepback appeared to be advantageous but

they still had to have reasonable handling qualities at low speeds. Pronounced sweepback necessarily involved a small span and low aspect ratio, factors associated with low maximum lift, rapidly increasing induced drag with increase in lift, and poor stability at the higher incidences needed for landing. As a result, landing speeds were being pushed up to dangerously high values with serious instability encountered at some stage on the landing approach. Sweepback that was adjustable in flight appeared to BGA to solve nearly all these stubborn aerodynamic problems.

BGA explained the study's prime objective was to show such an approach was worthy of trial. Detailed examination of the folding problem indicated it was not as difficult as first thought and the weight penalty incurred was small when measured against the aerodynamic gains from using two different planforms. The problem of the movement of centre of pressure and, therefore, of centre of gravity when folding the wings had been overcome quite simply by putting some of the fuel in the wings. The wing fuel weight was thus available to give the required centre of gravity movement during the folding and unfolding operations. The fuel was not used until after the wings had been unfolded in readiness for descent and landing, at the end of the high speed flight sequence.

An all-moving V-tail sat on the top of a fixed fin, directional control being provided by

differential movement of the two halves of the tailplane. Power was supplied by a Sapphire reheated to 1,800K, fed by side intakes which could be opened to provide more air during low speed flight. Mach 1.033, 683mph (1,099 km/h) was expected at 36,000ft (10,973 m) on dry power only. The forward fuselage, carrying pilot, instruments and armament (two 30mm cannon below the cockpit floor) could be jettisoned in an emergency.

Bodyside wing thickness was 9.6%; at the tip t/c was 8.6% spread, 6% swept. The wing planform and aerofoil sections were selected purely for the high-speed condition. For low speed flight the wing swung forward through a 40° angle about a hinge at the root, the change producing a fairly conventional low speed aerofoil section. On the low-speed wing trailing edge large chord split flaps extended from the fuselage side to the inboard end of the ailerons which in high speed flight were covered by skirts fairing the wing roots into the fuselage. As before, unfolding the wings for low speed avoided the tip-stalling of the swept version at larger angles of incidence. The aircraft had a tricycle undercarriage.

An independent assessment by RAE, dated 28th April 1949, expressed favour towards the lower landing speed achieved with the wing forward. However, it was still unhappy and felt the firm had under-estimated the weight problems of variable sweepback, nor had it given details of synchronising the wing motion. Despite this, overall criticism had moderated and official interest in the work began to grow.

After discussions at MoS on 2nd May BGA revised the layout to improve performance at both ends of the speed range. Issue 2 of the project followed in January 1950 (drawing dated October 1949) and now generally conformed to Specification E.16/49 (presumably used as a working limit). A Sapphire Sa.2 was chosen because of its more advanced stage of development and all-moving tip ailerons were introduced instead of Issue 1's conventional fittings which came into action in the high speed configuration. They gave an appreciable weight saving (the feature was similar to Hill's 'aero-isoclinic' wing developed a few years later). The cannon had moved to the wing roots and mean thickness was cut to 5.58%. BGA suggested that, though primarily for research, 'the time may not be too distant when this type of aircraft is in everyday use' and stressed how earlier successful mechanical changes of aerodynamic shape aimed at the problems of speed range included high lift flaps, variable pitch propellers and retractable undercarriages.

Blackburn and General 'Mk.3' projects

In June 1950, BGA advanced its ideas in two new layouts. The first had a Sapphire reheated to 1,500K and moved the wing up the fuselage with the mechanism inside the body following comments from E T Jones (below). The 'skirt' and faired wing roots were dispensed with and variable sweep was accomplished using a translating mechanism with flip-up/flip-down fairings at the bodyside. The fixed inner wing 'skirt' extending from the fuselage side and covering the wing pivot had provoked the most criticism and BGA acknowledged it involved a most difficult piece of detail design, but felt it was solvable. However, the firm's latest efforts had been directed towards eliminating the 'skirt' by a new system of hinging the wing to the body; here the single engine high wing machine partially suppressed the 'skirt', the mid-wing twin completely. BGA could see no possibility of deleting the 'skirt' from the earlier project.

All the previous brochures had a single engine but recent independent research by the Advanced Fighter Project Group and other bodies, and official Specifications, appeared to favour, for aspects of safety and performance, multiple powerplants. Hence a twin engine machine was offered which BGA recommended most strongly, duplicating the engines raising maximum Mach number from 1.13 to 1.29 at 36,090ft (11,000m) and 1,500K reheat.

The second aircraft had two Sapphires placed one above the other plus a butterfly tail fitted on top of a short vertical stub fin. This machine exhibited rare features in having two sets of intakes, each feeding its own engine, and jet pipes that joined a single orifice. The 'ear' intakes just behind the cockpit fed the top Sapphire, while identical intakes beneath the wing root supplied air to the more rearward lower engine. These aircraft shared identical wings and sweep range and, in his book *From Spitfire to Eurofighter*, Roy Boot stated these wings were 'clouded with uncertainty' because a lack of drag rise knowledge meant the predicted maximum speed might fall anywhere between Mach 1.2 and 2.0. Anything close to the lower figure nullified the value of the variable sweep.

–

Meanwhile, an astonishing variable sweep supersonic fighter appeared in 1949 from L E Baynes of Allan Muntz Ltd, Heston. This embraced an aeroplane using variable sweep wings integrated with variable sweep horizontal and vertical tail surfaces to overcome pitch moment changes, but also incorporating variable wing incidence, variable dihedral and differential wing sweep. It employed variable sweep for both lateral and

longitudinal control, replacing conventional ailerons. The former was effected by a differential change in wing sweep such as to cause an increase in span of one wing with a decrease in span on the opposite wing. This 'all-swinging, all-dancing' project with its highly complex mechanisms would surely have been impossible to develop and produce successfully using the technology of the time. It would be a handful for today's fly-by-wire systems. The project was discussed at MoS in January 1950, but much criticised. No action was taken as the firm could not be entrusted with the design and construction of such an advanced aeroplane.

From a Ministry point of view, Spring 1950 saw something of a coming together for the assortment of variable geometry projects that had appeared. The BGA ideas were never likely to be built, but the variety of studies now underway stimulated heavy discussion into the benefits of swing wings.

On 1st May, E T Jones PDSR(A), wrote to RAE explaining that the problems associated with variable sweep were many but he wondered if they were correct in not having a research aircraft underway with provision to vary the angle of sweep in flight. He listed the weaknesses of the four proposals received so far:

1: The Barnes Wallis projects had many novelties in addition to variable wing sweep and the whole concept might fail because of these novelties, not because of the wing sweep facility itself (author's note: Barnes Wallis' work at Vickers did not cover fighter projects).

2: MoS was not keen to support the Baynes project, partly because it duplicated the Wallis ideas.

3 The BGA layout was a clumsy design in that the stub wings might well obscure the otherwise good features of variable sweep.

4 The slow speed version of the English Electric (Short S.B.5) was rather outside the field as the wings would be fixed in flight, though changeable in sweep on the ground.

Jones felt there was a tendency to sacrifice adequate lateral control and stability when seeking high speeds. It was acknowledged that present variable sweep mechanisms implied extra weight, complication and probably expense, but Jones felt they should have a single research job for changing sweep in flight from, say, 20 to 60 degrees, with no other built-in novelty. The sweep mechanism should be entirely enclosed in the body, a necessary requirement despite needing a wider fuselage. No doubt, arguments would be forthcoming that the body of such an aircraft would be full of mechanism, but Jones countered by saying while this initially may be true, future development might reduce the problem.

Previous mechanical and structural changes such as the retractable undercarriage, constant speed propeller and landing flap had shown that should a worthwhile aerodynamic advantage accrue, ingenuity of design would eventually solve the structure bulk and weight problem. Jones pondered if the answer might lie with the delta wing, but that too was still somewhat in the prophetic stage. Two months earlier he had suggested to Professor Hill and Mr Crocombe that he would like their project more if the wing sweep

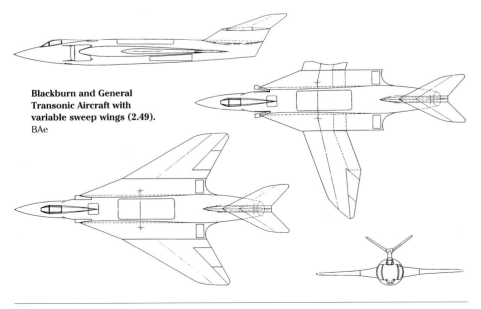

Blackburn and General Transonic Aircraft with variable sweep wings (2.49).
BAe

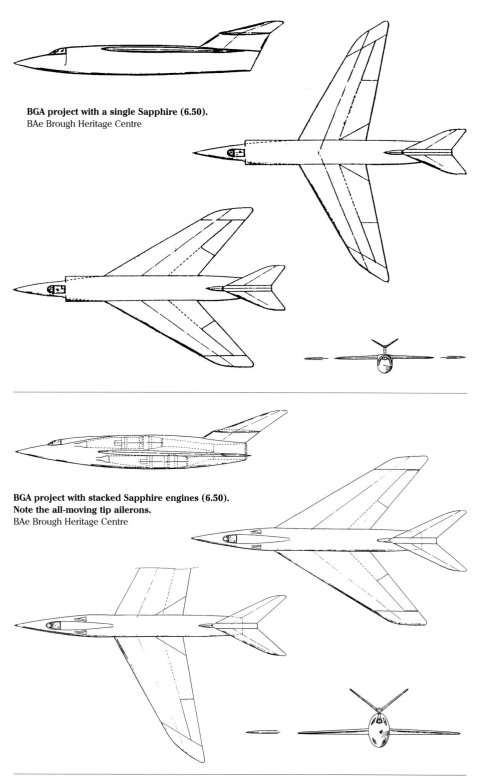

BGA project with a single Sapphire (6.50).
BAe Brough Heritage Centre

**BGA project with stacked Sapphire engines (6.50).
Note the all-moving tip ailerons.**
BAe Brough Heritage Centre

A meeting at RAE on 23rd May reported that work using variation in sweep as the method of control, as proposed by Vickers-Armstrong, was proceeding. Two other design studies submitted by Allan Muntz and Blackburn and General were somewhat less radical in conception, but were still so revolutionary that the firm's limited resources and experience in modern design led to doubts about their ability to bring them to fruition. Also there were severe technical criticisms of each submission. Thus, it was proposed to submit to wider tender a requirement for a design study on a variable sweep aircraft, hopefully to include a Mach 1.3 capability.

The choice looked set for sweepback at two positions, 25 and 60°, with change in sweep possible in flight up to speeds of 290mph (465 km/h). Considerable emphasis was placed on the necessity to tie the design study to an operational type and it was agreed that Specification F.23/49 would probably be the most satisfactory. Discussion also centred on firms suitable for doing the work and all present considered Vickers (Supermarine) to be the best firm with design capacity available. Bristol and Saunders-Roe also produced good structural work but Gloster, while short of project work, had few draughtsmen available.

Preparation of a draft requirement began in autumn 1950, the document to be broadly similar to F.23/49 but with variable sweep and no undercarriage. In December, Allan Muntz was told it could not expect Ministry backing for the Baynes design. In early January 1951 firms considered for the work included BGA, Boulton Paul and Armstrong Whitworth (who were short of work and often produced novel ideas). RAE suggested that a first class fighter firm should be consulted, but was told that Hawker, de Havilland and Vickers (Supermarine) were too busy.

ER.110T

Issued on 9th February 1951, this called for a *Supersonic Fighter with Variable Sweep Wings*. Only two positions were required; 25° sweep for take-off and landing, 60° for high speed flight. It was desired to have no speed limit for changing between the two positions, but realised this may be impractical and 290mph was made the lowest acceptable speed limit for sweep changes. The hinge and wing actuating system had to be outlined in detail so that its functioning, and influence on the rest of the aircraft's design, could be assessed; a small scale model was requested. Maximum level speed was not to be less than Mach 1.2 at 45,000ft (13,716m) with power supplied by either two Avon or Sapphire engines reheated to 1,500K. The aircraft had to be a single

mechanism was inside the body. Crocombe was also working at Feltham, but left the company to join Boulton Paul when the variable sweep work was moved to Brough. His efforts to continue in this area was one reason for Boulton Paul submitting to ER.110T.

The Aero Department at RAE doubted whether an aircraft with 60° sweepback was an overall practical proposition (quoting the

English Electric P.1's 58.5°). E L Ripley reported consideration of the idea for a variable sweep wing having two positions, say 30 and 60°. The mechanical and structural problems were discussed and it was realised that extensive development work was needed on the joint and associated local structure before a complete aircraft could go ahead, but it was recommended that work should start.

eater and fitted with a pair of 30mm guns. An undercarriageless design was acceptable provided adequate provision was made for take-off (catapulting to be considered) and landing on a carpet.

Armstrong Whitworth, Blackburn, Boulton Paul and Bristol plus one from de Havilland, English Electric, Hawker and Supermarine were to be invited to tender. In the event, Saunders-Roe also became involved. However, the list was poor in respect of fighter experience and PDSR(A) was emphatic that it was absolutely essential that one major fighter firm of the four listed should be included, despite the existing pressure on their capacity. Gloster was unsuitable on grounds of slowness. A 'mock-up' contract (the second stage in the programme) would only be placed with one or two firms selected from the design studies. Of the five companies to submit, several requested extensions to the tendering period and a further two months were granted. Blackburn for example found difficulty in keeping down weight, while at the same time was also preparing its B.89 project to N.114T.

Armstrong Whitworth AW.59

AWA identified two problems. Firstly, it believed the design of an equipped aeroplane capable of supersonic speed in level flight had yet to be solved without the aid of rockets. The second was a means of varying wing sweep with all the mechanical engineering difficulties involved in rotating a surface carrying heavy loads, which must at all times remain rigid in spite of the restricted depth of any pivot placed within the wing. To help solve the first, minimum frontal area was a primary objective and to reduce this, engine choice was a pair of fuselage mounted Sapphires placed in tandem and fed by a common frontal intake. AWA explained this gave an area comparable to that of one engine plus one intake, although additional area might be required to house the sweepback mechanism and undercarriage (if fitted). The frontal intake was preferred to a side intake for it offered a less uncertain performance at supersonic speeds, in spite of the considerable duct length required to supply air to the rear engine.

It was felt a logical step for variable sweep aeroplanes to omit the undercarriage and rely on catapult take-offs and mat landings. Housing a suitable undercarriage in a thin rotating wing was a difficult and perhaps impossible problem. The low sweep configuration would reduce both approach speed and corresponding incidence compared to a highly swept fixed wing, justifying the undercarriage's omission. It therefore followed that

the ability to dispense with the undercarriage was a major plus point for variable sweep, but a temporary non-retractable undercarriage would, however, be fitted for early flight tests. Fully duplicated power controls were applied to all surfaces and an all-moving tail sited halfway up the fin. There was no elevator. AWA was confident the required performance could be obtained using one engine with reheat and one without. The front Sapphire lacked reheat and used a bifurcated jet with inclined pipes emerging from the fuselage sides, the rear was reheated to 1,500K. Total fuel load was 700gal (3,182lit) and the two 30mm cannon with radar ranging were mounted in the upper nose.

To solve the second problem, varying sweep mechanically in a manner dictated by the aerodynamic requirements, AWA identified alternative approaches. One mounted the wings on a carriage inside the fuselage so that the fore and aft position changed whilst the wings varied their sweep angle about pivots within the fuselage sides (as adopted on the Bell X-5). This had the advantage that position could vary for a given sweep angle, hence maintaining trim during wing movement without relying on accurate predictions. This system did, however, give a number of problems, not least the extra volume required in the fuselage. The second and chosen method was to rotate the wing about a point well out from the fuselage. AWA's aim was to have no change of trim and static stability with a change of sweep at constant subsonic speed and they found the best rotation point to be about one third of a semi-span from the centre line of the aircraft.

A simple pivot strong enough to take the applied loads would not fit inside the wing so a track was provided in the form of a circular arc, the arc centre being at the desired centre of rotation. The moving parts of the track were attached to the wing, the outer parts

fixed to the fuselage and both were totally inside the fuselage. The system was so designed that wing motion would cease should extra loads be applied from gusts or manoeuvring, resuming when the load returned to more normal proportions. The limitations for changing sweep were given as 2g and Mach 0.9 at any height. In AWA's view the variable sweep aircraft was clearly a worthwhile step, although success was thought to depend on overcoming the mechanical difficulties, particularly with regard to rigidity.

Blackburn B.90

Since its E.16/49 work, BGA had moved its variable sweep personnel to Brough. The resultant B.90 had a chunkier appearance than its predecessors, principally through stacking the two Sapphire Sa.4s one above the other; both had afterburners. 1,150gal (5,228lit) of fuel could be carried and the Adens were fitted to the sides of the nose intake, the drawing shows no undercarriage. Spar type construction was used throughout the wing with variable sweeping effected by a system of links and guides. Ailerons and flaps were fitted although the latter became inoperable when the wings were in the maximum sweep position; a gap around the spread wing was to be closed using special doors. Sweep variation while flying was limited to 1.25g and Mach 0.8 and 518mph (834km/h).

Boulton Paul P.121

BP employed a different engine layout with a pair of reheated Avon RA.8 engines buried side-by-side in the fuselage. Fitted to the intake centre body was a pitot probe reminiscent of the firm's late version P.111a delta research aircraft VT935, first flown on 2nd July 1953. Total fuel load was 750gal (3,410lit) but only a single Aden was aboard mounted beneath the cockpit. Spar construction was used in the wing but the mechanism used a

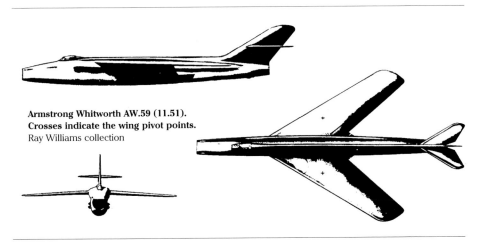

Armstrong Whitworth AW.59 (11.51).
Crosses indicate the wing pivot points.
Ray Williams collection

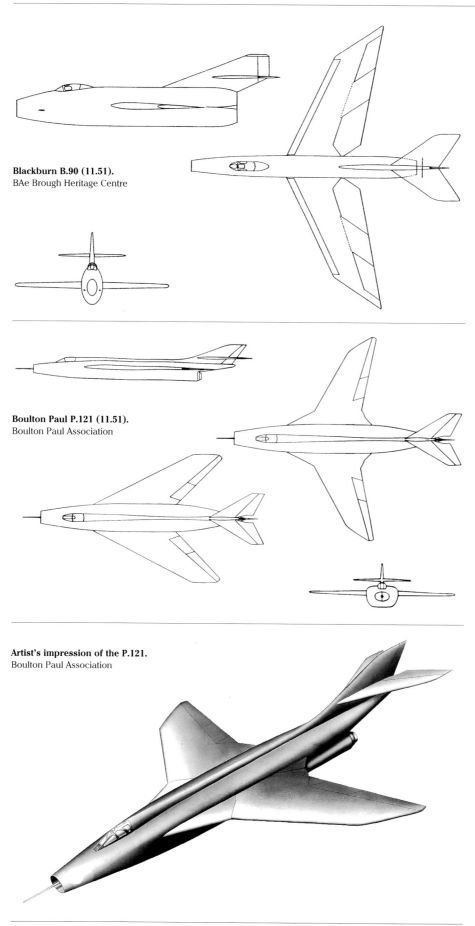

Blackburn B.90 (11.51).
BAe Brough Heritage Centre

Boulton Paul P.121 (11.51).
Boulton Paul Association

Artist's impression of the P.121.
Boulton Paul Association

single pivot with roller bearings. When th
wings were fully spread, the wing root ga
was filled by inflating a rubber tube necess
tating a pneumatic system in addition to th
hydraulics. Ailerons and flaps were provided
The only limitation to in-flight sweep variatio
was a speed of 575mph (927km/h). A nea
identical fixed wing P.121 was also offered b
BP with 64° sweep.

Bristol Type 183

On the side of the main D-section intakes c
this aircraft were supplementary auxiliary in
takes for use in subsonic running, but these
were closed during supersonic flight. It wa
felt the required performance could b
achieved without the use of reheat but fittin
reheat pipes was possible without changes t
the basic design, but then the fuel load c
430gal (1,955lit) would be a limiting factor.

No undercarriage was provided due to
lack of space, launching being by catapult o
from a trolley with landing on a mat. Existin
catapults were capable of launching the Typ
183 and Bristol expected that the mat landin
technique would be suitably developed i
time for flight test.

The extreme nose contained a scanner fo
the ARI.5820 radar ranging; immediately be
hind in the lower fuselage were the tw
30mm cannon. Two specified items in the
cockpit, an ejector seat and the GGS Mk.
gunsight, dictated a canopy of normal siz
which constituted a considerable drag iten
but could not be avoided.

Tailplane incidence was adjustable throug
10° for trimming purposes and the rudder and
plain flap elevator were power operated. The
two spar wing pivoted just inside the body a
approximately 0.52 chord and had power op
erated ailerons and single slotted flaps, the
latter for use in the swept forward position
There was a 3g limit for varying sweep i
flight. Each wing was mounted separately a
three points, one near the body side acting a
the pivot point and two others which move
around circular arc tracks. Operation was b
a hydraulic jack working a toggle mechanisr
so that the two wings moved together. All the
structure and operating mechanism was lo
cated in the top 2ft (0.61m) of fuselage depth
the space below filled by intakes and fue
tanks.

To complete its proposal, Bristol advanced
the argument that a 3% thick fixed delta win
aircraft without a tail would be better in alti
tude performance and approximately equa
in landing to the variable sweep machine
This became a parallel project study at Bristo
under Type 184 and displayed a marked fam
ily likeness to the 183.

British Secret Projects: Jet Fighters

Saunders-Roe P.149

Several schemes were studied by Saro before selection of a side-by-side engine format with two afterburning RA.12 Avons. An ARI.5820 radar ranging scanner was housed in the intake centrebody and two Adens mounted in the lower fuselage beneath the cockpit. Fuel capacity was 820gal (3,728lit). Saro's design, like Bristol's, utilised a box beam wing structure with heavy root ribs to carry the loads through a hinge. The wing sat on and moved along the top of the fuselage with movement actuated by hydraulic rams. The main pivot and rear pintles were linked together as a 'triangle' which moved forward 3ft (0.91m) as the wings switched from the 25 to 60° limits. A hinged fairing behind the cockpit enclosed the wing roots when swept back, but a gap appeared between this and the wing in the spread position. Movement in flight was limited to speeds below Mach 0.9 and 600mph (965km/h).

–

All submissions went to RAE for two departments, Structures and Mechanical Engineering (ME), to make a thorough assessment and give their opinions. From the structural viewpoint the most important feature of each design was the solution adopted for providing adequate strength and stiffness in the area required to accommodate the wing sweep mechanism. A single calculation applied a common factor to all five projects. On each design the total weight of the variable sweep equipment, wing and fuselage structure was compared to an equivalent aircraft with 60° sweep fixed wings, but keeping the dimensions unchanged. The weight increase or 'penalty' for having movable wings was then calculated as a percentage of that design's all-up-weight. The results were AWA 5.3%; Blackburn 10.0%; BP 11.9%; Bristol 7.3% and Saro 7.6% – the two companies using spar type construction showing the largest increase.

Hydraulically operated sweep mechanisms were adopted in all schemes, but ME reported on 11th February 1952, that estimates for the power required for sweep changing were vague and variable. The effects of wing flutter appeared to need careful investigation and ME advised that a full scale test rig of the wing sweep mechanism with representative loading should be set up.

It was found difficult to assess an order of merit, but judged on the basis of simplicity, expected reliability, maintenance, bulk and weight, the list was: 1st Bristol; 2nd Boulton Paul; 3rd Saro; 4th Blackburn & General; 5th Armstrong Whitworth.

RAE gave its overall impressions in a letter to ADARD(Res) on 22nd February. The weight

penalty for providing variable sweep was higher than envisaged at the time ER.110T was issued. Choosing from the five designs could only be made on engineering grounds, but no single design satisfied both structural and mechanical interests.

A meeting chaired by DMARD, A E Woodward Nutt, was held at MoS on 26th February to discuss the merits of the design studies and

to advise whether it was worthwhile proceeding with the project. The original plan had been to ask the firm producing the best proposal to make a full scale reproduction of the mechanism and wing structure, correct in detail for both size and strength, on which testing would be undertaken. If the results were satisfactory, an aircraft incorporating variable sweep would follow.

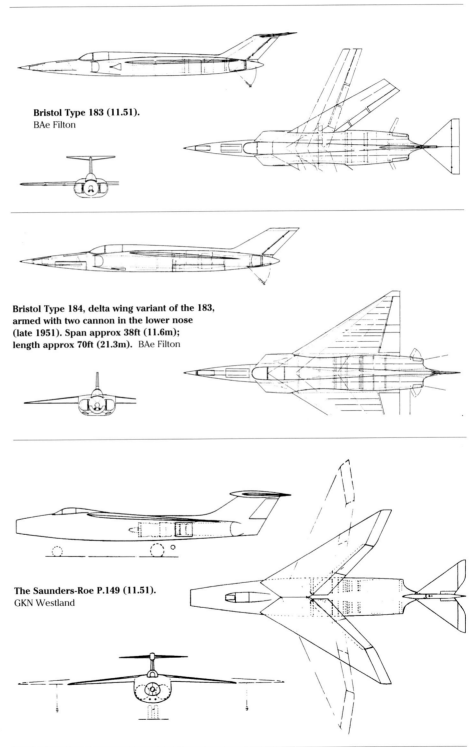

Bristol Type 183 (11.51).
BAe Filton

Bristol Type 184, delta wing variant of the 183, armed with two cannon in the lower nose (late 1951). Span approx 38ft (11.6m); length approx 70ft (21.3m). BAe Filton

The Saunders-Roe P.149 (11.51).
GKN Westland

Artist's impression of Saro's P.149. GKN Westland

Woodward Nutt commented that variable sweep-back work was underway in America where Bell's X-5 research machine and Grumman XF10F-1 Jaguar had been produced.

Variable sweep had been advocated because the low speed behaviour of highly swept supersonic aircraft was considered to be marginal and might prove to be unacceptable to the Services. Interest was linked with an assumed 4% weight penalty compared to fixed wing aeroplanes, the figure being derived from early work on the subject by Blackburn and General. The studies however, had shown an average of around 8%. It was expressed that an 8% penalty gave little favour to variable sweep high altitude fighters as called for in the Specification, but showed more benefit to the higher wing loadings generated from operation at moderate altitudes. Hence, the case for variable wing sweep was stronger for low and medium altitude aircraft than for higher altitudes and investigations were to move in this direction.

After reaching these conclusions it had not been thought necessary to carry out detailed aerodynamic analyses of the design studies submitted. Nevertheless some important points were raised. The Blackburn and Bristol designs had wing surface moving into or out of a large fuselage, whereas the Armstrong Whitworth and Boulton Paul projects involved parts of the wing moving relative to each other outside the fuselage which created difficult joints near the leading edge. It was agreed the latter was a severe disadvantage for high speed flight. An advantage from Blackburn and Saro was a reduced wing loading on landing.

Saro's design was thought to be the least meritorious as neither its structural nor mechanical engineering features were particularly good. The unfaired gap between the wing roots would give bad airflow during wing movement. Good aerodynamic features and the best structural work came from AWA, but its project was deemed to have the weakest mechanics. Boulton Paul's P.121 was good mechanically but heavy structurally. Bristol's performance estimate was thought to be very optimistic (remembering the machine had no afterburning) while other aspects were generally satisfactory without being outstanding. Blackburn's scheme was heavy and complex but quite good aerodynamically. The meeting felt unable to place the proposals in order of merit, neither did it consider any proposal was good enough to warrant a recommendation to proceed to a full scale aircraft.

Woodward Nutt pointed out that an average aircraft's payload was only 10% of its all-up-weight, so a penalty of 8% for variable sweep fittings would seriously reduce useful load. The extra weight also destroyed much of the advantage from a reduced landing speed. Since the variable sweep concept appeared less promising than originally hoped, a reassessment of the whole policy was needed with a thorough examination of the possible advantages for such aeroplanes, including lower level roles, before placing contracts with industry. H F Vessey added that the Air Staff was expressing concern because the F.23/49 (English Electric P.1) was unsuited for use in the ground attack role, so there might be a need here. A request for results of

American tests on these types of aircraft, particularly the Grumman machine, was to b made in order to avoid wasted effort in thi country. Information was received in Marc 1952 of the preliminary flights of the Bell X-5

It had been proposed that all firms migh examine each others models together t stimulate criss-crossing of thought. All agree except Blackburn who had been working o the concept for several years, mostly at i own expense, and believed it had made a least as much, if not more, progress than an other firm. Thus, the idea was rejected. I September 1952 the RAE prepared Technica Memorandum Aero 299, *The Application c Variable Sweep Wings to the Low Altitud Supersonic Fighter* after a short investigatior It reported that such fighters could have a use ful performance and there was a *prima faci* case for the inclusion of variable sweep. Bu in November, a final decision was taken nc to proceed with variable sweep aeroplane because of their structural complications, un less a subsequent Operational Requiremer forced an introduction of the feature.

These early and very raw attempts to de sign a swing wing aeroplane show severa British companies taking their first tentativ steps along a new and difficult road whicl eventually took over 20 years to produce in service hardware in the form of Tornado. The concept of varying sweep angle to satisfy the conflicting requirements created by a larg speed range seems simple enough, but a these studies have shown, there are acut mechanical problems. The hinge must be near or at the root of the wing, the poin where structural loads and bending momer are most severe. The Blackburn and Genera Transonic Aircraft looked a nice design over all but too big and heavy for a one-off re search aircraft. The problem with probably al early variable sweep designs was that the centre of pressure/centre of gravity move ments were difficult to balance when chang ing the sweep angle at transonic speeds Many had the wing pivot moving back anc forth on tracks as the sweep altered.

Bob Fairclough, of the North West Heritage Group, Warton, explains that, in essence variable geometry is a waste of time if the air craft is too small, as the extra weight nullifie the benefits of the movable wing. The Tornade was arguably as small as one could go depen ding on the engine and mechanism detail. Ir flight the biggest loads occur at the wing root nd to put in heavy features such as a swing wing mechanism concentrates these loads at the pivot point. Such a load concentration in aircraft is bad news and the worst feature that could be introduced. Pushing the pivot point out along the wing helps by reducing bending moment and taking out the fuselage slot, aspects which ease the mechanical, aerodynamic and structural problems.

Many years after ER.110T there was still world-wide debate about the choice of pivot position. Some problems needed solving before a satisfactory solution was obtained on Tornado; BAC's initial proposal in 1969 incorporated an inboard pivot and translating wing. Another vital mechanical problem on variable sweep wings is the need during movement to keep underwing stores, such as missiles, aligned with the airstream. This aspect appears to have been ignored by ER.110T which, although a research programme, was for a fighter type aircraft.

The results from these studies suggested that swing wings would most benefit aeroplanes specifically designed for operation at low and medium altitudes. In many cases this became a fundamental condition to making the selection of variable sweep in a new design worthwhile, the strike version of Tornado being a classic case. This machine was required to fly fast at low level and really needed a swept wing to help give a comfortable ride. A small highly swept wing with a heavy loading gives great benefit in dealing with the problems of gust effects because the increase in lift generated by the gust is reduced. This also helps to increase fatigue life. However, the specification further required Tornado to be operable from short runways no greater than 3,000ft (914m) long, something that was near impossible with a normal swept wing. Hence, the two requirements together made adoption of variable sweep practical, indeed almost a necessity, and the penalties could be accepted.

One is surprised the 'fighter' firms were not consulted for their opinions. It is believed Hawker and Supermarine were never happy working solely on research aeroplanes unless there was some benefit to the production of fighter aircraft, but ER.110T was proposed for a supersonic fighter. English Electric made no proposal despite the specification being based on the F.23/49 requirement to which it was building the P.1. Perhaps the fighter 'experts' did not favour variable wingsweep, or could see immediately the problems involved and wished to stay out until knowledge improved. The variable sweep specialist, Vickers-Armstrong, was not involved with ER.110T but maybe Barnes Wallis's work was

enough to cope with. Incidentally, no document consulted from 1948-52 used the term 'variable geometry' (VG) and it appears to have been some time before it was adopted. No design depicted here was ever close to being built but the effort and all the paper produced was not wasted. Much was learnt and the first steps taken towards developing top class VG aircraft in the future.

Beyond Wallis's work, between 1958 and the mid-1960s, Vickers designed an extensive series of variable geometry aeroplanes which included amongst many strike aircraft, the Type 583 in Chapter 11.

Panavia Tornado ADV

To date, the UK has possessed just one VG aeroplane, the Multi-Role Combat Aircraft later called Tornado. In 1967 the Anglo-French Variable Geometry aircraft (AFVG) was abandoned and, to fill the gap, Britain, Germany and Italy joined together to form Panavia Aircraft GmbH and build the MRCA in two versions, a strike aircraft and an air defence variant (ADV). The first prototype flew on 14th August 1974 and a month later the name Tornado was selected.

The entirely separate fighter version was developed to meet the UK's ASR.395 requirement for a long-range all-weather interceptor

and the prototype became airborne on 27th October 1979. Compared to the GR Mk.1 IDS (interdictor strike), it had a 4.45ft (1.36m) fuselage plug inserted aft of the rear cockpit. Traditional materials were used in construction and the main weapon was the British Aerospace Dynamics XJ.521 Sky Flash medium range AAM, a British adaptation of the American AIM-7E2 'dogfight' Sparrow with Marconi inverse-monopulse homing head. Work on this began in 1969 and the result was superior to the equivalent AIM-7M and particularly lethal at very low altitude. Four Sky Flash are housed semi-submerged in wells on the aircraft's underbelly to minimise drag; four short range Sidewinders are also carried on wing pylons.

The ADV's AI.24 Foxhunter radar provided numerous problems during the early years of service, but most are now cured. The F Mk.2 was the first fighter into service in 1985, but was quickly updated to the F Mk.3 with fully variable, fully automatic wing sweep operating as a function of Mach number. The slats and flaps were also fully automated replacing the old manual operation of controls. It was not the intention to make Tornado a close combat fighter, rather an interceptor of bombers, and at the time of writing, 227 Tornado ADVs have been built for the RAF and Saudi Arabia. Tornado will remain the only variable geometry combat aircraft to be built in this country for the foreseeable future. Swing wings, like the proposals to fit rockets in numerous 1950s projects, were for a period something of a fashion but are now pushed to one side by the advent of computer controlled unstable aeroplanes.

Fully variable, fully automatic wing sweep, operating as a function of Mach number was introduced on the Tornado F Mk.3. This particular aircraft is ZH559.

Swing Wing Projects – Estimated Data

Project	Span (Fwd/Back) ft (m)	Length ft (m)	Wing Area (Fwd/Back) ft² (m²)	All-Up-Weight lb (kg)	Powerplant Thrust lb (kN)	Max Speed / Height mph (km/h) / ft (m) x 1000	Armament
Transformable Delta (Feb 48)	42.0 (12.8) / 24.0 (7.3)	47 (14.3)	156 (14.5) / 268 (24.9)	13,000 (5,897)	1 x Avon 6,500 (28.9), 10,400 (46.3) reheat	Mach 1.29 at 36.0 (10.97)	None fitted
BGA Transonic Aircraft (Feb 49)	39.33 (12.0) / 25.1 (7.7)	46.0 (14.0)	345 (32.1) / 315 (29.3)	15,730 (7,135)	1 x Sapphire Sa.2 7,500 (33.3), ? reheat	Mach 1,375 907 (1,460) at 36.0 (10.97)	2 x 30mm Aden cannon
BGA (single jet) (June 50)	44.6 (13.6) / 27.2 (8.3)	48.0 (14.6)	324 (30.1) / 351 (32.6)	14,350 (6,509)	1 x Sapphire Sa.2	748 (1,204) at 35.8 (10.91)	None fitted
BGA (twin jet) (June 50)	61.6 (18.8) / 37.6 (11.5)	63.0 (19.2)	622 (57.8) / 600 (55.8)	27,500 (12,474)	2 x Sapphire Sa.2	852 (1,371) at 35.8 (10.91)	None fitted
Armstrong Whitworth AW.59	53.0 (16.2) / 37.5 (11.4)	68.67 (20.9)	480 (44.6) / 550 (51.1)	26,000 (11,793)	2 x Sapphire Sa.4 9,760 (43.4), c.12,000 (53.3) reheat	Mach 1.37 at 36.0 (10.97), Mach 1.35, 895 (1,440) at 45.0 (13.72)	2 x 30mm Aden cannon
Blackburn B.90	65.1 (19.8) / 35.3 (10.8)	61.1 (18.6)	? / ?	34,588 (15,689)	2 x Sapphire Sa.4 9,760 (43.4), c.12,000 (53.3)	Mach 1.35, 895 (1,440) at 45.0 (13.72)	2 x 30mm Aden cannon
Boulton Paul P.121	54.3 (16.6) / 34.3 (10.5)	65.4 (19.9)	? / ?	34,100 (15,467)	2 x Avon RA.8	Mach 1.34, 887 (1,427) at 45.0 (13.72)	1 x 30mm Aden cannon
Bristol Type 183	46.75 (14.2) / 32.0 (9.8)	65.0 (19.8)	? / ?	20,500 (9,299)	2 x Sapphire Sa.4 9,760 (43.3) dry only	Mach 1.39 918 (1,477) at 45.0 (13.72)	2 x 30mm Aden cannon
Saro P.149	58.25 (17.8) / 37.0 (11.3)	60.5 (18.4)	440 (40.9) / 440 (40.9)	32,000 (14,515)	2 x Avon RA.12 c12,000 (53.3) reheat	Mach 1.40 926 (1,490) at 45.0 (13.72)	2 x 30mm Aden cannon
Panavia Tornado F Mk.3	45.6 (13.9) / 28.2 (8.6)	61.3 (18.7)	323 (30.0) / ?	61,700 (27,987)	2 x RB.199 9,656 (42.9), 16,920 (75.2) reheat	920 (1,480)+ at low level Mach 2.27 at altitude	1 x 27mm Mauser cannon, 4 Sky Flash 4 Sidewinder AAM

The first prototype of the Tornado ADV, or F Mk.2 as it was termed at the time, shown on its maiden flight, 27th October 1979, with four British Aerospace Dynamics Sky Flash air-to-air missiles – its main offensive armament.

The First Fighters with Variable Sweepback

Chapter Ten

Rocket Fighters

Rocket and Mixed Power Fighters: 1952 to 1957

During the Second World War the Messerschmitt Me163 Komet, the world's first rocket powered fighter, made quite an impact in the European theatre. It made its first rocket powered flight in 1941 but had to wait until 1944 before entering service. There were plenty of problems but speed, climb and turn performance were impressive and left their mark on the Allies. The value of rockets in dramatically improving climb rate and speed at height was substantial because early jets could not provide such capability. Aircraft drag falls away with height, together with the turbojet's efficiency, but a rocket motor's effectiveness increases with height. The prize was too good to miss – rate of acceleration or time to height cut by perhaps 80% and ceiling pushed up to at least 80,000ft (24,384m). The RAF was keen to take on the concept.

Work started in Britain during 1946 on two rocket motors: the Armstrong Siddeley Snarler of 2,000lb (8.9kN) thrust, which oxidised methyl alcohol with liquid oxygen (lox) for a propellant; and the 5,000lb (22.2kN) de Havilland Sprite, that operated by decomposing concentrated hydrogen peroxide (HTP) to form a jet of steam and oxygen for thrust. No combustion took place with the Sprite, it was a 'cold' rocket, but the fuel itself was a nasty chemical. It was some time before the motors were ready.

Hawker's P.1072 (rocket powered P.1040) first tested the Snarler in November 1950 and demonstrated a striking rate of climb. The Sprite flew six months later and by now both Armstrong Siddeley and DH had begun development of more powerful 8,000lb (35.6kN) motors; the former was named Screamer and utilised lox as an oxidant, the latter was called Spectre and employed HTP, both mixing kerosene as the fuel. Now the Air Staff could issue a requirement for a Rocket Propelled Interceptor, OR.301 of 21st January 1952.

The first SR.53, photographed early in life, before dummy Firestreaks were fitted, mid-1957. The view shows to good effect the rocket and jet pipe arrangement. GKN Westland

F.124T (and OR.301)

The rocket interceptor was perceived as a countermeasure to high flying enemy aircraft, the concept arising from an anticipated inability to destroy them with normal interceptors; a task described as last-ditch defence. The Air Staff therefore requested an interceptor with an outstanding rate of climb (sea level to 60,000ft [18,288m] in 2.5 minutes) and high altitude performance which led quite naturally to the idea of rocket climb. It was realised there would be operating limitations, but the promise of tactical advantage outweighed this. Unconventional take-off methods were acceptable but in no way was the machine or its rocket motor to be considered expendable, gliding back to base if needs be.

In the first instance, the maximum operational speed was to be of the order of Mach 0.95, if this permitted substantial savings in design and development work, but ultimately the aircraft was to be capable of supersonic speeds at all heights above 30,000ft (9,144m). A high degree of manoeuvrability was required and the Spectre or Screamer considered the most suitable motors. Armament was to be a battery of 2in (5.1cm) air-to-air rockets but provision was requested for Blue Jay, then still in the project stage. Submission date was 30th April 1952 but, with the large manufacturing programme already underway, finding spare capacity at a suitable manufacturer presented a problem. The Specification went to Avro, Blackburn, de Havilland, Fairey and, on request, Saunders-Roe.

Avro 720

Since the present generation of bomber and reconnaissance aircraft could cruise up to at least Mach 0.9, Avro regarded it essential to design a supersonic aircraft from the start. Interception curves and times showed that the best Mach number for closing on a bomber was 1.2 to 1.5. The Screamer/Spectre's 8,000lb (35.6kN) thrust made the 720 supersonic in level flight at any altitude above 40,000ft (12,192m) and for subsonic cruise, only a small portion of the thrust was used. Avro felt the most promising aerodynamic form for flight in this region up to Mach 2.0 was the tailless delta, primarily because it permitted a combination of high sweepback with a thin wing. Having no tail avoided the buffet commonly associated with tailed aircraft in the transonic region while the low wing loading

ensured high manoeuvrability. Avro had acquired unequalled experience in delta wings after a thorough investigation of the 707 series test aircraft for the Vulcan bomber and was thus able to stress the satisfactory low speed qualities of the 720.

Structure was simple but both wing and fuselage employed sandwich construction, a process new to Britain, where two relatively thin metal sheets were separated and stabilised by a light metal core to which they were bonded. This saved weight, gave a stiff skin and helped ensure a good seal for pressurising the cockpit. The control surfaces comprised hydraulic power operated elevons but the rudder was manually operated. The 64 2in (5.1cm) rockets were housed in a fixed installation of four identical 16 rocket packs faired into the fuselage as a bulge, so arranged that a new unit could be clipped on to replace an empty one. The fairings were covered in doped fabric which shattered on firing.

Some delay was expected with the Screamer and, in view of the need to get the 720 in service as soon as possible, Avro proposed initial flight testing should be undertaken either as a glider or preferably using a Rolls-Royce Derwent jet. The machine could glide over 130 miles (209km) from 60,000ft (18,288m) but a Derwent permitted flight tests into the transonic region in shallow dives. The 2.5 minute climb to 60,000ft was met with the Screamer but just missed by the Spectre (2.7min) as the former gave slightly the better climb – 23,400ft/min (7,132m/min) at sea level, 52,600 ft/min (16,032m/min) at 60,000ft. Operationally, getting the 720 back to base in low cloud was a problem but substantially eased by using an auxiliary jet engine capable of 20 minutes cruising flight at low altitude. Avro estimated the prototype could fly 45 weeks from ITP.

Blackburn B.97

A broad analysis of the OR was made which stressed in particular the problems of landing aircraft propelled only by rockets. The wording of the specification implied that the risks connected with a powerless descent, approach and landing could be accepted. But these risks were great, leading inevitably to a high proportion of crash landings and/or landings away from base. After a powerless

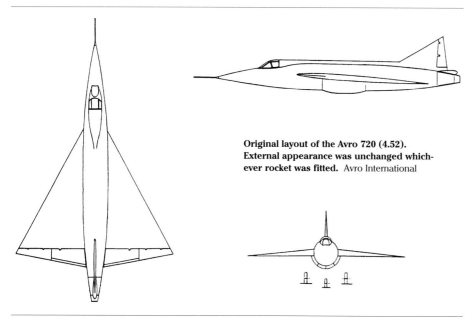

Original layout of the Avro 720 (4.52). External appearance was unchanged whichever rocket was fitted. Avro International

Messerschmitt Me 163 Komet '191904' on display in the UK, parked alongside a Javelin FAW Mk.4, XA634.

descent from altitude, the chance of breaking cloud within a reasonable approach distance of base was by no means high. A 2,000ft (610m) cloud base must be broken about 4 miles (6.5km) from home if a landing was to be effected, should a turn be necessary the accuracy had to be greater still.

Furthermore, operation of a large number of these aeroplanes within a general defence system would be complex if several arrived simultaneously. From these considerations, the case for providing power assistance for approach and landing was overwhelming, compounded by the psychological effect on the pilot knowing he has full control over his choice of landing ground. Using the rocket for approach was a solution but that cut the fuel available for combat.

Blackburn felt very strongly that to solve this situation a separate low thrust turbojet must be installed, which would also help the power operated flying controls. A modified Turboméca Marboré of 720lb (3.2kN) thrust increased the range after breaking cloud four-fold and was adequate to maintain the B.97 in level flight during descent. It also helped development of the prototype for getting the aircraft to an acceptable Service standard was likely to be a lengthy process. For early flying, Blackburn would install another Marboré in place of the rocket to provide a total of 1,600lb (7.1kN) static thrust, a step the firm felt would have enormous value. This made possible a level speed of 345mph (555km/h), high subsonic speeds in a dive and a ceiling of 20,000ft (6,096m).

A major function of the B.97 was the attack and destruction of a single target by visual search. Darkening of the sky at the zenith had been noted from very high flying aircraft, an effect associated with the absence of atmosphere dust and scattering of light. This made an upward visual search more difficult and stressed the need for the best possible pilot view. The logical conclusion was that attacks were best made from above and behind the target against the brighter horizon, when gunfire might prove a better method of attack than rocket projectiles thanks to superior aiming and range. Two Aden cannon were thus mounted in a nose installation that could be removed and replaced by 72 rockets. Provision for two Blue Jays on the wings could follow. Choice between Spectre or Screamer was likely to be a matter of policy; both could be fitted, but Blackburn based its design on de Havilland's Spectre. B.97 was supersonic at all heights above 20,000ft (6,096m) with Mach 1.2+ above 45,000ft (13,716m). Construction was conventional with light alloy sheet, extrusions and forgings.

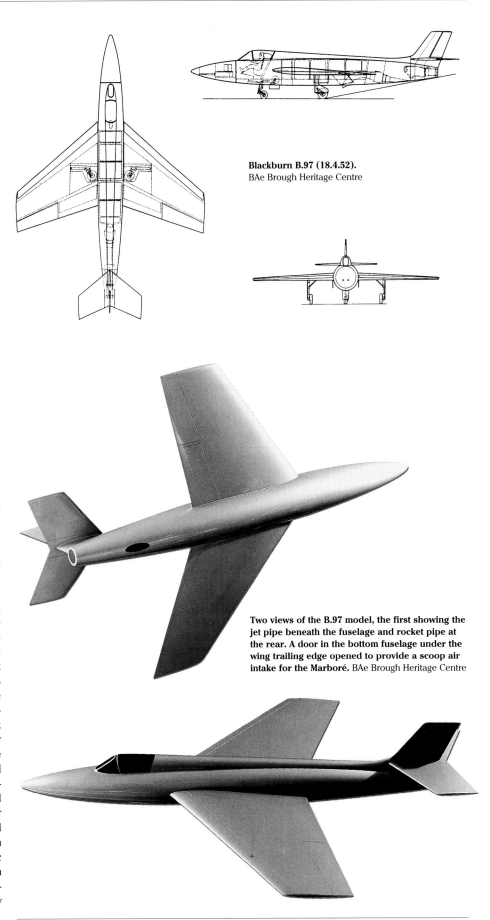

Blackburn B.97 (18.4.52).
BAe Brough Heritage Centre

Two views of the B.97 model, the first showing the jet pipe beneath the fuselage and rocket pipe at the rear. A door in the bottom fuselage under the wing trailing edge opened to provide a scoop air intake for the Marboré. BAe Brough Heritage Centre

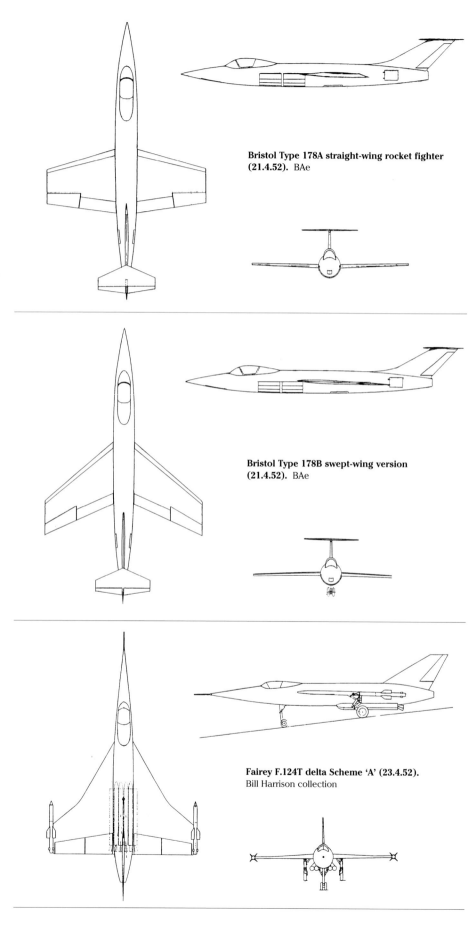

Bristol Type 178A straight-wing rocket fighter (21.4.52). BAe

Bristol Type 178B swept-wing version (21.4.52). BAe

Fairey F.124T delta Scheme 'A' (23.4.52).
Bill Harrison collection

Bristol 178

Two projects in one, straight and swept versions of the same Screamer powered aeroplane. Both shared the same basic layout with a drooped leading edge, single slotted flap and aileron on each wing plus an all-moving T-tail with elevators. The 48 rockets were housed in twin retractable batteries in the lower fuselage between cockpit and wing. Take-off was from a trolley, landing on the bicycle undercarriage. The swept project possessed the higher combat speed and manoeuvrability but both took just over 1.8 minutes to reach 60,000ft (18,288m).

Fairey F.124

Two more projects in one, but this time quite different shapes. Scheme 'A' was a delta with conventional undercarriage while Scheme 'B' had swept wings. 'A's fuselage showed a distinct family likeness to the later Delta II and was indeed based on the ER.103 project, but its cranked delta wing with wing tip Blue Jays would not look out of place in the Eurofighter chapter. Six rocket boosters were wrapped around the lower rear fuselage for take-off assistance and to cut time to 60,000ft down to 3 minutes, a technique used on the Delta I research aeroplane. The swept wing aircraft carried Blue Jays on underwing pylons and took off from a trolley under main rocket power; it also used the rocket for return and a conventional landing. Time to 60,000ft, 2.2 minutes.

Saunders-Roe P.154

Besides designing the fighter, Saro, one of the most innovative firms around, wished to produce its own 8,000lb (35.6kN) rocket to power it. This consisted of two 4,000lb (17.8kN) chambers fitted together with HTP as oxidant. High performance flying needed both units, but cruise just the one. Time to 60,000ft was estimated by MoS as 1.87 minutes (Saro – 2.18min) with the firm suggesting a climb rate of 13,600ft/min (4,145m/min) at sea level and 52,000ft/min (15,850m/min) at 50,000ft (15,240m).

Structure was conventional with full span drooped leading edges and slotted flaps, the latter with ailerons moving independently. A variable incidence tail had orthodox elevators. Take-off could be conventional undercarriage or on a trolley and utilised Mayfly cordite rocket boosters; a skid landing was planned to begin with. Two pods with 25 rockets each would extend from the rear fuselage for high speed firing. One hundred and sixteen weeks were estimated to build the first machine and Saro also advocated the advantages of an auxiliary 'get you home' jet.

Westland F.124

Another brace of quite different layouts, both using two Spectres, and a tricycle undercarriage. Design 'A' was a delta wing aeroplane with the Spectres either side of the rear fuselage, the second motor being used primarily to boost climb rate. The Ministry judged time to 60,000ft (18,288m) for 'A' and 'B' to be 2.05 min. Design 'B' was of the 'Duo Monoplane' or Delanne layout so favoured by Westland in the past with the Spectres stacked one-over-one in the rear fuselage. The idea of this 'bi-plane' arrangement was to reduce drag to a minimum. Only 36 rockets were carried on either project, but both had provision for a pair of underwing Blue Jays when further developed. For initial flight both types would use two Viper jets in place of the rockets, fed by air from intakes protruding from the sides of the rear fuselage; the Delanne's upper Viper had a third intake on top of the rear fuselage.

Three more companies prepared projects to F.124T, but the first two never submitted.

Boulton Paul P.122

A swept-wing design with twin tail-booms extending ahead of the wings to house the cannon. Take-off used a trolley, landing a central skid after a glide back to base. Climb to 60,000ft took 3.0 minutes, sea level climb rate was 12,000ft/min (3,658m/min) and at 60,000ft, 34,000ft/min (10,363m/min).

Hawker P.1089

The drawing shows a tail-less delta, one of several layouts including a swept wing effort. One finds it difficult to believe Sydney Camm would have been completely happy with a pure rocket fighter.

Short P.D.7 & P.D.701

On 30th June 1952, 12 days after the Design Conference, David Keith-Lucas of Short Brothers wrote to DMARD, A E Woodward Nutt, to explain how, at first, he had not wished to submit to F.124T because of work already in hand, but after re-assessing the document, had decided to design a project. The current workload included a Photographic Reconnaissance Aircraft, the P.D.8 with an aero-iso-clinic wing, and Keith-Lucas was interested in F.124 from the point of view of intercepting the P.D.8. From his investigations, he was struck by the relatively poor performance of the rocket fighter at low altitude compared to the jet fighter, a reverse of the situation at high level, and from these deductions had tried to get the best of both worlds by fitting a powerful jet engine as well as the rocket. His brochure was more of a report with its projects not to full tender standard.

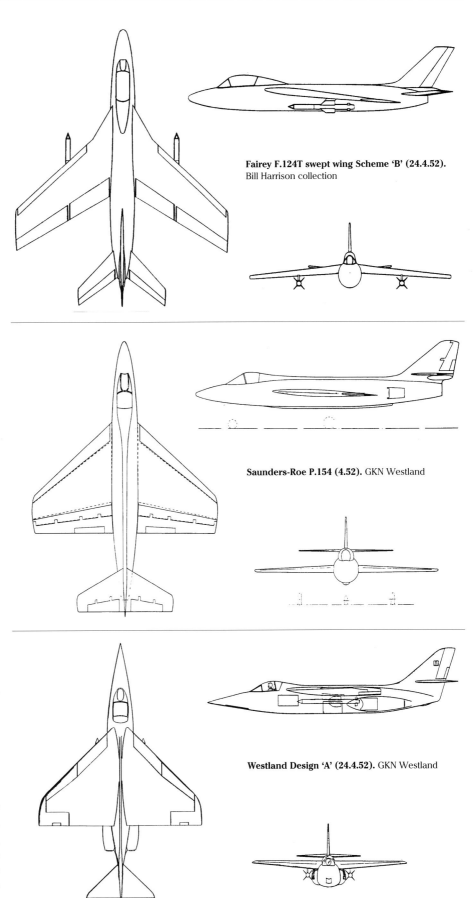

Fairey F.124T swept wing Scheme 'B' (24.4.52).
Bill Harrison collection

Saunders-Roe P.154 (4.52). GKN Westland

Westland Design 'A' (24.4.52). GKN Westland

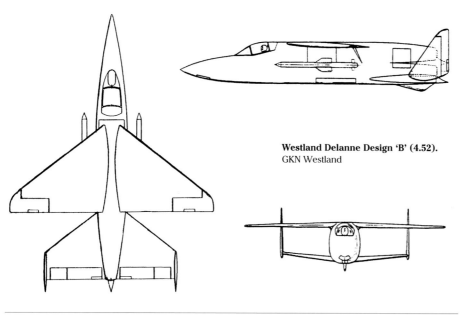

Westland Delanne Design 'B' (4.52).
GKN Westland

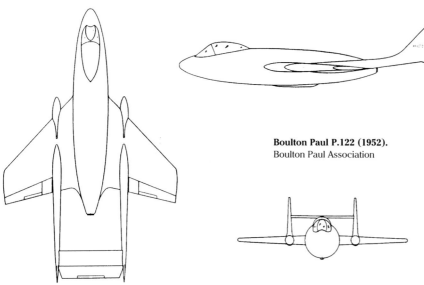

Boulton Paul P.122 (1952).
Boulton Paul Association

Artist's Impression of the P.122.
Boulton Paul Association

The report balanced fuel loads and weight with use of jet or rocket at different height and concluded that a jet capable of useful thrust at 60,000ft combined with a rocket gave a lighter aircraft thanks to the savings in fuel weight. The P.D.701 added two reheated 4,600lb (20.4kN) Bristol BE.22 jets, side-by-side in mid-fuselage, to the Screamer rocket.

The delta wing was chosen for its large fuel capacity and high speed qualities being theoretically capable of Mach 2.0. Keith-Lucas acknowledged a straight wing was the most suitable for Mach 2, but the transonic and low subsonic regimes were more important and the high swept delta offered the best solution.

The P.D.7 design offered a climb to 60,000ft (18,288m) in 3.72 minutes, the P.D.701 in 1.7 minutes. Climb rate was important as a Mach 0.9 bomber could travel about 20 miles (32km) in two minutes and the rocket only fighter at 60,000ft could gain just 10 miles before its fuel ran out. Using jets in conjunction with a rocket halved time to 60,000ft, reduced take-off weight and halved fuel load. Keith-Lucas had also realised that ferrying between bases needed a jet, the operation would be near impossible on rocket power alone and road transport was undesirable.

–

With several firms outlining the problems of rocket power only, the MoS began to appreciate the value of an additional jet engine and in May, everyone received extra time to redesign their projects with a mixed power plant. Everyone that is, except Blackburn who had pushed the idea more than anyone. As its B.97 already had a jet, it was denied another go, but the early time limit had prevented the firm from including some detail.

Avro's auxiliary Armstrong Siddeley Viper was sited in the base of the 720's fuselage Bristol opted for a Rolls-Royce RB.93 Soar engine while Westland replaced one of the bi-fuel rockets in both its projects with a Viper. In Design 'A' this raised questions of asymmetric thrust. For test flying with two 1,575lb (7kN) Vipers, Westland quoted 9,900lb (4,491kg) all-up-weight for both 'A' and 'B', 19 minutes to 30,000ft and a maximum level speed of Mach 0.82 (600mph [965km/h]). For the Delanne Design 'B' using one Spectre and one Viper, all-up-weight was 15,465lb (7,015kg), top speed at sea level Mach 0.89 and at 50,000ft (15,240m) Mach 1.4.

Val Cleaver, Special Projects Engineer at de Havilland Engines and responsible for its rocket motors, wrote to Woodward Nutt on

th July to confirm that the early worry of fit-
ing jets had subsided as the aircraft con-
tructors had chosen engines large enough
o be useful but still relatively small. He be-
eved F.124 had outstanding possibilities for
vhat the Germans had called a target-de-
ence interceptor, and earnestly hoped a spe-
ialised aircraft would be developed with
ome urgency. Prior assessment at RAE and
D Projects at MoS concluded that every F.124T
esign would be capable of reaching very
igh supersonic speeds (Mach 2.0 or above)
f they started accelerating at the end of the
limb. Probably the highest speeds, or alter-
atively the longest duration at a given speed,
vould be attained by the Avro 720 and straight
ving Bristol 178, largely on account of their
xtremely thin 4% wings, with the Avro possi-
ly flying more smoothly around Mach 1.

The Tender Design Conference took place
t Thames House South on 18th July 1952.
erodynamically and performance wise, the
aro and Avro projects were considered most
romising, both capable of reaching 60,000ft
n about three minutes from rest while having
ow touch down speeds. The Avro 720 should
ave a smaller turning circle than Saro's and
lightly better high speed performance. There
vas surprise at the large discrepancy be-
ween Bristol's weight assessments, and the
AE's – a hefty 6,000lb (2,722kg), caused large-
y by a mistake in fuel allowance. Blackburn's
.97 was a little slower than the others with-
ut compensating advantages, Westland's
rojects had the best climb performance (ex-
ept when switching one Spectre for a Viper)
ut poorer manoeuvrability. There were
oubts about the Delanne layout. One Fairey
esign called for rocket assistance on take-
ff, an undesirable feature, and the firm did
ot submit any ideas for fitting auxiliary en-
ines. The Fairey 'A' also had the highest
ouch-down speed.

There were no serious criticisms of any of
he proposed engine installations except
airey's take-off rocket assistance, but sur-
rise was expressed that some firms said they
ould easily use either Screamer or Spectre
ockets. Switching these motors would ne-
essitate a change of fuel, not necessarily
ossible with the same fuel system. It was
onsidered the Saro proposal to use a motor
ased on an RAE Westcott design would cre-
te delay.

As regards armament, a 2in (5.1cm) rocket
rojectile installation that did not increase
drag was desirable and the retractable type
vas the more favoured, particularly Bristol's.
nce Blackburn's B.97 had fired its RPs there
vould apparently be a large shift of CofG, the
ffects of which were uncertain.

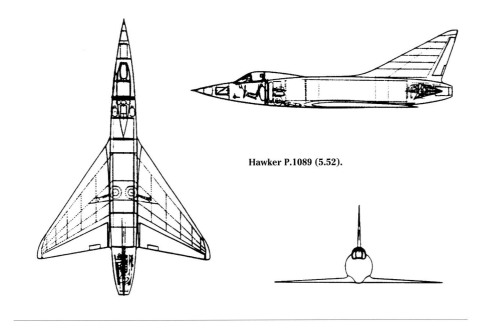

Hawker P.1089 (5.52).

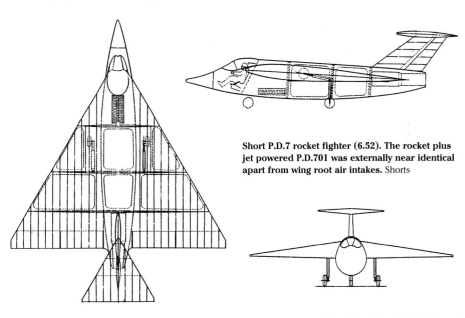

**Short P.D.7 rocket fighter (6.52). The rocket plus
jet powered P.D.701 was externally near identical
apart from wing root air intakes.** Shorts

From a production point of view, Bristol
badly needed a new project although its capacity might be used for the Red Rapier flying-
bomb and other guided weapons. However,
if Avro won a production order for the B.35/46
(Vulcan) bomber, as appeared likely, its main
effort would naturally go into that. Structurally,
Avro's 720 was rated first as the honeycomb
method of construction possessed great production potential. It was agreed that only the
Saro, Avro and straight wing Bristol 178 remained in the competition. Saro's had been
judged best by several independent assessments, they had submitted very good designs
on two previous occasions, so good that it
would be a mistake for their design team to
be disbanded, which would be the case un-

less the firm received a contract soon.

Scott Hall, DGTD(A), suggested Saro's project should be accepted against OR.301 with
the other pair considered for adoption as a research aircraft for flight up to Mach 2.

E T Jones, PDSR(A), pointed out that an RAE
paper on Mach 2 aircraft was forthcoming
(Chapter 7) and a research aircraft designed
for Mach 2 would accept a higher landing
speed than an operational machine. It would
also need sufficient fuel to make several runs
at high speed on one flight. But Jones thought
the Bristol 178 with thin straight wings was of
great interest and he placed it ahead of the
Avro 720, mainly because the Fairey delta
wing aircraft to ER.103 was already on order.
There would be merit in going ahead with the

Bristol design as a research aircraft, dependent on the content of the RAE paper, but a Mach 2 aircraft with two turbojets and reasonable endurance was more important.

The Bristol 178 was deleted from the competition with a view to its adoption as a research aircraft (in the event not proceeded with). The meeting finally recommended that both Saro's and Avro's projects should be ordered, one powered by the Screamer and the other by the Spectre, Saro's having priority should the Treasury turn down ordering both. In that situation, six Saros were to be built, three fitted with each motor for comparison. On 14th October Treasury approval was given for ordering two Avro 720s and three Saro aircraft.

Avro 720

The biggest change to the 720 as originally tendered was the addition of the auxiliary jet in a lower fuselage fairing with its own intake and pipe and at the Advisory Design Conference on 17th June 1953, a new specification F.137D was finalised to cover the machine. The 720's main armament was two Blue Jay AAMs carried under the wings, but the original air-to-air rocket packs or two cannon were alternatives. Normal role was still daytime interception of jet bomber and reconnaissance aircraft with reliance on ground control and visual search. The two prototypes were serialled XD696 and XD701 with a first flight planned for 1956. A mock-up was examined in late April 1954.

Saunders-Roe SR.53

Unlike Avro's 720, the Saro machine's appearance was to change quite drastically along with its new identity. The Viper was moved into the upper rear fuselage above the rocket and was fed by ear intakes behind the cockpit. Area ruling was applied and the two Blue Jays were tip mounted. Another new specification, F.138D, covered this machine like F.137D it demanded increased performance over F.124T to match expected Soviet developments during the five years before the fighter entered service. Serials XD145 XD151 and XD153 were allocated.

These projects highlighted the difficulties of ground control interception for high altitude fighters. Trials conducted in mid-1953 using de Havilland Venoms stripped out for high level flight up to c.51,000ft (15,545m) illustrated how much progress needed to be made, but the work eventually led to the sophisticated ground control systems in use today.

At the time the RAF's Central Fighter Establishment agreed airborne radar guidance was needed. The rocket fighters themselves were limited to 8/8th cloud with a 2,000ft (610m) base and 3 miles (4.8km) visibility; recovery in anything worse would be difficult.

By 1953, defence cuts aimed at making a 30% saving in 1955/56 had been requested and it was stated in February that both rocket interceptors would have to go. Debate centred on which should go and which might stay. AVM Geoffrey Tuttle, ACAS(OR), wrote on 3rd March that the Treasury would only allow one design to be built, so 'it is essential that this should be the best from every angle. I am very far from convinced that the Saunders Roe fills the bill, and I believe that we should change to the Avro before it is too late'. He reported that the Air Staff had always considered the Avro 720 the most promising, with Bristol a close second, but it had not dissented from the Tender Design Conference decision because there was no reason to believe then that prototypes of all three aircraft would not be built. In the event, the Treasury had approved the SR.53 but 'has stalled on the other two, and we are faced with the position that the design which is least favoured by the Air Staff is the only one likely to be built'. He felt this was unacceptable and requested the 720 to go ahead without delay, even if it meant dropping the Saunders-Roe.

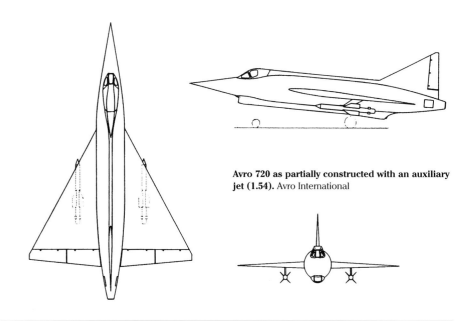

Avro 720 as partially constructed with an auxiliary jet (1.54). Avro International

Mock-up of the 720 built in light alloy. This is not the prototype; the picture does not reveal that it has no starboard wing. Avro International

British Secret Projects: Jet Fighter

In preparing the 1954/55 estimates later in the year, £11m was added to the Defence R&D Budget allowing one of the projected cuts to be restored. Thanks to the difficulty in choosing between the Saro and Avro, the former was returned to the programme but to effect some economy, the third SR.53 was cancelled on 23rd December.

The SR.53 Mock-Up Conference was held on 1st October 1953 and by 8th July 1954, 87% of the design work for first flight was finished. But on 7th May 1954, there were doubts in everyone's mind whether either would continue because thoughts were turning towards a mixed power interceptor for the next generation.

For some time neither the 720 nor SR.53 had been looked on as a full production machine for operational service, rather for limited production to give experience in rocket motors and operation at great heights. By 19th October a requirement for a new supersonic fighter with mixed power had appeared and the two earlier projects were now considered as lead-in aircraft.

It was assumed that the Russians would have by 1962 a bomber capable of flying at 60,000ft (18,288m) and in bursts at Mach 1.3 and this was the reason for the new requirement. Existing types of fighters under development, the P.1B (Lightning) and Thin Wing Javelin, were inadequate for the task.

The new requirement was OR.337/Specification F.177, but the original threat that led to the concept of the rocket fighter still remained and, to fill the gap, it was felt a possible development of the Avro 720 might suffice. The new de Havilland Gyron Junior engine would be available in 1958 and a pilot operated AI radar by 1959, so fitting these into a 720 with redesigned fuselage should be possible within the timescale. This would prove a valuable insurance against a high altitude threat which, even on a small scale, would be devastating if the H-bomb were used. In its current form the 720 would be of limited operational value.

The result was the modified 720 shown in the drawing which had a Vee windscreen, area ruling, AI radar in the nose which increased length to 45ft (13.7m) and the Viper replaced by the Bristol Orpheus turbojet as an interim substitute for the Gyron Junior. A similar naval version called the Avro 728 had wing area increased from 360 to 460ft² (33.5 to 42.9m²); both had two Blue Jay missiles.

However, Saro's P.177 project to OR.337 was considered superior and on 21st April 1955, it was recommended that the Avro 720 should be cancelled. This was later accepted.

Avro 726

Before closing on Avro, there was another project in its fighter family, the 726 interceptor and escort fighter proposal of January 1954. The chief difference from the 720 was the introduction of a light 30in (76cm) diameter jet engine instead of the rocket that was currently under consideration by several manufacturers, and more powerful than the 'get-you-home' unit. Avro's brochure figures were based on the proposed Armstrong P.151 engine, but others such as the Bristol BE.30 Zeus and de Havilland PS.37 gave similar performance. It was hoped to produce these engines at little more than half the cost of a conventional Avon or Sapphire. The 726 was really a Light Fighter, a concept brought by the cost of current Western fighters which prevented adequate numbers from being built, and it was around half the weight of existing machines.

Honeycomb sandwich construction was retained and two Adens were placed in the wing roots with RP pods or alternative Blue Jays under the wing. The interceptor variant used the reheated engine and could climb to 50,000ft (15,240m) from rest in 4 minutes. The escort fighter deleted reheat for extra endurance.

For the record, the Bristol Zeus was a two shaft engine with contra-rotating 3 stage LP and 7 stage HP compressors that was particularly suited for operation under full reheat conditions at Mach 2.

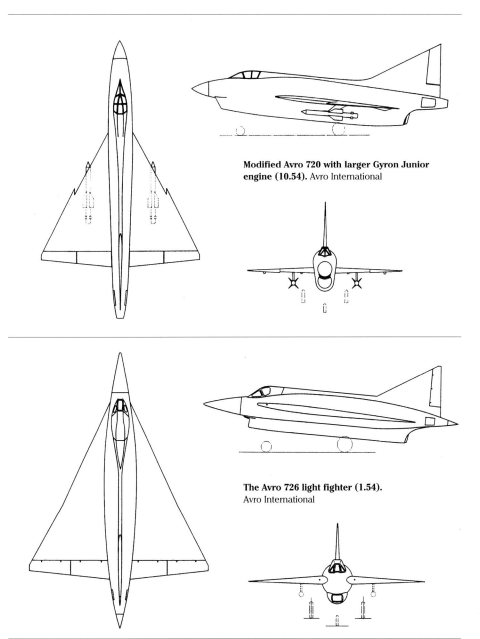

Modified Avro 720 with larger Gyron Junior engine (10.54). Avro International

The Avro 726 light fighter (1.54).
Avro International

Model of the P.177 prototype XL905 in naval colours with Red Tops.

The Director of Engine Research and Development had invited proposals for an 8,000lb (35.6kN) engine suitable for several types of aircraft including a light interceptor capable of Mach 1.4, the NR/A.39 subsonic naval strike aircraft and a Mach 2 supersonic fighter.

F.177D (and OR.337)

The next generation of mixed power fighters moved away from the pure rocket with auxiliary jet, the emphasis switching to a larger cruise jet plus a rocket for acceleration and combat. The aircraft had to reach Mach 1.6 at 65,000ft (19,812m) in 4 minutes with the maximum sustained level speed to be at 60,000ft (18,288m). It should be capable of Mach 2 for short periods and supersonic above 40,000ft (12,192m). Two Blue Jay missiles were to be carried with RP batteries to OR.1126 the alternative weapon, there were no guns. This specification for a *Mixed Powerplant Interceptor Fighter* was completed on 17th May 1956, and was also taken on board by the Admiralty who wrote a sister requirement NR/A.47. Every effort was to be made to keep the two versions as close as possible.

Saunders-Roe P.177 / SR.177

A design study was requested in early 1955 and to begin the powerplants were arranged as per the SR.53 with jet above and rocket below. But the Admiralty requested a deflected jet in addition to the blown flaps required by the Air Ministry which needed the jet in the lower position. This was adopted and, in fact, produced an intake of better form than originally planned. G W H Gardner, DGTD(A), felt the Saro aircraft in developed form with the Gyron Junior had an attractive performance and, on 23rd March he strongly recommended ordering it. The third SR.53 was reconsidered for tactical testing in July but rejected as this would delay the P.177.

An ITP for P.177 was received in September and on the 30th, the 27 aircraft programme listed below was outlined, covering prototypes for both services:

Group 1 – 5 a/c – Flying shells for basic aerodynamic and engine development to prove the aircraft as a weapon platform;
Group 2 – 3 a/c – Weapon system development;
Group 3 – 5 a/c – Development of special features for the Navy and RAF;
Group 4 – 6 a/c – Final CA weapon system clearance, delivered to A&AEE as a group;
Group 5 – 8 a/c – Service trials, 4 to each service as P.177R and P.177N.

The first five aircraft were to be given serial numbers XL905 to XL907 and XL920 and '921. Airframes 10 to 13 were to be the first with reheated Gyron Juniors.

As a firm, Saunders-Roe presented some difficulties. It had no flight test team nor adequate facilities for development work at Eastleigh Aerodrome. Despite this and a lack of experience with such aircraft, P.177 first flight was promised for 1957 with squadron service a further two to three years in 1960. It was suggested if this was achieved, Saro would have established a record in this country that would be difficult to approach. By 3rd May 1956, Saro was working flat out on the project and, later in the summer, came the first signs of German Air Force and Navy interest. First flight was now projected for Spring 1958 and a production programme of 150 aircraft for each service was laid down. The P.177R was to re-equip half of the RAF's short range Hawker Hunter force, the rest being replaced by the Lightning. Jigging the first machines had started by early 1957 .

The United States had frequently expressed interest in the P.177 and through the Mutual Special Weapons Programme was already supporting the SR.53. Hence, a request was made in early February to MWDP requesting support to the tune of $11.71m by 30th June 1959, the largest single project to date for which support had been solicited. However, the April Defence White Paper cancelled the RAF prototypes and cut the development batch to 18 aircraft.

A revised MWDP funding submission explained that the first eleven aircraft were for purely development purposes, the remaining seven were to be handed over for service use. The Scimitar and Sea Vixen just coming into service had neither the speed nor ceiling to deal with the threat while the new Seaslug guided weapon had limited range and no high altitude performance. Without the P.17? there would be a gap in the Fleet defences until 1970; no other supersonic high altitude fighter was being developed for the navy. In addition, a German technical mission had visited the UK in April and made a detailed examination of the P.177.

On 4th June MWDP replied that the project did not fall within its terms of reference since it was in the production phase of development, not research and development. A restructured submission was requested but never completed as the P.177N was now cancelled. The MoS's J R Christie explained to Admiral Marion Kelley in Paris how Her Majesty's Government had concluded that the cost of the project was outside the resources the UK had available and the request for aid was thus cancelled. It was the Government's intention to continue with the SR.53 project and keep the first five P.177s for trials purposes, but the latter were ultimately cancelled at Christmas.

The SR.53 first flew on 16th May 1957, but after the P.177 cancellation, the Air Staff did not know what to do with it. When re-appraised in August 1958 it was fully intended to keep the aircraft flying for, in its present form it was capable of greater altitudes, and Mach numbers as high as any aircraft now flying in the UK. Its 45° of sweep nicely filled the gap between the straight wing Bristol 188 and 60° Lightning. Both prototypes flew but the second crashed on take-off on 5th June 1958 after just 12 flights totalling 5.25 hours.

A limited programme of flight research was planned on 2nd February 1959 as the Ministry was anxious to get as much out of the aircraft as possible. This went ahead, but the period 5th October 1959, to 11th March 1960, brought a series of stop/go decisions on a further programme before Contract Action was suspended in view of the doubts about the value of proceeding. Twenty-seven flights had been planned covering the transonic speed range Mach 0.8 to 1.3 and heights up to 55,000ft (16,764m) to examine lift and buffet boundaries, and thrust and drag measurement. RAF pilot familiarity was another aspect, but the decision came on 26th July 1960, to stop flying the SR.53.

In the event, the expected high flying bombers that brought forth the rocket interceptor switched to low level. Other proposals for fitting rockets to aircraft such as the Lightning to boost altitude performance were dropped once jet engine and reheat power improved to a sufficient level.

Rocket Fighter Projects to Specification F.124T– Estimated Data

Project	Span ft (m)	Length ft (m)	Wing Area ft² (m²)	t/c %	All-Up-Weight lb (kg)	Powerplant Thrust lb (kN)	Max Speed / Height mph (km/h) / ft (m) x 1,000	Armament
Avro 720	28.25 (8.6)	48.0 (14.6)	385 (35.8)	4	14,500 (6,577) (Screamer) 15,200 (6,895) Spectre	1 x Screamer or Spectre 8,000 (35.6)	Mach 2.0, 1,320 (2,125) at 40.0 (12.2) Mach 3.0, 1,980 (3,186) at 60.0 (18.3) (fuel limited)	64 x 2in RP
Blackburn B.97	33.25 (10.1)	47.67 (14.5)	360 (33.5)	8	17,805 (8,076)	1 x Spectre	Mach 1.57 at 60.0 (18.3)	2 x 30mm Aden or 72 x RP
Bristol 178 (straight wing)	28.0 (8.5)	49.1 (15.0)	252 (23.4)	4	12,420 (5,634)	1 x Screamer	?	48 x RP
Bristol 178 (swept wing)	29.0 (8.8)	50.2 (15.3)	268 (24.9)	5	13,043 (5,916)	1 x Screamer	?	48 x RP
Fairey Scheme A (Delta)	27.5 (8.4) [29.83 (9.1) with AAM]	52.67 (16.1) with pitot	387 (36.0)	5	20,305 (9,210) (MoS estimate)	1 x Screamer	?	52 x RP or 2 x Blue Jay
Fairey Scheme B (swept Wing)	30.5 (9.3)	40.25 (12.3)	266 (24.7)	8	15,629 (7,089) (MoS estimate)	1 x Spectre	?	52 x RP or 2 x Blue Jay
Avro P.154	26.0 (7.9)	37.1 (11.3)	272 (25.3)	6	13,260 (6,015)	1 x rocket 8,000 (35.6)	Mach 2.44 at 60.0 (18.3) (fuel limited), Mach 1.17 at 30.0 (9.1)	50 x RP or (later) 2 x Blue Jay
Westland 'A'	29.2 (8.9)	46.6 (14.2)	340 (31.6)	7	21,035 (9,541) (MoS estimate)	2 x Spectre	?	36 x RP or 2 x Blue Jay
Westland 'B' (Delanne)	28.5 (8.7)	38.0 (11.6)	208 (19.3) + 125 (11.6) tail	?	21,806 (9,891)	2 x Spectre	?	36 x RP or 2 x Blue Jay
Boulton Paul P.122	21.5 (6.6)	36.67 (11.2)	?	?	?	1 x Screamer	?	2 cannon + ?
Hawker P.1089	24.25 (7.4)	37.75 (11.5)	336 (31.2)	?	16,000 (7,258)	1 x Spectre	?	?
Short P.D.7	30.0 (9.1)	39.75 (12.1)	420 (39.1)	9	19,934 (9,042)	1 x Spectre	?	?
Short P.D.701	30.0 (9.1)	39.75 (12.1)	420 (39.1)	9	16,184 (7,341)	1 x Spectre + 2 x BE.22, 4,700 (20.9)	?	?

Mixed Power Fighters

* (to be 8,000 [35.6] but not achieved)

Project	Span ft (m)	Length ft (m)	Wing Area ft² (m²)	t/c %	All-Up-Weight lb (kg)	Powerplant Thrust lb (kN)	Max Speed / Height mph (km/h) / ft (m) x 1,000	Armament
Avro 720	27.3 (8.3)	43.23 (13.2)	360 (33.5)	4.5	17,575 (7,972)	1 x Screamer + 1 x Viper 101/ASV.8 1,640 (7.3)	Mach 2.0	2 x Blue Jay (Firestreak)
Avro SR.53 (flown)	28.1 (8.6) with AAM	46.4 (14.1)	271 (25.2)	6	18,400 (8,346)	1 D.Spe.1A Spectre 7,000 (31.1) * + 1 x Viper 101, 1,640 (7.3)	Mach 2.1 at 60.0 (18.3)	2 x Blue Jay (Firestreak – dummies only)
Avro 726	27.3 (8.3)	39.25 (12.0)	385 (35.8)	4.5	14,340 (6,505) – Escort 13,100 (5,942) – Interceptor	1 x P.151 8,000 (35.6), 10,500 (46.7) reheat	Mach 1.48+	2 x 30mm Aden + 40 x RP or 2 x Blue Jay
Avro P.177	30.3 (9.2)	50.5 (15.4)	327 (30.4)	6	25,786 (11,697) RAF 27,348 (12,405) Navy	1 x DGJ.10R Gyron Junior 10,000 (44.4), 14,000 (62.2) reheat, + 1 D.Spe.5A Spectre 8,000 (35.6)	Mach 2.35 (structure limit)	2 x Red Top

Chapter Eleven

A Quiet Period

No More Fighters and a Reorganised Industry: 1957 to 1974

The 1957 Defence White Paper is a somewhat unfortunate landmark in British aviation history detailing, as it did, the future of military aircraft development in Britain, or rather the lack of it. When one reads any book or article covering this period, the deep scar that this document left on the aviation scene is always visible. The author is not old enough to remember these events but the pain and frustration is clear to see.

Defence – an Outline of Future Policy was presented to the House of Commons on 4th April 1957, by the newly appointed Minister of Defence Duncan Sandys. The section on Research and Development stated 'In view of the good progress made towards the replacement of the manned aircraft of Fighter Command with a ground-to-air guided missile system, the RAF is unlikely to have a require-

ment for fighter aircraft of types more advanced than the supersonic P.1 and work on such projects will stop'.

Extracts from a memorandum written on 11th March 1957, by Air Commodore J F Roulston, DOR(A), clarify the situation. 'In view of recent technological advances and the fact that the major threat to this country is changing fairly rapidly from aircraft carrying nuclear weapons to one of ballistic missiles with nuclear warheads, it has now been decided that the contribution which future manned fighters could make is insufficient to warrant their development. In place of manned fighters it has been decided that surface-to-air guided weapons should be introduced as soon as possible. The developed F.23 (Lightning) is expected to be able to deal with the manned aircraft threat within its timescale and its development is therefore to be continued. The development of the aircraft to OR's 337 and 329 (Saunders Roe SR.177 and Fairey 'Delta III') is no longer required by the Air Staff'.

Other projects closed down included the

VG Lightning model for the RAF, with Red Tops, as displayed to officials in a secret mini-exhibitio[n] at Warton in April 1964 (1963).
North West Heritage Group

manned supersonic bomber (Avro 730) whi[ch] high priority was to be given to the develop[-]ment of British nuclear weapons for initial d[e-]livery by the V-bombers and then by strateg[ic] missiles. Just about every published work o[n] British combat aircraft has poured scorn o[n] this document, but why did it come about?

To the Government, the 1956 Suez Crisi[s] crystallised sharply how Britain was living be[-]yond her means with so many expensiv[e] world-wide Imperial and NATO commi[t-]ments. Britain's world status was now threa[t-]ened more by economics and politics than b[y] military factors while foreign aid had de[-]creased. The situation was complex but th[e] main problem was crystal clear, the cost o[f] defending British interests in Europe, Afric[a] and Asia had to be reduced and in Januar[y]

957, Prime Minister Harold Macmillan appointed Sandys as Defence Minister with the dict to formulate a new defence policy that vould secure a substantial reduction in expenditure and manpower; an awesome task.

Defence expenditure, the composition of the Armed Services, their equipment in light f new technical and operational developments and the UK's changing world role were ll to be assessed. The announcement brought nease throughout the industry, but such a substantial shift in policy was totally unexpected and, ever since, Sandys has been oundly criticised for the consequences. Vhether he was right or wrong, thanks to a vartime role on the periphery of the British Var Cabinet and experience as Minister of upply from 1951, Sandys actually knew nore about the subject than most who hold ne position.

Sandys' great interest in rockets and misiles may have clouded his judgement on nanned aircraft. Emphasis shifted to the ever rowing nuclear threat and an emerging conept was that Britain had become indefensile to missiles and bombers when attacking n sufficient numbers. It would be impossible o shoot everything down so, in the Government's eyes, dismantling Fighter Command eemed a reasonable move. From now on, onventional forces were looked on primariy to enhance credibility for the nuclear deerrent and an overriding factor in the White aper was 'to prevent war rather than preare for it'. But there were counter arguents. Manned fighters were more flexible nan missiles. Fighters could move swiftly to trouble-spot; they could identify an unidenified intruder (a frequent RAF job during the o-called 'Cold War'); they could escort transorts overseas; missiles could not. The prospect f a small local war like the 1982 Falklands ampaign does not appear to have been aken into account either.

The effect of this policy on Britain's aircraft ndustry was severe, not least that the essenial continuous process of design, test and nanufacture was cut. Morale was damaged, s were export prospects. Germany was very nthusiastic about the Saro P.177, but bought he American Starfighter when the British mahine was cancelled; Australia had exressed interest in the Sea Vixen while the ightning's export potential was lost until audi Arabia bought it 1965. There is a strong ossibility that a multi-mission Lightning ould have sold well. The theory was also aken on board overseas. Canada wiped way its CF-105 Arrow fighter, possibly the nost advanced and capable interceptor ever uilt by a Western country, wrecking in the

process the ability to design its own fighters. The idea was discussed in Sweden but here the argument's weaknesses were recognised and that country's superb range of combat aircraft continued. The USA did cut back some fighter programmes and replace them with missiles.

Economies were needed in British defence expenditure, but a more selective process would surely have been more suitable. Besides the cancellation of brand new aircraft, many airworthy fighters in RAF service were withdrawn and scrapped and incomplete orders for Hunter F Mk.6s cancelled. The number of RAF Squadrons was slashed, though in fact this was a process already underway, the Sandys Paper just accelerated it. In July 1955, the RAF declared 1,338 fighters operational; two years later this had dropped to 908; five years after that the total was 335. In some areas, Sandys' proposals were not quite so revolutionary as many think; they were more evolutionary but at a quicker pace.

Contributors to the problem included the Air Staff and Ministry with their regular changes of policy on what and what not to build, and the industry which had too many individual firms and design teams. Perhaps the only constructive outcome of the White Paper was the biggest ever reorganisation of the industry with many famous names disappearing. For the workforce, this must have been awful, but amalgamation removed much of the waste from internal competition. With the growing world-wide export successes of America and France, it was important to work together from now on.

To be fair to the Air Staff and Ministry, the 1950s must have been difficult. With so much technological advance, one never knew what was coming next and when it did, somebody had to decide what to do with it. Consequently there was an ever growing number of requirements to accommodate it all and many were badly planned. The Operational Requirements Branch was staffed by medium to senior rank serving RAF officers and the intention was to keep a continuous flow of current experience running through with a parallel line of permanent civil servants, many of whom stayed for long periods. With RAF staff changes maybe every three years, personal whims and fancies, changes in the perceived threat and 'political' pressure from Government and industry, there was bound to be confusion and so development programmes rarely ran straight and true.

One is struck by how stories are repeated. A new design comes along or wins a competition which looks very attractive (a favourite description), so go-ahead is requested with

enthusiasm and all haste. After a while, problems start and the project gets held up. Then a rival appears or the designer reveals changes that look even better and so the earlier programme fizzles out. Is it any wonder there was indecision when the Air Staff had to handle a line such as Supermarine's Attacker, 510, 535, Swift and 545, each apparently better than before and competing with someone else's design?

There are two sides to this. 'Freezing' a design might be an error if the pace of technological advance quickly makes it inferior to its competition. But construction has to begin at some stage. Several outstanding fighters and bombers were lost, one or two when close to completion, but there are others that should never have been started. Easy to say all this with hindsight, but the experts were paid to make the correct decisions.

The plethora of parallel projects and the effort and time consumed on assessing brochures was wasteful. It has been suggested that perhaps 1,000 brochures covering every type of aircraft were prepared for the Ministry in the 12 to 15 years from 1945. Air Marshal Sir Thomas Pike, DCAS, wrote on 18th April 1956, while discussing the AW.169 interceptor to F.155T, that a 'frequent criticism, which may be thought to some extent to be justified, was that too many projects were embarked upon, particularly in the defensive field'. Too many prototypes were built and there were numerous bomber projects as well. The V-bombers were a success but the Sperrin and Valiant were ordered as an insurance against both the Victor and Vulcan. The Swift was an insurance against failure of the Hunter but was to become an even bigger problem itself. Such a policy of duplication was expensive and covered engines as well as airframes. Numerous programmes ran over time and over budget, Britain could not afford it all and the cancellations continued until 1965.

The industry had too many firms and only now was anything really done to sort this out. The one manned combat aircraft to survive the 1957 White Paper was the proposed 'Canberra Replacement' which led to the TSR.2 strike aircraft (itself cancelled in 1965), but prospective airframe and engine manufacturers could only win orders if they amalgamated. The outcome was the formation of two airframe companies: the British Aircraft Corporation (BAC) and Hawker Siddeley Aviation (HSA) and two engine companies, Rolls-Royce and Bristol Siddeley Engines. BAC comprised Bristol, English Electric, Percival, Vickers and Supermarine; the Hawker Siddeley Group had been established in the mid-1930s by

Hawker and Gloster, and quickly added Armstrong Whitworth, Avro and High Duty Alloys. Blackburn, de Havilland and Folland completed the formation of HSA in 1959-60. Amalgamation should have occurred much earlier, but that would have halved this book's size! BAC and the airframe side of HSA were nationalised in 1977 into British Aerospace (BAe).

–

Whatever the arguments for and against the new policy, the fact was there were to be no new fighters and some pretty good projects were sent flying out of the window. These might have become a handful financially, but that will forever remain conjecture.

OR.346

It was not until 1959 that the first signs of the 'policy' fading against the real world appeared in the form of the Joint Naval/Air Staff Target OR.346, in effect a 'wonderplane' for the 1970s and an outgrowth of TSR.2. The primary requirement was about 70% strike but there was also a 30% loiter interceptor-fighter element with a required four-hour Combat Air Patrol, carrying air-to-air missiles.

The projects offered included those summarised below, though because of the high percentage strike role, they would all qualify for coverage in full in a companion volume on strike/bomber aircraft:

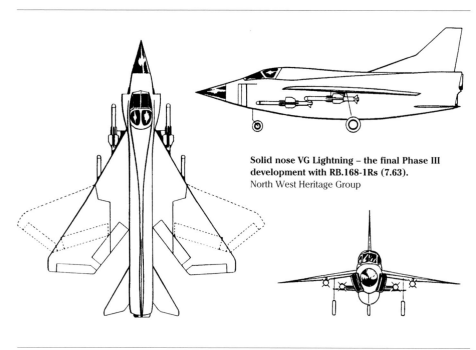

Solid nose VG Lightning – the final Phase III development with RB.168-1Rs (7.63). North West Heritage Group

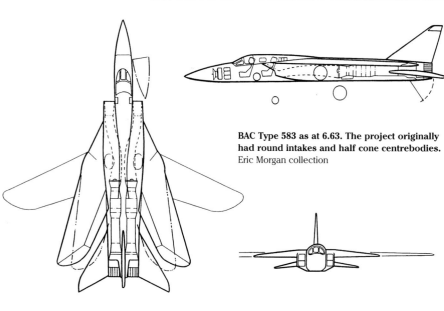

BAC Type 583 as at 6.63. The project originally had round intakes and half cone centrebodies. Eric Morgan collection

Blackburn B.123 – delta wing aircraft with two Rolls-Royce RB.168 military Spey engines for propulsion and two small RB.162 engines in the front fuselage for extra lift;

HSA (de Havilland) DH.127 – a tail-less delta with two RB.168s as the main powerplant and two RB.162 lift engines, sited ahead of the cockpit;

Hawker P.1152 – a supersonic aircraft with a variable incidence wing, one deflected vectorable main engine and four RB.162s;

BAC (Vickers) Types 581 & 582 – a variable geometry twin engine machine, and a curious twin fuselage design with the centre wing between the bodies, housing eight 1,800lb (8kN) dry thrust engines.

A research specification, ER.206, was written to cover these advanced concepts and in May 1959 Vickers received a contract to examine variable geometry in more depth. Any of these projects would probably have been as big a mouthful as the TSR.2 and there was never any chance of metal being cut, but they represented another stage in the line of development leading to the MRCA Tornado. The OR.346 work introduced separate lift jets for a vertical or short take-off and landing (V/STOL) capability. It was followed by NATO's NBMR.3 strike aircraft requirement that invited proposals from all over Europe, and the Navy's AW.406.

AW.406 (and OR.356)

Another combined strike and interception requirement but with emphasis on the fighter role as a successor to Sea Vixen for fleet defence in 1969-70. The RAF wished to replace the Hunter in 1968. As an interceptor, the machine had to be able to destroy a Mach 2.5 target at 65,000ft (19,812m) and low level targets at various speeds. Initial armament was four Red Tops but these were to be replaced by a new all-weather AAM to GDA.103 when available. For the strike role a weapon load of up to 8,000lb (3,629kg) on six weapon stations was specified including a lightweight nuclear depth bomb or WE.177. A reconnaissance capability was also outlined. Top speed at sea level had to be Mach 0.92 continuous cruise with a supersonic dash capability, and Mach 2.0 at the tropopause. A two-man crew was essential and maximum all-up-weight without stores was not to exceed 40,000lb (18,144kg). There was no gun. The full Joint Service OR.356/AW.406 was raised in April 1962.

British Aircraft Corporation (English Electric) Naval Lightning

The first 'swing wing' Lightning actually originated from Vickers at Weybridge under Type 588 and was part of an all-embracing study for converting current service aircraft including the Swift and Scimitar. The work was undertaken to NBMR.3 in 1961.

A naval Lightning appeared from Warton in about the middle of 1963 and was an unnumbered variable geometry project based on the two-seat T Mk.5 trainer. Changes from the T Mk.5 included the variable sweep wing, an enlarged dorsal fin fairing, arrestor hook, an inwards retracting undercarriage and an extended ventral pack with more fuel.

The existing Lightning wing was replaced by one where the outer portion had variable sweepback between 25° and 60°. At the higher angle, the new wing presented almost exactly the same planform as the fixed wing and thus required no new development flying. The wing had double slotted flaps and its fuel capacity was increased for a total aircraft capacity of 1,810gal (8,230lit), the sweep pivot and mechanism were based on work done at Weybridge. Variable sweep provided the Lightning with a low speed performance suitable for operation from existing aircraft carriers. The fin folded downwards to assist below deck accommodation.

For interception, a forward weapons bay housed either two Red Top, two Firestreak, two Matra R.530 or two Sidewinder AAMs (or 60 2in rockets for ground attack); two more AAMs could go on underwing hardpoints. For strike, 1,000lb (454kg) bombs, Nord AS.30s, Bullpups or Napalm tanks could go both underwing and/or in a ventral pack that replaced the central fuel tank. Because the weapon systems, structure and powerplant were fully-developed, development time would be minimal while the machine would benefit from the Avon being in service with the Navy already. From an ITP of January 1964, estimated first flight for a fixed wing prototype was spring 1966 with the first VG aircraft following in the autumn. At this stage, the aircraft carried the existing AI.23B radar but the need for a new system was acknowledged. The machine did not carry WE.177. An RAF version appeared later.

There followed in July 1963 a Phase III development with a solid nose to permit the installation of the 30in (76cm) radar dish required by AW.406. More efficient engines were now available and to take advantage both the intake and rear fuselage had been redesigned. Alternative engines in the same positions to the Avon were the Rolls RB.168 /1R, a reheated version of the Buccaneer Mk.2 Spey engine, and the smaller RB.153/61C. The latter could be incorporated in the existing Lightning rear fuselage except for the larger reheat nozzles which needed a small local increase in fuselage depth confined to the last

6ft (1.8m) of fuselage length. To accommodate the greater diameter RB.168/1R, a completely new rear fuselage was required which included an integral ventral pack and increased intake area. On both the new side intake system was of the double shock variable ramp type with separate ducts to each engine.

Two Red Tops were carried on fuselage pylons beneath the wing roots with two more on underwing hardpoints just inside the hinge. Usable fuel capacity was 2,000gal (9,094lit) for the RB.168 machine, 1,800 (8,184lit) for the RB.153. An all-up-weight with RB.168s and four 1,000lb (454kg) bombs of 47,450lb (21,523kg) was quoted for the strike role. The RB.153/61C version possessed the better subsonic performance, albeit by a very small margin, but supersonic performance was no better than the existing Phase 1 aircraft with Avon 300 series (RB.146), so no supersonic development was expected. Warton felt the RB.168/1R version was much more attractive with ample thrust at both subsonic and supersonic speeds and had scope for further advance. Performance improvement over the Phase 1 aircraft was substantial and the new 30in (76cm) radar dish was also now aboard.

British Aircraft Corporation (Vickers) Type 583

Weybridge's effort towards a Vixen replacement centred on two variable sweep schemes – the Type 583 CTOL aircraft and a vectored thrust VSTOL variant called Type 583V. Work started on the 583 as part of the firm's large on-going variable sweep programme which encompassed all the strike fighter requirements including Types 581 (OR.346) and 584 (NBMR.3). The Type 588 proposal had suggested converting two standard Lightnings with variable sweep wings but, as a second stage, these were to be followed by a new research aircraft. It was this desire to build a variable sweep research aircraft that dominated the effort described below.

In early June 1962 it was suggested the research aeroplane might be aimed at AW.406/ OR.356 and rough outlines were drawn for both a Vixen replacement at 40,000lb (18,144 kg) and a larger Buccaneer replacement (to OR.346) at 50,000lb (22,680kg), both having much in common with early TSR.2 studies. The research aircraft would be powered by two Avon engines, but in service the RB.153/61 then under development for Germany would be substituted.

According to the brochure, in general form the design was suitable for development to level speeds and heights to the order of Mach

4.5 at 85,000ft (25,980m). The smaller project quickly became the Type 583 but a version with two additional RB.162 lift jets placed behind the cockpit was prepared to the requirements of OR.355.

The 583 could operate from existing carriers and, apart from the needs of AW.406, be used with alternative equipment in the early warning role. Considerable advantages were suggested over a single engine fixed wing VTOL design (Hawker's P.1127 had by now made its appearance) and BAC felt the 583 was worthy of consideration on the grounds of operational capability. However, a disadvantage was that full development costs would be in addition to the RAF's OR.346 aeroplane. Ministry support enabled the firm to reach an advanced stage in the design and development of the airframe including full-scale structural and mechanical testing of the variable sweep features.

The wings were set at 25° for take-off, landing and low speed and swept through to 74° when fully supersonic, with an intermediate position used for transonic and high subsonic flight. The wing could also be 'over-swept' to reduce width for carrier stowage, the variable sweep provision taking the place of the normal wing fold with its associated systems. The moving wings carried blown trailing-edge flaps, leading edge slats and ailerons while the torsion box, of conventional construction, was sealed to contain fuel.

BAC envisaged the 583 as a multi-role design but initial service would be as the Navy's Vixen replacement. It was considered the Type 583 represented a third generation supersonic aeroplane and a second generation modern weapon system which involved an exacting process of equipment integration. The proceeding generation, TSR.2, had the same flight and temperature boundaries as the 583 which eliminated much of the development work required and helped BAC to achieve a high cost effectiveness. When, in 1965, the new Labour Government cancelled the Hawker P.1154 and announced an intention to order the Phantom, Weybridge swiftly submitted a brochure outlining the advantages of the variable sweep 583 over the American aircraft. The document indicated that the first service interceptor could be delivered in July 1970 from an ITP of May 1965, but the project died soon afterwards.

BAC (Vickers) Type 583V

The VSTOL 583V first appeared in two-seat form in a note dated 23rd August 1963. Besides OR.356's ground attack/all-weather interception, it could also be adapted to do the airborne early warning job. Powered by twin

Two-seat Type 583V with square intakes.
North West Heritage Group

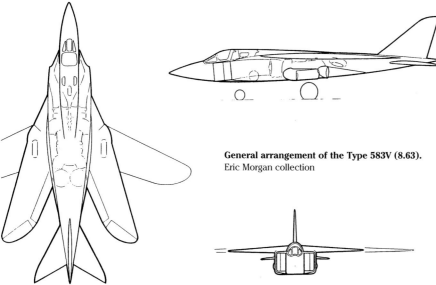

General arrangement of the Type 583V (8.63).
Eric Morgan collection

RB.168-32D vectored thrust engines, it displayed some benefits over single engine fixed wing designs, one being a substantial improvement on the Navy's required patrol times, range, take-off and landing performance. Another was a big reduction in aircraft lost from engine failure and the subsequent cost of their replacement.

Both Weybridge and Warton naval aircraft studies stressed the value of two engines in the event of engine failure. Previously it had been taken for granted naval aircraft operating for long periods over water should always be twin engined, but suggestions for the adaptation of a single engine aircraft to AW.406 had triggered severe debate. Much of it was political, but the good safety record of the single engine Hunter was an influence. In its VG Lightning brochure, Warton reported that in 24,000 sorties there had been 47 occasions when a Lightning had recovered with one engine shut down. In 24 of these cases there had been a total loss of power in one engine – a condition which would have resulted

in the loss of a single engine aeroplane. At a typical cost of £1m each, a considerable sum of money had been saved.

The Type 583V was estimated by Weybridge to meet or exceed with a single aircraft the requirements of OR.356 in almost all areas, but an in-service date of 1971 was given instead of the RAF's requested 1968 and Navy's 1970. The firm summarised, 'although the RAF and RN duties of the Joint Staff Requirement are at first sight incompatible, the design described comes very near to fulfilling them literally. It is a practical aeroplane which is suitable for both services'. At the request of the Ministry of Aviation, BAC completed preliminary estimates of a single-seat design to OR.356 on 7th November. This had round intakes with half-cone centrebodies and only two Red Tops were carried. The vectored thrust arrangement showed similarities to Kingston practice and one version even envisaged using a Bristol Pegasus engine. Another had a Rolls RB.141 Medway turbofan with switch-in thrust deflectors.

These variable sweep projects was hampered by a pending Government decision on the future of Britain's aircraft carriers and by the one British 'fighter' to gather real support during this period, the Hawker P.1154. None of these combined RAF/Navy combat aircraft were built but the 'commonality' concept now popular in America (same aircraft for both Air Force and Navy) exerted a powerful influence in Britain and reached a peak with the P.1154. Such a policy contrasted strongly with the separate service bomber and fighter requirements issued during the 1940s and 1950s.

With the passing of the P.1121, the Kingston design team had to look for new work. Fortunately, the concept of Vertical and Short Take-Off and Landing (VSTOL) had literally taken off and the firm's design of the P.1127 around the Bristol Siddeley BE.53 (Pegasus) engine is well documented. OR.345 was initially written around the P.1127 for a tactical ground attack aircraft and development proceeded into the Kestrel for evaluation by Germany and the USA in 1965. Further advance turned this into the Harrier close support strike aircraft which entered RAF service in 1969. In parallel with these subsonic aircraft, Kingston also worked on a more ambitious supersonic development.

Hawker (Siddeley) P.1150

In October 1960 discussions between Hawker and Rolls-Royce on future VTO projects finally centred on the P.1144 multi-engine supersonic strike fighter grossing 30,000 to 40,000lb (13,608 to 18,144kg). At the same time, the Air Staff turned towards a long range fighter for 1970 capable of Mach 4.5, 100,000ft (30,480m), multi-weapon strike, reconnaissance and interception.

When made aware that this was likely to gross upwards of 100,000lb (45,360kg), the Air Staff was somewhat surprised. Moving on the Hawker Board agreed on 13th April 1961 that preliminary design should proceed on a supersonic P.1127 called P.1150 and this was prepared to NBMR.3. But when the requirements were upgraded, the project was found to be too small and a new version, the P.1150/3, was drawn powered by a BS.100/9 engine of 33,000lb (146.7kN) static thrust. This was quickly renumbered P.1154.

Hawker (Siddeley) P.1154

A Defence Committee meeting on 6th December 1961 decreed that 'in future aircraft were to be developed to meet the needs of both the Royal Navy and RAF. Development of a supersonic version of the P.1127 should therefore, proceed with the requirements of both services in mind'. On the following 8th January Hawker's submission to NBMR.3 was delivered to the MoA for transmission to NATO when it was understood that, out of eleven submissions, the principal contender was the French Mirage IIIV which was being sponsored by BAC.

On 13th February 1962 a presentation was given to the Air Ministry, with representation from the Admiralty, and great interest was expressed in the aircraft. To Hawker, it was evident that the simplicity of vectored thrust with its ability to give good conventional flight performance was at last being appreciated and, in addition, considerable interest was now developing in the old fashioned interceptor because of the obvious limitations of a pure missile defence.

Soon afterwards the RAF was told it must accept the successful NBMR.3 aircraft in a version to suit both the RAF and Navy and it became keen to discuss the P.1154.

On 9th April Hawker's Assistant Chief Designer (Projects) was asked to visit the Director of Operational Requirements to discuss BAC propaganda against the vectored thrust concept as it was suggested that this was doing considerable harm to its cause. The Air Ministry was disturbed since it now openly supported the P.1154.

The first draft of OR.356 for a joint RAF/Navy Hunter and Sea Vixen replacement based on NBMR.3 was received at Kingston in late April, but as far as the naval aspects were concerned, anything less like NBMR.3 was hard to find.

Air Marshal Hartley, ACAS(OR), reported to Hawker that politically and financially the RAF was committed to sharing a requirement with the Navy. However, the RAF was to be allowed to keep its single-seater, when the Navy wanted two seats, provided it used the same large AI radar required by the Navy. Meanwhile, according to First Sea Lord Sir Caspar John, the Navy was accepting the P.1154 with its VTOL concept under protest.

Reports in the daily and technical press during July stated that the P.1154 had won the NBMR.3 competition, but for political reasons both the P.1154 and the Mirage IIIV would be recommended for development. Hawker learned that its aeroplane was technically coming out top but that political compromise might water down the choice of a single winner.

P.1154 was to be supersonic thanks to plenum chamber burning (PCB) in the low pressure fan air duct of the new bigger engine, a feature that would produce a very large and hot exhaust plume but deliver much higher thrust.

The firm's Joint Services OR.356/AW.406 submission around P.1154 was made on 8th August but criticism from the Navy centred around the bicycle undercarriage and its effects on catapulting and ship deck strength. Within a month, a wing mounted tricycle undercarriage had been investigated which appeared entirely practical. During December 1962 Rolls offered to fit the P.1154 with two PCB side-by-side Spey engines with crossover pipes and Hawker agreed to examine the scheme in more detail to compare it with the BS.100. A meeting with the Ministry on 24th January 1963 however, agreed that the Spey version was inferior and should be considered no further.

P.1127 deck trials on the carrier *Ark Royal* were made between 8th and 13th February to support the P.1154 project and proved very successful. Plans were underway to modify a Sea Vixen for testing the nosegear tow catapult launch but weight was now becoming a problem. Between March and July, P.1154's weight grew by almost 3,000lb (1,361kg) – roughly 1,000lb (454kg) 'natural' weight growth, 1,000lb from navalising and 1,000lb more from changes in role and equipment.

In early July the Navy criticised a new single-seat P.1154 then being offered and believed the RAF was stupid by sticking resolutely to V/STOL. The Navy said it would be content only with a 50,000lb (22,680kg)

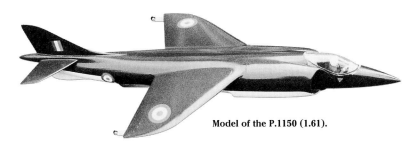

Model of the P.1150 (1.61).

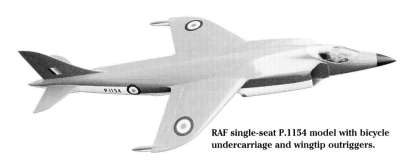

RAF single-seat P.1154 model with bicycle undercarriage and wingtip outriggers.

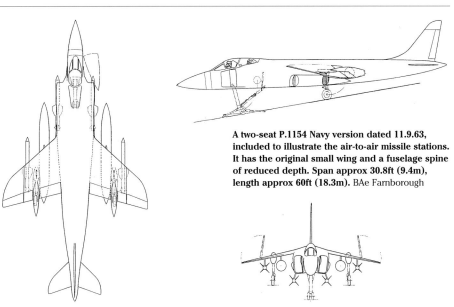

A two-seat P.1154 Navy version dated 11.9.63, included to illustrate the air-to-air missile stations. It has the original small wing and a fuselage spine of reduced depth. Span approx 30.8ft (9.4m), length approx 60ft (18.3m). BAe Farnborough

'swing-wing' fighter. Yet on the 30th, the Minister of Defence, Peter Thorneycroft, announced in the House of Commons that 'the RAF and Royal Navy have reached agreement on the characteristics of a common aircraft which will replace both the Sea Vixen and Hunter'. In fact, on the 16th a full-scale meeting of the MoA, RAF, RN and HSA had clarified that this would be a completely common aircraft except the two Services would need different nose radars owing to their differing in-service dates. The machine would have nose and wing folding, a high strength bicycle gear with catapulting and arresting (the RAF's was not to be catapulted however), Red Top and AI radar. The RAF accepted a 21in (53cm) pulse AI set because of its 1968/69 date, the Navy being unsatisfied with anything less than the 30in (76cm) Aspinall CW radar not expected to be available until 1971/72.

A new brochure requested from Hawker was completed on 21st August but the firm expressed concern that these new changes were taking the aircraft some way from a possible NBMR.3 export version. Next day, the Navy made it clear it was convinced that the P.1154 being offered was a second-rate interceptor while the RAF was most disappointed about the loss of strike performance. Discussion also began regarding installation of the BS.100 in the Vulcan flying test bed, Hawker stressing the need to include the intakes and most of the P.1154 lower fuselage as well so that early results on the aircraft as well as the engine could be obtained.

By October there was concern in the Ministry about the way the project was progressing, getting the same aircraft for both services was clearly going to be difficult. The Chief Scientist's Committee now recognised that attempting to combine a strike aircraft and fighter into a single airframe and attempting to make such a machine cross-capable between the RN and RAF was unsound. Towards the end of October the Air Staff began consideration of an alternative and on the 29th, the Minister of Defence and Chiefs of Staff agreed to proceed with two versions of the P.1154 involving substantial but not complete commonality. The 'common' aircraft was to be postponed until the late 1970s and plans for the immediate future now included a cheap subsonic aircraft for the RAF and the Phantom for the Navy. On 11th November both P.1127 and P.1150 were discussed for the RAF but declared technically and operationally unattractive. The best solution appeared to be the P.1154 for the RAF and the Phantom F-4C for the Navy.

Hawker learnt on the 18th that work was to concentrate on the RAF version, but a month later the Drawing Office began a full navalised twin Spey P.1154 with a big 350ft (32.6m²) high aspect ratio wing because Rolls-Royce had undertaken substantial work on the engine since the previous February. By mid-January 1964, Rolls' Cyril Lovesey had promised Spey 32D engines two years from go-ahead complete with contra-rotation, PCB and Mach 2+ capability. Engine weight had risen by just 90lb (41kg) from the previous year and 20,000lb (88.9kN) thrust per engine was promised for short periods, although 17,000lb (75.6kN) was likely for the prototypes (dry rating around 13,000lb [57.8kN]).

Preliminary performance indications for the big wing Spey P.1154 RN with 1,850gal (8,412lit) internal fuel plus another 450 (2,046) external and four Red Tops was a CAP endurance of 2.7 hours and a top speed of Mach 1.6 (1,400K PCB) or Mach 1.95 (1,600K PCB). The aircraft was well within catapult limits and Naval representatives who examined the P.1154 RN seemed quite interested. However, Rolls duly reported it could get 19,200lb (85.3kN) using 1,400K PCB but were unable to support 1,600K as the NGTE would not agree to the higher temperature at this stage. Ultimately the Navy aircraft was expected to achieve Mach 1.75 with the BS.100 Phase 3 and Mach 1.8 with two Speys at weights ranging from 48,000 to 49,500lb (21,773 to 22,453kg). The Phase 3 BS.100's take-off thrust was 39,700lb (176.4kN).

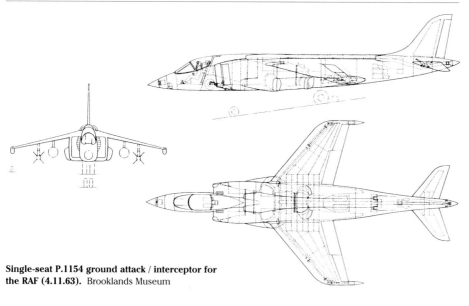

Single-seat P.1154 ground attack / interceptor for the RAF (4.11.63). Brooklands Museum

P.1154 in Royal Navy Colours. Note the wing fairings to accommodate the tricycle undercarriage main wheels and the two-seat cockpit.

Hawker generally favoured the BS.100 as it gave the better overall performance and was a little closer to hardware, but the firm was informed on 28th January that the choice between the naval variant and the Phantom was close. On 26th February Thorneycroft opened the House of Commons debate with the news that he was intending to place a development contract for the P.1154 with BS.100 for use by the RAF as a single service aircraft. This was to be predominantly a strike aircraft to specification SR.250D (replacing F.242 which had incorporated interceptor fighter elements). The document called for a strike and low level aeroplane able to sustain Mach 0.92, but capable of Mach 1.6 on the level. Four Red Tops on underslung pylons were still included. Hawker stated that first flight of the prototype would be two years from issue of first drawing. At this point, the Navy was allowed to begin negotiations for buying Phantoms.

The BS.100 engine ran for the first time on 30th October but contracts had yet to be placed with Ferranti for the nav/attack and radar system and there were worries that this would cause delay. At the end of the year, AVM Hartley visited the USA and, on his return, was able to inform Kingston that the P.1154 would more than hold its own with other aircraft, including the Phantom, in terms of performance in the strike role. He explained 'the closer one got to American aircraft the more we obtained information which suggested that they were not so marvellous as the view of them from this side of the Atlantic appeared'.

By now the Labour Government under Harold Wilson was in office and on 21st January 1965, Sir Arnold Hall visited the Prime Minister to discuss the Government's intentions for Hawker Siddeley aircraft. The interview suggested the position was felt to be 'reasonably satisfactory'. But on 2nd February Wilson announced in the House that the P.1154 was to be cancelled on grounds of cost and a timescale too late for RAF purposes. The RAF was going to be allowed to buy Phantoms and the Kestrel was to be ordered into Squadron service. The Kestrel was redesigned into the Harrier, the name having been reserved for the P.1154. Photographs show the P.1154 prototype's first fuselage frames were in their jigs at Kingston by November 1964 and, by cancellation, the front and centre fuselage framing was complete with the first skins in place. At Hamble, work began in early January 1965 on jigging the first pair of wings; two more sets were underway by the end.

This has been a most complex story to write and one guesses that the situation over

Royal Navy Phantom FG Mk.1, serial XT596, just after touchdown. An immensely successful type with over 5,000 built; no British jet fighter has ever seen such numbers. Ken Ellis collection

these three years was, at times, tough to keep under control. At one stage there were several P.1154s including single and two-seaters for the Navy and the most clear-cut moment appears to be Wilson taking over with his axe. With the end of P.1154, the Government bought the tried and tested McDonnell Douglas F-4 Phantom but had Spey engines fitted which proved to be such a difficult and expensive modification that, in the words of Bill Gunston, 'we had the biggest, most powerful, most expensive and slowest Phantoms in the world'. Britain was the first foreign customer for the aircraft and eventually got 170, split between the Royal Navy and RAF. The first machines, for the Navy, arrived in 1968.

The author has often wondered if Harold Wilson and several of his Ministers were really up to the task of dealing first hand with the complex problems of Aviation and Defence. However, cancelling P.1154 was probably a good move since a supersonic V/STOL fighter is yet to enter squadron service anywhere in the world. Research machines have flown (Russia's Yak-41 and the tilt-engine VJ-101 from Germany) but their careers suggest that, technically, P.1154 may have been a difficult and expensive objective for the time. Hopefully, the Joint Strike Fighter (Chapter 14) will one day make supersonic V/STOL squadron service a reality. A curious result of losing the P.1154 was that Hawker, the most famous and successful of all UK fighter firms, never built and flew a supersonic fighter, surely one of the oddest facts in British fighter history. Neither, of course, did de Havilland, Gloster or Supermarine.

HSA / BAe Sea Harrier

Hawker Siddeley Kingston continued with subsonic V/STOL to produce the Harrier; in fact it had little non-V/STOL work until the HS.1182 Hawk trainer arrived in the 1970s. In 1966 the projected CVA-01 class of fleet aircraft carriers was cancelled and the Navy's carrier force axed, the service being faced with the prospect of having no more seaborne fixed-wing combat aircraft. Its Phantoms were transferred to the RAF after a relatively short stay in Navy colours. However, new studies for helicopter carrying cruisers capable of taking an air group of more than nine machines showed that a clear flight deck or 'through deck' was needed, the proposals being labelled 'through-deck' cruisers to keep the politicians at bay. In April 1973 the first of what was to become the *Invincible* class was ordered, by which time the Harrier GR Mk.1 was established in RAF service.

Initial proposals for a Maritime Harrier to go with *Invincible* came in the early 1970s and in 1975 it was announced that the new ships would carry the Sea Harrier; a decision made sometime earlier. The name was chosen against an alternative of Osprey. Similar in appearance to the RAF's attack machine, the big difference was a new front fuselage and raised cockpit fitted with fighter avionics including the Ferranti Blue Fox radar. Main armament was the Sidewinder AAM. The first of 73 FRS Mk.1s flew on 20th August 1978 and the aircraft was highly successful, particularly in the 1982 Falklands War, despite being something of an improvisation to fill a need. But then the UK aircraft industry has always been adapting and improvising its products to suit a situation.

Go-ahead for an upgraded Sea Harrier, originally FRS Mk.2 but today the F/A.2, came in 1984 with AMRAAM for beyond visual range capability and the new Blue Vixen radar which needed a larger radome. It carries four

AMRAAMs, the initial plan to have only two was doubled, purely from the Falklands War experience. The Service's complement of F/A.2s will comprise both FRS Mk.1 conversions and new build aircraft, the first upgraded pre-production machine flying on 19th September 1989. At the time of writing, this latest Sea Harrier is described by many as one of the world's best air combat aircraft, thanks to its small size, agility and versatility. If Hawker's P.1121 fighter had gone ahead in 1957, would we have seen the P.1127 and all the Harrier variants that followed? Pass – but it's a fascinating subject to discuss.

The 1957 White Paper pretty well put an end to national fighter development in the UK for the best part of two decades. No pure fighter aircraft was pursued by the Air Staff or industry from the late 1950s to the 1970s; yet during this period the Americans developed and flew the excellent F-14, F-15 and YF-16. Thanks to the long series of early 1960s multi-role aircraft requirements, the acquisition of the Phantom and the subsequent multi-role Anglo-French Variable Geometry (AFVG) and Tornado programmes, the lists for the surviving fighter teams at Brough, Kingston and Warton show few fighter projects for the per-

iod. Not until the mid-1970s when Tornado was up and running did fighter design start again in earnest. Today British Aerospace Farnborough has replaced the now extinct Kingston site and still designs fighters, but not independently. Instead the team provides input with Warton and Brough into a country wide design organisation.

Projects from 1957 to 1974 – Estimated Data

Project	Span ft (m)	Length ft (m)	Wing Area ft² (m²)	All-Up-Weight lb (kg)	Powerplant Thrust lb (kN)	Max Speed mph (km/h) / ft (m)	Armament
VG Lightning (Interceptor)	48.2 (14.7) 36.6 (11.2) swept	50 (15.2)	?	43,000 (19,505)	2 x Avon 301 11,100 (49.3) 16,300 (72.4) reheat	Mach 1.06 at sea level Mach 1.9 at tropopause	4 x Red Top, Firestreak, Matra R.530 or Sidewinder
VG Lightning (Solid Nose)	48.2 (14.7) 36.6 (11.2) swept	50 (15.2)+	?	44,950 (20,389)	2 x RB.168/1R 10,360 (46.0) c.18,000 (80) reheat	Mach 1.43 at sea level Mach 2.2 at 44,000ft (13,411m)	4 x Red Top
Type 583 AW.406 (July 1964)	49 (14.9) 27 (8.2) swept	53 (16.2)	?	43,300 (19,641)	2 x RB.153/61R	Mach 1.1 at sea level Mach 2.5 at 55,000ft (16,764m)	4 x Red Top
Type 583V AW.406 (August 1963)	c.43 (13.1) c.25 (7.6) swept	c.52 (15.8)	250 (23.3) (25° sweep)	45,100 (20,457)	2 x RB.168-32D	Mach 1.1 at sea level Mach 2.5 at altitude	2 x Red Top
P.1154RN (Big wing, two-seat)	36.0 (11.0)	58.5 (17.8)	350 (32.6)	BS.100 – c.48,000 (21,773) Spey-32D – c.49,000 (22,226)	1 x BS.100 39,700 (176.4) PCB or 2 x RB.163-32D Spey 19,200 (85.3) reheat	Mach 1.75 Mach 1.8	4 x Red Top
Sea Harrier FRS Mk.1 (flown)	25.25 (7.7)	47.6 (14.5)	201 (18.7)	26,200 (11,884)	1 x Pegasus 104 21,500 (95.6)	c.Mach 0.97 at sea level Mach 1.25 at height in a dive	4 x Sidewinder, 2 x 30mm Aden in pods

The 'prototype' Sea Harrier FRS Mk.1, XZ450, shown in the hover.

Sea Harrier F/A.2 with AMRAAMs in August 1990. BAe Brough Heritage Centre

No More Fighters and a Reorganised Industry

Chapter Twelve

Nonconformists

The third Folland Gnat development aircraft, XK740.
Brian Kervell collection

Ideas outside the General Trend

This chapter covers items that do not fit neatly into the general course of events but demand deeper coverage than addressed in Appendix 1. Some are important, others just caught the author's eye.

Gloster CXP-1001 China Fighter, 1946

This project differs from all others in the book for it was designed purely for an overseas customer – what the Ministry describes as an 'offshore' purchase (i.e. an export).

The Chinese Nationalist Government was eager to modernise its Air Force and in mid-1946 sent missions to both the United States and Great Britain. The British Mission was split into three with one section investigating the design and construction of a jet fighter, the second a bomber and the third a jet engine. Negotiations brought proposals to collaborate with Gloster on the fighter.

An agreement dated 18th July 1946, stated that, as part of a plan to assist the build-up of a Chinese aircraft industry, 30 Chinese personnel were to be given facilities for 12 months instruction at the Design and Drawing Offices at Hucclecote (Sterling credit was already available). After six months, the Chinese Government could request Gloster to design and build three prototype fighter aircraft to a specification supplied by China and agreed by the firm. The aircraft were to have Rolls-Royce engines and be delivered in 30 months. China then had the option of acquiring the manufacturing rights to the aeroplane.

The 30 trainees arrived in September and a section of the Brockworth factory, complete with workshop and offices, was set aside for the visitors. It is thought each Chinese draftsman received an Austin 8 car. However, during these early days the security aspects presented formidable difficulties. For example, the Gloster Meteor and E.1/44 Ace fighters and Rolls AJ.65 and Nene II engines were all secret with little likelihood of information

on them being cleared for the Chinese. In fact there would be problems with any document marked Secret. Approval of a manufacturing licence for the Nene I was given but, as a result of misgivings expressed by the Air Ministry, Rolls-Royce was asked to defer completion of the contract for as long as possible. In November the Chinese Government asked Gloster to prepare a contract for the design of a single Nene powered fighter aircraft to be schemed with the assistance of the Chinese draftsmen.

Gloster requested Ministry permission to adapt to Chinese requirements the E.1/44 aircraft already building, but not to go into production, and this was agreed (the proposal was called CXP-102, dated 14th May 1947). But Colonel Ku, who conducted the negotiations with Gloster, wished to secure a more advanced design in view of the length of time needed to get a Chinese factory in operation.

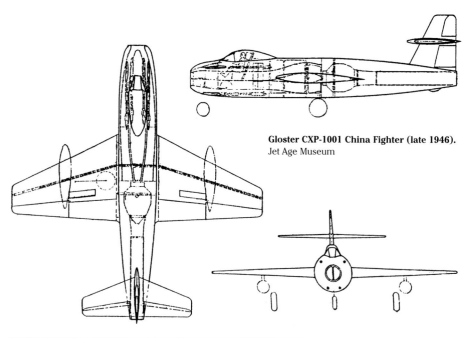

Gloster CXP-1001 China Fighter (late 1946).
Jet Age Museum

The Ministry refused because it objected to an overseas Air Force being equipped with a British design comparable to or in advance of that currently in UK service and, with available design capacity in the UK limited and the E.1/44 rejected, Gloster was to be invited to prepare a design to one of the specifications (F.43 and 44/46) shortly to be released. The Foreign Office opposed exporting arms to China because of the conflict between the Kuomintang (Nationalists) and the Communists, but did not object to a manufacturing licence as production was at least two or three years away.

In the end, the E.1/44 was thoroughly redesigned as the CXP-1001 though, at one stage in late 1946, the Meteor and Nene Vampire were considered as alternatives by the MoS. The biggest change from the E.1/44 was the nose intake. Length was 41.9ft (12.8m), span 38.0ft (11.6m), wing area 360ft² (33.5m²), normal gross weight 13,900lb (6,305kg) and overload 18,700lb (5,700kg). All-up-weight received considerable attention in the early design stages, a target weight having been set at 14,000lb (6,350kg). When the project closed it had reached 14,250lb (6,464kg). CXP-1001 was considered a fairly efficient design, power coming from a single 5,000lb (22.2kN) Nene engine. Four 20mm Hispano cannon were placed in the nose, two above and two below the intake, and top speed was expected to be 600mph (965km/h) at 10,000ft (3,048m) with sea level rate of climb 6,000ft/min (1,829m/min).

Progress was slow and by early 1949, with just two prototypes on order, only a mock-up and some components had been manufac-

tured. By now the Nationalists were suffering at the hands of the Communists and on 3rd February Colonel Lin contacted Air Marshal Coryton to inform him that the contract was to be cancelled and all work cleared up by the month's end. (This at last allowed Gloster to increase Drawing Office strength on the F.4/48). Gloster received confirmation to discontinue work on 28th February except for the completion and despatch of unfinished drawings, a model and part of the mock-up.

In fact, after the Chinese Communist takeover in 1949 the project continued for the Nationalists in Formosa, but release of drawings and components was frozen in October 1950 after Nationalists attacked a British merchant ship, the *Achises*. On 25th November 1952, Gloster decided to dispose of all remaining material without consulting the Chinese Central People's Government. The MoS said this should be acceptable as the aircraft was now an out of date design, but also stated it was not responsible for the firm's actions.

Saunders-Roe P.121
Hydro-ski Naval Fighter

Over many years, Saunders-Roe had built a strong reputation for producing flying-boats and on 16th July 1947, expanded the theme by flying Britain's first boat jet fighter, the SR/A.1 to Specification E.6/44 (also called P.113 and SR.44 in Saro files). The machine flew well and three prototypes were built, but was to remain something of a curiosity as equivalent land-based fighters were superior. However, before the firm moved on to the mixed-powered interceptors that were to make it famous by the middle of the next

decade, it was to try another type of water borne high performance fighter.

During 1949/50, Saro began to examine the merits of the hydro-ski and after intensive work in the experimental tank, was confident enough by mid-December to state that an aircraft with retractable water-planing surfaces was a practical proposition and to submit a project brochure for the P.121. The firm's study emanated from the idea of an undercarriageless fighter launched by an accelerator and landing on a flexible deck (next section) but research led to the realisation that retracted water-planing skis gave a body as clean as a conventional land fighter.

Take-off of a high speed aircraft on water was possible with a ski or skis extended under the surface like seaplane floats which as aircraft speed increased, pushed the fuselage upwards clear of the water so allowing it to skim the surface until take-off. The bonus was that once retracted into a relatively small space as an integral part of the body, the skis offered much less drag than either buoyant floats or a flying-boat hull. The smooth, rounded underbody presented when the planing surfaces were retracted also lent itself to use from carriers equipped with the accelerator and flexible deck.

P.121 had its skis mounted beneath the forward fuselage and small wing tip skis were fitted that deployed for lateral stability. When afloat but static, the wing trailing edges were level with the water surface. Four 30mm cannon were placed either side of the cockpit watertight doors fitting over the gunports. For production, power was to be a Sapphire 4 of 12,500lb (55.6kN) reheated thrust, but provision was made in the prototype to have an unreheated Sapphire 3 of 7,500lb (33.3kN) to reduce weight. This machine also lacked the guns. Emphasis was placed upon simplicity and ease of maintenance and all major components such as wing, engine, tailplane, etc were readily detachable. The overall dimensions were kept inside the necessary limits for storage to avoid any need for wing folding. Span was 39.75ft (12.1m), length 51.5ft (15.7m), wing area 490ft² (45.6m²) and all-up-weight for the 'light' prototype was 16,500lb (7,484kg), increasing to 22,000lb (9,979kg) for the full aircraft.

The wing planform was chosen for a best performance of Mach 0.94 at altitude and 1.1 in a shallow dive. The dry Sapphire 3 was expected to give the first aircraft a maximum speed of 617mph (993km/h) at sea level and 542 (873) at 45,000ft (13,716m), and an initial rate of climb of 6,700ft/min (2,042m/min). For the reheated Sapphire 4 these figures became 705 (1,134) and 615mph (989km/h)

The first prototype Saunders-Roe SR/A.1
flying-boat jet fighter, TG263, moored outside
its hangar at Cowes.

and 16,200ft/min (4,938m/min). The two versions were expected to show a take-off distance on water of 980yds (896m) and 840yds (768m) respectively which equated in time to 9 and 28 seconds. For carrier only operations, all-up-weight could increase to 25,000lb (7,620kg) with extra fuel for long range work.

A G Smith of the MoS stated that Saro had achieved a logical and very practical solution to providing a high subsonic fighter designed primarily for aerodynamic performance, but with a secondary role of being able to land on sheltered water for tactical reasons and training. Overall performance, particularly stability, was probably better than one would expect on most current seaplane designs, but the need for it would be assessed once comments on a parallel American aircraft, the Convair Sea Dart, were received. Drag was rather more than one would normally accept because of the high wing loading and it was doubted if the P.121 afloat would behave well in cross swells. Behaviour should be satisfactory in choppy seas of the type experienced in harbours and sheltered waters. Recommended practice would always be to land across wind, along a swell, and so it would be important to provide adequate cross wind handling characteristics. Smith stressed there was no doubt the P.121's water performance would improve but emphasised this was essentially a landplane with an auxiliary water device.

RAE studied the proposals and felt confident the design could achieve a satisfactory water performance. After much debate, how-

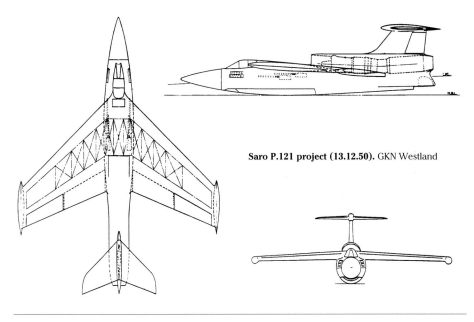

Saro P.121 project (13.12.50). GKN Westland

ever, it was agreed that using a wing as thin as the P.121's could show high Mach number problems similar to those exhibited by Hawker's P.1052 and the Supermarine Swift. By mid-June 1951, Saro was expressing some anxiety to get moving, but the MoS's Chief Scientist, H M Gardner, felt the retractable skis may be a failure and suggested that first experiments should determine the efficiency of the ski system. The MoS stated that the skis, tip floats and water rudder were responsible for a 3% increase in all-up-weight. By July no one could decide what to do with the P.121 as further model trials could serve no purpose.

On 29th January 1952, the decision was reached not to build an aircraft specific for research purposes. The real problem was the cost of a new aircraft when there was nothing currently available that could be readily converted. The earlier SR/A.1 was considered hydrodynamically 'quite unmobile'. P.121 was made public in mid-1953 by Saro's in-house magazine. The only water-ski jet fighter to fly was American's delta wing Convair Sea Dart which made its maiden flight on 9th April 1953 and reached about Mach 1.2 at 36,000ft (10,973m). Single and twin ski arrangements were tested and a modest production order placed, but the project was abandoned after problems with the skis and the growing development programmes for carrier-borne supersonic fighters. Watching a jet fighter take-off on full power from water must have been quite something.

Undercarriageless Fighters and Flexible Decks

The earliest jet engines were so thirsty that the first generation of jet fighters were handicapped by poor range and endurance and, consequently, a substantial effort was targeted towards improving this situation. Jet engines would ultimately appear with a much improved fuel consumption, but how long this would take was unknown and so one remarkable theory was thoroughly tested as a possible short term solution.

Discussions for operating aircraft without landing gear were underway before the end of the Second World War, primarily for carrier machines but also for land-based aircraft. The landing gear represented about 5% of a land-based fighter's all-up-weight, this figure increasing to 7% for naval fighters because of the extra strength needed in carrier landings. If that weight could be turned into fuel, range and endurance would improve drastically.

At an RAE meeting on 1st January 1945, Major Green outlined his idea for using a rubber carpet stretched between shock absorbers for landing naval fighters with their undercarriage removed, the fighter catching an arrestor wire and then pitching onto the carpet. It was then removed on a trolley.

'Belly' landing full size dummy aircraft proved successful and a decision followed to modify some de Havilland Sea Vampires for trials, initially on a flexible deck sited at RAE and then on HMS *Warrior*.

The Meteor was rejected as being unrepresentative of future high performance aircraft due to its engine nacelles. Trials began at RAE in late 1947, and the first successful operation achieved on 17th March 1948. The first successful undercarriageless landing on *Warrior* followed on 3rd November and the experiments continued through to the end of 1949. Two hundred landings on *Warrior* without serious accident clearly demonstrated how undercarriageless fighters were a practical proposition and by January 1950, proposals had moved on to testing Hawker Sea Hawks ready for a fully operational machine expected by end 1952. But, the experiment stopped for it was realised building lots of flexible decks everywhere and modifying aircraft would prove costly when only a small performance gain resulted.

The tests thus brought forth no service aircraft, but for a while brochures appeared for new undercarriageless fighter projects including the swing wing submissions to ER.110T (in Chapter 9). Should a winning design to that specification have proceeded, it would have been torpedoed by the abandonment of the flexible deck.

Artist's Impression of the Supermarine Type 543.

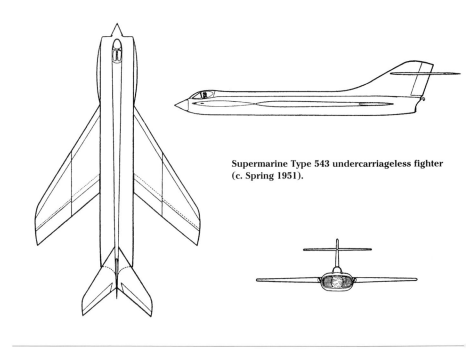

Supermarine Type 543 undercarriageless fighter (c. Spring 1951).

Supermarine Type 543

This brochure described a supersonic fighter designed to reach 45,000ft (13,716m) from sea level in 3 minutes and utilising a catapult take-off and carpet landing. Alternative armaments comprised four 30mm Aden cannon or two Adens and 20 recoilless 50mm guns each firing a spin stabilised rocket. Maximum level speed was 882mph (1,420km/h), Mach 1.16, at sea level and 1,013mph (1,630km/h), Mach 1.53, at 36,000ft (10,973m). Sea level rate of climb was 37,000ft/min (11,278m/min). The use of reheat to 1,800K was expected to increase speed to 1,117mph (1,797km/h), Mach 1.69, at 36,000ft. Span was 32.5ft (9.9m), length 58.5ft (17.8m), wing area 450ft² (41.9m²) and normal all-up-weight 30,300lb (13,744kg).

Both Naval and RAF versions were offered and Supermarine explained that with the aircraft carrier already available for conversion, the latter required the bigger changes in existing practice. The firm envisaged two possibilities:

1. Highly camouflaged and substantially bomb-proof permanent bases for defence;
2. Mobile advanced bases from where high performance aircraft with approach speeds of 170mph (273km/h) could operate, but needing relatively small areas of flat surface.

Proposals for ground handling airframes without undercarriages comprised a special eight wheel trailer for each aeroplane with a suitable number of tractors. Carpet, catapult and hanger facilities and movement between them were fully mechanised, but it was acknowledged the problem of handling undercarriageless aircraft was still open and a solution acceptable to all involved, operators, ship constructors and aircraft designers, would not emerge until the whole thing had been thrashed out.

Forty-six years on, it is clear that lifting and moving the 543 would have been a far slower process than taxying around an airfield, but the advantage was that a runway was no longer needed and thus no longer vulnerable; one of the main reasons for vertical take-off aircraft becoming important a few years later. In addition, the construction of forward airfields for aircraft of this class would be a formidable problem for civil engineers, expensive in both time and labour. The light mobile equipment necessary for the 543 was easily picked up and put down elsewhere, the firm comparing the operation to moving a circus or fair.

Removing the undercarriage obviously offered gains in performance, but Supermarine highlighted the less obvious alternative of a reduction in aircraft size and cost and suggested that achieving the same performance as the 543 with an undercarriage would need an aircraft at least 35% larger. Both single and twin engine designs were considered initially, but the latter, as expected, showed substantially the better performance for the same military load. The single engine did not achieve the maximum speed aimed for by Supermarine and was inferior in time to height and ceiling. As to twin engines, three wing loadings, 48, 60 and 72lb/ft² (234, 293 and 352kg/m²) were investigated and while there was a difference of 192mph (276km/h) between the most lightly and heavily loaded designs, the gain in ceiling for a 2g level turn was only 2,800ft (853m). Supermarine did not feel this small increase justified such a large loss in maximum level speed. Studies also suggested there was little advantage in using wing sweep angles beyond 55°.

Drawings and performance were based on two Bristol BE.15 engines mounted side-by-side which was the largest axial jet available with the highest possible degree of reheat, but alternatives were an Avon development, the Sa.50 Sapphire development or Napier's E.143. Engine arrangement followed the basic layout and experience of the Type 525 N.9/47 then under construction, stacked engines being rejected in favour of the horizontal position as the latter gave less total drag for a constant wing area. But supersonic requirements necessitated nose intakes and jet pipes through to the extreme rear fuselage.

The wing was very thin (from 5 to 7% t/c ratio root to tip) but structural methods developed for the swept wing Swift and 525 were capable of meeting the severe strength and stiffness requirements imposed by supersonic flight at low altitude. A droop-nose high lift device stretched along the entire leading edge and double slotted flaps were fitted from wing fold to fuselage side. A cruciform variable incidence tail was provided and the normal 'sting' type arrestor hook was relatively short due to the absence of the undercarriage. The guns were housed in the fuselage side and were 'extremely accessible', while the 50mm rockets were stored in the wing roots. Opinions of the Type 543 at the Ministry could not be traced, but the passing of the undercarriageless fighter and flexible deck concept ensured it remained a 'paper plane'.

Armstrong Whitworth AW.165

When the author first saw this project brochure in the old museum at RAE Farnborough, someone had scribbled in pencil around 40 years earlier 'this might be worth looking into if something blows up'. If something had 'blown up', say with the Soviet Union, there would have been little time to do anything with the AW.165 for this was a *big* fighter. In fact its size did not register immediately and it would have been quite an aeroplane if built but, at the time, there was no requirement. This unsolicited brochure, dated November 1952, described an aircraft that became the first in a short series of supersonic fighters from AWA, the others being the AW.166 and AW.169 (see Chapters 7 and 8).

AWA explained its theories for future all-weather fighters. In the past, the fighter had always been able to overtake the bomber by accepting a short range, relatively large power units and a small fuel supply. Where rate of climb was not the primary factor, typically in escort fighters, range was increased with drop tanks. The latest jet bombers all appeared to rely on the same general principle of evasion, i.e. fly as high as possible and at the greatest subsonic speed to avoid an appreciable rise of drag coefficient. To overtake its adversary therefore, the opposing fighter would need a high rate of climb and the ability to fly supersonically on the level. To achieve supersonic speed, which appeared essential, the fighter must accept the penalty of a drag coefficient which may treble itself between Mach 0.9 and 1.1 and require reheated engines that consume fuel very quickly.

Thus it was clear to AWA that the fighter must accept a shorter range than current types and use supersonic speed only during pursuit and combat. The high altitude aircraft showed great gains in efficiency if its low altitude performance was restricted and ideally high and low interceptions would require different aircraft. Wing loading was critical since although a high loading increased speed and reduced structure weight, a low loading was essential for high altitude manoeuvrability.

At this time no jet engined combat aircraft in Britain or America was capable of supersonic speed in level flight and AWA thought it impractical for a fighter carrying armament and all-weather search equipment to exceed the speed of sound by a large margin. A Mach number of 1.1 or 1.2 was felt adequate to catch the fastest subsonic bomber. The long range bomber was likely to remain subsonic for some time and the need for a Mach 2.0 fighter was questioned. AWA considered if the minimum time to height was achieved by a subsonic climb, the subsequent period of acceleration formed an important part of the total time and distance to intercept. Acceleration thus became of overriding importance when a jet fighter was forced to attempt an interception at an altitude not far below its ceiling.

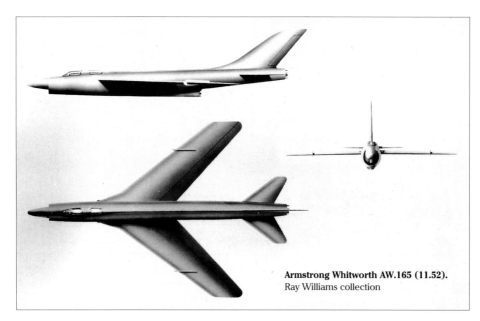

Armstrong Whitworth AW.165 (11.52).
Ray Williams collection

For the AW.165, considered a possible successor to the Javelin, the equipment required by a two-seat all-weather fighter ruled out a small aircraft. Layout was conventional bar heavy sweep back on wing and tail but a high lift for manoeuvrability at altitude was attained by means of wing fences. Low speed performance was improved by fitting plain trailing edge flaps. Two Sapphire Sa.7 engines of 11,000lb (48.9kN) dry thrust were mounted in tandem in the fuselage using a common frontal intake which divided internally to feed both engines, AWA's research showing this was the optimum arrangement for high speed. The rear engine only was reheated, the forward engine pipe protruding from the bottom of the fuselage. The upper nose housed the airborne interception radar scanner, equipment AWA considered a big handicap to supersonic aeroplanes but there was no evidence that a better way of locating enemy aircraft would be available in the future.

AW.165 artist's impression. Wing fences had been added when the brochure was issued.
Ray Williams collection

The undercarriage retracted into the fuselage because the wing, only 5% thick at the root and decreasing sharply towards the tip, had insufficient depth. An all-moving tail was mounted on a special ring which encircled the rear jet pipe and all controls were power operated using a system that was fully duplicated as long as one of the engines continued to run. Span was 46.75ft (14.2m), length 80ft (24.4m), wing area 730ft² (67.9m²), total fuel was 800gal (3,638lit) and gross weight 31,500lb (14,288kg). Maximum speed was 834mph (1,342km/h), Mach 1.25, at 40,000ft (12,192m) and a climb to 50,000ft (15,240m) would take 4.5 minutes. Armament comprised two wing root mounted 30mm Adens or two batteries of 40 unguided rockets in the fuselage or two underwing Blue Jays.

Substantial private venture aerodynamic research was completed on the AW.165 well into 1954, despite no official support by mid-1953. According to Ray Williams' Armstrong Whitworth records, the MoS's lack of interest in the fighter was that it offered 'too short a step in performance and too large and complex an aircraft compared to the then official concept'. As Ray says, 'somewhat of a contradiction'.

Lightweight Fighters

A lightweight fighter aircraft was an idea often pushed by designers and the example of this type to come closest to RAF service was the Folland Gnat. The concept of a simple interceptor had been discussed for several years prior to the Gnat's appearance and was certainly under consideration at the MoS in 1949. The first requirement for a Light Interceptor Fighter was issued in July 1951 based on proposals from Folland.

OR.303

An aircraft that could be produced quickly and in great numbers was required to meet an anticipated and most serious threat to the UK, that of massed raids by Soviet Tupolev Tu-4 bombers (Boeing B-29 copy), of which 1,000 were expected to be in service by 1954. This created the possibility of a 'Power Pack' turbojet of about 50 hours life and a light fighter to attack the enemy bombers in the height band 25,000 to 30,000ft (7,620 to 9,144m). An order for 24 light fighters for tactical trials was requested with production underway by July 1953.

W E W Petter left English Electric and his P.1 supersonic fighter behind in 1950 to join Folland Aircraft. He immediately began work on a lightweight fighter called the Gnat whose transonic performance was equal to that of a larger aircraft, the project was the stimulus that brought forth OR.303. Other proposals to the OR included a stripped de Havilland Venom with the same military load and endurance as the Gnat while Freddie Page, who had succeeded Petter at English Electric wrote on 20th September that his suggestion would have the wing configuration lauded by the North American F-86 and the Hawker P.1067. It would be powered by two of the new little expendable Rolls-Royce RB.93 engines developed from the RB.82, one in each wing root. The Venom was still 100% heavier than the Gnat but had a better take-off performance thanks to its straight wing.

The MoS decided to award a development contract to Folland in October without resorting to design tender, the geometry of the Folland project being broadly the same as the eventual Gnat Mk.1. The aircraft also used two 1,500lb (6.7kN) thrust RB.93 Soar engines, but Rolls-Royce decided not to proceed with the development of this missile engine for use in manned aircraft because of other commitments. This move forced the Air Ministry to abandon the idea of a light Tu-4 interceptor for a brief period in December as no other suitable engine was available. Bristol, however, put forward a plan to develop a suitable engine (the BE.22 Saturn) and the light fighter programme continued with this new engine. The craft was seen as an ideal carrier of two infra-red homing missiles.

By July 1952, the MoS had concluded that the Requirement would result in an aircraft approaching Hawker Hunter dimensions and whose weight would ultimately rise to the same level should guided weapons be mandatory along with a full endurance. It was felt Folland's project went some way to meeting equipment and performance targets but its ability to carry Blue Jay was doubted. Throughout 1952 the Air Staff tried to state a minimum requirement that Folland's proposals could meet, but failed to produce a suitable document.

In July 1953 the Air Ministry stated it was no longer interested in a light interceptor for financial and other reasons, but the 'Gnat' flew on 11th August 1954 as the private venture Fo.139 Midge with a 1,640lb (7.3kN) Viper 101 engine. The change of name signified a preliminary version of the Fo.141 Gnat because the engine earmarked for the aircraft, the Bristol Orpheus, was not ready. The Saturn powered Fo.140 had been abandoned when the engine, really planned for Bristol's Type 182 flying bomb, was stopped. A little later Bristol had introduced the new more powerful Orpheus that perfectly suited the Gnat.

The Midge was assessed by A&AEE Boscombe Down, whose enthusiastic comments noted excellent basic handling qualities and good longitudinal characteristics. It made a sound foundation for the more highly developed Gnat and, on the basis of these results and estimates of the performance of the Orpheus engine, the latter had every prospect of being a good fighter provided the equipment carried proved adequate for operational roles. As a consequence, a development batch of six Gnats was ordered in March 1955.

Folland Fo.141 Gnat

The full lightweight day fighter made its maiden flight on 18th July 1955 and really was a small aeroplane. Span was 22.1ft (6.7m), length 29.67ft (9.0m) and maximum weight 8,233lb (3,734kg), but the single 4,520lb (20.1kN) BE.26 Orpheus 701 allowed it to reach a maximum level speed of Mach 0.97 and climb to 45,000ft (13,716m) in 5 minutes. Beyond the threat, the major driving force behind this aircraft's conception was a need to stop the ever increasing cost and complexity of each new generation of fighters. Intensive effort over several years at Folland had evolved this small high performance machine at a fraction of the cost of a large conventional fighter and it was capable of performing most single-seat fighter operations. Weight saving measures utilised new features such as a one-piece wing with no landing gear, weapons or fuel, the main armament being two Adens in intake fairings. Ground attack weapons could be carried.

The RAF could not be persuaded to buy the Gnat, particularly when deeper inspection at Boscombe Down brought criticism of the tailplane and elevator control systems. Bitter controversy resulted but after modifications, export orders were won by the fighter, in particular Finland and India, the latter eventually building 150 machines of its own. A trainer version of the Gnat, the Fo.144, was ordered by the RAF in 1958 and became the Service's standard advanced training aircraft. There were, however, further proposals for Gnat fighters including, initially, a naval Gnat with the Mk.1 fuselage and the larger wing of the trainer, but the long saga in Chapter 1 ensured little time was spent considering that option.

Folland Fo.143 Gnat Mk.2

A big change from the original Gnat with the 8% thick wing replaced by a similar one of 6%, reheat added to the Orpheus to give a substantial increase of thrust to 5,750lb (25.6kN), plus some additional integral tankage. Project development was concurrent with the Mk.1 and both a structural test and a flight wing were built, the former being successfully tested. Several proposals for reheat were considered, the most favoured from Bristol Siddeley Engines which necessitated modification of the rear fuselage.

This project was felt suitable for meeting the requirements of the Yugoslav Air Force with an optional alternative armament of air-to-air rockets in external pods and, eventually, replacement of the Gnat's simple radar ranging set by an interception radar, probably Ferranti's AI.23 which gave a fatter nose. With this radar, this aircraft was called the Gnat Mk.2/4. Another weapon choice was two Sidewinders.

Level speed stretched well into the supersonic region, the MoS estimating Mach 1.1 at 36,000ft (10,973m) with the manufacturer quoting 858mph (1,380km/h), Mach 1.28, at 35,000ft (10,668m) together with a 2.7 minute climb to 40,000ft (12,192m). Span was 22.2ft (6.8m) and wing area 137ft^2 (12.7m^2). All-up-weight was 7,865lb (3,568kg). The Air Ministry asked the MoS in October 1954 for an evaluation of the Mk.2 which showed the aircraft was promising.

By January 1955, the Air Ministry was preparing an Operational Requirement around the Mk.2, specifically naming the aircraft, and Folland was estimating an in-service date of 1957. But the aircraft was never built.

The Folland Midge (G-39-1), private venture predecessor of the Gnat.

Gnat Mk.4 and Mk.5

The Mk.4 was another supersonic Gnat with a new 160ft^2 (14.9m^2) 5% wing and full span flaps. This was expected to have the high speed performance of the small thin wing (in fact Mach 1.5) and the low speed performance of the large trainer wing. The engine was a reheated Orpheus 6 of about 8,000lb (35.6kN) thrust and interchangeable with the 701. The Mk.5 followed after slow progress at Bristol on the Orpheus high altitude reheat system brought the decision to find an alternative powerplant, the choice falling on two RB.153s, an engine only slightly behind the Orpheus 6 in development. Little structural change was required and top speed was increased to Mach 1.7+. Later the project developed into a Mach 2.4 high altitude interceptor with a much changed and streamlined shape that showed little of its Gnat ancestry. Span and length were both 24ft (7.3m) and

all-up-weight 11,100lb (5,035kg). Reheated to 2,000K, the RB.153s gave 5,400lb (24kN) thrust each and the machine carried AI.23 radar and Firestreak or Sidewinder missiles.

In January 1955, a memo from R H W Bullock at the MoS in reply to a *Sunday Chronicle* newspaper article highlighted several points that counted against the Gnat being ordered for the RAF. First, there never was an Operational Requirement stated by the MoS that the Gnat could meet, while the lack of a suitable lightweight engine, on which the whole project depended, meant an in-service date of 1956-57, so ordering Gnats would not have made a quick contribution to the defence of the UK. In some respects the Gnat would probably have a better performance than the Hunter and Swift, but in others it did not meet the requirements that they did, despite being three years later. Finally, the Gnat's take-off and landing advantage over those aircraft

was not as good as had been suggested [Hunter take-off with drop tanks is 5,100ft (1,555m) – Gnat 3,500ft (1,067m); landing distance similar although a Gnat tail parachute would considerably reduce this]. A NATO Working Party had criticised the Gnat's take off and landing characteristics when the aircraft had always been designed to operate from concrete runways.

A 1954 NATO requirement for a light fighter and tactical aircraft had also been based on Petter's concept and the Gnat was considered, but the competition was won by the Italian Fiat G.91. In the RAF there were thoughts that the Gnat was so small it was not worth putting a fully trained pilot in it. A weakness of the Gnat was that it was too small for some pilots, an important point when pilots come in all shapes and sizes.

BAe Hawk

Today, the British lightweight fighter is represented by the Hawk 200, a development of the Hawker Siddeley HS.1182 Hawk trainer. The Gnat trainer's most famous role was as a mount for the Red Arrows aerobatic display team until replaced by the Hawk in the late 1970s. An immensely successful design that has sold all over the world, the Hawk was designed from the start as an advanced trainer and light ground attack aircraft, first flying in 1974. A private venture redesign by British Aerospace into the relatively cheap single seat Hawk 200, reversed the Gnat's evolution path, the prototype flying on 19th May 1986. Powered by the 5,845lb (26kN) thrust Rolls Royce Turboméca Adour Mk.871, Hawk 200 carries an Aden gun pod below the fuselage and four Sidewinders, for a maximum take off weight of 20,062lb (9,100kg) in the Airspace Denial Role. It can reach 540 knots / 621mph (999km/h) at sea level, Mach 1.2 in a dive; sea level climb rate is 11,510ft/min (3,508m/min). At the time of writing, Hawk 200 is the last all British fighter.

A Lead-In Fighter Trainer (LIFT) development of the Hawk was announced by British Aerospace in September 1998. Much-modified, it offers specially instrumented cockpits for training pilots progressing to Eurofighter Typhoon, Saab Gripen, F-16, F/A-18 etc.

Ideas Outside the General Trend

Chapter Thirteen

Trails to Typhoon

Eurofighter, (DA.2), ZH588, has had
its RB.199s replaced with EJ.200 engines.
Export aircraft are called 'Typhoon'. BAe

The Return to Real Fighters: 1975 to 2000

The next few years should see the introduction into service of Eurofighter, an event long awaited by Governments, Manufacturers, Air Forces, pilots and enthusiasts alike. It has been a long wait. The story of the European Fighter Aircraft (EFA) or Eurofighter 2000 (EF2000) or Typhoon, names which actually relate to the same aircraft, really began during the early 1970s. Gestation spreads across something like 25 years from before the birth of British Aerospace, although work on the aircraft itself began in the mid-1980s. Many delays resulted from the decisions and non-decisions of the Governments involved but for once (so far) without a big cancellation. It makes a fascinating story, but one must stress that a fully detailed account is some time away.

The previous chapters have reported fighter developments from over 30 years ago for which there is a liberal supply of accessible records both public and private. On reaching the 1970s, the situation changes for it is likely to be at least another ten years before the first files of official documents on this subject are opened under the 30 year rule. Consequently, one has to rely on company archives (where material also remains secret), personal reminiscence and contemporary magazine and newspaper items to piece together a part complete account. For a subject loaded with politics, a good deal of the Ministry's behind the scenes role will have to wait. It is possible to report on many of the designs that were prepared, but detail is limited and important weapon system and avionics information must remain classified for as long as is necessary, which in many cases will comprise Eurofighter's entire career.

AST.396

The first seeds for Eurofighter came with the publication of Air Staff Target 396 in late 1971. This called for a Jaguar/Harrier replacement low level interdictor capable of full battlefield support against the massive Warsaw Pact armoured forces; air-to-air was a minor role. To later issues of the AST, BAC Warton forwarded developments of the Jaguar strike aircraft under its P.86 and P.87 and all-new blended body fixed wing, delta and VG designs under P.88, P.89 and P.91 respectively (P.90 was a comparative non-blended body design).

HSA at Brough began a series of single RB.199 powered light combat aircraft with its P.153 and P.154, whilst also persevering with the tried and tested Buccaneer in a variant

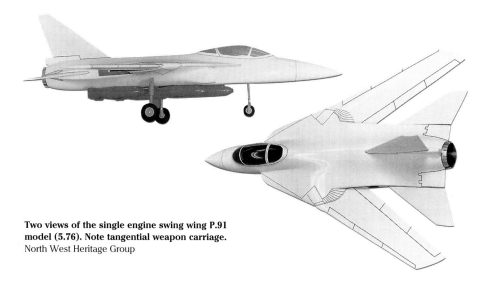

Two views of the single engine swing wing P.91 model (5.76). Note tangential weapon carriage. North West Heritage Group

The twin engine P.92 model (1976). North West Heritage Group

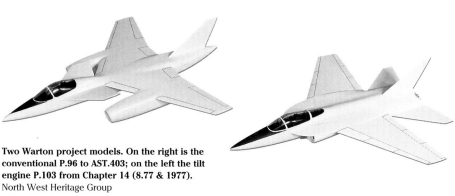

Two Warton project models. On the right is the conventional P.96 to AST.403; on the left the tilt engine P.103 from Chapter 14 (8.77 & 1977). North West Heritage Group

Designed as a strike aircraft, not a fighter, the Jaguar, which is still in front-line service today, was nevertheless the main subject for replacement by AST.403. XZ356 was photographed during its time with 14 Squadron. North West Heritage Group

called HS.1197. HSA Kingston was much involved with advanced Harriers and offered at least two versions, plus another of the Hawk trainer. AST.396 caused the industry much anxiety for it was considered in many ways to be flawed. A major element was the STOVL capability which, mixed with complex avionics and the required range, predicted a heavy technology problem and huge costs. There was some relief when the document was withdrawn and superseded by AST.403.

AST.403

Dated 8th July 1975, this was still called *Offensive Aircraft to Replace Harrier and Jaguar* but air-superiority was becoming the primary element. Progress was gradual and on 10th February 1978, AVM Harold Bird-Wilson (now working for BAe) discussed the requirement with ACAS(OR), AVM D P Hall, to find there was still hesitation on the fighter's true primary role. Air combat and all that it entailed in the Second World War, and offensive support with a call from the Army Staff for a fighter to 'keep the enemy air off our backs', were factors highlighted. It was understood that even the Battle of Britain and then Dunkirk air tactics came within the discussions. Hall also stated that vectored thrust was a high penalty to pay for a short take-off requirement. Collaboration with another country was really 'the name of the game' for AST.403.

AST.403 marked the redirection of MoD interest from ground attack to air-to-air. The impact made by the General Dynamics F-16 influenced the outcome because here was an aircraft developed for dogfighting with a performance close to the RAF's attack specification. Airfield performance was duly relaxed to allow a big increase in air combat capability; air-to-ground became secondary but was still important. Supersonic speed up to at least Mach 1.6 was requested from a single-seat aircraft with advanced radar and navigation/attack systems. A wide range of air superiority fighter projects was forthcoming from the three fighter design teams still functioning, HSA at both Brough and Kingston and BAC Warton. Hawker Siddeley did more work to the Staff Target than has been appreciated but much of it began before the document was issued and was not always fully related so is therefore examined in Chapter 14. The following Warton projects resulted from many studies.

British Aircraft Corporation
P.91 and P.92

With design of the variable geometry MRCA Tornado out of the way, it was only to be expected when Warton's Advanced Project Office turned its thoughts to new fighters that studies would include high aspect ratio swing wing aeroplanes such as the P.91 and P.92. This pair were essentially single and twin RB.199 versions of the same project, the second certainly to AST.403, the long movable wings extended from a large fairing around the fuselage. For ground attack, P.91 could use its 'wide' fuselage to carry six bombs.

P.93

Another single RB.199 project, but this time with a delta wing. The P.92, P.93, P.95 and P.96 families all had side intakes which were located under large wing strakes similar to those fitted later to the unstable fly-by-wire Jaguar (see p.137). All were studied in parallel and were, apart from the lifting surfaces, near identical. P.96 shared the fuselage and tail of the P.92. Variables such as single or twin engines were investigated, one parameter at a time being changed, but the P.93 delta was dropped as a 'non-runner' quite early on.

P.95 and P.96

Two conventional fixed wing layouts from 1976-77 with one and two RB.199s, the single engine P.95 repeating Brough's work on lightweight fighters but disliked by the RAF who felt it had 'half the effectiveness of the twin-engined aircraft at two-thirds the cost'. There were arguments against this, not least that you could buy more aircraft for the same money. However, export potential rarely features in Operational Requirements and, like the earlier Gnat, the lightweight fighter still entertained little support. The twin engine P.96 resembled a scaled McDonnell Douglas F-18 Hornet with single fin and gothic leading edge extension and was altogether more popular with the RAF and Ministry. Comparison with the F-18 meant competition and in some ways the P.96 was superior, the large leading-edge strake enabling P.96 to be agile at high incidence.

Considerable attention was paid to weapon carriage without resorting to semi-conformal mountings within the aircraft's structure and the final arrangement of flat-bottom areas with stores touching their surface was simpler and gave little extra drag over the conformal arrangement, and much less than previous methods. With a short take-off and landing performance, the P.96 looked good and fitted the Staff Target well. It became the 'datum' solution agreed for AST.403 but was the end of the line in 'conventional' layouts and would probably not sell abroad. Both P.92 and P.96 concepts were duly overtaken by the canard delta, a step ahead of the pure delta and repeated the world over by the Gripen, Rafale, Israel's Lavi and others. All the twin engine designs were quite big and heavy, but that ensured the weight of a full weapon and avionics load presented no difficulties.

P.97 'Super Jaguar'

A Jaguar with a new big wing, composite construction, fly-by-wire and a pair of RB.409-07 or Adour 63 engines. This was a complete update of the Anglo-French strike aircraft, but considered a long shot for the Staff Target.

–

These studies fell within what was called the Pre-Feasibility phase (the American F-15 Eagle and F-18 Hornet were also considered early on). In the 1970s the F-15, F-16 and F-18 set the standards around the world and most or all of Warton's studies possessed excellent agility to give better combat capability than the F-16. Agility is an essential characteristic for achieving air combat superiority and was described by Ivan Yates as 'exceptional manoeuvrability, that is very high rates of climb, turn, roll and acceleration throughout the very wide speed range involved and up to exceptionally high aircraft incidences'. High subsonic and supersonic agility was deemed essential to survive air-to-air combat against the latest advanced missiles. A very long debate took place in the UK on whether to put the agility into the aircraft or just the missile, but the US was satisfied it was the aircraft that needed the agility and by making the F-16 and F-18 so capable, ended the argument, although similar conclusions were reached in the UK.

To simplify matters, the Harrier Replacement component of AST.403 was withdrawn in early 1979, rewritten as ASR.409 and later satisfied by the order of 60 GR Mk 5 Harriers based on the McDonnell Douglas AV-8B.

AST.403 was re-titled *An Offensive Aircraft to Replace Jaguar* and was endorsed by the Operational Requirements Committee on 19th April 1979 which approved commencement of Feasibility Studies over a 12 month period from July. It confirmed both conventional (P.96F) and vectored thrust (HS.1205-11 [see Chapter 14]) concepts had been studied during the Pre-Feasibility phase before endorsement.

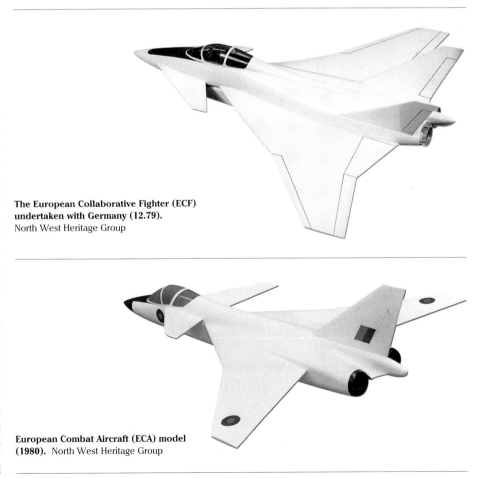

The European Collaborative Fighter (ECF) undertaken with Germany (12.79). North West Heritage Group

European Combat Aircraft (ECA) model (1980). North West Heritage Group

An in-service date of 1984 was requested but the Warton team felt a suitable advance in materials and technology to make a new project worthwhile would set the earliest achievable date at 1987.

The Staff Target became a demanding document and no purely British project could be built to it because of the cost; declared UK policy was that any major new national project could not be funded alone. At the time of writing, most official opinion of the AST.403 studies remains under wraps but none were at any stage considered starters. The only affordable option was an F-16 or F-18 purchase. Up to about 1985, the drain on the Air Vote from variants of Tornado meant that little money was available for any other new manned fixed wing project, and in this climate the Air Staff could do little with AST.403 (or 396 before it). It was ACAS(OR) who insisted on the performance standard and the various propositions from the three firms were either too far below requirements, too expensive, had too big a timescale, or all three. None proceeded beyond initial study phase despite the enthusiasm and hopes of the designers.

AST.403 was effectively cancelled by John Nott's June 1981 White Paper, entitled *The UK Defence Programme: The Way Forward*, but not withdrawn until 1st May 1984 when it was succeeded by ASR.414 for an Agile Combat Aircraft. Nott, the Conservative administration's Defence Secretary, had ordered a full defence review and the Paper explained there was to be 'no direct and early replacement of the Jaguar Force [but] we are continuing work and discussion with potential partners on future combat aircraft'.

ECF

Other European nations were now working on new fighters, not least Germany who by 1979 had prepared the concept definition and general requirement for its TFK.90 aircraft to replace the Phantom after 1990. Dornier, Messerschmitt-Bölkow-Blohm (MBB) and VFW-Fokker all offered conventional or canard delta projects and with such like ideas, and the close links forged from the Tornado programme, thoughts moved swiftly towards a joint Anglo-German fighter. A proposal by BAe and MBB was formally presented to the British and German governments as the European Collaborative Fighter (ECF) in December 1979, the study having taken three months.

This had a cranked delta with all-moving canard, a chin intake for the two RB.199s and twin fins, and was constructed in mock-up. The engines were positioned such that deflection of the main propulsive thrust was possible (i.e. thrust vectoring nozzles could be added) to enhance airfield and combat performance. Twin versus single fins was studied closely at this time; the conclusions were marginal but the twin was more modern. Some support was forthcoming but the politicians wanted more partners, in other words France who had recently begun its *Avion de Combat Tactique* (ACT.92) requirement. Thus the ECF was soon pushed aside by the European Combat Aircraft or ECA.

ECA

Merging three separate requirements into a common design presented plenty of problems, but the new technology of fly-by-wire (FBW) was seen as an important part of the solution. A tri-national study team was set up in October 1979, Dassault-Bréguet joining the ECF partners. Co-operation was discussed in London in January 1980 by the French and British Defence Ministers, M Yvon Bourges and Francis Pym (Nott's predecessor), and agreement on a common airframe and tentative programme for ECA was reached and announced in mid-April by the firms. The parties involved described talks as 'extremely

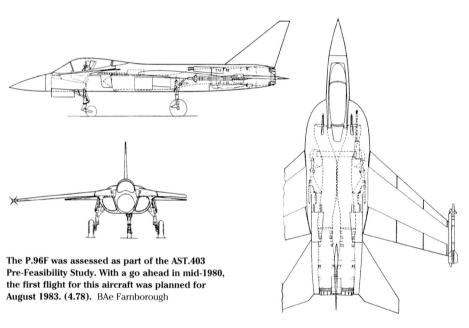

The P.96F was assessed as part of the AST.403 Pre-Feasibility Study. With a go ahead in mid-1980, the first flight for this aircraft was planned for August 1983. (4.78). BAe Farnborough

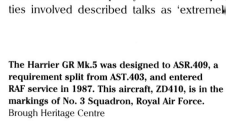

The Harrier GR Mk.5 was designed to ASR.409, a requirement split from AST.403, and entered RAF service in 1987. This aircraft, ZD410, is in the markings of No. 3 Squadron, Royal Air Force. Brough Heritage Centre

uccessful', a common aim being to increase he fighter content across the requirements of ll three air forces. A work-share framework or a 700 aircraft production run was drawn up with a predicted in-service date of 1991-92. Test-bed aircraft were to fly in 1982 and two prototypes in 1984. No suitable radar was available in Europe, the solutions being a derivative of the F-18's APG-63 or an expensive start from scratch. It was on this aircraft that he name Eurofighter was first coined.

Work proceeded until March 1981 when the Ministries re-examined their requirements and mission priorities and declared ECA unaffordable, a shortage of cash (particularly by Germany who has suffered from this problem ever since) preventing a development launch. General Friedrich Obleser, *Luftwaffe* Chief of staff, stated the three nations' requirements were too far apart to justify economically a joint project, while Dassault declared its participation depended on having 'design leadership'. It never even tabled any configurations. ECA had the now usual canard cranked delta but with a single fin and side intakes beneath the wing roots. ECF and ECA were good designs and capable of much of what Eurofighter can do now, their structure and fly-by-wire differed slightly from today's aeroplane but in the early 1980s presented a greater risk. Eurofighter's avionics have now matured and are a generation later giving a more effective fighting machine, but the earlier avionics would have benefited from a mid-life update.

The period embraced by AST.403, ECF and ECA saw the first movements away from some conventional methods of design and construction. The canard delta became a favoured layout due to its manoeuvrability, but the gains were bigger still when full time fly-by-wire was introduced which delivered artificial stability to a aircraft purposely designed to be unstable. In other words the demand for inherent airframe stability was relaxed but kept controllable by electronic means, a situation known as Relaxed Static Stability (RSS). A normal delta relies on a big vortex over the upper surface to act as a lift generator as it flows from a sharp leading edge, the method used by the French Mirage III in 1956. A slab-type canard foreplane ensures this vortex is produced when used with a sharply swept wing, but Eurofighter has been made very unstable and the control surfaces need active control from a computerised system, like an auto-pilot, that continuously monitors and reacts to airflow disturbance.

The benefits of artificial stability can be dramatic and include enhanced performance, or reduced size and weight for a given performance; for a strike fighter perhaps 8 to 10%. The canard wing plan benefits as much as any and British Aerospace found that artificial stability made it competitive to other configurations at subsonic speeds and superior when flying supersonically. Such systems need to be totally reliable and ensuring the software was free from bugs caused delays to the Eurofighter programme in the 1990s, a vital step since software problems had caused the loss of early examples of Sweden's JAS 39 Gripen and America's YF-22A Raptor prototype. Key elements of British research in the early 1980s included active controls, FBW, digital cockpits and lightweight materials. To help mature the new technologies, test flying followed in an adapted Jaguar demonstrator (see pages 137-8). The digital cockpit reduced weight and, very important, pilot workload.

The new properties of relaxed stability and continuous automatic control of high lift devices had, when combined with engines giving thrust-to-weight ratios in excess of 1:1, given a big step forward to fighter design, comparable perhaps to regular flight above Mach 1.0 20 years earlier. Programmed leading and trailing edge flaps provided camber for combat agility, the all-moving canard stability as a weapon platform. The potential manoeuvrability of these new aeroplanes for dog fighting was tremendous, the aerodynamics being fine tuned before manufacture by computer-aided design (CAD). CAD has made it much easier to get an optimum shape than in the 1950s by cutting the need to calculate/recalculate internal volume and surface area for weight and performance. The cost of developing the software does mean, however, that combat aircraft prices have risen enormously, but an offset is increased capability.

New lightweight airframe materials such as carbon fibre composite and aluminium lithium alloys (the lightest aluminium ever), coupled with advances in engine materials and technology, ensured big reductions to predicted weight of around 15 to 20% which translates into increased performance and manoeuvrability. Carbon fibre prevents many parts having to be made in metal and allows complex shapes to be made cheaply. Many projects specified the Turbo-Union RB.199 which was designed for the Tornado bomber, but the 199-62R was to have a modified compressor, new fan and reheat improvements tailoring it to the fighter role with 15 to 20% more thrust.

This was the preferred engine of Britain and Germany, but the French were working on the SNECMA M.88, an engine rather larger than the RB.199 and specifically designed for new fighters. It prevented interchange on the ECA and was another factor in that aircraft's demise, this opening series of collaborative proposals ending with the collapse of the European Combat Aircraft. Much knowledge had been acquired, but only stacks of paper produced. Just about every major aviation project becomes political and CAD and advanced technology are no help when that stage is reached. The biggest problem for Eurofighter, and for the projects that proceeded it, was to ensure that full political support was forthcoming. Years were to pass before this was accomplished.

BAe P.110

Early AST.403 studies were funded by the Procurement Executive of the MoD who declined payment for unconventional projects which meant industry had to pay for some of its own ideas. Once the Harrier element had

Model of the P.110 agile fighter (1980/81). North West Heritage Group

been withdrawn from the Staff Target, government support became more concrete on ECF and ECA. As these faded, Warton shelved the 'datum' P.96 while continuing studies on a wide front and then bounced back with the P.110, a project it took very seriously but one that had to be solely company financed again. Important improvements were identified for the RB.199 and these, coupled with a size reduction from the defunct ECA, led to a potentially very attractive agile fighter. Roy Boot, Executive Director New Aircraft, prepared the P.110 concept during February and March 1981 and by year's end the design had largely been frozen. With funding, it could fly in about three years.

To cut risk, maximum commonality with the engine and airframe systems of Tornado was derived together with the advanced structures and avionics of the ECA and fly-by-wire of the Jaguar demonstrator. The avionics were prepared solely for air combat as envisaged by the Industrial Avionics Working Group, but the addition of ground attack items was foreseen and catered for. Rolls-Royce had proposed three stages of engine development beginning with the current RB.199 unit and finishing with a largely new engine tailor-made to the requirements of advanced fighters. The cranked delta-canard stayed after what were by now very in-depth studies into the configuration. To avoid regular changes of requirement and political interference, a separate and dedicated project team was visualised for the following UK national programme:

1. Initial studies to continue to mid-1982;
2. Drawing issue to commence late in 1982;
3. Manufacture of six development aircraft to begin 1983 with first flights through 1986;
4. Start of production during 1985 with first flight of first production aircraft late 1988;
5. Initial release to service early 1989.

–

BAe felt there was a strong need for a P.110 type aircraft with superior manoeuvrability over the F-16. Around 40% of the structure was to be made of carbon fibre including the forward fuselage, wing, canard and fins while the quadruplex digital fly-by-wire active control system was based on the Jaguar test bed's. Full project support for initial design work up to a £9m limit was forthcoming from Rolls, Ferranti, Marconi, Smiths Industries, Dowty and Lucas from mid-1981 until December 1982, Ferranti starting work in March 1981 on a pulse Doppler radar for a 'European Fighter Aircraft'.

The extra thrust given to the RB.199 would raise thrust-to-weight ratio in excess of one ensuring the aircraft's STOL characteristics would be rather better than Tornado's. BAe hoped this would stimulate MoD funding as it felt the aircraft had substantial export potential, but would not sell without a clear statement of support from the government. The official MoD attitude was no cash for a Jaguar replacement in the short term so BAe would have to find the initial funding costs and wait to see if the RAF eventually placed an order. There were still many in the RAF and MoD who favoured a supersonic V/STOL machine not a 'redesigned F-18', and a project like the P.110 was looked upon as wasteful.

It was now something of a stalemate. King Khalid of Saudi Arabia was approached during a UK visit in mid-June 1981 to help split the predicted £1,000 million cost (Oman was another possible contributor). Work proceeded on a single engined light fighter, the P.106 (see p.140-1), as a possible alternative collaborative programme with India and Sweden. At the time however, the Saudis were receiving F-15 Eagles as replacements for Warton built Lightnings and were not interested. Possible purchases would be considered by Middle East nations if a flying P.110 could be viewed, but not for a 'paper plane', so lobbying resumed for domestic support (four years later the Saudis did order the Tornado).

Acceptance of a P.110 type by RAF chiefs as a future service aircraft was secured, and some political interest was also forthcoming, but John Nott completed a close examination of the P.110 at the end of March 1982 and stated BAe would need an international partner for final development. A full scale mock-up of the P.110 to focus attention was the only 'hardware' completed.

A separate BAe team still had direct contact with MBB and one difference of opinion centred on the intake position. BAe favoured the side intakes of the P.110 because they gave a lower cockpit/front fuselage for easier maintenance, better undercarriage layout and improved under-fuselage stores carriage. The Germans favoured the ECF's chin intake with

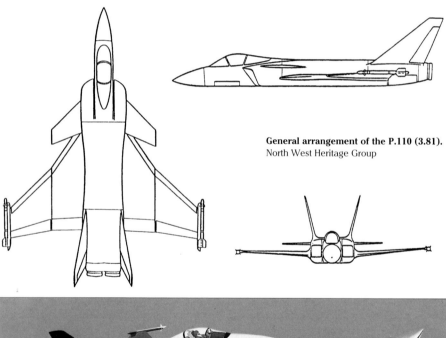

General arrangement of the P.110 (3.81).
North West Heritage Group

Two views of the Agile Combat Aircraft (ACA) that had much in common with P.110 except for the chin intake and closer canted fins (1982).
North West Heritage Group

forward canard for good handling at high an-gles of attack well past the normal stall. P.110's side intakes would not be acceptable for this and BAe agreed to relocate them be-neath the fuselage; a compromise that con-siderably assisted the next phase.

ACA

During April 1982 BAe, MBB and Aeritalia re-vived their Tornado partnership with the all-weather capable Agile Combat Aircraft (ACA) which closely resembled the P.110 except for the chin intake. Equipment was to include a long range Marconi pulse-Doppler look-down/shoot-down radar derived from the Tornado ADV's Foxhunter plus integrated ad-vanced communication, navigation and weapon systems. Ferranti was to furnish an inertial navigation system developed from Tornado's and the Blue Falcon strike radar as an alternative to the intercept equipment. The baseline RB.199 was to have a 14in (35.6cm) afterburner extension for improved high altitude performance giving ACA a sea level thrust to weight ratio better than 1.2:1. It was designed to out-perform any other pro-duction aircraft within the same time-scale and for the primary air superiority role carried cannon, four AMRAAM on low drag partly submerged fuselage hardpoints and two wing tip ASRAAM, with further missiles such as ALARM on wing pylons. Bombs, guided weapons and munition dispensers were al-ternatives for ground attack work.

Along with these advanced fighter projects, work was in hand on a new generation of air-borne missiles including the Advanced Medi-um Range Air-to-Air Missile (AMRAAM) to replace Sparrow and Sky Flash, the later Ad-vanced Short Range Air-to-Air Missile (AS-RAAM) under SR(A).1234 to supersede Sidewinder, and the Air Launched Anti-Radi-ation Missile (ALARM) to AST.1228 which was designed to seek out and destroy enemy radar sites. Technology was moving ahead in all areas. ACA could deploy from a Quick Re-action Alert state or Combat Air Patrol and employ exceptional climb and acceleration. Take-off could be accomplished in 1,640ft (500m). It was publicly unveiled in full size mock-up in September's SBAC Farnborough Show and shown again at Paris the following May when the French presented some re-markable competition in the shape of Das-sault's *Avion de Combat Experimental* (ACX) mock-up placed nearby. This had a single fin and different style intakes, but otherwise was strikingly similar. It was later named Rafale.

In July Geoffrey Pattie, Under Secretary of State for Defence Procurement, stated that 'the Air Staff has considered the type of air-

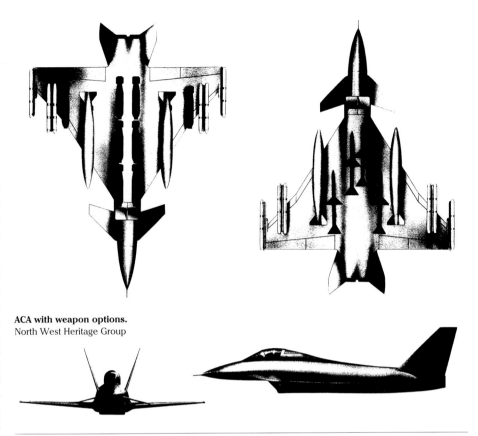

ACA with weapon options.
North West Heritage Group

craft to AST.403. It was found impossible to fund the costs of such a project in the defence programme. Nevertheless, studies had been initiated to assess how far the development of new technology allows the performance tar-gets of a future combat aircraft to be met, at what cost and in what time-scale [and] tech-nology programmes were started to explore more accurately these new possibilities. An aircraft project of that type is likely to be be-yond our national resources; without some major cost-sharing, through joint ventures with industry, both nationally and interna-tionally, it would be impossible for the de-fence budget to meet unaided the heavy front-end investment associated with new high technology combat aircraft'.

Pattie, Air Chief Marshal Sir Douglas Lowe (Controller Aircraft) and the Permanent Sec-retary at the Ministry of Defence, Sir Frank Cooper, became key supporters for con-structing a UK experimental aircraft once col-laboration with MBB became possible. After full preparation of the case for such an air-craft, John Nott gave the go-ahead just before the outbreak of the Falklands War in spring 1982. Funding was 50:50 between the MoD and industry with BAe left to decide on its in-dustrial partners. Germany and Italy joined in on a two aircraft programme, one to be built at Warton and one by MBB. Having started as ACA, BAe disclosed on 26th May 1983 that a

contract had been signed for development and construction of what was to be called the Experimental Aircraft Programme (EAP). Such a step could not have been made with-out constant support and investment from Sir Frederick Page and the British Aerospace Board.

FBW / ACT Jaguar

Before describing EAP, we must tie in anoth-er line of development. Fly-by-wire has been described, but a Jaguar aircraft was modified to test the theories for the first time on an es-tablished airframe. BAC Warton and HSA had both assessed FBW way back in 1975/76 with proposals for modifying a Jaguar and Bucca-neer respectively. The former was chosen, the MoD deciding to proceed with an active control technology (ACT) programme in 1977. This was the consequence of some promis-ing results from studies at Warton and a gov-ernment specification and requirement were laid down. All funding was to be paid by the Ministry. A standard GR Mk.1, XX765, was loaned as a test airframe in which a digital quadruplex fly-by-wire control system was in-stalled. This was a one-off modification; there were no plans to upgrade the Jaguar fleet, in-stead just the gathering of knowledge for the next generation of warplanes.

XX765 flew in modified form on 20th October 1981 as the first practical digital ACT

The fly-by-wire Jaguar in 1981, as first modified.
North West Heritage Group

aircraft to fly with production standard equipment. Software development problems had delayed the first flight by about a year. The unstable condition was created initially by putting around 560lb (254kg) of lead in the tail to move the CofG back beyond the centre of lift (centre of pressure). This induced -4% instability but had limits as the aircraft would eventually sit on its tail when the CofG moved beyond the main wheel centre of contact.

A second stage moved the centre of lift forward by fitting large leading edge root extensions or strakes, similar to the P.96's, forward of the wings along the intake boxes which destabilised the aircraft by -10% in the longitudinal axis and turned it into what was called a control configured vehicle (CCV). A standard Jaguar was never less than +2% stable. In de-stabilised form the aircraft was manually unflyable due to instant pitch up or nose down, but the pilot was linked to the control surfaces by computers which made flight corrections 50 times per second to generate artificial stability. Flight testing began on 15th March 1984, and was a great success, the strakes introducing a 'marked improvement in performance, especially at low speeds during take-off and landing, with less drag and significantly improved turn rate'. The programme continued until 1985.

EAP

The Experimental Aircraft Programme was the rather uninspiring title given to a technology test aircraft designed to demonstrate as much 'state-of-the-art' as possible, although there was no doubt that a European fighter was to be the main beneficiary of the research. It also helped to keep the design team in being. Manufacturing costs were cut to a minimum with numerous firms supplying parts or services free. For example, the author's company, High Duty Alloys, received free aluminium forging stock for processing into rough shape forged parts at no cost. Existing components were adopted where appropriate, not least the fitting of an adapted Tornado rear fuselage and fin.

MBB withdrew most of its support in December 1983 on German government instruction, although other German firms and Aeritalia (against advice) stayed in, and so only the Warton aircraft, ZF534, was built. Losing MBB meant the centre and rear fuselage were made in light alloy instead of carbon fibre and standard Tornado ADV engines were used. Major British players (and payers) were the MoD (who contributed costs for manufacture and first flight only), BAe, Ferranti, GEC Avionics, Dowty, Smiths Industries and Lucas. Final assembly was underway by late 1985 and unveiling took place at Warton in April 1986 to near complete ignorance by the general media, a sad fact for what was the first British single-seat 'fighter' prototype since the 1960s. ZF534's maiden flight took place on 8th August 1986 and it eventually completed 250 flights, support work closing in 1991.

To illustrate the potential problems of multi-national aeroplanes, the port wing was made by Aeritalia and the starboard by BAe using different CAD programmes, but worries that the resulting wings might be different were alleviated when both developed a minor leak in the same place. It was easily cured. As a flying laboratory, EAP saved substantial Eurofighter development costs in gathering experience in new materials and construction methods, unstable aircraft, flight control systems and delta canards at speeds up to Mach 2 and in areas such as radar stealth. Much of the risk was taken away and

a House of Commons Accounts Committee stated publicly that £850m had been saved by reducing Eurofighter's development time by a year (a figure now rather smaller perhaps thanks to delays in Eurofighter's software). EAP confirmed the value of the technology demonstrator and looking back, can be considered one of the most successful research aircraft ever built. One is reminded of the knowledge available to the P.1B Lightning from the P.1A 40 years before.

Demonstrators were used in other areas too. Back in 1982, an unknown factor was how plastics and composites would behave after battle damage (when good experience was available with aluminium and titanium) and a model was used to create realistic conditions. This proved to be difficult research, but much was learnt including the ability to repair broken joints that then passed the required destruction tests. Another vital step was development of a generic engine called the UK Advanced Core Military Engine (ACME or XG.40) in a demonstrator programme which took place in the early 1980s and totalled over 200 hours running time. The knowledge gained found its way into Eurofighter's EJ.200 engine. This and other research work ensured that by the early 1980s, all the key engine and airframe technologies necessary for a new supersonic fighter were underway.

Eurofighter 2000 (Typhoon)

EAP's first public demonstration was at the Farnborough Air Show in September 1986 when BAe also displayed a full size mock-up of EFA, the European Fighter Aircraft, to show what it might look like. New feasibility studies for a European fighter had begun during 1983 and an Outline European Staff Target for a Future European Fighter Aircraft (FEFA) specified a twin engine, canard cranked delta single-seat agile machine with STOL capability to be in service in the mid-1990s. Primary role was air defence with air-to-surface a secondary consideration. Empty weight was set at around 9,500kg (20,950lb) to balance Britain's desire for an 11,000kg (24,250lb) machine and France's 8,500kg (18,745lb) aircraft for export. Further studies realised the more definitive European Staff Target (EST) on 11th October 1984.

But France's needs would not allow a configuration agreeable to everyone and in February 1985 two concepts were offered, one by Dassault alone and another jointly agreed by the other four nations; the main difference lay in the relative positions of the intakes and canards. The four-nation concept closely followed EAP with an engine based on the XG.40, France's was almost exactly derived from the Rafale demonstrator and had a compromised performance to ensure a naval version could be developed with ease. It was clear all five nations could not settle on a single configuration and at a meeting of Ministers at London on 17th June no decision was taken to enter the Project Definition Phase.

When the five nation's Armament Directors met at Turin on 1st August three, Britain, Germany and Italy, decided to proceed into Project Definition using the EAP based datum design. A month later Spain chose to stay with the programme, but France opted for a purely national programme for a combined navy and air force Rafale fighter. Once again France had demanded design leadership and a 46% share in the programme. The Turin Agreement launched the European Fighter Aircraft (EFA) and the main Project Definition study was completed in September 1986.

To manage the collaborative design and development, Eurofighter Jagdflugzeug GmbH was established in the Panavia office block in Munich on 2nd June 1986 and comprised BAe, MBB / Dornier, Aeritalia and CASA (Panavia was responsible for the Tornado). This was followed by the NATO European Fighter Management Agency (NEFMA) which was set up by the four governments in February 1987.

A new engine, the EJ.200, was to be built by a consortium formed in September 1986 called Eurojet Turbo GmbH, a combination of Rolls-Royce, Dasa MTU-München, Fiat and ITP.

Full development contracts for both airframe and engine were signed on 23rd November 1988. At the June 1987 Paris Air Show, it was announced that EAP was to become the official 'airborne test rig' for the new fighter; an important step because further Ministry funding was now available for flight tests. Since EAP's first flight, all flying had been paid for by British Aerospace on a 'private venture' basis. EAP had persisted with the cranked delta with canard, EFA eventually became more of a pure delta. Both had a single fin and the chin intake, EAP's was straight but EFA smiles at its victims.

Progress at times has been painfully slow for various reasons. EFA is the largest industrial collaborative programme in the world and perhaps the most 'political' military programme ever which makes it an easy target for critics; it is much easier to disagree than agree on decisions that will cost an awful lot of money.

Early model and layout of the Experimental Aircraft Project (EAP), (1983). North West Heritage Group

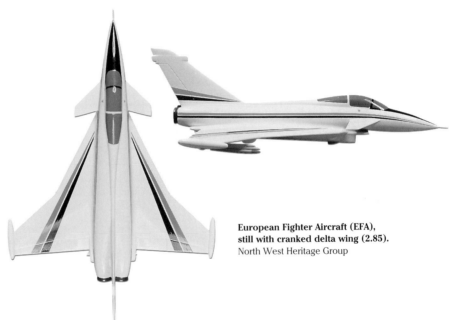

European Fighter Aircraft (EFA), still with cranked delta wing (2.85). North West Heritage Group

Eurofighter DA.2, ZH588, reveals its intake and leading edge detail. North West Heritage Group

The Return to Real Fighters

View of a P.106 model (1980).
North West Heritage Group

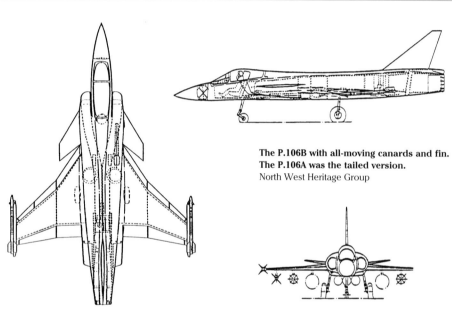

The P.106B with all-moving canards and fin.
The P.106A was the tailed version.
North West Heritage Group

The aircraft is very expensive which itself led to near collapse of the programme during 1992 when Germany threatened to withdraw because of cash shortages (significantly prior to an election campaign). Alternative studies with reduced capability were considered to ease the cost burden, but in the same year the desire to continue was reaffirmed and the aircraft was renamed Euro-fighter 2000. Considerable additional time has been purposely spent on getting the software right to prevent the fly-by-wire accidents that affected the Gripen and F-22 – much better to get it right first time, despite moans about delay, than have the worry of a crash.

A 1995 programme revision detailed quantity production from 2001 with service entry in 2003; the first production contracts were signed in early 1998. On 2nd September 1998 the export variant was named Typhoon but Eurofighter was retained within the four European customer nations (the media's desire for Spitfire II was quietly ignored since that would go down like a lead brick in Munich). The aircraft will carry a big range of weapons for air-to-air work Sidewinder or ASRAAM short range missiles, AMRAAM or FMRAAM (the future advanced medium range air-to-air missile to SR(A).1239, to which the Matra-BAe Dynamics Meteor was selected on 16th May 2000 in an announcement by British Defence Minister Geoff Hoon); and a 27mm Mauser cannon in the starboard wing root, which controversially may now be omitted on later aircraft as a cost-saving measure. Eurofighter Typhoon can reach Mach 1.5 at 35,000+ft (10.668m) from brakes off in 2.5 minutes but the key criterion in the design became the ability to climb, dive and turn sharply at supersonic speed, i.e. to have supersonic agility. It is possibly the first fighter designed to have this vital capability.

It was a relief when the first of seven prototypes flew for the first time from Manching in Germany on 27th March 1994. The first British prototype, DA.2, followed at Warton ten days later. In its own way Eurofighter tells the story of British fighter design since the beginnings of aerial warfare. Stop, start, delay, go-ahead and endless wrangles over cost seem to have been a fact of life since the First World War. One worry was how Eurofighter seemed to be repeating the TSR.2 story from the 1960s, but the project is now well advanced and with production orders placed for over 600 aircraft, it now seems beyond cancellation. The fact that Americans have criticised it confirms it must be a good aircraft.

–

ASRAAM air-to-air missile aboard Eurofighter in 1997.

Eurofighter's French rival, the Dassault Rafale.
Dassault

pure fighter role, the tailed aircraft had the edge when carrying ground attack stores, but in both cases the difference was marginal. The newer canard configuration however, was bound to be attractive in the marketplace and became the chosen option.

P.106 was basically a scaled down single engine P.110 at about 70% of the cost with trade offs between performance and price, but using all the new technology. First flight could have been in 1985/86 with service entry about three years later, but work did not proceed for several reasons. One was the lack of knowledge about plastics and their resistance to damage. The authorities again showed little interest in the lightweight fighter despite a big effort from BAe, compounding the firm's frustration with the slow progress on the larger projects. A similar aircraft but with forward swept wings called P.107 was discussed at an FSW conference held at Bristol in March 1982.

The P.106 concept was similar to Sweden's JAS studies for a Viggen replacement and Warton saw the opportunity for collaboration. The subsequent discussions culminated in BAe winning the contract to help design, and to build, the wings of the first JAS 39 Gripen fighter. The partnership worked so well that in June 1995 Saab and BAe signed a further agreement centred on Gripen exports but also covering future technology co-development.

here are further Warton projects from this period that deserve mention. As the organisation grew in size, several design teams were set up working concurrently but in different areas. For example the P.104 was a parallel and separate study to the ECA and was used for comparison purposes as an independent baseline'. Outside and later than the AST.403 designs, one group worked on an advanced technology light combat aircraft under the collective title P.106. An altogether different aeroplane was the P.103 described in the next chapter.

BAe P.106

In early 1981 some tabloid newspapers carried a feature that Britain might get a new Spitfire and reproduced an impression of a light fighter that was actually the P.106. It all sounded so easy. The project had in fact started in 1980 and for a period Warton and Brough worked together to pool their knowledge. Studies included a trapezoidal wing plus tail layout (favoured at Brough) and variations of the canard delta. Performance estimates were similar for both. The delta's manoeuvrability made it more suited to the

BAe P.112

Fighter design never stops. At the 1990 Farnborough Show BAe revealed details and a model of a highly-agile single-seat multi-role fighter which came from a series of ASTOVL studies made under a US/UK Memorandum of Understanding signed in 1986. P.112 utilised a promising new advanced engine configuration called RALS (remote augmented lift system) which, besides the main rear nozzle, had a pair of remote nozzles at the front taking bleed air from the main jet. Another canard delta, it carried AMRAAM, ASRAAM and air-to-ground weapons, plus a cannon in the starboard wing root.

P.112 model (1986).
North West Heritage Group

The first British-built Eurofighter, (DA.2), ZH588, powered by RB.199 engines. BAe

BAe Projects from 1977 to 1999 – Estimated Data

Project	Span ft (m)	Length ft (m)	Wing Area ft² (m²)	All-Up-Weight lb (kg)	Powerplant Thrust lb (kN)	Max Speed mph (km/h) / ft (m)	Armament
P.95	25.0 (7.6)	43.0 (13.1)	240 (22.3)	Up to 26,000 (11,793)	1 x RB.199	Mach 1.06+	4 x Sidewinder 27mm cannon, bombs
P.96F	36.8 (11.2)	47.2 (14.4)	409 (38.0)	c.31,085 (14,100) (air combat role)	2 x RB.199-34R	Mach c.2.0 at 36,000ft (10,973m)	4 x AAM, 27mm cannon, bombs
ECA	39.0 (11.9)	49 (14.9)	c.600 (55.8)	Up to 35,000 (15,875)	2 x RB.199	Mach 2	AAMs, cannon
P.110	33.0 (10.14)	50.2 (15.3)	476 (44.3)	Up to 30,845 (14,000)	2 x RB.199 (developed)	Mach c.2.14 at 36,000ft (10,973m)	AAMs, cannon, bombs
ACA	35.75 (10.9)	48.6 (14.8)	c.570 (53.0)	c.34,832 (15,800) –	2 x RB.199-103 19,100 (84.9reheat	Mach 2.0	6 x ASRAAM, 1 x cannon, + 4 x Sky Flash or 2 x Alarm and 8 bombs
EAP (flown)	38.6 (11.8)	48.2 (14.7)	560 (52.1)	37,400 (16,965)	2 x RB.199-104D 9,000 (40) 17,500 (77.8) reheat	Mach 2.0 at 36,090ft (11,000m)	4 x Sky Flash, 2 x ASRAAM (all dummies)
Eurofighter (flown)	35.9 (10.9)	52.33 (15.95) (wing t/c ratio c. 4%)	538 (50.0)	33,737 (15,300) (6 missiles)	2 x EJ.200 13,500 (60) 20,250 (90) reheat	Mach 2.0	Air-to-Air – Max 10 AAM mix of short & med range + 1 x 27mm Mauser cannon
P.106A (conventional tail)	26.3 (8.0)	43.4 (13.23)	269 (25)	Up to 25,500 (11,000)	1 x RB.199 21,500 (95.6)	?	At least 2 x AAM, 1 x 27mm cannon
P.106B (canard delta)	28.1 (8.57)	45.8 (13.96)	Up to 344 (32)	Up to 26,500 (12,020)	1 x RB.199 (developed)	Mach c.2.0 at 36,000ft (10,973m)	At least 4 x AAM, 1 x 27mm cannon
P.112	40.0 (12.2)	52 (15.8)	?	c.22,045 (10,000)	Single engine	?	2 x AMRAAM, 2 x ASRAAM, 1 x cannon

Chapter Fourteen

Hawker Siddeley's Fighter Family

Steps beyond Harrier: 1975 to the 1980s

British interest in Eurofighter centred on Warton, but from 1975, Sydney Camm's successors at Kingston, by then Hawker Siddeley, were also getting stuck into some good old fighter design which, in the shapes of HS.1200, HS.1201 and HS.1202, involved more conventional (CTOL) combat aircraft studies than had been made at Kingston for some time, apart from advanced trainers. The work is both important and interesting but generally had little to do with Eurofighter, and so is gathered together under its own chapter. Again, the following projects involved many studies over several years.

Hawker Siddeley HS.1200

A series of light fighter projects with single RB.238, RB.346 or RB.409-50R engine, not specifically prepared to AST.403 but overlap-

ping. Some were really single engine versions of the HS.1202 layouts. An early example, the HS.1200-2, carried wing tip Sidewinders plus two cannon above the intakes. Later versions had chin intakes and the HS.1200-6 (RB.409-50R) of August 1976 was very similar to, but of course smaller, than the HS.1202-9 illustrated, right down to twin fins, cannon and the four missile positions.

HS.1201

A small battlefield air superiority fighter which absorbed considerable effort and reminds one of the wartime Heinkel He162. All studies shared a podded RB.199 on top of the fuselage, fly-by-wire, a V-tail, variable incidence wing and semi-supine pilot. Great attention was given to the 65° pilot seat, the primary reason for the project, as this permitted a slim fuselage of about half the sectional area of conventional aircraft (a position universally adopted in racing cars and sailplanes for the same reason). This meant the pilot's

Model of the P.1216 project with bomb load.

tolerance of high 'g' (his resistance to blackout) was expected to increase. The HS.1201 was also an exercise in leaving behind the Harrier and moving on to something quite different, but it was never likely to be built.

This study commenced after surprising claims were made for increased 'g' tolerance in the F-16's 30° seat. HSA started with the type of cockpit used in sailplanes and could have stayed with a 'normal' airframe, but to make the aircraft more interesting, a fuselage slim enough to banish the engine to the external pod was also examined. To keep the fuselage substantially level, and relatively undisturbed air flowing into the intake, the wings were made variable incidence with full span leading and trailing edge flaps and this required the guns to be wing mounted (from consideration of circling air-air combat). In the HS.1201-6, the cannon were mounted

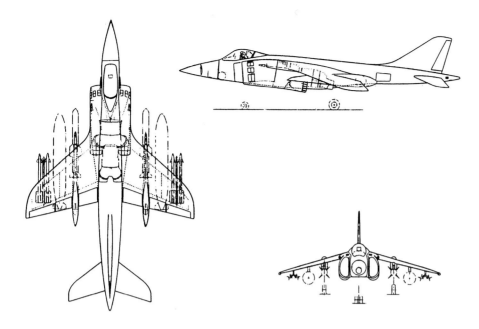

A 1970s solution to supersonic STOVL was the AV-16-S6 project or HS.1185-6 (1974). Work began in 1973 on the subsonic AV-16 strike aircraft, a joint UK/USA study, as a next generation Harrier, but was abandoned in late 1974. Later there were joint studies by Kingston and McDonnell Douglas for a supersonic fighter for the US Navy called

AV-16S which used a Pegasus 15-13 and PCB (naval Harriers were always fighters). It is a significant design for it shows the first steps in divorcing the jet streams from the fuselage. Span 31ft (9.4m), length 53ft (16.2m). The weapon load includes two guns on the intake sides and four Sidewinders. Brooklands Museum

HS.1200-2 layout (28.8.75). Later versions had chin intakes and the -6 (6.8.76) closely resembled the HS.1202-9. Brooklands Museum

along with the main undercarriage in win pods which were locally area ruled, a featur previously used in some HS.1185 Harrie developments. This helped give a simpl structure, kept the machine small and le room for more fuel.

Kingston pondered why engine pods wer rarely used in combat aircraft when the dominated civil aviation as the firm felt th HS.1201 possessed an ease of engine acces without parallel in other fighters. For pitc and yaw control, a butterfly tail was fitte which helped shield the jet exhaust and pro vide some protection from beam attack hea seeking missiles. The most serious work wa done at RAE who built a mock-up cockpit (a did Kingston) and tested the reclining sea and the F-16's 30° seat, in the centrifuge. Fron the results, the Institute of Aviation Medicin came to disbelieve the claims made for th F-16 as the benefit of the reclining seat wa less than hoped for. Pilot tolerance was dis appointing and HSA concluded the gain di not justify the need to design smaller pane and console areas and a new type of ejectio 'bed'. The MoD expressed some interest i the variable incidence wings which were n the primary design feature.

HS.1202

An altogether larger aircraft, this comprised long series of designs over three years, most outside AST.403 requirements. Power cam from two reheated RB.199s or single RB.43 (essentially a straight-through Pegasus). Th first HS.1202 was drawn in November 1975 an featured a canard with square side intake (there was also a tailed version with intake above the fuselage). Two 27mm cannon an the forward undercarriage were housed in lower fuselage bulge beneath the canard four bombs were placed in a low drag reces behind it. A year later, studies had advance to layouts more akin to the McDonnell Dou glas F-18 which introduced leading edge roo extensions. In 1977 the aircraft became British 'F-16' and, with a single fin, looked re markably like the General Dynamics machine Four Sidewinders were carried, two 27mn in the LERX and a variety of ground attac weapons on four more underwing hardpoint

HS.1204

This was Brough's P.159 for a lightweight a superiority fighter with a single reheated RE 409-5R, dated May 1976. It succeeded Brough AST.396 proposals with few external differ ences, and indeed was originally offered t the earlier requirement as HS.1190. Startin with the P.156, the Brough team had unde taken a long study of light fighters, alway with a great emphasis on air combat. When AST.403 was introduced, it was well placed to offer the P.159 / HS.1204 as a low risk minimal approach which was close to meeting the requirement. It had fly-by-wire active controls and a bigger wing than P.153 after a decision to introduce an unblown leading edge flap. Two cannons were mounted in lower fuselage bulges and the RB.409-5R replaced the 16,455lb (73.1kN) reheated thrust RB.199-34R.

HS.1205

The type of project one would have expected from Kingston; a supersonic ASTOVL fighter with four nozzle Pegasus 11 and plenum chamber burning, LERX and a chin intake. Somewhat behind the CTOL proposals, work began during the long hot summer of 1976 and lasted until 1979. The project envisaged a highly manoeuvrable aircraft for dog-fighting and the team believed vectored thrust was the best configuration for this class of aircraft, a philosophy that found good support within the RAF. PCB research continued throughout this period and in 1984 a complete Harrier airframe, mainly consisting of GR Mk.1 XV798 and T Mk.2 XW264 (both damaged beyond repair in landing accidents) and modified for PCB at Kingston, was hung from a test rig at Shoeburyness for trials. This composite airframe was held by the Bristol Aero Collection at Kemble, Gloucestershire, early in 2000.

The earliest configurations are summarised by the HS.1205-5 with four wing mounted Sidewinders and the combined cannon/undercarriage pylon-like fairings of the HS.1201. The engine was placed beneath the fuselage keeping the latter free for more fuel, and PCB was applied to the front nozzles. Tests were made in the tunnel to try and prevent hot gas ingestion, i.e. hot gases from the twin deflected nozzles entering the air intake. The similar HS.1205-11 was publicised in numerous brochures, more than any other 1205 variant, and had a single cannon in the starboard root extension. Later, the HS.1205-15 employed the more traditional Harrier style side intakes.

The HS.1205 was trapped between two difficult restrictions. If the four nozzles were raised as high as possible beneath the fuselage, the rear fuselage and tail surfaces received a rough time from vibration and heat effects caused by the jet energies. If the nozzles were lowered to give a deep fuselage with up-swept rear, drag increased and the offset of horizontal thrust and CofG became excessive. There was also a possibility of nose-up pitching in conventional flight. These factors brought abandonment of the HS.1205 concept, in essence a P.1154 derivative, and a move to the P.1212 / P.1214 / P.1216 series.

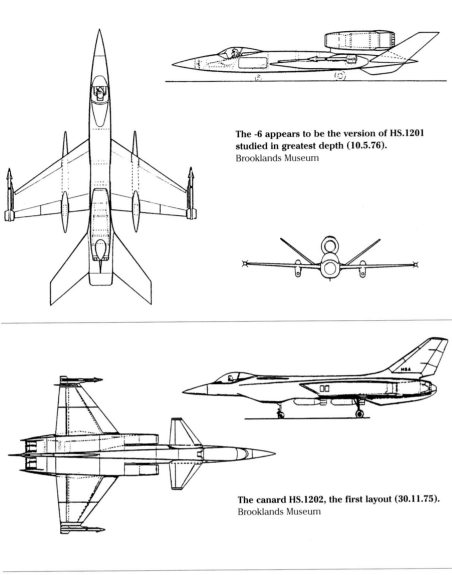

The -6 appears to be the version of HS.1201 studied in greatest depth (10.5.76).
Brooklands Museum

The canard HS.1202, the first layout (30.11.75).
Brooklands Museum

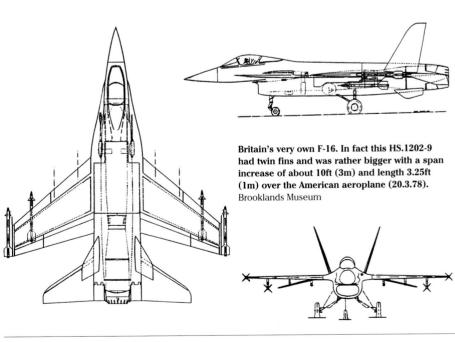

Britain's very own F-16. In fact this HS.1202-9 had twin fins and was rather bigger with a span increase of about 10ft (3m) and length 3.25ft (1m) over the American aeroplane (20.3.78).
Brooklands Museum

HS.1207

Another Brough project (the P.158) begun in 1974 which had twin RB.199s but shared many of the features of the smaller Brough designs. In all probability, this would not have been profitable for the aircraft industry, for it lacked export potential. Initially, the most favoured projects at Kingston were the HS.1202 and HS.1205, with the latter way out in front.

'Third Generation' V/STOL fighters

A long debate during Eurofighter's development concerned whether it should be designed for short take-off and landing (STOL) or short take-off and vertical landing (STOVL). However, aerial photographs of badly damaged airfields showed short strips were still available that were suitable for operating aircraft capable of taking-off and landing inside about 500 metres. The high power to weight ratio and fairly low wing loading needed to give Eurofighter the necessary agility also, as a by-product, conferred the capability to operate from such short strips and the decision was taken not to go for STOVL.

Once ASR.409 had been written for the second generation Harrier AV-8B/GR Mk.5, AST.410 was raised for a Mach 2 V/STOL fighter. Details so far are scarce, but the Ministry wanted a 'broad brush and washy colours' to make the fighter as adaptable as possible while the Navy wanted much more fuel. The document was eventually withdrawn but not before a quantity of design work had been undertaken which embraced, to a certain extent, the following.

BAe Warton P.103

The brainchild of Ivan Yates (later BAe's Engineering Director), it started in about 1977 as a very unconventional tilt wing ultra-STOL fighter. Eventually it became tilt engine only. Maximum advantage was taken of the very short length of the RB.199, which when tilted gave the required vertical thrust, allied with a thrust to weight ratio necessary for a level performance that satisfied AST.403. Engine tilt plus thrust deflection at the nozzle gave an ultra short take-off and possible vertical landing.

Computer control systems were essential to make the substantial complexity inherent with the idea work and getting all of the services across the hinge, whilst the flying control system was a very difficult problem to solve. The hot and high pressure jet efflux ground footprint also gave problems, but the concept was considered feasible after tunnel testing, flight simulation and hot gas reingestion tests. A full size mock-up was built, engine rotations demonstrated and after several years work the firm knew it had a practical idea.

BAe Kingston P.1212

The HS.1205 series was succeeded by a set of ASTOVL fighters and this 1979 project was the first to have a 3 nozzle PCB Pegasus 11F-33, fed by a chin intake, and LERX and tail booms merging with the pylons that carried the twin fins, main undercarriage and weapons. Cannon were mounted within the pylons and Sidewinders on the wing tips but after tunnel testing, the Kingston team was not satisfied that the outboard trailing edge controls were sufficient for all the pitch and roll demands

and P.1212 was superseded. Typical span 34ft (10.4m), length 50ft (15.2m).

BAe Kingston P.1214

These studies formed a family of projects in pursuit of supersonic V/STOL capability. The P.1214 ASTOVL fighter from 1979-80 covered the forward-swept wing component of a common format and used a 3-nozzle PCB engine, swept tail and twin boom fins. Forward sweep was used to assess if the feature showed any practical advantages. It did no

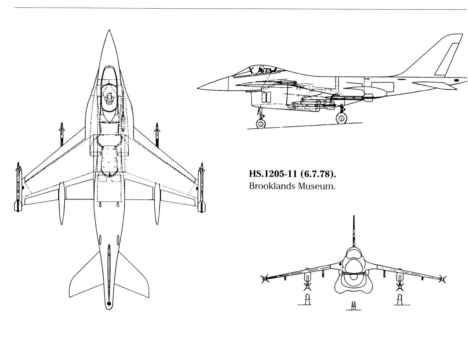

HS.1205-11 (6.7.78).
Brooklands Museum.

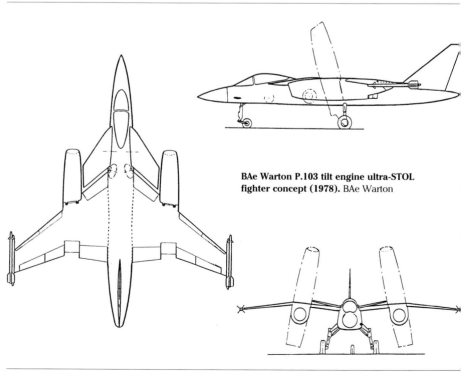

BAe Warton P.103 tilt engine ultra-STOL fighter concept (1978). BAe Warton

and, as a consequence, P.1214 consumed the least work in the series and failed to proceed beyond general layout. The aircraft was dubbed the 'Star Wars Fighter' and captured the public's imagination when used for publicity purposes in the early 1980s. The last version, P.1214-4 had wing tip ASRAAMs and could carry missiles and bombs on the forward boom extensions. It was quickly realised the configuration held no advantage, but came as a shock to Kingston's competitors who took great pains to try and photograph the model when it was privately displayed at an air show.

BAe Kingston P.1216

From the P.1127 of 1957 to this project from 1981 onwards, Kingston made near continuous studies of supersonic STOVL aircraft and considered every conceivable lift concept, but found none better than thrust vectoring by rotating engine nozzles. The firm felt the P.1216 was a logical outcome of this work and incorporated PCB to boost the thrust sufficiently to provide the supersonic performance.

PCB burns fuel in the fan bypass air flow and is thermodynamically very efficient since burning takes place only in the cold gas stream. Reheat is not necessary and, in fact, cannot be used due to the need for balance in V/STOL flight. With PCB lit, specific fuel consumption rises to about 2.5 times that of a dry Pegasus, but in flight is only two-thirds the figure for a CTOL afterburner. For V/STOL hover, thrust boost is 35-40%, the figure becoming much bigger in high speed flight. However, the system develops a great deal more jet exhaust energy than the Harrier which means on a normal Harrier type layout, the rear fuselage and tail would suffer from the noise, heat and vibration induced, so Kingston sought ways of removing as much airframe as possible from behind the powerplant.

Thus, on these studies, the fuselage was separated from the 3-nozzle single intake Pegasus and split into twin booms to take the outboard mounted tailplanes and avoid the vectoring jet exhaust, so completing the process of splitting fuselage and jetstream. P.1216 makes an interesting comparison to Russia's Yak-41 experimental V/STOL fighter displayed at the 1992 SBAC Show, although the Yak-41 was unknown in Kingston when P.1216 was drawn. Yakovlev appeared to have gone only part way to separating the exhaust from the airframe. Despite the radical new configuration, P.1216 was therefore able to retain the same simple, reliable and effective thrust vectoring idea as the Harrier. The booms could carry a wide variety of weapons in low drag installations (including guns in the front)

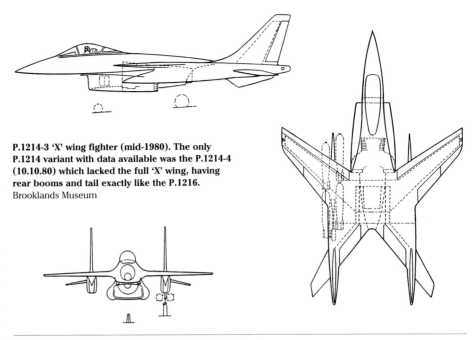

P.1214-3 'X' wing fighter (mid-1980). The only P.1214 variant with data available was the P.1214-4 (10.10.80) which lacked the full 'X' wing, having rear booms and tail exactly like the P.1216.
Brooklands Museum

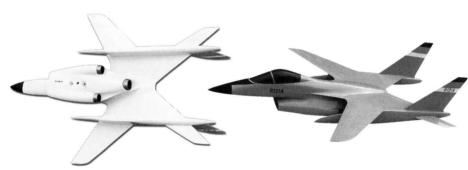

Two views of the P.1214-3 model which, because it reached this stage of 'hardware' was probably the most important. The jet pipe arrangement on the P.1216 was very similar.

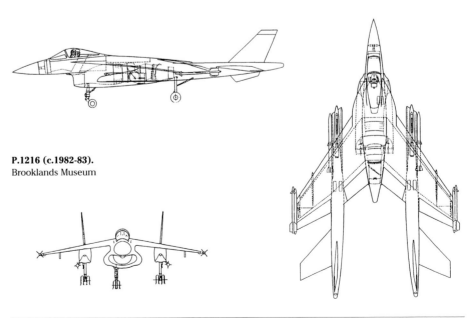

P.1216 (c.1982-83).
Brooklands Museum

while shielding the jets from IR seeking missiles. The front portion of each boom was detachable to form an armament module and two more underwing pylons were available.

The central fuselage aft of the cockpit had become nothing more than an engine nacelle. With no need to split the single rear nozzle, it could exhaust directly aft for maximum efficiency yet be vectorable through 90° for STOVL operation. The Pegasus dated back to the late 1950s and was clearly no longer suited for a 1990s fighter, so a new Rolls-Royce engine called RB.422 was installed with PCB on the front nozzles and rear nozzle unboosted. The massively powerful RB.422 two-spool turbofan with contra-rotating shafts represented 'state-of-the-art' and, unlike the Harrier, could be installed and removed without removing the wing. A light airframe was obtained by using carbon fibre composite, lithium based aluminium alloys and superplastic formed/diffusion bonded titanium (a special way of making complex titanium parts for areas requiring good heat resistance and employed on Eurofighter).

Similar to the P.1212, this fighter rectified

that aircraft's control problems by introducing all-moving differential tailplanes outboard of the booms. Handling and operation were also aided by active controls and all-moving fins. P.1216 offered a short take-off from small strips and could land vertically at the end of a mission while having good in-flight manoeuvrability. A naval version proposed after members of the Naval Staff had made approaches had a nose-mounted multi-mode radar for a primary role of the air-to-air and air-to-ship. Their interest in such aircraft received a big boost from the Falklands War and a successor to the Sea Harrier was needed. For the anti-armour role, the main requirement for the RAF and other NATO users, an alternative FLIR sensor/designator system could be fitted. Each version offered the other as a secondary capability.

The P.1216 was examined seriously at Kingston during the first half of the 1980s and the considerable amount of work done confirmed the machine held many practical advantages. It showed promise despite some hot gas recirculation problems and probably being a bit short of stealth, although with

radar absorbent paint and other coatings it would have matched the 1980s Eurofighter projects in this respect. A full scale mock-up was built after extensive tunnel testing and versions were drawn with side intakes, a conventional fuselage or twin engines for comparison. A collaborative programme between the US and the UK was assumed, the British and American services being the initial customers.

–

The 1970s were very busy and difficult years at Kingston; busy thanks to the introduction of the Harrier into RAF and US Marine Corps service, development and introduction of Sea Harrier into naval service, design and development and introduction of the Hawk trainer into RAF and overseas service and the work leading to the Harrier II; difficult due to changes of government, the 1973 oil crisis, Nationalisation (followed by Privatisation) and a general background of raging inflation, wage freezes and a high staff turnover. To quote Ralph Hooper, it was 'not surprising that nothing new was launched'.

Third Generation V/STOL Fighters – Estimated Data

Project	Span ft (m)	Length ft (m)	Wing Area ft² (m²)	All-Up-Weight lb (kg)	Powerplant Thrust lb (kN)	Max Speed mph (km/h) / ft (m)	Armament
HS.1201-6 'Wing Waggler'	34.0 (10.4)	50.75 (15.5)	300 (27.9)	?	1 x RB.199-34R 15,300 (68.1)	Mach 1.0+	2 x 27mm cannon, 2 x Sidewinder
HS.1202-	33.0 (10.1)	63.5 (19.4)	340 (31.6)	?	2 x RB.199-34R 15,300 (68.1)	Mach 1.6 (?)	2 x 27mm cannon, 2 x Sidewinder, 6 bombs
HS.1202-9	41.0 (12.5)	52.5 (16.0)	?	?	1 x RB.431-11R	Mach 1.6 (?)	2 x 27mm cannon, 4 x AAM, bombs
HS.1204 / P.159	26.9 (8.2)	43.25 (13.2)	220 (20.5)	24,285 (11,016) (air combat role)	1 x RB.409-50R c.9,700 (43.1) dry 16,595 (73.8) reheat	Mach 1.6 (?)	2 x 27mm, 2 x Sidewinder, bombs
HS.1205-11	36.1 (11.1)	52.8 (16.1)	?	30,732 (13,940)	1 x Pegasus 11F-33 c.30,000 (133.3)	Mach 1.6 (?)	1 x 27mm, 4+ AAM, bombs
HS.1207 / P.158	40.2 (12.3)	50.6 (15.4)	420 (39.1)	c.30,000 (13,608)	2 x RB.199	Mach c.2.0 at 36,000ft (10,973m)	1 x 27mm cannon, 4 x AAM, bombs
P.103 (BAe Warton)	42.0 (12.8)	50.0 (15.2)	?	Up to 36,155 (16,400)	2 x RB.199 (developed)	Mach c.2.0 at 36,000ft (10,973m)	2 x Sidewinder, 1 x 27mm Mauser cannon, GA Weapons
P.1214/4	32.0 (9.8)	49.2 (15.0)	352 (32.7)	?	1 x RR PCB 3 nozzle engine	Supersonic	2 x 27mm cannon, 2 x Wing-tip ASRAAM + AMRAAM, or bombs on pylons
P.1216	34.75 (10.6)	55.9 (17.0)	421 (39.2)	c.31,000 (14,062) [Air combat role - 2 x ASRAAM + 2 AMRAAM]	1 x RB.422-60 31,400 (139.6), 44,600 (198.2) with full PCB	Mach 1+ at sea level, Mach c.1.8 at 36,000ft (10,973m) [air combat role]	2 x 27mm Mauser cannon, 2 or 4 x Wing-tip ASRAAM or Sidewinder; 2xAMRAAM or Sky Flash, or 2 Sea Eagle on boom pylons; bombs

Chapter Fifteen

Future Directions ?

Possibilities for the Next Decades

Where will fighter design turn next? So often the direction taken is the opposite to that expected. It has always been dangerous to try and predict the future of aviation when politics and technology have such a strong influence. Works written 30 and 40 years ago make fascinating reading when one looks at their predictions for the future; some are close, others miles off target. So this short piece just briefly examines the steps into the future that are already being made.

On today's evidence, the biggest influence will be Stealth technology. This is the ability to make an aircraft as difficult to detect as possible and does not, as many imagine, just mean detection by radar. Reducing the size of a fighter's radar cross-section (RCS – the spot on the screen) is a big factor, but stealth takes in aircraft size, the noise it makes, the heat it creates and how clearly it can be seen visually.

Painting an aircraft black for night flying is just as important.

Today's radars are highly sophisticated and, for some time, fighter radars have had a look-down, shoot-down capability. This gives a fighter at medium to high altitude the ability to scan downwards for aircraft flying at very low level, pick them out amongst all the other ground objects that reflect echoes and then deploy weapons to shoot them down. Radar works on the principal that when radio waves are emitted from a scanner, any aeroplane within range will reflect some of the waves back to the source and reveal information on its speed, height and direction. An aircraft with radar stealth is designed to deflect these waves away in all directions and, combined with skin coatings to absorb radio energy, ensure as few as possible return to their source. This should result, at most, in a signal that is not large enough for the receiver to interpret usefully. As yet, few aircraft have been designed with stealth in mind and those that have such as America's F-117 look very un-

British Aerospace joined the Lockheed Martin team competing for the Joint Strike Fighter contract in mid-1997. If built, a Royal Navy version of their aircraft might look something like this.

conventional. They are manually unflyable and need fly-by-wire systems to work. Not until such systems were available did aircraft like the F-117 become possible, but in the 1991 Gulf War they proved a great success.

Stealth also applies to reductions in engine noise, and heat emissions to lessen the chance of detection by infra-red systems. Finally, a fighter can give away its position thanks to the waves being transmitted by its own radar. The solution to that, of course, is to leave the radar out, but such a move prevents the fighter from doing its job. Consequently, new fighters such as Eurofighter are something of a balance between size of aircraft to ensure sufficient space is available for all the equipment and applying enough stealth to keep radar signature, etc, as small as possible.

The desire to make aeroplanes 'invisible' is not new. In 1912, von Petroczy, an Austro-Hungarian, replaced the doped fabric of a Taube aircraft with a transparent material (a type of Cellophane) to reduce the chance of visual detection. One of the first stealth weapons was the submarine which became practical at the beginning of the century and it is worth remembering that, despite the defeat of Germany's U-boats in the Second World War, a colossal amount of effort still had to be put into developing methods of finding and killing submarines throughout the 'Cold War'. It is quite possible that developments in radar and other detection systems will eventually cancel out the lead held by today's F-117 and its sisters, but the radar technology battle is sure to continue.

An important engine development is vectored thrust. Swivelling the nozzles on a Harrier has been with us since the early 1960s, but fitting a conventional fighter's jet pipe with thrust vectoring nozzles that deflect the jet exhaust to give 'super-manoeuvrability' is a new property altogether. Thrust vectoring control has been tested on the Rockwell/MBB X-31 first flown in 1990, Russia's Sukhoi Su-37 development of the Su-35 *Flanker* first tested in April 1996, and specially modified F-15, F-16 and F-18 aircraft.

The X-31 and Su-37 have performed spectacularly and unforgettably at recent Air Shows, but the value of vectored thrust is still in debate. The author is in no position to offer an opinion, but fears it will need actual combat to help settle the argument. Eurofighter does not have vectored thrust, but it could be fitted in a mid-life update.

Joint Strike Fighter (JSF)

Fighter design never stops. The Joint Strike Fighter is predominantly an American project but the UK has been involved from an early stage and the need to replace the F-14, F-16, F-18, Harrier II and the Royal Navy's Sea Harrier makes it a potentially enormous programme. Some quite diverse requirements must be met by the same aeroplane. Most USAF and US Navy aircraft will land and take off conventionally, but the US Marines and Royal Navy need to replace their Harriers with another V/STOL aircraft. At the same time the US Department of Defence has designated JSF a paperless project with a virtual co-location of the companies involved by maximum use of Information Technology.

JSF started in 1994 as a study into a next generation USAF/USN combat aircraft following two earlier projects, the Common Affordable Lightweight Fighter (CALF) and the Joint Advanced Strike Technology (JAST) programme. In the meantime, ASTOVL technology research between British and America for a supersonic successor to Sea Harrier and AV-8B was well underway. As a result of merging the projects into JSF, a service aircraft for about 2008 onwards has emerged rather than an experimental technology demonstrator.

The UK agreed to fund 35% of the ASTOVL portion of JSF and on 28th October 1994, BAe teamed alongside McDonnell Douglas and Northrop Grumman as a partner in one of three submissions, the competitors being Lockheed Martin and Boeing. The first hurdle was selection of two out of three as weapon system Concept Demonstrator Aircraft but BAe had the opportunity to join one of the others should its project be the one to fall. The MDNG/BAe design used a near standard 35,000lb (155.6kN) Pratt & Whitney F.119 main engine with vectoring nozzle, labelled SE615, backed up in STOVL mode by a projected 16,000lb (71.1kN) General Electric/Allison/Rolls-Royce lift engine designated GEA-FXL sited behind the cockpit. The aircraft had no fin.

Having two different engines was one of several factors to count against the project and it was eliminated when the first phase winners were chosen on 16th November 1996. After close assessment, BAe joined Lockheed Martin in June 1997, first information indicating that BAe would receive a 12% share of complete JSF development and production should the aircraft win the fly-off competition.

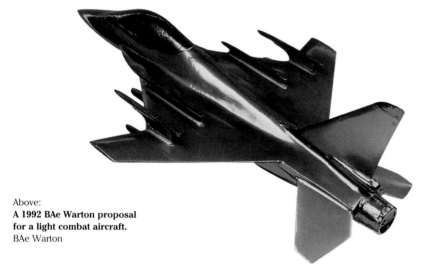

Above:
A 1992 BAe Warton proposal for a light combat aircraft.
BAe Warton

The McDonnell Douglas / Northrop Grumman / BAe contender for JSF, as envisaged at the time of the 1996 Farnborough Air Show. This computer-generated image shows how the Royal Navy version would have appeared.

Above: **An artist's impression of a pair of the Lockheed Martin JSF contender.**

Left: **An early subsonic stealth penetrator study by BAe Warton. This project, from around 1994, a rather attractive design with a chin intake, was more of a strike aircraft than a fighter, but it illustrates one of the shapes that have been looked at as 'future concepts'.**

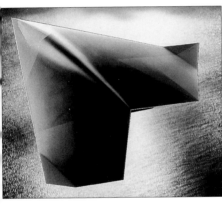

Lockheed Martin's Configuration 220 will use for both cruise propulsion and vertical thrust an F.119 development called SE611; for STOVL operation a shaft-driven lift fan behind the cockpit works in concert with the vectored cruise nozzle. With twin fins, its looks the more 'normal' of the competitors. The two groups will build and test CTOL (conventional) and STOVL versions of their aircraft under designations X-32 (Boeing) and X-35 (Lockheed Martin and partners).

Flight testing should begin in 2000 with an Engineering and Manufacturing Development contract for the winner about a year later. Top speed for the Lockheed Martin and Boeing contenders will be Mach 1.4 and 1.6 respectively, less than current aircraft though subsonic and transonic manoeuvrability must be superior to the aircraft being replaced. In a maximum stealth air-to-air role, JSF will carry two AIM-120C cropped AMRAAMs internally and a gun. Predicted maximum weights are 50,000lb (22,680kg) for the USAF version and 60,000lb (27,216kg) for the Navy. The current UK plan is 60 STOVL JSFs to replace Sea Harriers, small fry compared to the US's indicated total of nearly 3,000 machines, but adoption by the RAF is possible. Has a 'common' aircraft for Navy and Air Force arrived at last? Maybe, but JSF has a long way to go yet.

Not all British Aerospace eggs are in one basket. Talks with Dassault of France over future combat aircraft began in 1992 and saw the signing of a Memorandum of Understanding in 1996: collaboration was continuing in mid-2000. During 1995, BAe and Saab of Sweden announced their joint marketing agreement for the JAS.39 Gripen lightweight fighter. This prompts the question, will the British Services totally embrace the JSF or will the flow into a combined Europe see a European collaborative programme to succeed Tornado as well? In late 1999 BAe joined forces with Marconi and early in 2000 this global consortium sadly dropped all reference to its British ancestry (and aviation) in its new name, BAE Systems. Although the new concern continues to design projects of its own, a new all-British fighter would surely be the biggest surprise of all.

Forty years after Sandys, is the manned fighter approaching the end of the road? Will JSF be the last manned fighter as we know it? Will the following generation of fighters be unmanned? The colossal cost of Eurofighter makes the author wonder if development of manned fighters will continue beyond JSF; there is talk already of the benefits from unmanned combat aircraft. The great progress in technology, capability and sophistication has added enormously to the cost of designing any combat aircraft and maybe the next fighter will prove just too expensive to produce. But who can say if, as computer design capability moves on to even higher planes, the cost of designing fighters might not fall; just compare state-of-the-art technology in 2000 to that of 1980 and then try to imagine where we might be in 2020. By then we might know some of the answers.

It is staggering to see the progress of fighter development since the 1930s. Could Reginald Mitchell, watching his lovely Spitfire make its first flight at Eastleigh in March 1936, have imagined that nearly 20 years to the day, Fairey's beautiful Delta II would be careering over Christchurch, just a few miles away, at an average speed of 1,132mph (1,821km/h).

And what about fighters that take-off vertically or fly on computers? Mitchell, of course, was denied the chance to design jet fighters; he might well have produced something different from the Attacker. Stimulating thoughts indeed, but whatever the future holds, I look forward to the next fighter developments with great anticipation.

Possibilities for the Next Decades

Glossary

A&AEE Aeroplane and Armament Experimental Establishment, Boscombe Down.
AAM Air-to-air missile.
ACA Agile Combat Aircraft.
ACAS(OR) Assistant Chief of the Air Staff (Operational Requirements).
ACT Active control technology.
ADARD Assistant Director of Aircraft Research and Development [Ministry of Supply position].
AI Air Interception.
ALARM Air-launched anti-radiation missile.
AMRAAM Advanced medium range air-to-air missile.
AoA Angle of attack – the angle at which the wing is inclined relative to the airflow.
AS Armstrong Siddeley.
ASM Air-to-surface missile.
aspect ratio Ratio of wingspan to mean chord, calculated by dividing the square of the span by the wing area.
ASR Air Staff Requirement.
ASRAAM Advanced short range air-to-air missile.
AST Air Staff Target.
ASTOVL Advanced short take-off and vertical landing.
AVM Air Vice-Marshal.
AWA Armstrong Whitworth Aircraft Ltd.
BAC British Aircraft Corporation.
BAe British Aerospace.
BGA Blackburn & General Aircraft Ltd.
BP Boulton Paul Aircraft Ltd.
BS Bristol Siddeley.
CA Controller of Aircraft (UK).
CAD Computer-aided design.
CAP Combat air patrol.
CCV Control-configured vehicle.
CofG Centre of gravity.
CNR Chief Naval Representative. [MoS post]
Critical Mach Number Mach number at which an aircraft's controllability is first affected by compressibility, ie. the point at which shock waves first appear.
CS(A) Controller of Supplies (Air).
CTOL Conventional take-off and landing.
DARD Director of Aircraft Research and Development. [MoS post]
DCAS Deputy Chief of the Air Staff. [Air Ministry post]
DDARD(S) Deputy Director of Aircraft Research and Development (Supply). [MoS post]
DDGSR(A) Deputy Director General of Scientific Research (Air). [MoS post]
DD.OPS (Fighter) Deputy Director of Operations (Fighters).
DGSR Director General of Scientific Research. [MoS post]
DGTD(A) Director General of Technical Development (Air). [MoS post]
DH de Havilland.
DMARD Director of Military Aircraft Research and Development. [MoS post]
DCNR Deputy Chief Naval Representative (Air). [MoS post]

DOR(A) Director of Operational Requirements (Air).
DTD Director of Technical Development. [MoS post]
EAP Experimental Aircraft Programme.
ECA European Combat Aircraft.
ECF European Collaborative Fighter.
EE English Electric.
EFA European Fighter Aircraft.
FAA Fleet Air Arm.
FBW Fly-by-wire.
FLIR Forward looking infra-red.
FRAAM Future medium range air-to-air missile.
FSW Forward-swept wing.
GAL General Aircraft Limited.
HAL Hawker Aircraft Limited.
HMG His/Her Majesty's Government.
HSA Hawker Siddeley Aviation.
HTP High-test peroxide (rocket fuel).
incidence Angle at which the wing (or tail) is set relative to the fuselage.
IR Infra-red.
ITP Instruction to Proceed.
kinetic heating Heating of the airframe by friction created by its passage through the air. This can take the surface temperature towards the heat-resisting limit of the constructional materials.
LCA Light Combat Aircraft.
LERX Leading edge root extensions.
LWF Lightweight fighter.
MAP Ministry of Aircraft Production – created May 1940 to relieve the Air Ministry of its role of procuring aircraft, equipment and supplies associated with them. Functions transferred to Ministry of Supply in 1946.
MBB Messerschmitt-Bölkow-Blohm.
MoA Ministry of Aviation – created October 1959 when the civil aviation functions of the Minister of Transport and Civil Aviation were transferred to the Ministry of Supply and merged.
MoD Ministry of Defence – created late 1940s to co-ordinate the policy of the three Armed Services. In April 1964 the MoD was reconstituted to absorb the functions of the Air Ministry, Admiralty and War Office; the Air Ministry (the civilian body that governed the RAF) ceasing to exist.
MoS Ministry of Supply – created August 1939 to provide stores used by the RAF (and Army and Navy). Disbanded and reconstituted as Ministry of Aviation in 1959.
MRCA Multi-Role Combat Aircraft; later the Tornado.
NACA National Advisory Committee for Aeronautics (of America). Today is NASA, National Aeronautics and Space Administration.
NATO North Atlantic Treaty Organisation.
NBMR Nato Basic Military Requirement.
NGTE National Gas Turbine Establishment (merged with RAE, 1983).

OR Operational Requirement.
PCB Plenum chamber burning.
PDRD(A) Principal Director of Research and Development (Air). [MoS post]
PDSR(A) Principal Director of Scientific Research (Air). [MoS post]
PDTD(A) Principal Director of Technical Development (Air). [MoS post]
R&D Research and Development.
RAE Royal Aircraft Establishment, Farnborough (today part of DERA – the Defence Evaluation and Research Agency).
RCS Radar cross-section.
rh reheat.
RP Rocket projectile.
rpm revolutions per minute.
RR Rolls-Royce.
RSS Relaxed static stability.
RTO Resident Technical Officer.
SBAC Society of British Aircraft Constructors (now Society of British Aerospace Companies).
s.l. sea level.
SR(A) Staff Requirement (Air).
STOL Short take-off and landing.
STOVL Short take-off and vertical landing.
telemetry Transmission of in-flight test data from aircraft to ground station by radio link.
t:c Thickness/chord ratio. Ratio of the maximum thickness of a wing to its chord at the same spanwise station; the chord being the distance from leading edge to trailing edge at that station. Any reduction in the ratio will increase the critical mach number.
transonic flight The speed range either side of Mach 1.0 where an aircraft has both subsonic and supersonic airflow passing over it at the same time.
TRE Telecommunications Research Establishment, Malvern (became RRE – Royal Radar Establishment; then RSRE – Royal Signals & Radar Establishment; today part of DERA).
USAF United States Air Force.
VG Variable geometry.
VTOL Vertical take-off and landing.

Useful conversion factors:

x 0.093	square feet (ft²) to square metres (m²)
x 0.3048	feet (ft) to metres (m)
x 0.4539	pounds (lb) to kilograms (kg)
x 1.2	Imperial (UK) gallons to US gallons
x 1.609	miles to kilometres (km) (also for mph to km/h)
x 1.853	knots to kilometres/hour (km/h)
x 2.54	inches (in) to centimetres (cm)
x 4.5469	Imperial/UK gallons (gal) to litres (lit)
÷ 225	pounds (lb) to kilonewton (kN)

British Secret Fighter Colour Chronology

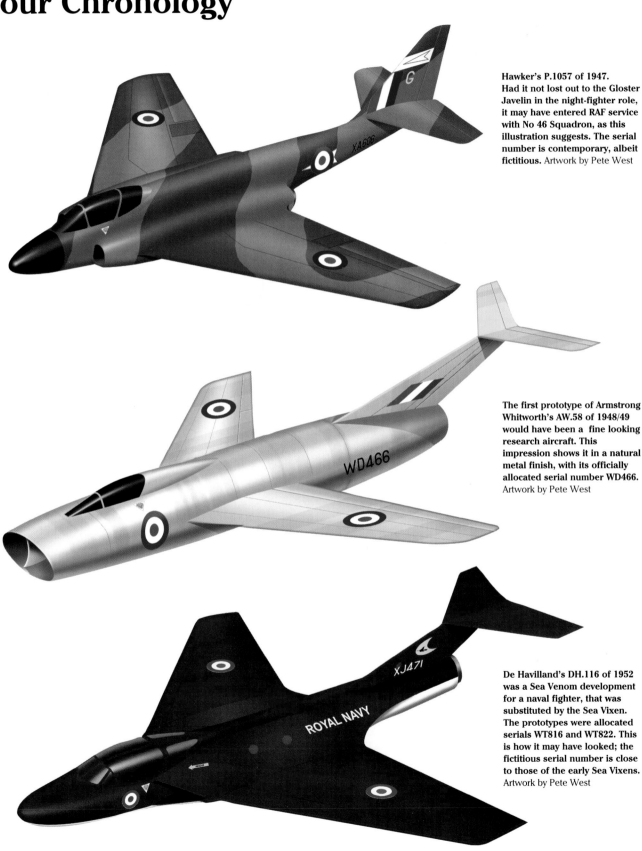

Hawker's P.1057 of 1947. Had it not lost out to the Gloster Javelin in the night-fighter role, it may have entered RAF service with No 46 Squadron, as this illustration suggests. The serial number is contemporary, albeit fictitious. Artwork by Pete West

The first prototype of Armstrong Whitworth's AW.58 of 1948/49 would have been a fine looking research aircraft. This impression shows it in a natural metal finish, with its officially allocated serial number WD466. Artwork by Pete West

De Havilland's DH.116 of 1952 was a Sea Venom development for a naval fighter, that was substituted by the Sea Vixen. The prototypes were allocated serials WT816 and WT822. This is how it may have looked; the fictitious serial number is close to those of the early Sea Vixens. Artwork by Pete West

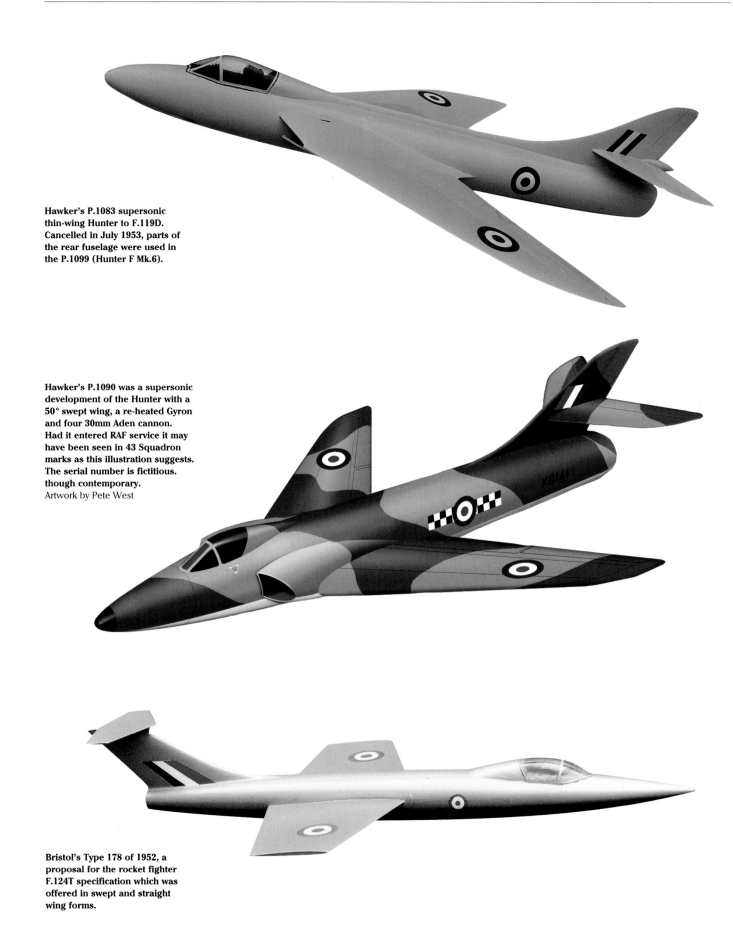

Hawker's P.1083 supersonic thin-wing Hunter to F.119D. Cancelled in July 1953, parts of the rear fuselage were used in the P.1099 (Hunter F Mk.6).

Hawker's P.1090 was a supersonic development of the Hunter with a 50° swept wing, a re-heated Gyron and four 30mm Aden cannon. Had it entered RAF service it may have been seen in 43 Squadron marks as this illustration suggests. The serial number is fictitious, though contemporary.
Artwork by Pete West

Bristol's Type 178 of 1952, a proposal for the rocket fighter F.124T specification which was offered in swept and straight wing forms.

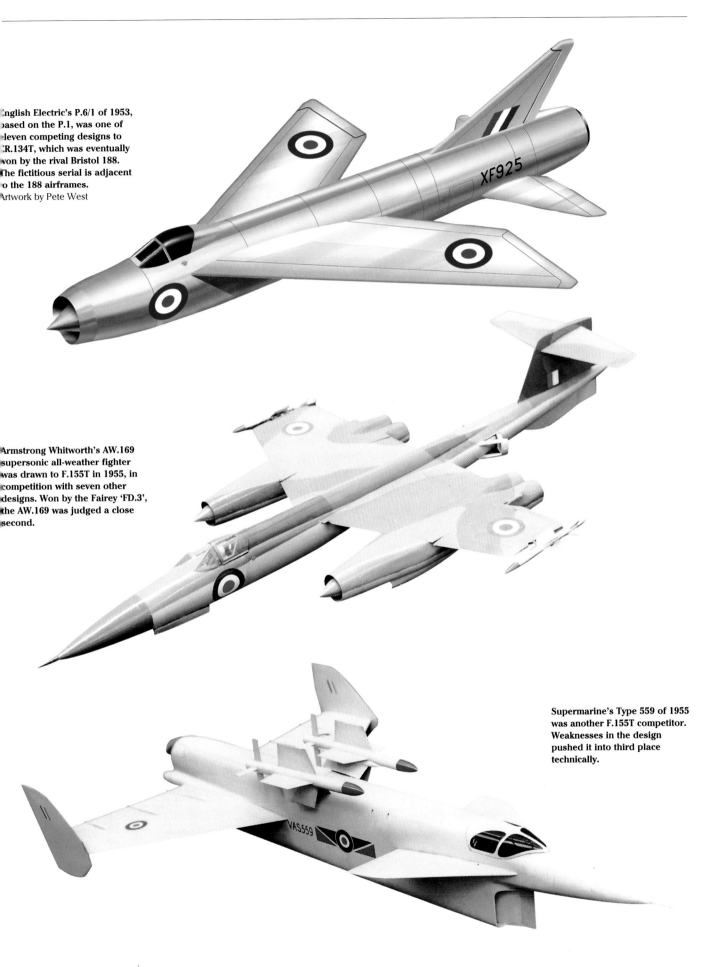

English Electric's P.6/1 of 1953, based on the P.1, was one of eleven competing designs to ER.134T, which was eventually won by the rival Bristol 188. The fictitious serial is adjacent to the 188 airframes.
Artwork by Pete West

Armstrong Whitworth's AW.169 supersonic all-weather fighter was drawn to F.155T in 1955, in competition with seven other designs. Won by the Fairey 'FD.3', the AW.169 was judged a close second.

Supermarine's Type 559 of 1955 was another F.155T competitor. Weaknesses in the design pushed it into third place technically.

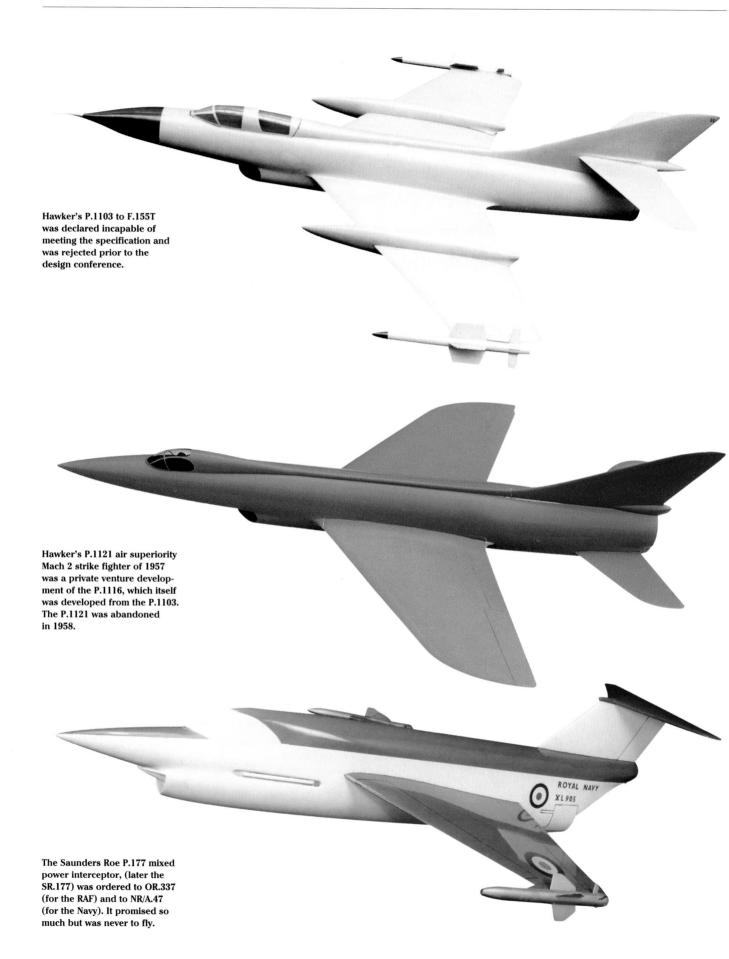

Hawker's P.1103 to F.155T
was declared incapable of
meeting the specification and
was rejected prior to the
design conference.

Hawker's P.1121 air superiority
Mach 2 strike fighter of 1957
was a private venture development of the P.1116, which itself
was developed from the P.1103.
The P.1121 was abandoned
in 1958.

The Saunders Roe P.177 mixed
power interceptor, (later the
SR.177) was ordered to OR.337
(for the RAF) and to NR/A.47
(for the Navy). It promised so
much but was never to fly.

Hawker's private venture Hunter FR Mk.4 led to the R.164D Specification of 1957, and a mix of 33 Hunter Mk.6s and 9s were subsequently converted to FR Mk.10 for RAF service, most of them with Nos 2 and 4 Squadron in 2nd TAF, Germany. No 2 Sqn was equipped with FR Mk.10s between 1961 and 1971, based at RAF Gütersloh, which is probably where that unit's XF458 was pictured. Eric Morgan collection

Colour views of a production Supermarine Swift F Mk.7 armed with Fireflash missiles are very rare. This particular aircraft, believed to be XF123, the penultimate production F Mk.7, was one of those allocated to the Guided Weapon Development Squadron at RAF Valley for AAM trials during 1957-58. Note the leaking fuel. Alan Curry

This evocative photograph, taken between January 1961 and November 1962, shows the RAF's three main fighter types at that time: the Gloster Javelin (represented by FAW Mk.9, XH912, 'S' of 33 Sqn); the Hawker Hunter (XG274/'P' and XJ636/'S', two 4 Sqn, 2nd TAF, F Mk.6s); and the English Electric Lightning (three F Mk.1As of No 56 Sqn, coded 'S', 'D' and 'H' respectively). Eric Morgan collection

Above: **This lovely view of Lightning F Mk.3 XP755 in the markings of 74 Squadron, taken in the mid-1960s, emphasizes just why it was one of the most glamorous fighters of all. This English Electric aircraft marks one of the peaks in British fighter design.** North West Heritage Group

Left: **The ADV (Air Defence Variant) of the Tornado was introduced into RAF service with 229 OCU at RAF Coningsby in November 1984. In July 1986 the interim F Mk.2s were superseded by the improved F.3s which have continued to serve in that role, albeit under a variety of shadow squadron designations ever since. This example, which is carrying four AMRAAM and two Sidewinder missiles, also wears the markings of No 65 Squadron on the forward fuselage.** North West Heritage Group

Below: **The Royal Navy Sea Harriers proved their capabilities as fighter aircraft in the Falklands War of 1982. FRS Mk.1 XZ493 is seen here in the markings of 801 Squadron, FAA, while based aboard HMS *Invincible* in 1981.** BAe

British Secret Projects: Jet Fighters

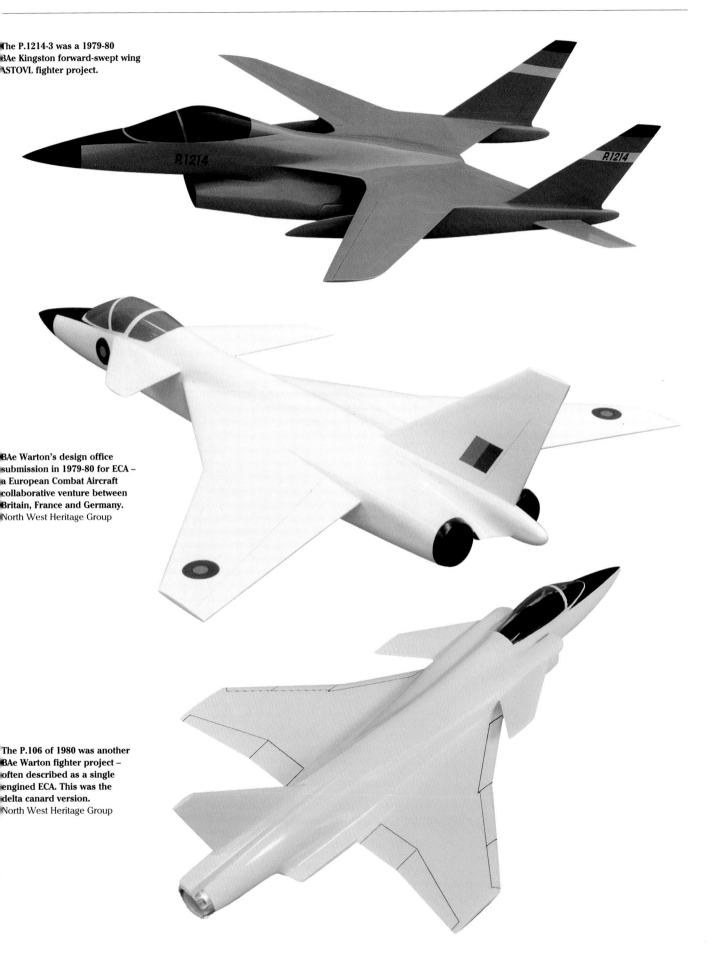

The P.1214-3 was a 1979-80 BAe Kingston forward-swept wing ASTOVL fighter project.

BAe Warton's design office submission in 1979-80 for ECA – a European Combat Aircraft collaborative venture between Britain, France and Germany.
North West Heritage Group

The P.106 of 1980 was another BAe Warton fighter project – often described as a single engined ECA. This was the delta canard version.
North West Heritage Group

Above: **The EAP – an Experimental Aircraft Programme technology demonstrator, was born out of the Anglo/German/Italian ACA of 1982, and although built and first flown at Warton in August 1986, it did have support from the German and Italian aerospace industries. It proved a very valuable test platform, being involved in around three dozen technology developments for the EFA programme, and six flights in 1989 were to test the airbrake for Eurofighter. Its 259th and final flight was in May 1991; it was stored at BAe Warton until June 1996 whereupon it was transferred on loan to Loughborough University and housed within the Department of Aeronautical and Automotive Engineering and Transport Studies.** North West Heritage Group

Left: **The Jaguar ACT (Active Control Technology) test-bed (XX765), funded by the British MoD, was the first aircraft in the world to fly with no reversionary control, relying on only fly-by-wire inputs – doing so for the first time on 20th September 1981. It went on to play an important role in the development of EAP and EF2000 before retiring to Loughborough University. With the arrival of the EAP in 1966 it moved on to the Aerospace Museum at RAF Cosford, where it was placed on display in September that year.** North West Heritage Group

Below: **The EFA was being touted as the EF 2000 by the time the first development airframe first took to the air, on 27th March 1994. This, the second prototype, DA.2, and the first to be built in Britain (at Warton) made its first flight on 6th April 1994.** BAe

British Secret Fighter Colour Chronology

British Fighter Projects Summary

During their years of independence, many of Britain's aircraft firms became wedded to certain types of aeroplane or areas of manufacture. For example, Hawker was a fighter specialist and features throughout the book while Avro was inclined towards bigger game and built large numbers of heavy bombers (this explains why the famous name Handley Page does not feature at all). Blackburn was just one manufacturer to regularly supply aircraft to the Fleet Air Arm and this was a major influence on its lines of development.

The following tables list jet or rocket powered fighters, fighter-bombers, strike fighters and research aircraft developed mainly to advance the fighter designer's art. Reconnaissance developments, trainer versions and suchlike are omitted in an effort to keep the list to a manageable size. In theory, all projects are 'official' despite some schemes lasting for such a brief lifetime (perhaps just a day or two) that they really have no right to be here, but sneak in as one cannot always determine which they are. For quite a number of the projects, little or no information is known to have survived and has probably been lost forever. Others of course are still secret. The list of unbuilts contains some potentially outstanding aircraft, plenty of good ones and a few that are quite appalling. But more than anything perhaps, it shows so clearly that at one stage there were just too many firms designing too many projects.

ARMSTRONG WHITWORTH

AW.58   Swept (ordered, but suspended 11.49) and delta transonic research aircraft to E.16/49, 11.48 and 13.1.50. Cancelled 5.50.

AW.59   Experimental variable geometry aircraft to ER.110T, 11.51.

AW.60 to AW.64 Variants of Meteor night fighter, early 1950s. Respectively AW.60 Sapphire engines; AW.61 RR Nene engines plus thin wings; AW.62 DH Goblin engines; AW.63 APQ.43 AI radar; AW.64 staggered side-by-side seating.

AW.165   All-weather supersonic fighter, 11.52.

AW.166   Supersonic research aircraft to ER.134T, 5.53.

AW.169   Supersonic all-weather fighter to F.155T, 10.55.

AVRO

720   Rocket fighter to F.124T, 4.52. Construction to F.137D started, flight planned 1956, programme cancelled 5.55.

724   High speed research aeroplane designed as comparison study to Avro Canada Project Y aircraft, 7.53. Twin RB.106 powered tail-sitting VTOL with tripod standing gear and prone pilot. Radar carried and provision made for wing tip Blue Jays. Span 24ft (7.3m), length 37ft (11.3m), wing area 375ft² (34.9m²), gross wt. 24,500lb (11,113kg). Top speed full reheat Mach 2.65 at 45,000ft (13,716m); without reheat sufficient power for Mach 1.6 at 50,000ft (15,240m) but insufficient power to accelerate over the 'hump' at Mach 1.0.

726   Development of 720 for interception or escort duties with turbojet only, 1.54.

728   Naval variant of 720, early 1955.

729   Supersonic fighter to F.155T, 1.55.

765   Lift fan powered VTOL fighter, 1959.

BLACKBURN / HAWKER SIDDELEY / BRITISH AEROSPACE, BROUGH

This firm was designing fighters right through to the 1980s and many of its later projects are still classified, but the last design was the P.183. Some of the later Brough projects, where only a Hawker Siddeley 'HS' number is known, appear in the Kingston list.

B.50   Two variants of Fleet Air Arm strike fighter with single Nene. Conventional layout, span 40.5ft (12.3m), length 41.8ft (12.7m); twin boom, tricycle undercarriage same span, but 39.1ft (11.9m) long. Armament of bombs or torpedo, and four nose cannon. Brochure submitted to Air Ministry 17th February 1945.

B.67   Naval fighter to N.40/46, 2.47.

B.68   Naval fighter proposal, 11.46.

B.71   Flexible deck landing version of B.67, 30.4.47.

B.74   Naval fighter believed prepared to N.9/47, 1947.

B.82   Preliminary naval fighter scheme to N.14/49, 3.49.

B.89   Full naval fighter submission to N.114T, 6.7.51.

B.90   Experimental swing wing aircraft to ER.110T, 11.51.

B.94   Undercarriageless version of B.89 for use on flexible decks, 10.51. Span 46ft (14.0m), length 53.75ft (16.4m); four cannon under cockpit floor.

B.95   Major revision of B.89 with reduced take-off weight, 3.52. Span 40ft (12.2m).

B.97   Rocket fighter to F.124T, 18.4.52.

Armstrong Whitworth AW.169 model. Ray Williams

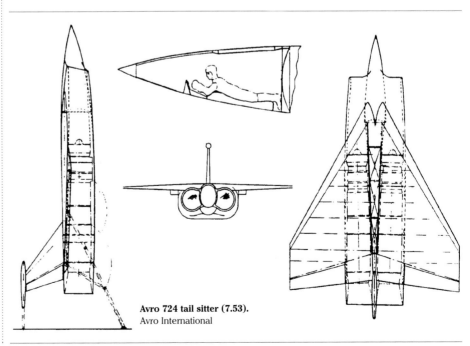

Avro 724 tail sitter (7.53).
Avro International

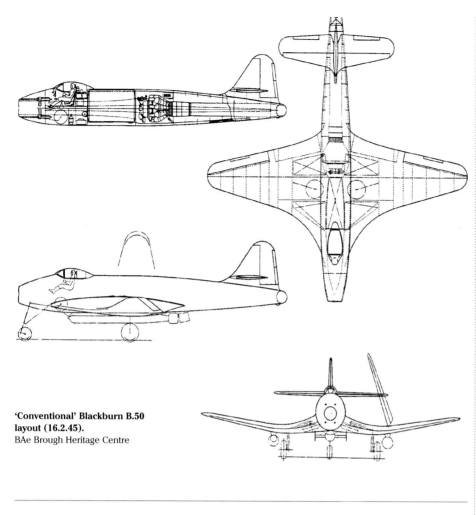

'Conventional' Blackburn B.50 layout (16.2.45).
BAe Brough Heritage Centre

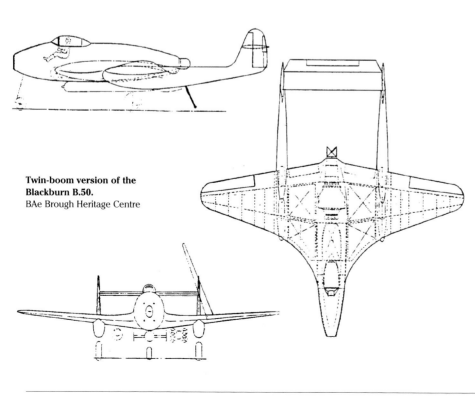

Twin-boom version of the Blackburn B.50.
BAe Brough Heritage Centre

B.99 Follow-on development of B.97, 1952.

B.102 Mixed powerplant naval all-weather interceptor based on B.89/B.95, possibly to N.131T, 10.52.

B.109 Interceptor / strike variant of Buccaneer for Canada, 1958. Span 42.5ft (13.0m), length 71.67ft (21.8m), two reheated Avon RB.146 engines, Mach 1.65.

B.112 Combat air patrol fighter Buccaneer for Royal Navy, Mach 1.5, 1958.

B.117 High altitude fighter Buccaneer, 1960.

B.129 / P.140 Mach 1.8 fighter version of Buccaneer, 1962 & 1964.

P.138 Counterinsurgency strike fighter, 1962.

P.153 Lightweight fighter to AST.396, 2.73. Developed into P.159.

P.156 Lightweight fighter with reheated Spey RB.168-73R, 1972. Similar to P.159 / HS.1204 but with LERX. Span 35.2ft (10.7m), Length 48ft (14.6m). One cannon, four Sidewinder. Designated HS.1206 at Kingston.

P.158 All-Weather fighter, 12.74; developments to AST.403, 1976. Designated HS.1207 at Kingston.

P.159 Light fighter, 1973, and to AST.403, 5.76. (HS.1190 and HS.1204 at Kingston).

P.160 Various designs to AST.403 with vectored lift, c1976. Power supplied by twin RB.199 lift/thrust arrangement using PCB. Still secret.

P.161 Unstable canard v conventional fighter design study, rough drawings only, late 70s.

P.163 Light combat aircraft developed from P.159, 1979.

P.171 Technology demonstrator, 11.83. Still secret.

P.173 Advanced stealth configuration studies. Still secret.

BOULTON PAUL

P.111 Delta wing research prototype to E.27/46 first flown 10.10.50.

P.113 Prone pilot transonic research aircraft powered by single Avon (P.113A) or Sapphire (P.113S), 10.48.

P.114 Transonic research aircraft, similar layout to P.113 but conventionally seated pilot and two Avon (P.114A) or Sapphire (P.114S) engines, 10.48.

P.118 Highly swept wing aircraft, single RR Nene engine, c1951.

P.120 Delta wing research prototype developed from P.111, first flown 6.8.52.

P.121 Experimental variable geometry aircraft to ER.110T, 11.51.

P.122 Rocket fighter to F.124T, 1952.

P.126 Research proposal for experimental thin wing for fighters. Work lasted from 11.52 to at least 3.57 following RAE request for structural research on 3% thick wing felt necessary for supersonic speed. Problem to find adequate torsional stiffness for typical supersonic fighter specification of 25,000lb (11,340kg) all-up-weight and 300ft² (27.8m²) wing area. Tied in with RAE report Aero 2462 which investigated Mach 2 aeroplanes and was stimulant for ER.134T. Various materials examined – steel, titanium, magnesium – as replacement for DTD364 aluminium alloy; steel gave the lowest weight but manufacturing difficulties were prohibitive (as found later on Bristol 188). Wing displayed at 1955 SBAC show.

P.127 Interceptor fighter resulting from P.126 thin wing research, c1953.

P.128 Supersonic research aircraft to ER.134T, 5.53.

P.129 Research aircraft planned as development model for P.128, 11.53. Initially powered by wing-mounted 880lb (3.9kN) Turboméca

Marboré turbojets with Snarler rocket in tail, the machine was to test a variety of outer wings, or have no outer wings fitted. Aircraft then to be re-engined with 1,750 lb (7.8kN) AS Viper 5s and aircraft re-tested, but experiment probably abandoned once P.128 failed to win ER.134T. Using Marborés or Vipers ensured the P.129 had much in common with French lightweight fighter Sud-Ouest SO.9000 Trident, first flown 2.3.53. Marboré – max. span 32.5ft (9.9m), without outer wings 18ft (5.5m); Viper – 28.33ft (8.6m) and 20.1ft (6.1m), length 53ft (16.2m) approx. Top speed Mach 1.1 at height; top all-up-weight 9,000lb (4,082kg).

P.133 Powerful dart shaped fighter and strike aircraft designs for RAF and Navy evolved from Government-sponsored research on VTOL fan-lift systems. First fighter version P.133 (6.56) with tip mounted reheated Gyron Juniors coupled to six lift fans for VTOL capability. Spectre rocket fitted in extreme rear fuselage. The P.133A (8.96) was smaller and had just four lift fans. Larger P.133B was a pure strike aircraft for Navy. P.133 Span 25.83ft (7.9m), length 69.83ft (21.3m), P.133A 18.5ft (5.6m) and 50.25ft (15.3m). Estimated performance unknown.

P.134 Dedicated lift fan research aircraft for supersonic flight associated with P.133, 2.57. Brief studies made applying fan-lift principle to Naval Requirements NA.47 (Supersonic fighter [SR.177]) and NA.39 (Strike aircraft [Buccaneer]). Two Bristol Orpheus turbojets, 76° sweep delta, span 26ft (7.9m), length 64.5ft (19.7m), Mach 1.23 at 33,000ft.

P.135 Similar to P.134 but designed for subsonic flight with reduced wing sweep, 5.57. P.135A had Saab Draken style double delta, P.135B 67.5° delta. Span 38.33ft (11.7m) and 35ft (10.7m) respectively, length 65ft (19.8m). Performance identical Mach 0.96 at sea level.

BRISTOL

177 Supersonic fighter reportedly to F.3/48 but not indicated on drawings; versions A and B both 2.11.48. 177A two stacked Bristol BE-10 engines with large nose orifice reminiscent of Russian practice at its most ugly. 56° sweep wing, two 30mm cannon below intake, gun laying radar scanner in orifice centre, span 36.67ft (11.2m), length 66.0ft (20.1m), wing area 580ft² (53.9m²), performance unknown but supersonic. 177B similar but BE-10s side-by-side, length 59.75ft (18.2m). Modified Type 177C (24.2.49) solid nose for radar, side intakes, 65° wing, single engine, bicycle u/c with outriggers, span 32.0ft (9.8m), length 58.5ft (17.8m), area 435ft² (40.4m²), gross weight 32,000lb (14,515kg), supersonic.

178 Rocket fighter to F.124T, straight and swept wing forms, both 21.4.52.

180 Supersonic development of Type 177, 1953.

183 Experimental variable geometry aircraft to ER.110T, 11.51.

184 Parallel research study to Type 183 with delta wing, late 51/early 52.

185 Rocket powered interceptor, 1952. Pilot in prone position. For trials, Meteor F Mk.8 fitted with extended nose incorporating prone position cockpit. Flown 10th February 1954, second pilot always sitting in regular cockpit as precaution, not a success and Type 185 dropped.
Firm studied numerous other rocket fighters.

188 Supersonic research aircraft to ER.134T, 5.53, first flown 14.4.62. Type 188F fighter proposed 9.53.

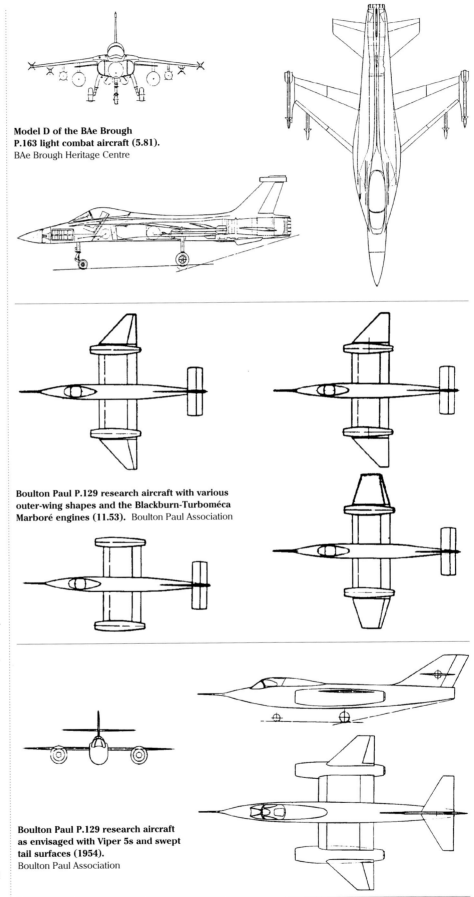

Model D of the BAe Brough P.163 light combat aircraft (5.81).
BAe Brough Heritage Centre

Boulton Paul P.129 research aircraft with various outer-wing shapes and the Blackburn-Turboméca Marboré engines (11.53). Boulton Paul Association

Boulton Paul P.129 research aircraft as envisaged with Viper 5s and swept tail surfaces (1954).
Boulton Paul Association

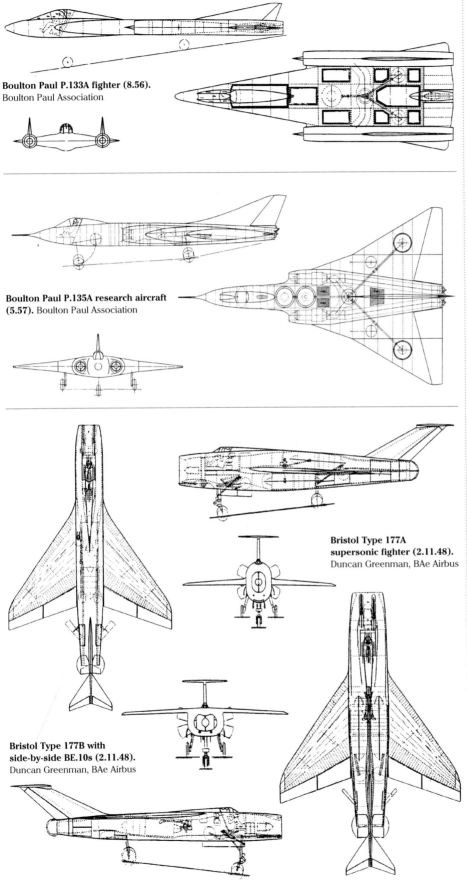

Boulton Paul P.133A fighter (8.56).
Boulton Paul Association

**Boulton Paul P.135A research aircraft
(5.57).** Boulton Paul Association

**Bristol Type 177A
supersonic fighter (2.11.48).**
Duncan Greenman, BAe Airbus

**Bristol Type 177B with
side-by-side BE.10s (2.11.48).**
Duncan Greenman, BAe Airbus

DE HAVILLAND

For a period in the 1950s, there were two de Havilland fighter design teams, the original Hatfield group and one at the former Airspeed factory at Christchurch. The latter was mainly responsible for modifying fighters already in production and did not allocate new project numbers, but its modifications to the DH.110/Sea Vixen constituted new projects.

DH.100 Vampire fighter built to E.6/41, first flown 20.9.43.

DH.107 Proposed Vampire development eventually turned into the Venom.

DH.108 Swallow tail-less research aircraft to E.18/45, flown 15.5.46. Based on Vampire fuselage. Designed primarily to probe unknowns of transonic flight for Comet airliner but results benefited aviation in general.

DH.110 Initially designed as RAF night fighter to F.44/46 (3.47) but prototypes eventually ordered for RAF to F.4/48 and Navy under N.14/49 (latter cancelled 11.49), first flight 26.9.51. Eventually became Sea Vixen to N.139D and first pre-production flown 20.3.57. Mk.2 version with RB.168 engines proposed 2.60 but Avons retained and FAW Mk.2 flew 1.6.62. Work on thin-wing supersonic variants 12.53 to 1954. RAF high-altitude development with additional rocket capable of Mach 1.43 proposed 7.11.55; all work carried out under DH.110 designation.

DH.112 Venom fighter, begun as thin-wing Vampire, built to Spec. 15/49, flown 2.9.49.

DH.113 Vampire private venture night fighter first flown 28.8.49.

DH.116 Sea Venom development for naval fighter to N.131T, 21.1.52. Replaced by DH.110 Sea Vixen.

DH.117 Supersonic all-weather fighter to F.155T, 10.55.

ENGLISH ELECTRIC /
BRITISH AIRCRAFT CORPORATION /
BRITISH AEROSPACE, WARTON

This is probably the only project list with new items still being added during the 1990s. There are gaps because of security considerations and the lack of fighter work in the 1960s. How far the series has gone is unknown, and that some of the work will remain secret for many years is certain. Latterly, depth of project investigation depended on whether the work was undertaken to an MoD requirement or just an internal study.

P.1 Transonic research aircraft (P.1A) to F.23/49 first flown 4.8.54. Fighter prototype development P.1B flew 4.4.57.

P.3 Side intake development of P.1, 3.51.

P.5 Development of P.1 with single reheated RR Avon RA.12, 3.52.

P.6 Supersonic research designs to ER.134T, 11.5.53 and 17.9.53. Two based on P.1.

P.8 Supersonic all-weather fighter to F.155T, 4.10.55.

P.19 Interceptor variant of Lightning, c1957.

P.23 Lightning modified to carry Douglas AIR-2 Genie nuclear-tipped unguided air-to-air missile, 5.59. Weapon available as part of United States Aid Funding and go-ahead given by Ministry to modify the aircraft. Decision deferred 1.60.

P.25 Lightning F Mk.2 – first flight 11.7.61.

P.26 Lightning F Mk.3 – first flight 16.6.62.

P.33 Lightning Strike fighter variant for Australia, c1960.

Lightning VG Interceptor – Unnumbered variable geometry project for Royal Navy to AW.406, and later for RAF, based on T Mk.5 trainer, 1963. Ultimate development had radar in solid nose with side intakes, 7.63.

P.51 Advanced combat aircraft. Immediate successor to UK Variable Geometry Aircraft (UKVG), immediate predecessor to MRCA, 1968.

P.53 Fixed wing version of MRCA/UKVG aircraft, 11.68.

P.68 Air Defence Variant (ADV) of joint British/German/Italian Multi-Role Combat Aircraft (MRCA), later Tornado, to ASR.395, prototype flew 27.10.79.

P.88 Blended body fixed wing aircraft, 10.75.

P.89 Blended body delta wing aircraft, 1.76.

P.90 Non-blended body variable geometry aircraft for comparison purposes, 10.75.

P.91 Blended body VG strike fighter, single engine, 5.76.

P.92 Twin engine variable geometry fighter to AST.403, 1976.

P.93 Single engine delta design to AST.403, 11.76.

P.94 Twin RB.199 delta design, 6.78.

P.95 Fixed wing, single RB.199 lightweight fighter to AST.403, 11.76.

P.96 Fixed wing, twin RB.199 fighter to AST.403, 8.77.

P.97 Super Jaguar with new wing and pair RB.409-07 engines to AST.403, 11.76.

ECF European Collaborative Fighter; Britain and Germany, 12.79.

ECA European Combat Aircraft; Britain, France and Germany, 1979/80.

P.103 Tilt-wing fighter, also forward swept wing variant, 1977. Believed started with tail-aft layout.

P.104 Delta canard design – parallel but separate comparison study to ECA, c1980. Much work done on the project which satisfied many of the requirements of the time.

P.106 Fighter described as single engine ECA, conventional and delta canard versions, late 1980.

P.107 Forward swept wing development of P.106, 1980/81.

P.109 Harrier replacement with vectored thrust, 1980. Similarities with Harrier layout but large chin intake and two main swivelling nozzles faired into wing trailing edge strake. Reheat/PCB avoided for subsonic/transonic capability but reduced supersonic. Tricycle undercarriage nosewheel slightly offset to starboard, avionics similar to P.106 and P.110, wing tip Sidewinders. Span 32.7ft (10.0m), length 47.4ft (14.4m), all-up-weight 24,250lb (11,000kg), top speed Mach 1.4. Early version had side intakes.

P.110 Medium size agile combat aircraft, 3.81.

ACA Agile Combat Aircraft developed from P.110, German/Italian collaboration, 4.82.

P.112 Advanced STOVL canard delta project, 1986.

EAP Experimental Aircraft Programme. Technology demonstrator born out of ACA, first flown 8.8.86.

P.120 UK European Fighter Aircraft (EFA). Eurofighter flown 27.3.94.

JSF Design prepared in collaboration with McDonnell Douglas and Northrop Grumman for United States Joint Strike Fighter (JSF) requirement, c1994. When rejected, BAe joined Lockheed Martin team in 1997.

FAIREY

Fairey did not use project numbers, in applicable cases just the specification number. Consequently, the following is the best available list but it is impossible to know what may be missing, particularly regarding private venture work.

Type K Research aircraft. Brochure dated 19.5.46 submitted for short chunky swept wing aircraft with no horizontal tail and stubby fin blended into dorsal spine. Side-by-side RR AJ-65s, nose intake, top speed 650mph (1,046km/h) at sea level, 13,500lb (6,124kg) all-up-weight, optional two 30mm cannon or one recoilless gun.

Above: **De Havilland DH.100 Vampire FB Mk.9 fighter-bomber, seen here in a later training role, (sometimes designated FB(T) Mk.9).**

Below: **WM515 is a DH.112 Sea Venom FAW Mk.20. The DH.116 Super Venom was based on the forward fuselage of the Sea Venom.** BAe Farnborough

Type N proposed 27.6.46 as powered scale model or glider of 5,240lb (2,377kg) maximum weight. Decision by MoS 27.9.46 not to proceed with construction of Type K because of firm's commitments.

Delta I Aircraft to E.10/47 for delta wing and vertical launch research, first flown 12.3.51. Originally presented to MoS in brochure form as Type R, 2.47. At that stage, span 15.4ft (4.7m), length 28.67ft (8.7m).

N.40/46 Naval fighter, 11/47. Modified 16.11.48.

N.14/49 Naval fighter, twin engined N.40/46 renumbered as N.14/49 3.49; two versions of single engine design, 19 & 20.12.49.

Delta II Supersonic delta wing research aircraft to ER.103, first flown 6.8.54. Resulted from long series of transonic and supersonic research aeroplanes, the first prepared in response to Ministry request of 8.48.

N.114T Naval fighter submission, 3.7.51.

F.124T Rocket fighters, delta and swept wing versions, 23.4.52 and 24.4.52.

F.155T Supersonic all-weather fighter, small and large developments of Delta II (larger dubbed 'Delta III'), 10.55.

Below: **Impression of the original Fairey Type R (2.47) as submitted to the Ministry of Supply, and which eventually turned into the Delta I.**

Top: **Gloster E.28/39 Pioneer, W4041/G, Britain's first jet aircraft and an immensely successful research aeroplane. This view shows it late in its career, with tailplane fins.** Eric Morgan collection

Centre: **The first jet fighter to fly in the UK was the Gloster Meteor. Over 3,900 were built, in many versions. This view shows WH453, an F Mk.8.**

Bottom: **Gloster E.1/44 Ace third prototype TX148 in February 1949.** Ken Ellis collection

FOLLAND

Fo.139 Midge private venture interceptor fighter, first-flight 11.8.54.
Fo.140 Gnat private venture ground attack fighter with BE.22 Saturn, 1.52. Abandoned.
Fo.141 Gnat lightweight day fighter first flown 18.7.55.
Fo.142 Private venture general study for high performance light fighter with jet deflection begun 3.53. Embraced two distinct engine configurations labelled as 'parallel' and 'series' installations for deflected thrust control at low speeds. Combined under Fo.142 10.53. Two 5,000lb (22.2kN) static thrust engines, equipped weight 11,732lb (5,322kg), 737mph (1,186km/h) at sea level, span 30.9ft (9.4m), two Aden cannon.
Fo.143 Gnat Mk.2 with re-heat, 10.53.

GENERAL AIRCRAFT

Series of variable geometry research projects, began with 'Transformable Delta' of 7.2.48, prepared before and after the Company came under the control of Blackburn. Some work to E.16/49 before concentrated into Blackburn B.90 project to ER.110T, 11.51.

GLOSTER

This fighter specialist's list suggests that before its disappearance, many Meteor and Javelin developments were prepared but with few all-new designs. The P numbers list drawings, not projects, and so many of the gaps are not projects but rather specific details of others. For example P.261 shows component assembly for the three-view P.259. The 'G' numbers were introduced retrospectively.

G.40 Pioneer Research aircraft to E.28/39 and Britain's first jet, flying on 15.5.41.
G.41 Meteor Britain's first jet fighter to F.9/40, flown 5.3.43.
G.A.1 Fighter to E.5/42, mid-1942. Some similarity to G.40 but solid nose, four 20mm cannon, wing root intakes and T-tail. Mock-up and some components produced before abandoned 1944. Replaced by G.A.2.
Rocket E.5/42 development with two Rolls B.37 Derwent I or B.38 engines in fuselage behind pilot, 7.43.
P.171 & P.172 Single Halford engine projects between E.5/42 and E.1/44 fighters, late 43.
P.181 Development of G.A.1 to E.1/44, Halford H.2 engine, 2.7.44.
P.190/G.42/G.A.2 Ace P.181 with B.41 (Nene) engine, flown 9.3.48. Name little used.
G.47 Meteor Night Fighter Full prototype to F.24/48 first flew 31.5.50. Design and production assumed by Armstrong Whitworth.
CXP-1001 Collaboration with Chinese Nationalist Government for single-seat fighter agreed 7.46. Work frozen 10.50 and surviving material disposed of 11.52.
P.199 AJ.65 (Avon) powered version of E.1/44, 1945.
P.209 Fighter with two AJ.65 engines, 1946.
P.212 G.A.2 Ace third prototype fitted with tail high on fin, flown 1949. Tail later adopted for Meteor F Mk.8.
P.228 RAF night fighter to F.44/46, 3.47.
P.231 Naval fighter to N.40/46, 2.47.
P.234 RAF day fighter to F.43/46, 2.47.
P.238 Combined day/night interceptor covering both F.43/46 and F.44/46 with delta wing, slab tail, four 30mm cannon and Metro-Vickers F.9 Sapphire, 3.47.
P.240 Variant of P.238 with 30° swept wing, 18.4.47.

Top: **The prototype of the Hawker Sea Hawk jet fighter was the P.1040 (serial VP401), seen here.**

P.241 Refined variant of P.238, 21.4.47.
P.248 RAF day fighter to F.43/46 with one 4.5in (11.5cm) recoilless gun, 8.47.
P.250 RAF day fighter to F.43/46 with two 30mm cannon, 8.47.
P.258 Delta wing fighter designed to carry battery of six rocket projectiles or single Red Hawk AAM, 14.10.47.
P.259 Fighter with Sapphire or Avon engines, 10.47.
P.262 Modified Meteor with delta wing, slab tail and two RR Derwent 5 engines, 11.47.
P.263 Developed P.262, 19.11.47.
P.272 RAF night fighter to F.4/48, 15.4.48.
P.275 RAF day fighter to F.3/48, 13.4.48.
P.276 F.4/48 night fighter, believed the first real G.A.5 Javelin prototype flown 26.11.51.
P.279 RAF night fighter to F.4/48 with two Sapphires, 5.7.48.
P.280 RAF day/night fighter to F.4/48, 23.7.48. Final Javelin prototype drawing.
P.281 Meteor development with improved range and altitude performance, 5.8.48.
P.284 Prone pilot transonic research aircraft powered by single Sapphire, 26.10.48.
P.285 Transonic research aircraft, as P.284 but conventional seating, 26.10.48.
P.295 Meteor with reheated Derwent 8s, 8.49.
P.297 As P.295, 9.49.
P.298 All-weather Meteor variant with reheated Derwent 5s, cannon mounted outside engine nacelles in broad-chord wings, 9.49.
P.300 Variant of P.298 with narrow chord wings, 10.49.
P.315 Long range fighter variant of F.4/48 with radar; very like Javelin prototype, 5.50. Span 52ft (15.8m), length 57ft (17.4m), all-up-weight 39,500lb (17,917kg).
P.316 Long range variant of F.4/48 without AI radar, 5.50. As P.315 but length 58.8ft (17.9m) and weight 39,700lb (18,008kg).
P.318 Long range rocket armed fighter, 1950.
P.322 F.4/48 Interceptor variant with 9,760lb (43.4kN) Sapphire Sa.50s, 7.50. Minimal structural alteration but 30% more thrust. Mach 0.92 at sea level, Mach 0.94 at 50,000ft (15,240m), sea level rate of climb 19,800ft/min (6,035m/min).
P.323 Long range fighter version of P.322, 7.50.
P.325 High altitude escort fighter variant of standard F.4/48, 3.51. Designed to escort Vickers B.9/48 Valiant bomber. Span 66ft (20.1m), length 57ft (17.4m), Sapphire Sa.3s, all-up-weight 45,440lb (20,611kg), Mach 0.92 at 40,000ft (12,192m).
P.356 First transonic proposal for Thin Wing development of Javelin with Sapphire Sa.7, tendered 7.53.
P.359 Javelin FAW Mk.1 & 2 first flown 22.7.54.
P.364 Further Thin Wing Javelin development with Olympus, 9.53.
P.370/G.50/G.A.6 Transonic Thin Wing Javelin to F.153D, powered by two Olympus Ol.6 or Ol.7. P.371 carried twin Red Deans, P.372 had four Firestreaks, 9.54.
P.376 Final enlarged supersonic Thin Wing Javelin with Olympus 21R, 5.56. Project cancelled 31.5.56.
P.382 Mk.7 Javelin with two 2,250lb (10kN) Scorpion rocket packs replacing ventral tanks, 2.57. Improved climb and turn rate; time to 50,000ft (15,240m) halved.

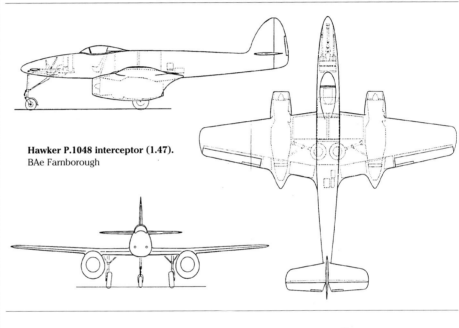

Hawker P.1048 interceptor (1.47).
BAe Farnborough

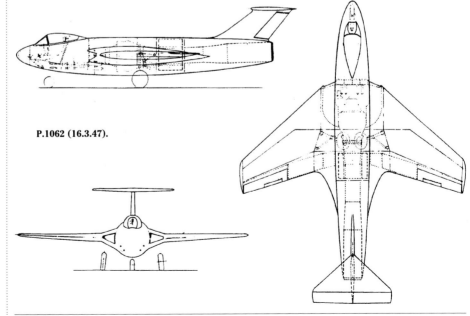

P.1062 (16.3.47).

HAWKER / HAWKER SIDDELEY / BRITISH AEROSPACE, KINGSTON

One of the most famous of fighter firms. This series of projects spread over 40 years illustrates really well how fighter development proceeded within a design set-up and shows a constant mix of new projects and modifications of established designs. Fighters are a bit thin in the mid-1960s because once the vertical take-off P.1127 and Harrier were flying, much of Kingston's effort centred on advanced versions which predominantly fit into the attack aircraft category. If air-to-air combat formed just a small component of a project's capability, it has been omitted. On the formation of British Aerospace, the prefix reverted to P.

P.1031 Fighter based on piston Sea Fury with one RR B.40 (later B.41) engine in nose, 1944.

P.1035 Fury (P.1026) fitted with single RR B.41 (later Nene) in central fuselage, 1944.

P.1040 Modified P.1035, became Sea Hawk prototype, serial VP401, first flown 2.9.47.

P.1042 P.1040 variant, 1944.

P.1043 Undercarriageless P.1040 for flexible deck landing trials, 1944.

P.1045 Fighter with AJ.54 engine, 7.45.

P.1046 Swept P.1040 with rocket boost, 9.45.

P.1047 Swept wing interceptor version of P.1040, B.41 plus rocket engine in extreme rear fuselage, two 20mm cannon, 9.45.

P.1048 Interceptor fighter tendered to Ministry 1.46. Span 39.5ft (12.0m), length 41.0ft (12.5m), two podded AJ.65 Avons, twin nose mounted 30 mm Aden cannon. A similar and contemporary aircraft, the Russian Sukhoi Su-9, appeared in mock-up early 1946 and flew 13.11.46.

P.1049 Interceptor investigation; fleet fighter re-schemed around one AJ.65, highly swept wings for high subsonic performance, 1.46. Results to DGTD 14.1.46.

P.1052 Swept wing P.1040 to E.38/46, flown 19.11.48.

P.1053 Rocket fighter project, 1946.

P.1054 RAF day fighter to F.43/46, originally drawn 23.9.46.

P.1056 RAF night fighter to F.44/46, straight wing, drawing dated 7.3.47. One version had cockpit offset to port.

P.1057 RAF night fighter to F.44/46, swept wing, 7.3.47.

P.1059 & P.1060 Naval variants of P.1056 with, respectively, wing and fuselage engine nacelles, 1947.

P.1061 RAF day fighter to F.43/46, straight wing P.1054 development, 5.47.

P.1062 Studies for swept wing P.1040 as interim interceptor before more advanced types available, 16.3.47. Main project had T-tail, all-through jet-pipe, 6,200lb (27.6kN) thrust RR RB.44 Tay engine (reheat available later), four 20mm Hispano cannon below cockpit as per P.1040, span 31.5ft (9.6m), length 38.33ft (11.7m), wing area 260ft² (24.2m²), all-up-weight 11,800lb (5,352kg). Top speed 690mph (1,110km/h) at sea level. Was first project study leading to P.1081.

P.1063 Fighter to F.43/46 and possibly N.9/47, late 47.

P.1064 RAF day fighter to F.43/46, 16.1.48.

P.1065 Mixed jet/rocket powered fighter to F.43/46, early 48.

P.1067 Series of designs to F.3/48 culminating in the Hunter first flown 20.7.51.

P.1068 Straight wing version of interim P.1062; the two forming a combined study using results of P.1040 flight tests, 16.3.47. Powerplant and weapons identical to P.1062, span 36.5ft

(11.1m), length 38.33ft (11.7m), wing area 256ft² (23.8m²), all-up-weight 11,700lb (5,307kg). Top speed 650mph (1,046km/h) at sea level.

P.1069, P.1070 & P.1071 Transonic research aircraft with reheated Avon or Sapphire, 1948. P.1070 had additional rocket motor, P.1071 rocket motor and two 30mm Adens.

P.1072 P.1040 prototype fitted with Snarler rocket, first flew 16.11.50 – first British mixed-power experimental prototype to fly. Trials successful but technical problems, and realisation that reheat not rocket boost was the way forward, terminated programme.

P.1073 P.1062 variant, 1949. Tay engine, span 31.5ft (9.6m), length 36.33ft (11.1m).

P.1074 Modified straight wing P.1040, 17.2.49. Span 36.5ft (11.1m), length 38.1ft (11.6m).

P.1075 P.1062 with reheated Nene, 16.2.49. Span 31.5ft (9.6m), length 37.25ft (11.4m).

P.1076 Investigation into developing the P.1067, no drawings, 1949.

P.1077 Tail-less swept wing (Combat Patrol?) fighter with outrigger undercarriage and mid-wing vertical fins, 1949. Two stacked reheated Avons, span 58ft (17.7m), length 55ft (16.8m), wing area 750ft² (69.7m²), four cannon beneath cockpit, nose radar, 1,000gal (4,547lit) fuel. Hawker did much work on 'hidden' intakes – here split above and below the wing.

P.1078 P.1052 fitted with Screamer rocket motor and swept tail, drawing dated 18.5.51. Span 31.5ft (9.6m), length 40.2ft (12.3m).

P.1080 P.1052 to Australian requirement, 1950.

P.1081 Modification of second P.1052 prototype with swept tail, single jetpipe (Tay engine planned), flown 19.6.50.

P.1082 Supersonic fighter designed to F.23/49, 5.50.

P.1083 Supersonic 'thin-wing' Hunter to F.119D, due to fly late summer 1953, cancelled 7.53, part of fuselage used in P.1099 (Hunter F Mk.6).

P.1084 Two designs for small lightweight low delta wing fighter, 1951.

P.1085 High delta wing, undercarriageless, rocket powered fighter, 14.2.51. Span 25.5ft (7.8m), length 38.25ft (11.7m), all-up-weight 11,280lb (5,117kg).

P.1087 Navalised P.1081 interceptor development with reheated Nene, 22.3.51. Span 36ft (11.0m), length 39.1ft (11.9m), wing area 287ft² (26.7m²), four cannon beneath fuselage.

P.1088 Light fighter with cockpit in base of T-tail fin, 5.7.51. Two 3,000lb (13.3kN) RR engines in nose, span 24ft (7.3m), length 28ft (8.5m), wing area 120ft² (11.2m²), gun or rocket armament.

P.1089 Rocket fighter to F.124T, 5.52.

P.1090 Supersonic development of Hunter with 50° swept wing, one reheated Gyron and four 30mm Aden cannon, 5.8.51. Span 35.33ft (10.8m), length 51.75ft (15.8m), wing area 358ft² (33.3m²).

P.1091 F.3/48 Hunter with 60° delta wing, one reheated 8,000lb (35.6kN) Sapphire 4, four 30mm Aden cannon, 15.10.51. Max. speed Mach 0.98, span 33ft (10.1m), length 41.92ft (12.8m), wing area 510ft² (47.4m²). Study undertaken with Avro (presumably to use the sister company's delta experience).

P.1092 With P.1082 and P.1083, Hawker began push for fighter with supersonic capability, either as Hunter development or new design. One effort was P.1092 blended delta, two-seat all-weather fighter of 5.11.51 and not dissimilar in concept to Avro Canada's Arrow. Powered

by single reheated Avon, expected to reach Mach 1.5 at 36,000ft (10,973m) and have ceiling of 55,000ft (16,764m). Four 30mm cannon mounted in wings. Span 35.0ft (10.7m), length 55.0ft (16.8m), wing area 580ft² (53.9m²). Initial investigations complete by December 1951, but Javelin dominated RAF planning and P.1092 proved to be of academic interest only, the fate of most fighter projects.

P.1093 Supersonic blended delta all-weather fighter with single Avon RA.14 or Gyron fed by pitot intake, 8.2.52. Six wing mounted 30mm guns, Span 41.0ft (12.5m), length 49.67ft (15.1m), wing area 750ft² (69.7m²).

P.1094 P.1072 given 4% thick wings, Nene plus Snarler rocket, 6.3.52.

P.1095 P.1083 fitted with Sapphire 4 or reheated Avon RA.14, 1952.

P.1096 & P.1097 Supersonic research aircraft to ER.134T, 5.53.

P.1099 Hunter with 200 Series Avon, became Hunter F Mk.6, flown 23.1.54.

P.1100 Supersonic 'thin-wing' Hunter with RA.24 Avon plus two rocket motors in trailing edge wing roots, 1953. Two 30mm Aden cannon, two Firestreak under wings, AI.20 radar, Mach 1.5. Span 35.5ft (10.8m), length 52.0ft (15.8m), wing area 343ft² (31.9m²), 680gal (3,092lit) fuel.

P.1102 Hunter development with reheated Avon RA.19R and undercarriage in extended wing root fairings, 27.10.53. Span 34.33ft (10.5m), length 47.4ft (14.4m), wing area 368ft² (34.2m²).

P.1103 Studies for supersonic all-weather fighter to F.155T, begun 2.54, tendered 10.55.

P.1104 Large Mach 2 fighter with two reheated Gyron Juniors, 12.54. Two 30mm Aden under cockpit. Span 44.0ft (13.4m), length 71.5ft (21.8m). Outrigger u/c. Earlier layout 2.54 similar but delta wing and further 12 34mm single-shot upward-firing guns in upper fuselage near wing trailing edge.

P.1105 Hunter F Mk.6 with two underwing podded Napier TRR/37 rocket engines, 1954.

P.1106 Hunter with thin large span wing, Sapphire Sa.10, AI.20 radar, two underwing Firestreaks, no guns, 5.10.54. Span 38.0ft (11.6m), length 48.1ft (14.7m).

P.1107 Two similar designs for supersonic fighter, 7.54. Four 21in (53cm) diameter supersonic turbojets in underwing groups, outrigger undercarriage, two Firestreak. Shown – span 36ft (11.0m), length 60ft (18.3m). Alternative had engine groups extended well beyond wing trailing edge and underwing Firestreaks.

P.1109 Hunter F Mk.6 with two underwing Firestreak and AI.20 radar. Two prototypes only, first flown 1956.

P.1114 & P.1115 All-weather fighters based on two-seat Hunter trainer with long nose for search radar, tip tanks; Avon 203 and Sapphire Sa.6 respectively. Brochures completed 11.11.55. Two Adens, span 33.67ft (10.3m), length 50.5ft (15.4m).

P.1116 Mach 2 interceptor and long range strike fighter developed from P.1103, 14.5.56.

P.1118 Brief study for high speed Hunter with straight wing, 3.56. Reheated Avon, extended pointed nose, span 27ft (8.2m), length 53ft (16.2m), wing area 270ft² (25.1m²).

P.1121 Mach 2 air superiority strike fighter developed from P.1116, 6.56. Private venture construction begun 1957 but abandoned by end 1958.

P.1122 Near identical to P.1121 but all-steel wing, more powerful engine, Mach 3 capable, late '58.

P.1127 Vertical take-off research aircraft to ER.204D, first flown 13.3.61. Developed into Kestrel, Harrier and Sea Harrier.

P.1130 Hunter all-weather fighter based on T Mk.7 trainer, AI.23 radar, 1957.

P.1133 Hunter F Mk.6 all-weather fighter, AI.23 radar in long nose, Avon Mk.203, 1.8.58. Two underwing Firestreak, two Aden. Span 33.67ft (10.3m), length 49.1ft (14.9m).

P.1135 Thin-wing Hunter with RB.146 engine, 1959.

P.1141 Supersonic V/STOL fighter reminiscent of Gnat, one reheated BE.53/11, 5.60. Span 25ft (7.6m), length 49ft (14.9m).

P.1142 Supersonic STOL fighter with Bristol Siddeley Pegasus BE.53/1, 1960.

P.1147 Naval STOL fighter with two RB.173 and four RB.162 engines, 1960/61.

P.1148 Variant of P.1147 with variable sweep wing, 1960/61.

P.1150 Supersonic V/STOL fighter with BS Pegasus 5/6 PCB vectored thrust turbofan, 1.61. Developed into P.1154.

P.1154 Originally P.1150/3 – Supersonic V/STOL fighter with BS.100 PCB vectored thrust turbofan to NATO requirement NBMR-3, and AW.406 / OR.356, 1.62. Prototype construction begun, but project cancelled 2.65.

P.1160 Unusual fighter with cockpit placed just ahead of tail and single engine in forward fuselage fed by conical intake with jet pipe below middle fuselage, 20.3.62. Four Sparrow AAM, two above, two below square fuselage.

Sea Harrier Initial proposal for Maritime Harrier made early 1970s, eventually Sea Harrier developed based on RAF's attack Harrier. First FRS Mk.1 flew 20.8.78; upgraded FRS Mk.2 (later F/A2) flew 19.9.89.

HS.1185 Supersonic V/STOL strike aircraft with Pegasus 15 and PCB, 1973. Final version -6 (AV-16-S6) joint study with McDonnell Douglas for naval fighter 1974.

HS.1190 HSA Brough project P.159 to AST.396, 1973.

HS.1200 Air superiority fighter projects, various engines including RR RB.238 and RB.346, 8.75 to 1.77.

HS.1201 Simple lightweight air superiority fighter, 7.75 to 1.77.

HS.1202 CTOL designs for air superiority fighter, in part to AST.403, 7.75-12.78. First drawings had canard; from late 77 resembled large General Dynamics F-16.

HS.1203 'Super Gnat' air superiority fighter with single unreheated RB.231-07, 13.11.75. No detail examination.

HS.1204 Brough project P.159 to AST.403, 5.76. Slightly improved HS.1190.

HS.1205 ASTOVL designs for air superiority fighter to AST.403, 6.76 to 5.79.

HS.1206 Brough project (P.156) for an air superiority fighter with advanced Spey engine; work began 1972.

HS.1207 Brough project (P.158) for air superiority fighter to AST.403, 1974-76.

P.1208 V/STOL ground attack fighter with Pegasus 11-35 and chin intake, 15.9.78. Swept foreplanes, forward swept wings, two cannon in wing roots, two tip mounted Sidewinder. Span 29.0ft (8.8m), length 44.5ft (13.6m), wing area 290ft² (27.0m²). Appearance of forward swept HS.1205.

P.1210 Brough project for air superiority fighter with two podded RB.199s, 1978.

P.1211 Brough project for air superiority fighter with single advanced engine, 1978.

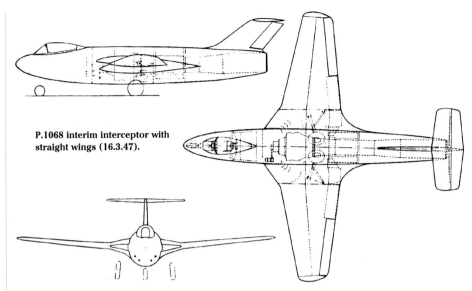

P.1068 interim interceptor with straight wings (16.3.47).

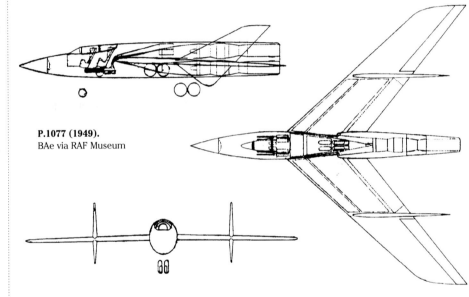

P.1077 (1949).
BAe via RAF Museum

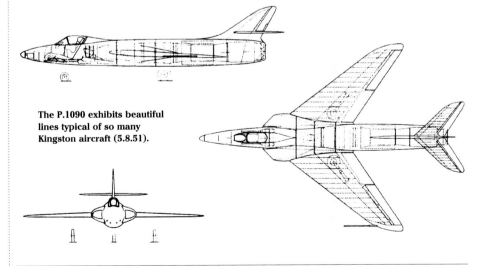

The P.1090 exhibits beautiful lines typical of so many Kingston aircraft (5.8.51).

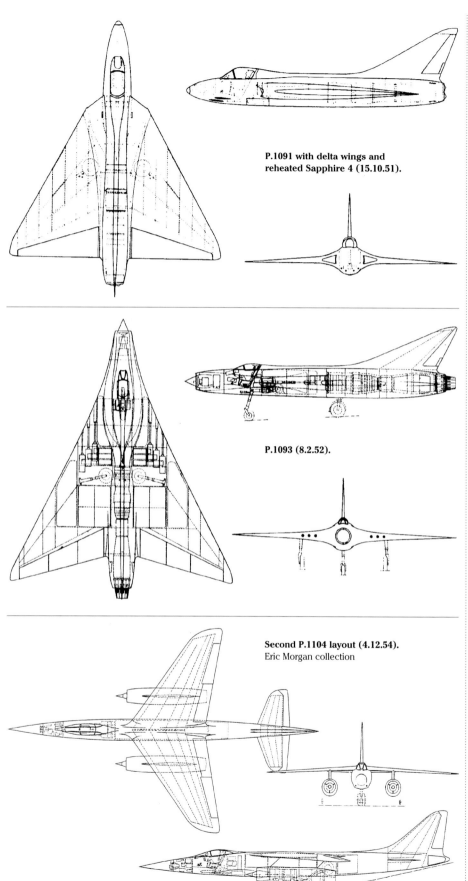

P.1091 with delta wings and reheated Sapphire 4 (15.10.51).

P.1093 (8.2.52).

Second P.1104 layout (4.12.54).
Eric Morgan collection

P.1212 ASTOVL fighter with PCB Pegasus 11F-33, 3.79 to 9.79.
P.1214 'Star Wars' forward swept wing ASTOVL fighter, 1979-80.
P.1215 Brough project for conventional canard fighter, RB.236 engine, 1979/80.
P.1216 Designs for Mach 2 ASTOVL fighter for RAF and Navy, 1981-84.
P.1219 Lightweight VSTOL fighter, 1981/82.
P.1220 Lightweight VSTOL fighter with canard, 4.1.82.
P.1221 Half scale P.1216, 1982/83.
P.1226 Subsonic P.1216 layout, 1984.
Hawk 200 Lightweight fighter based on HS.1182 Hawk trainer, flown 19.5.86.

MARTIN-BAKER

MB.6 Single engine low wing fighter with four 20mm Hispano cannon, c1945. Cigar shape fuselage with nose intake. Two skids fitted in lieu of optional tricycle undercarriage. Engine unspecified and no performance figures available. Length 36.25ft (11.0m), wing area 263ft² (24.5m²).
F.43/46 Delta wing fighter, 1947.

MILES

M.52 High speed experimental aircraft to E.24/43. First attempt to build aircraft to fly faster than sound. Flight planned for 1947, project cancelled March 1946.

SAUNDERS-ROE

Saro had long experience designing flying-boats but thanks to the requirements for rocket powered fighters in the early 1950s, and the unlikelihood of selling passenger aircraft like the Princess, it became a modest player in the fighter world for a short time.

P.103 Swept SR.A.1 with Sapphire engines, c1947. Nose intakes flanked radome.
P.113 / SR.44 / SR.A.1 Experimental flying-boat fighter to E.6/44, flown 16.7.47.
P.114 / SR.44 Long jet pipe version of P.113 but rejected in favour of that project's twin pipes, 1.44.
P.121 Hydro-ski fighter project with reheated Sapphire, 13.12.50.
P.122 Larger, faster and more heavily armed SR.A.1, 10.50. Reheated Sapphire, swept wings, cheek intakes, nose radome, four 30mm Aden. Span 46.4ft (14.1m), length 51ft (15.5m).
P.127 flying-boat research aircraft powered by Metro-Vickers Beryl engine, 1949/50.
P.142 Twin-hydro-ski amphibious fighter, 27.6.50. Alternative hydro-ski, or undercarriage for carrier operations; pilot housed in centre section cupola, reheated Napier E.137 jets in twin fuselages or booms which also carried fins and high-set tail; two cannon in upper nose of cupola. Span 48ft (14.6m), length 40ft (12.2m), wing area 543.5ft² (50.5m²), all-up-weight 27,800lb (12,610kg).
P.148 Naval fighter to N.114T, 7.51.
P.149 Experimental variable geometry aircraft to ER.110T, 11.51.
P.151 High performance fighter, 1951. Main layout had wings tapered on leading and trailing edges. Various powerplants with one proposal to carry fighter to operational height by turbo-prop aircraft.
P.154 Rocket fighter to F.124T, 4.52.
P.155 Delta wing fighter with high performance, little detail work, 1952.

P.161 Two versions of mixed powerplant delta wing fighter, 1952. Heavy – two BE.22 jets, one Spectre rocket, span 28ft (8.5m), length 44ft (13.4m), all-up-weight 15,300lb (6,940kg); Light – one BE.22, one Spectre, span 20ft (6.1m), length 34.33ft (10.5m), all-up-weight 8,800lb (3,992kg).

P.163 Supersonic research aircraft to ER.134T, 5.53. Further developed into P.177.

P.167 Development of P.154 which bridged gap to eventual SR.53, 1953.

SR.53 Mixed power interceptor to ER.138D, first flown 16.5.57.

P.177 Mixed power interceptor which became SR.177 and ordered to OR.337 (RAF), NR/A.47 (Navy) and F.177D, 5.55. First flight planned spring 1958 but cancelled in stages, 4.57 to 12.57.

P.179 Delta wing strike fighter with Orpheus or PS.37 Gyron Junior, 1954. Span 26.5ft (8.1m). Similar in appearance to SR.53.

P.180 Supersonic interceptor, one Gyron Junior, 1954. Span 26ft (7.9m). Appearance again showed similarity to SR.53 but with nose radome.

P.187 Supersonic all-weather fighter to F.155T, 10.55.

P.209 Developments of SR.53, two Spectre or RB.93 Soar rocket motors, 1958.

SHORT BROS & HARLAND

This firm's main number sequence, the S series, embraced projects from Rochester and Belfast over many years, but only one jet fighter. The P.D series applied to Belfast preliminary designs originating from 1947 onwards as schemes or tenders. If the latter progressed beyond this stage, a number was allocated in the SBAC designation system, the only relevant example here being the S.B.5 research aircraft.

S.41/S.A.3 Naval fighter to N.7/46, 1946.

P.D.5 Naval fighter to N.114T, 7.51.

P.D.7 Rocket fighter to F.124T, 6.52.

P.D.701 Rocket plus jet version of P.D.7 to F.124T, 6.52.

S.B.5 Low speed research aircraft to ER.100, first flown 2.12.52.

P.D.10 Supermarine Swift fuselage fitted with 'aero-isoclinic' wing for high speed research to ER.145, 7.53. One reheated Avon RA.7R, span 43.0ft (13.1m), length 41.5ft (12.6m), all-up-weight 17,000lb (7,711kg). Maximum speed 716mph (1,152km/h), Mach 0.97 at 10,000ft (3,048m); 677mph (1,089km/h), Mach 1.0 above 30,000ft (9,144m). Project to follow earlier low speed testing with S.B.4 Sherpa and expected to fly 18 months from go ahead, but project not proceeded with and specification remained unwritten. As speeds increased with jet power, bending of the wing (aeroelasticity) recognised as serious problem in future design. Main feature of 'aero-isoclinic' wing was use of rotatable 'all-moving' outer wings replacing conventional elevators and ailerons for both lateral and pitching control, the incidence remaining constant whatever the distortion caused by flight loads. The P.D.10 was also planned to demonstrate possibilities for the wing on high altitude fighter but no military equipment carried. The wing was conceived by Professor Geoffrey Hill.

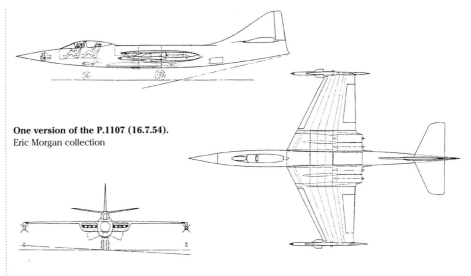

One version of the P.1107 (16.7.54).
Eric Morgan collection

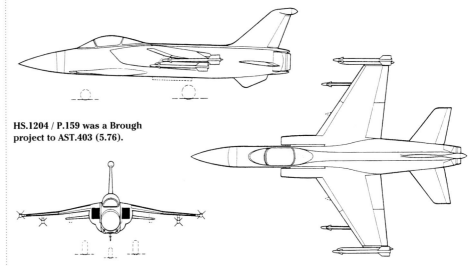

HS.1204 / P.159 was a Brough project to AST.403 (5.76).

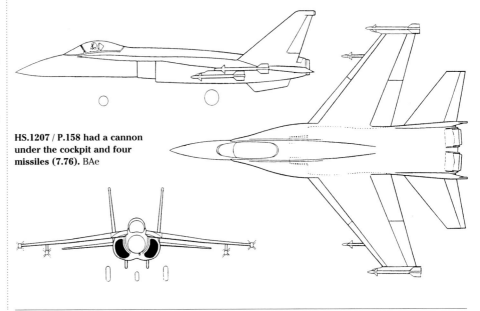

HS.1207 / P.158 had a cannon under the cockpit and four missiles (7.76). BAe

VICKERS SUPERMARINE

Accurate dates for many of these projects (referred to as 'Types') are unavailable as brochures were often undated. Designs from about 1959 onwards originated from the Vickers / BAC team at Weybridge.

392 Attacker fighter to E.10/44, flown 27.7.46.
398 Attacker F Mk.1 naval fighter to E.1/45, first flown 17.6.47.
500 Variant of Type 392, c1946.
505 Undercarriageless naval fighter, early 1946.
508 Development of Type 505 with undercarriage to N.9/47, first flown 31.8.51.
510 Experimental swept wing variant of Attacker, first flown 29.12.48.
511 Swept and straight wing versions of RAF night fighter to F.44/46, 3.47.
515 Projected Attacker F Mk.2 with DH Ghost II engine, 1947.
516 Attacker variant, c1947.
517 Fuselage modification of Type 510 prototype, all-moving tailplane, 7.53.

519 Attacker fitted with jet deflection, c1948/49.
520 Projected conversion of second Type 510, c1948/49.
525 Third prototype N.9/47 given swept wings and V-tail, 6.49. Flown with conventional tail 27.4.54.
526 Interceptor variant of Type 525 to F.3/48, 9.8.49.
527 Proposed Attacker Mk.2 variants with Avon or Tay engine, 1949.
528 Modified Type 510 second prototype provisioned for reheat, flown 27.3.50.
529 Second Type 508 fitted with cannon and other changes, August 29.8.52.
531 Proposed modifications to Types 510 and 528, eventually flown on Type 535, 1950.
532 Type 510 proposed with Ghost engine, 1950.
535 Modified 510 second prototype (Type 528) with tricycle undercarriage, flew 23.8.50.
541 Swift fighter to F.105D developed from Type 535, prototype flown 1.8.51.
542 Attacker variant with floats, c1951.
543 Undercarriageless fighter with two Bristol BE.15 engines, 1951.

544 Scimitar F Mk.1 fighter to N.113D, first flown 19.1.56.
545 Supersonic development of Swift to F.105D.2, first flight planned spring 1954, programme cancelled 1955.
546 Swift F Mk.4, first flown 27.5.53.
548 Project for naval 'hooked' Swift to N.105D and NR/A.34, 3.52. 20 ordered but cancelled late 52.
552 Swift F Mk.7, first flown 4.56.
553 Supersonic research aircraft to ER.134T, 9.4.53.
555 Third N.9/47 / N.113 Scimitar prototype with form of lift augmentation, 1953.
556 All-weather fighter Scimitar, 3.54. Adapted to carry two Red Dean, four Blue Jay, four cannon or Blue Jay and cannon mix; AI.18 radar.
558 Mark 2 Scimitar project with developed Avon RA.24 engines, 4.55. Span increased, main weapon Firestreak.
559 Supersonic all-weather fighter to F.155T, 29.9.55.
560 De-navalised Scimitar, c1956.
562, 567 & 574 Scimitar developments, late 50s.
563 De-navalised Type 544 Scimitar variant prepared for Swiss Air Force, c1958. Series of studies carried out by Swiss resulted in purchase of French Mirage III fighter.
576 Supersonic Scimitar with reheated RB.146 Avons, or dry RB.146s boosted by Spectre rockets, 12.58.
583 Variable geometry naval strike fighter to AW.406, mid-1962 onwards.
583V VTOL study for naval strike fighter to OR.356, 8.63 onwards.
588 Studies to fit swing-wings to the Swift, Scimitar and English Electric P.1B Lightning, c1961. Study work on Lightning completed 2.62.

Supermarine Type 556 (19.3.54).
Eric Morgan collection

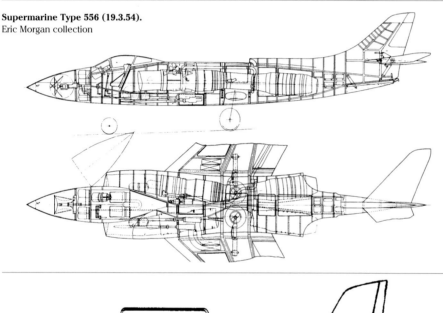

Main version of the Saunders-Roe 'catamaran' fighter was the P.142/1 (27.6.50). GKN Westland

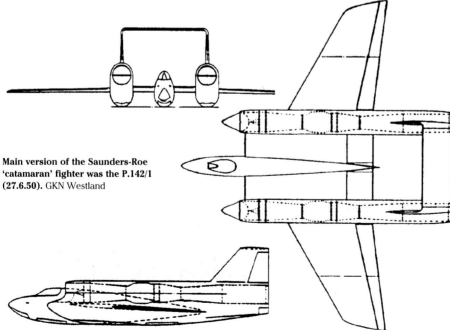

WESTLAND

A firm that never actually built a jet fighter, but who submitted to several specifications. Westland was in fact designing jet fighters by the middle of the war before Sydney Camm at Hawker had taken the type aboard, steps which gave designer Teddy Petter experience for his move to English Electric where it was put to good use on the P.1. This is another company where one does not know how many designs were prepared and what might be missing.

P.15 Fighter with single 3,000lb (13.3kN) Halford H.1 turbojet to E.5/42, 1942. Twin boom configuration which, apart from inner wing leading edge intakes, gave appearance similar to de Havilland Vampire. Span 46ft (14m), wing area 240ft² (22.3m²), all-up-weight 9,600lb (4,354kg), top speed 490mph (789km/h) at 35,000ft (10,668m).
N.7/43 Naval P.15 with same engine, 6.42. Span 40ft (12.2m), all-up-weight 11,000lb (4,990kg), maximum speed 390mph (628km/h). Reason for performance loss unknown.
F.11/45 Naval interceptor with mid-fuselage swept wing, single AJ.65 (4,860lb [21.6kN]), 1945. Span 35ft (10.7m), wing area 280ft² (26.0m²), all-up-weight 12,500lb (5,670kg). To operate from carrier with flexible deck; variant had bifurcated jet pipes and tail mounted booster rocket.
N.40/46 Naval night fighter, several designs, 2 and 11.47.
W.37 Naval fighter submission to N.114T, 20.7.51.
F.124T Rocket fighters, two designs, conventional or 'Delanne' delta layouts, 4.52.

Post-War British Fighter Project Specifications

The Air Ministry (the main functions of which were absorbed into a reconstituted Ministry of Defence in April 1964) has traditionally signalled expected future requirements to the British aircraft industry via a series of specifications against which tenders were invited.

Until the end of 1949 the sequential system used to issue these specifications was a 'letter/number/year' arrangement. One of the last to be issued was F.23/49: 'F' stood for fighter (in fact what became the Lightning); '23' indicated it was the 23rd specification issued in that year, which was 1949. Alternative prefix letters included B (bomber), E (experimental) and N (naval).

From 1950 the system changed and at the same time was declared 'Secret' in an effort to prevent any public insight into the thoughts of the Air Council and Admiralty. The new specifications were also prefixed by one or two letters, these again being an indication of the intended role of the aircraft, ie: F, B, N plus ER (experimental research), MR (maritime reconnaissance), T (trainer). The second element was a number in a series that began at 100 and by the 1980s had passed 300. A suffix letter, for example T (for tender), D (development) or P (prototype), usually completed the specification. There was no longer any reference to indicate the year of issue.

ER.103 was one of the first of these new-style specifications to be issued, written for the experimental supersonic research aircraft from Fairey that became the Delta II. In the case of F.155T, the suffix 'T' indicated that this was the basic document to which industry would have tendered for that new fighter, and had the winning Fairey 'Delta III' been built, then a more detailed F.155D would have been written around it.

Specifications for an aircraft required for military service were usually accompanied by an Operational Requirement with its own 'OR' number, for example OR.329 in the case of F.155. Naval requirements were 'NR/A's, for example NR/A.38 for N.131 and N.139.

Further details of the aircraft specifications issued are in *The British Aircraft Specification File* by Meekcoms and Morgan; details of ORs etc appeared in *Aeromilitaria*, issues 4/96 and 1/97 – all published by Air-Britain.

N.7/46 Hawker P.1040 Sea Hawk,
Shorts S.41/S.A.3.
E.38/46 Hawker P.1052.
E.41/46 Supermarine Type 510.
N.40/46 *First Stage:*
Blackburn B.67,
Gloster P.231,
Westland N.40/46.
Second Stage:
Blackburn B.67,
de Havilland DH.110,
Fairey N.40/46,
Westland N.40/46.
F.43/46 Gloster P.234,
Hawker P.1054 & P.1061,
Martin Baker F.43/46,
Supermarine modified Type 508.
Later:
Gloster P.248, P.250, P.258 & P.259.
F.44/46 de Havilland DH.110,
Gloster P.228 & delta wing project,
Hawker P.1056 & P.1057,
Supermarine Type 511.
N.9/47 Supermarine Type 508 & 525.
F.3/48 Hawker P.1064, P.1065 and later P.1067,
Also Gloster P.275,
Supermarine Type 526.
F.4/48 de Havilland DH.110,
Gloster P.272, P.279, P.280 & G.A.5 Javelin.
N.14/49 Blackburn B.82,
de Havilland DH.110, Fairey N.14/49.
E.16/49 Armstrong Whitworth AW.58,
Blackburn & General swing wing project.
F.23/49 English Electric P.1A & P.1B Lightning,
Hawker P.1082.
ER.100 Shorts S.B.5.
ER.103 Fairey Delta II.
F.105P Supermarine Type 535,
F.105P2 Supermarine Type 541 Swift,
F.105D2 Supermarine Type 545.
ER.110T Armstrong Whitworth AW.59,
Blackburn B.90,
Boulton Paul P.121,
Bristol Type 183,
Saro P.149.
N.113D Supermarine Type 544 Scimitar.
N.114T Blackburn B.89,
Fairey N.114,
Saro P.148,
Shorts P.D.5,
Westland W.37.

F.119D Hawker P.1083.
F.124T Avro 720,
Blackburn B.97,
Bristol Type 178 (two),
Fairey F.124 (two),
Saro P.154,
Westland F.124 (two),
Also:
Boulton Paul P.122,
Hawker P.1089,
Shorts P.D.7 & P.D.701.
N.131T de Havilland DH.116.
ER.134T Armstrong Whitworth AW.166,
Boulton Paul P.128,
Bristol Type 188,
English Electric P.6/1, P.6/2, 'P.6/B' and '/D'.
Hawker P.1096 & P.1097,
Saro P.163,
Supermarine Type 553.
F.137P Avro 720.
F.138P Saro SR.53.
N.139P de Havilland DH.110 Sea Vixen,
Supermarine Type 556.
F.153D Gloster P.356, P.364, P.370, P.371, P.372 &
P.376 Thin-wing Javelin.
F.155T Armstrong Whitworth AW.169,
de Havilland DH.117,
English Electric P.8,
Fairey Delta II development & 'Delta III',
Hawker P.1103,
Saro P.187,
Supermarine Type 559.
Also:
Avro 729.
F.177P Saro P.177.
OR.356 and/or AW.406 BAC Warton VG Lightning,
Hawker Siddeley P.1154,
BAC Weybridge Type 583 & Type 583V.
ASR.385 McDonnell Douglas F-4 Phantom.
ASR.395 Panavia Tornado ADV.
AST.403 BAC P.91(?), P.92, P.93, P.95, P.96, & P.97
Super Jaguar,
Hawker Siddeley HS.1202 (in part),
HS.1204 (P.159 – in part),
HS.1205 & HS.1207 (P.158 – in part).
AST.410 To a certain extent BAe Kingston P.1212,
P.1214 & P.1216,
BAe Warton P.103.
ASR.414 and later SR(A).414
BAe Warton EAP (indirectly),
Eurofighter Typhoon.

Select Bibliography

During the research for this book a great deal of primary source material has been consulted, including original documents held by the Public Record Office (AVIA 53, 54, 65, AIR 20), and Museums, Heritage Centres, Groups and individuals, as per the Acknowledgements (see page 6). Drawings and photographs are credited individually unless from the author's collection. Important secondary source material helped to get things started and fill gaps:

Armstrong Whitworth Paper Planes: Ray Williams; *Air Enthusiast* No.43, 1991.

Avro Aircraft since 1908: A J Jackson; Putnam 1965.

Blackburn Aircraft since 1909: A J Jackson; Putnam, 1968

Boulton Paul Aircraft since 1915: Alec Brew, Putnam, 1993.

Boulton Paul Aircraft Unbuilt Projects: Alec Brew; 1996. (Several drawings were reproduced from this booklet, with permission).

Bristol Aircraft since 1910: C H Barnes; Putnam,1964.

British Aerospace EAP: Bill Gunston; Linewrights, 1986.

The British Aircraft Specifications File: K J Meekcoms and E B Morgan; Air-Britain, 1994.

British Experimental Jet Aircraft: Barry Hygate; Argus Publications, 1990.

De Havilland Aircraft since 1909: A J Jackson; Putnam, 1962.

Design Problems for Interceptor Fighters: J S Bailey; RAeS Journal, June 1952.

The Early Development of Guided Weapons in the United Kingdom, 1940 to 1960: Stephen R Twigge; Harwood, 1993.

Early Wing-Swingers: Tony Buttler; *Air Enthusiast* No.69, May 1997.

English Electric Aircraft and their Predecessors: Stephen Ransom and Robert Fairclough; Putnam, 1987.

Evolution of the New European Fighter – A British Industrial Perspective: Ivan Yates; (unpublished lecture papers).

From Sea to Air – the Heritage of Sam Saunders: A E Tagg and R L Wheeler; Crossprint, 1989.

From Spitfire to Eurofighter: Roy Boot; Airlife, 1990.

The Frustrating Fifties: William Green; *Flying Review International*, September 1964.

Futile Rivals: Tony Buttler; *Air Enthusiast* No.61, January 1996.

Gloster Aircraft since 1917: Derek James; Putnam, 1971.

Hawker Aircraft since 1920: Francis K Mason; Putnam, 1971.

Hunter: Roy Braybrook; Osprey, 1987.

Interceptor: James Goulding; Ian Allan, 1986.

Kingston's Fighters – the Jet Age: Ralph Hooper; (40th R K Pierson Lecture – text unpublished).

The Next Combat Aircraft: Roy Boot; *Aerospace*, April 1981.

Operational Requirements: Ray Sturtivant; *Aero-militaria*, Air-Britain, April 1996 & January 1997.

Planemakers 2 – Westland: David Monday; Janes, 1982.

Project Cancelled: Derek Wood; Janes, 1986.

RAF's Rocket Fighters: Michael J F Bowyer; *Air Pictorial*, October and November 1996.

Research Rivals: Tony Buttler; *Air Enthusiast* No.60, November 1995.

The Role of Missiles in British Concepts of Defence – The Influence of Duncan Sandys: Cecil James; (from *Seeing off the Bear: Anglo-American Air Power co-operation during the Cold War*); USAF, 1995.

Seaplane Jet Fighter: Michael J F Bowyer; *Air International*, October 1996.

Shorts Aircraft since 1900: C H Barnes; Putnam,1967.

Sir James Martin: Sarah Sharman; Patrick Stephens, 1996.

Supermarine Aircraft since 1914: C F Andrews and E B Morgan; Putnam, 1981.

Tactical Jet V/STOL – Its Future in a CTOL World: John Fozard; British Aerospace publication, 1985.

The Ten-Year Gap: Bill Gunston; *Flight International*, 19th December 1963.

Three Centuries to Concorde: Charles Burnet, MEP, 1979.

Westland Aircraft since 1915: Derek James; Putnam 1991.

Wings of the Weird and Wonderful: Captain Eric Brown; Airlife, 1983.

Contemporary issues of *Aeromilitaria,* *The Aeroplane, Air International, Aviation Week, Flight and Flight International, Interavia,* and *The Times* were also consulted.

Early 1950s artist's impression of Saunders-Roe P.122 flying-boat fighters on patrol over the fleet. via Peter Green

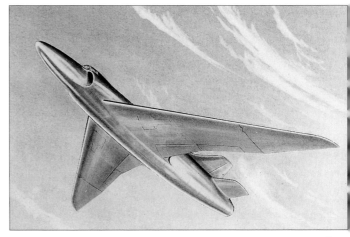

Short P.D.10, which used a Supermarine Swift fuselage with 'aero-isoclinic' wing (7.53). Shorts

Index

We hope that you have enjoyed this book . .

Midland Publishing book titles are carefully edited and designed by an experienced and enthusiastic team of specialists. A catalogue detailing our aviation publishing programme is available upon request from the address on page two.

Our associate company, Midland Counties Publications, offers an exceptionally wide range of aviation, railway, spaceflight, naval, military, astronomy and transport books and videos, for purchase by mail-order and delivery around the world.

To order further copies of this book, or to request a copy of the appropriate mail-order catalogue, write, telephone or fax to:
Midland Counties Publications
Unit 3 Maizefield, Hinckley, Leics, LE10 1YF
Tel: 01455 233 747   Fax: 01455 233 737